SOULFORCE

SOUL FORCE

HOW TO DISCOVER YOUR ARTISTIC PURPOSE, CREATE MORE FREELY, AND MAKE ART THAT MATTERS

Joseph Arnold

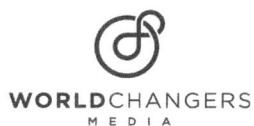

Copyright ©2024 by Joseph Arnold. All rights reserved. No part of this book may be reproduced or used in any manner without the prior written permission of the copyright owner, except for the use of brief quotations in a book review. To request permissions, contact publisher@worldchangers.media.

DISCLAIMER: This is a work of nonfiction. Nonetheless, some of the names and identifying character traits of people featured in the stories herein have been changed in order to protect their identities. Any resulting resemblance to persons either living or dead is entirely coincidental.

The publisher and the Author make no representations or warranties of any kind with respect to this book or its contents, and assume no responsibility for errors, inaccuracies, omissions, or any other inconsistencies herein. The content of this book is for informational purposes only and is not intended to diagnose, treat, cure, or prevent any condition or disease, including mental health conditions. The use of this book implies your acceptance of this disclaimer.

At the time of publication, the URLs displayed in this book refer to existing websites owned by Joseph Arnold, excepting URLs referenced in citations which are owned by third parties not affiliated with the author. WorldChangers Media is not responsible for, nor should be deemed to endorse or recommend, these websites; nor is it responsible for any website content other than its own, or any content available on the internet not created by WorldChangers Media.

Paperback ISBN: 978-1-955811-68-2
E-book ISBN: 978-1-955811-67-5
LCCN: 2024901333

First paperback edition: August 2024
Author photo: Leslie Hermans
Cover artwork: Penji & Bryna Haynes
Cover design, layout, and typesetting: Bryna Haynes
Editors: Bryna Haynes, Audra Figgins, Paul Baillie-Lane

Published by WorldChangers Media
PO Box 83, Foster, RI 02825
www.WorldChangers.media

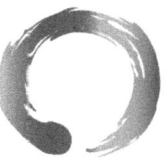

*To the place where your art, well-being,
and the world's hunger meet.*

PRAISE

"In *Soulforce*, Joseph Arnold courageously confronts the dominant mainstream paradigm which so afflicts art and artists no less than anyone else: a malign fantasy of hyper-control over a meaningless world. Arnold's advice releases our innate creative energies, gives co-creative relationships the central place they deserve, honors wildness, and restores hope, both individual and collective. His account is both deeply spiritual and eminently practical. We are lucky to have it."

— Patrick Curry, PhD, author of *Art and Enchantment: How Wonder Works*

"Deeply moving and wonderfully practical, *Soulforce* affirms our heart's wisdom about the power of art. Joseph Arnold's message empowers artists to address their creative and physical blocks to make the kind of art the world needs right now."

— Marci Shimoff, #1 *New York Times* bestselling author, *Happy for No Reason* and *Chicken Soup for the Woman's Soul*

"A deeply inspiring and hopeful vision for how a more fulfilling creative process can create a better world."

— Raji Malik, fingerstyle guitarist

"This is a book for artists who sometimes feel helpless in this chaotic world. With *Soulforce*, Arnold lays out his methods for artists of all stripes to crank up their creative energy, to fulfill their personal purpose, and share that energy with the world."

— **Mark Baldwin, Borealis Press**

"This book will help you as an artist develop a new mindset that will provide a path for personal growth and artistic mastery. Arnold's unique perspective is based on his own experience seeking artistic fulfillment and satisfaction, in both his own career and in helping others. The ideas in this book will benefit any artist, at any level, seeking greater achievement and contentment."

— **D.W. Fearn, producer, product designer, engineer, and founder of D.W. Fearn Professional Audio Equipment**

"*Soulforce* lands with the *whomp* of an ocean wave! I've always believed that we're in this world for a reason and it's our task to discover that reason and then make our contribution. Joseph has done this with *Soulforce* and has shown you the reality of interbeing. It's his gift for all of us."

— **Bob Lada, Alexander Technique teacher and Professor at Berklee College of Music**

"Joseph Arnold presents an impassioned plea for the necessity of the arts in our fragmented society. Though written with musicians in mind, all creative people will benefit from Joseph's beautifully written and practical suggestions."

— **Martha Hansen Fertman, EdD, Director of the Philadelphia School for the Alexander Technique**

"Joseph Arnold shares and validates many of my thoughts about the creative process and the tensions artists face in a culture that is largely anthropocentric, ethnocentric, and egocentric. Soulforce strives toward creative integrity."

— Phyllis Purves-Smith, perceptual painter,
New York Academy of Figurative Art Faculty 2000–2007,
Associate Professor, University of the Arts 1976–2010

"Joseph Arnold's book, *Soulforce*, invites us step by step with vivid examples and practical explorations, like 'The Magic Pause,' into a refreshing new approach and experience of hope and celebration. In putting his own journey into a larger context, he instills the confidence that opening to our Soulforce is the healing medicine out of the present Separation model, and that everyone is a vital link within a whole web of interconnectedness. The artist thus becomes the midwife to a soulful world through their own active creative aliveness. This is a powerful proposition."

— Zoana Gepner-Müller, Alexander
Technique teacher and Reiki Master

CONTENTS

Introduction: The Call to Soulforce 1

SECTION I: FOUNDATIONS

CHAPTER 1 | Does Your Art Really Matter? 15
CHAPTER 2 | The Arts in a World Gone Mad 35
CHAPTER 3 | The Foundations of Soulforce 55
CHAPTER 4 | The Soulforce Arts Approach 73

SECTION II: PRACTICE

CHAPTER 5 | Your Artistic Purpose 103
Mind-Body Interlude #1 | Spacious Awareness 133
CHAPTER 6 | Playing from the Heart 139
Mind-Body Interlude #2 | Two Percent Easier 167
CHAPTER 7 | The Yoga of Art 173
Mind-Body Interlude #3 | Exactly As It Is 203
CHAPTER 8 | The Spirit of the Gift 209
Mind-Body Interlude #4 | The Thing Mode and The Being Mode .. 237

SECTION III: EVOLUTION

CHAPTER 9 | Spiral Dynamics and the Arts 243

   Mind-Body Interlude #5 | Four Thoughts, Four Bodies 287

CHAPTER 10 | Second-Tier Artistry 293

   Mind-Body Interlude #6 | The Four Permissions 319

CHAPTER 11 | Ancient Roots, New Life 325

   Mind-Body Interlude #7 | The Magic Pause 367

CHAPTER 12 | Aligned Livelihood 373

Conclusion 429
Resources 435
Recommended Reading 437
Endnotes 441
Acknowledgments 449
About the Author 451
About the Publisher 453

INTRODUCTION

THE CALL TO SOULFORCE

I've always loved playing the violin. The joy I found in the instrument when I was young inspired me to perform at every opportunity, whether at a school concert or for the plumber who was fixing a leaky pipe at our home. Some of my most cherished memories are learning fiddle tunes at a music camp in the redwood forests of California and jamming with friends on the moonlit and ocean-battered cliffs of Monhegan, an island in Maine. In all these moments, I felt: *Yeah, this is what life is all about!*

So, when it was time to go to college, these joyful experiences inspired me to pursue a violin performance degree. However, my inspiration quickly faded in the face of the intensive training and highly competitive environment I encountered. The anxiety and tension I felt as a result led to repetitive strain injuries in both arms. This prevented me from playing the violin for anything more than a few minutes at a time. It was possibly the worst imaginable situation for a budding violinist.

When I first realized that the intensifying pain in my arms wasn't going to go away on its own, I sought help from my violin teacher. His response, "You should learn how to relax," was of little practical benefit. I tried my family doctor who told me that I had "lateral epicondylitis," which I discovered translates to "pain in the forearm"—something I was already well aware of, thanks very much. He prescribed a round of physical therapy, my first of many. My anxiety only grew when I discovered that the relief I found in these sessions was entirely temporary—as soon as I picked up my violin again, I noticed every bit of pain that I had felt before.

I then visited dozens of specialists including chiropractors, physical therapists, various types of myofascial therapists, Pilates and yoga teachers, and many others. I tried relaxation techniques, strength training, stretching, wearing physical supports, and over-the-counter pain medications. After more than a year of this, I was still in pain, and I had no clear answers as to either the root cause of the problem or how to solve it. At the time, it seemed like my career in music was over, and I could feel that my pathway to finding and fulfilling my life's purpose was blocked.

As it turned out, this was not the end. It was just the prelude to an amazing series of discoveries.

The first discovery took place in an Alexander Technique course I attended as a last resort. I remember lying on a table with my teacher's hands placed gently on my chest, waiting for something to happen. I felt the gentle, "listening" quality of her hands, but nothing more. Then, right when I was about to suggest that we try something else, the tension in my body released all at once. I was shocked! Previously, I had accepted this tension as a permanent part of who I was. Now, it had all been released. At that moment I understood that the tension that had been causing my pain was a *choice*, one which I had been unconsciously making, and not a structural or physiological problem with my body as I had assumed.

Never had I been aware of the capacity for this choice, and it shed a whole new light on the inner workings of my body. Over the course of many subsequent Alexander Technique lessons, I discovered a newfound agency over the muscular tension in my body, one that gave me a clear path toward pain relief. The freedom of movement I could now access changed the quality of my entire life. It was a bit like those stories where the hero grows up as an adopted child in a poor family but is later shown that, in fact, they were royalty all along. Before, I had thought of my body as a sort of malfunctioning machine. I now saw it as a rich source of learning, growth, and artistic pleasure.

Now, with many years of experience behind me, I know well the incredible breadth and depth of benefits that this method offers. In my case I found pain relief so absolute that I have long been able to play violin as much as I want without restriction. My performances also benefited from the ease and fluidity of movement I gained, which improved my technique, sound quality, and stamina tremendously. In short, the Alexander Technique restored my life as a violinist.

There was still more to come. The most magical discovery I made in applying the Alexander Technique to music was the difference in expressive power—my ability to open a channel within and effortlessly translate felt emotion into music. I also observed this while training to become an Alexander Technique teacher alongside other injured musicians, dancers, actors, wellness professionals, and others. I recall countless moments where, aided by an almost imperceptible release of muscular tension, the other student's performances, while already quite good, became positively luminous.

This shift was so striking, so moving, and so transformative for both the performer and the audience that I was captured. I dedicated myself to discovering how to tap into and cultivate this power, both in my own playing and when supporting students. When I learned of the term "soul force" in reference to Mahatma Gandhi's philosophy about the latent potency for change in society (discussed in Chapter 3), I realized that I finally had a name for this magical source of transformation. The Alexander Technique, by showing me how to release excess tension present in musical expression, helped facilitate a connection to my own latent potential. It revealed to me that this luminous quality, Soulforce, was already fully formed inside me, always ready to spring forth with soul-stirring power.

REVEALING THE SOURCE WITHIN

Deep down, what everyone wants in a work of art is Soulforce. When you sit in rapt attention at a concert, with chills going up and down your spine, that's Soulforce. When you become mesmerized by a painting so that you can't tell if you were looking at it for a minute or an hour, that's Soulforce. When a poem breaks your heart open and shows you an expansive freedom you never thought possible, that's Soulforce.

Soulforce is also what every artist longs to tap into during the creative act. When you release "trying to get it right" and instead get lost in a joyful, spacious, creative flow, that's Soulforce. When your body is relaxed and you feel like your art is creating itself, that's Soulforce. When you stop being afraid of what your audience is thinking and instead allow yourself to give voice to the depths of your heart, that's Soulforce.

Soulforce is the defining feature of all the greatest works of art. It's the X factor, the secret sauce, what makes your jaw drop and lifts you into an experience of awe. It's the real reason audiences seek out artistic experiences and also what inspires artists to expand the creative horizons of the human experience. Soulforce is what makes art, and life, worthwhile.

Even though you, I, and countless others may instinctively know this to be true, unfortunately there are many forces in our society that act to block the flow of Soulforce. My own rude awakening to these forces came during my stressful, and eventually physically painful, experiences during my music education. At the time, these painful experiences seemed like a problem I couldn't overcome. In a funny way, however, they are exactly what led to my greatest connection with Soulforce.

My essential discovery was simple: there is a source of wisdom, creativity, ease, and love that already exists within all of us. One whose expression leads to the transformative energy of Soulforce. Importantly, I learned that even though this source sometimes gets temporarily blocked, it can never be fully extinguished. It exists as a powerful, creative potential that is simply waiting to be called upon.

I have seen this source of wisdom, creativity, ease, and love in every one of my Alexander Technique students over the years. Often, their injuries have been stubbornly resistant to conventional treatments, and they're worried they won't be able to find lasting relief. What I tell them is what I learned myself: that their injuries are the result of how they are using their body. I then show them a new way of using their body, one that taps into the natural ease inherent to the structure and functioning of their body. The ease, comfort, and fluidity that result is often surprising to them. Not only is moving freely a new experience, but it becomes obvious that the very freedom they have been seeking has been lying in wait. They simply needed to learn how to get out of the way.

Of course, this is easier said than done. Most of my students arrive at my studio so used to trying hard and getting it right that, at first, they have a difficult time trusting that anything less than one hundred percent effort could work at all. All that changes when they experience how a single moment of greater freedom of movement brings bigger improvements in their technique, poise, and sound quality than could have otherwise been achieved through six months of diligent practice.

The question then becomes not finding a new way of trying harder, but how to get out of the way of what's inside that wants to be expressed. Through questions like, "How does your body want to do this?" or "What do you need to let go of to allow more freedom of movement?," my students gradually open themselves to a greater freedom, ease, joy, and connection in their creative life than they previously thought possible.

The process of revealing the source within has always put me in mind of the famous quote from fifteenth-century artist Michelangelo: "I saw the angel in the marble and carved until I set him free." What I have learned is that this is true not just of blocks of stone, but of artists themselves. The truth is that your Soulforce is already within you. Your task now is simply to learn to tap into it.

In writing a book about Soulforce, I would be remiss if I didn't share how I understand the word *soul*. This is obviously a term with countless interpretations, so I want to be clear about how I use the word in this book.

I do not use this term in reference to any specific religion, set of beliefs, or practices. *Soulforce* is not a religious book, but it does touch on matters of spirituality, which to me simply means an interest in the big questions of life. I define *soul* as an aspect of consciousness that is the source of your deepest truths and desires. Soul has both personal and universal aspects. It is specific to your own life circumstances, your background, culture, and where you call home. At the same time, it also comprises universal needs, such as acceptance, love, play, and healing, as well as the universe's own evolutionary forces.

Many traditions assume that what is spiritual must be fundamentally different from that which is worldly, but to me this is just another example of separation that is unhelpful and untrue. I believe that all aspects of the soul can be found in everyday life and directly engaged and experienced in a variety of ways. Experiences like creativity, vibrating energy inside the body, intuition, or synchronicities in daily life are all soul experiences.

I sometimes use the terms *soul* and *heart* interchangeably as I consider them to be pretty much one and the same. The heart is experienced as an emotional center, and it is the main channel for your soul to communicate with you. Soulforce could then also be understood as Heartforce, and for some this might be a more resonant way to think of it.

I also want to offer clarity about the term "Soulforce" itself. In this book, I repeatedly make the point that many artistic challenges arise from the use of excess force in the creative act. So why, if force is to be avoided, do I use a term that contains the word "force"? It's because Soulforce is an active energy, a flow, a source of creative momentum—and, yes, a force. But it's a mysterious, connected, and alive kind of force, very different from the constricted, effortful, and controlling kind of force that interferes with the creative act. If you find the word "force" confusing in this context, try to remember that there are different kinds of force in this world and that no term, Soulforce included, is fully adequate to fully capture an ineffable experience.

WHO THIS BOOK IS FOR

This book is for artists and creatives of all kinds, abilities, and backgrounds: musicians, visual artists, dancers, writers, designers, composers, actors, sculptors, directors, photographers, poets, producers, gardeners, chefs, and others. It is for artists who want to improve their artistic lives across three core dimensions:

- *Personal:* This book will help you navigate many of the physical, emotional, and spiritual obstacles that artists commonly face.
- *Professional:* This book will introduce you to new values and methods that will make your artistic life richer, more joyful, and more impactful. It will help you discover your artistic purpose, create with greater physical and emotional freedom, and cultivate a career that is financially rewarding and which matters to our world today.
- *Communal:* This book will redefine your life as an artist so that you know and see yourself as an active participant in a community and in the healing and growth of the world at large.

Many of the examples I use in this book are about music and musicians. If you are not a musician, do not be concerned; it's all the same process, all the same feeling. For example, while the Playing from the Heart technique discussed in Chapter 6 might sound like something only a musician can do, a sculptor or painter can do the same thing with a chisel or brush. Build from the heart, paint from the heart, sing from the heart.

In fact, you don't need to consider yourself an artist at all to get something of value from this book. Being an artist has little to do with a specific activity but is rather an orientation to life characterized by a devotion to beauty and creativity. You might be an artist in your garden, or in your cooking, or in how you play with your children. So, whether your art is with a violin, a camera, a pen, or a garden spade, you will certainly be able to find ways of relating each section and its practices to your own life circumstances.

One more note on who this book is for. This book puts forth the idea that many artistic challenges are the result of certain attitudes inherited from our society. Which society is this? In this book, when I say "our society," I mean the individualist, consumerist, industrialized society that evolved in the United States and which now spans the globe. My primary audience comprises creatives who, like me, have grown up in this society and have experienced its Soulforce-draining effects. If you hail from another society, then some of the examples and practices in this book may not resonate with you. However, you may still find it useful or inspiring because Soulforce is a universal human experience.

HOW TO USE THIS BOOK

It is a cliché that you are most called to teach what you have most needed to learn, and this book certainly lives up to that for me. In a sense, this book contains all the guidance I would have liked to have had when I was in music school, something that could address the struggle and doubts I faced and orient me to what was most important in my music and in life in general.

I wrote this book in part to address such a need for guidance in other young artists and anyone seeking answers and a means of reconciling their creative life with the world as it is today. My goal is not to teach the specifics of any artistic craft. I assume that you already have some level of competence in the basic skills and techniques of your art.

Rather, you can think of this book as a compendium of all the most vital aspects that your formal artistic training overlooked. This book is, in short, not necessarily about *what* you do as an artist, but *how* you do it and *where* you're coming from as you do it.

This is a psychoactive book. It is meant to provide more than an intellectual understanding, instead transforming your artistic life so that you can channel your Soulforce in your every creative act. This transformation can happen in two ways. The first is by the simple act of reading this book. Doing so will open your mind and heart to new artistic possibilities and touch on ones that have long been hidden in your heart. To aid this process, take your time reading. Let things sink in and work on you before you move on.

You can also speed your transformation by engaging with the practices. Practice is where intellectual ideas become an embodied reality, and in the end, this book is about practical, embodied change. So, integrate what you learn in this book into your daily life with patience, curiosity, and regular practice. This is the quickest and richest way to achieve a genuine personal transformation.

People have different relationships with practice. Some may be used to skipping over the practices, eager to get to the "good stuff" in the main body of the text with the idea to return to the exercises later. If this is you, then your growth edge may be to do all the practices at least once so you can get the full benefit.

Others feel a sense of responsibility to do things right, to read every page, and do all the practices. When this comes from a place of pressure and anxiety, this can make even the right methods lead to the wrong results. If this is you, then your growth edge may be to relax and just do the practices that speak most to you. This will be sufficient.

In addition, remember that it's better to adapt than adopt. In other words, feel free to adapt any given exploration to suit your needs, rather than trying to make it work when it really doesn't. Some things will work better for certain people or at certain times, so don't worry if one of the practices doesn't work for you right away. Perhaps they will make more sense with time.

There are two kinds of practices in this book:

- *Mind-Body Interludes:* These appear in Sections II and III between the chapters. These are essentially lessons in the Alexander Technique, ones that over the course of my twenty-plus years of studying and teaching have proven to be particularly effective. They are presented in an order to complement the material of each chapter. You can think of these as the centerpieces of your self-care and Soulforce toolkit. Once you've tried the Embodied Practices as written in each Mind-Body Interlude, attempt them while doing a low-stress everyday activity (such as brushing your teeth or making your coffee), and then while doing a challenging artistic activity (such as with a tricky technique). Practice each exploration at least once. If it works for you, consider making a point of practicing it daily for a few weeks. The more you experiment with it, the more it will infuse every area of your life with effortlessness, awareness, and renewed creative flow.

- *Soulforce Inquiries:* These are practices embedded throughout the chapters, and relate directly to the material being explored. Some are journaling exercises meant to help you get clearer on who you are and what you want as an artist. You may wish to obtain a journal specifically for the exercises contained herein. Others are meditations meant to give you a direct experience of the ideas in this book. (You don't need to have any prior experience with meditation to do these.) Each will help you flesh out and deepen your skills as a Soulforce artist.

You will also find many stories in this book. On one level, their purpose is to bring the ideas and practices in this book to life, to make them feel more relatable and tangible. On a deeper level, these stories are a form of medicine that will act on your creative soul if you allow them to. So, as you read, make note of any thoughts, emotions, or connections that come up for you and bring those into your next creative session. (Note: To protect the privacy of the people in these stories, I have changed their names and other identifying characteristics.)

Ultimately, your artistic transformation is as much a collective effort as an individual one, so it cannot be achieved alone. We need others to support and inspire us along the way. You can begin by sharing your journey into Soulforce with your friends and colleagues. You can also share your progress on social media, using #soulforcearts so we can all find each other. If this book changes your life (as I hope it does), give a copy to someone else; it might change their life, too.

In addition, if you want a more tangible sense of togetherness in your journey to Soulforce, you can join the Soulforce Arts Community, an online community and learning platform that brings together conscious artists of all kinds, abilities, and backgrounds to help you embrace your artistic purpose, create free from blockages, and make art that matters to a world in need—together. As a member, you gain access to regular Soulforce arts classes featuring the Alexander Technique and other methods of enhancing your creative Soulforce, all Soulforce Arts Institute online course recordings at no extra charge, and a vibrant community of like-minded and like-hearted creatives. Learn more at SoulforceArts.com/community.

I also offer two additional resources to enhance your journey to Soulforce artistry. One is the Recommended Reading section, a list of books I have found transformative in my own journey to Soulforce and which may be useful to you, too. The other is a link to access additional materials directly relevant to this book, including a guided meditation into your creative Soulforce, recordings of the Mind-Body Interludes that go into greater detail than space allowed in this book, and other bonus content that won't be available elsewhere. Visit SoulforceArts.com/bookextras or scan the QR code below.

 Scan to access your Soulforce resources, audio meditations, videos, and more!
https://SoulforceArts.com/bookextras

MY GREAT HOPE

My great hope in writing this book is to help you to find the aliveness, joy, and purpose that you desire, and to give you the tools you need to embody and express this in all your creative life. I'm sure that you, like so many, intuitively feel that this is what the arts are ultimately about, that this is what makes for truly transformative art as well as a fulfilling life as an artist. This book will help you reconnect with all that creative magic by affirming its value, showing why it seemingly disappeared in the first place, and what you can do to cultivate it in your life.

Ultimately, my goal is to support the emergence of a new way of being. A soulful one. A creative one. An unabashedly joyful one. One that will allow humanity to live in greater harmony: people with each other, and all of us with our planet. I believe that humanity is currently at a crisis point, and that as with all crises, there is both danger and opportunity. The danger is that we continue to become even more disconnected: from ourselves, each other, and nature. The opportunity is that we could instead reconnect, and from there experience a world of beauty, awe, and goodness that I believe is our birthright. All that is required to fulfill this opportunity is that each of us follow our soul's guidance, our Soulforce.

We begin our journey with one of the most painful, poignant, and urgent questions in the hearts of artists today: does your art *really* matter?

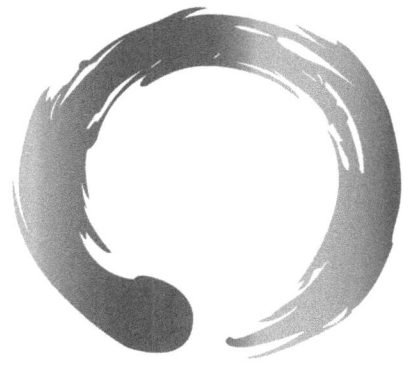

SECTION I

FOUNDATIONS

"It's either soul force—or bust."

— JAMIE WHEAL, *RECAPTURE THE RAPTURE*

CHAPTER 1

DOES YOUR ART REALLY MATTER?

On August 9, 2021, I woke up in my friend's sun-filled guest room, surrounded by the whispering of trees, the chirping of birds, and the fresh air of rural Maine. When I stepped outside with my morning coffee, the clear sky and the sounds of life all around filled me with a sense of well-being I rarely felt in the city.

So, when I heard the gravel crunching under the tires of my friend's Subaru as she rolled up her driveway, I was ready to burst forth with relief and gratitude for such a beautiful day.

However, her face was anything but serene as she made her way up to the porch. "Have you heard the news?" she demanded. "There's a report from the Intergovernmental Panel on Climate Change saying, 'Code red for humanity.'[1] The climate's screwed!"

The beauty around me suddenly felt fragile, ephemeral, and even more precious—like it could all go up in flames at any moment.

I had been aware of ecological issues since I was a little boy. I remember celebrating Earth Day in elementary school and feeling a vague anxiety that grew every year as the destruction and pollution of our environment accelerated. I felt a deep grief at the diminishment of Earth's ecosystems at humanity's hands, and while I made it a point to do what I could to understand the issues and minimize my own contribution to this diminishment, I also felt helpless to stop it.

That morning, the emotional impact of the Intergovernmental Panel on Climate Change report swirled through me. I felt an intense mixture of fear, grief, confusion, and anger. Amid these emotions, I thought, *Well, the rehearsal is over. It's finally here.* It was time to do something real—but what could I do? As a musician and Alexander Technique teacher, it's not as if I had the political clout to sway policymakers. Nor did I have millions of dollars to invest in ecological protection or millions of social media followers to influence.

I wondered, *Does my art really matter in the face of global climate change? What can I possibly do to help?*

At first, there seemed to be no satisfying answers. The societal messages I grew up with placed the arts far down the totem pole of tools to effectively address humanity's challenges. The arts were regarded as something "nice" but essentially frivolous—definitely not something that could address planetary or societal issues such as climate change or inequality. So, I was faced with a terrible choice: abandon the arts in favor of a more "practical" field like climate science or political lobbying, or isolate myself from global issues and continue a life in the arts in the naïve hope that my art could, somehow, make a positive difference.

Neither option appealed to me. Ever since I was little, I have known, deep in my heart, that I was meant to be an artist. Over the years, I turned down many opportunities to move into a more hardnosed, utilitarian, or financially stable career. I also know that, while the arts have played a crucial role in societal change around the world (for instance, energizing the revolutionary movements of many Latin American countries), creating yet another socially or environmentally conscious piece of music isn't something my creative soul is called toward. Nor, for that matter, are "protest songs" necessarily the most effective channel for artists' creativity in general; such works are great

Chapter 1 | DOES YOUR ART REALLY MATTER?

for energizing those who already care about the issues, but otherwise seem to have little effect on the social and political ills they decry.

I knew I needed a different kind of answer to my dilemma, one that reached to the root cause of the destruction in our world today, and that also considered the true meaning and value of the arts. My heart rebelled at the thought that all of the time, joy, love, and training I had poured into my artistic pursuits would be wasted—that I would essentially be a passionate bystander while the Earth burned. I knew, with unshakable certainty, that there *must* be a role for artists in resolving humanity's many crises, one that went beyond engaging in the rat race of money and influence, that didn't rely on wishful thinking, and that every artist could embrace in their current life. But what was that role?

My friend and I were sitting on the grass, discussing all this and what the "code red" meant. It was then that the memory of soul force rang through my mind.

Two years earlier, at the beginning of the COVID-19 pandemic, I listened to a podcast episode in which the guest, flow expert Jamie Wheal, was asked, "What chance does humanity have of surviving the next few decades with all the climate destruction, political division, and inequality?" Wheal's reply changed my life. He said, "To me, it's either soul force—or bust."[2] He went on to explain that "soul force" meant to face life's challenges from a deeper truth, and that this term was coined by Mahatma Gandhi during the movement to free India from British colonial rule. According to Wheal, our usual ways of fighting the symptoms have failed and are only causing more problems. It's time to step into a new story and guide our choices from a place of soul force, because our lives depend on it.

Despite previously knowing the broad outlines of Gandhi's philosophy, this was the first time the idea of "soul force" hit home for me. Once I learned more about this term, I coined my own version, *Soulforce*, to reflect the underlying unity of the soul and its transformational force.

I immediately loved this term because it gave form to a hidden connection I had long intuited, deep in my soul. I realized that Soulforce was the luminous quality I had witnessed and experienced in my Alexander Technique school: it was what made my favorite works of art so moving and transformative; and it was at the core of the wisdom teachings I had studied and cherished over the years. My first thought after listening to this podcast was, *What if I could have a Soulforce Arts Institute and guide musicians and artists to share this world-changing quality more effectively in their own art? How amazing that would be!*

I realized with newfound optimism, curiosity, and joy that the time for Soulforce arts had apparently arrived. Soulforce arts seemed to answer all the challenges I, along with so many others, had ever faced as artists. I saw how Soulforce could help artists relieve the physical tension that causes injuries and undue strain. I saw how Soulforce could help artists turn performance anxiety and impostor syndrome into flowing, creative energy. I saw how Soulforce could help artists create art that inspires, heals, and connects. Vitally, I also saw how Soulforce could answer the despair and helplessness so many artists and others had been feeling about the state of our climate.

All of this came to me in a flash that summer morning in Maine. Sitting on the grass with my friend, coffee cup in hand, I saw how my entire life had led up to this moment. I suddenly understood my life's purpose: to bring the message of Soulforce to artists worldwide to help create the kind of art that makes the world a more peaceful, beautiful, and life-affirming place—so that we could create art that *matters*.

I spent the two years following that epiphany developing ideas and methods related to channeling Soulforce in the creative act. I explored the creative impact of discovering a deeper artistic purpose; how to release the physical and emotional blockages that interfere with the free flow of Soulforce; the relationship between individual actions and global impact; the true—and often forgotten—purpose of the arts, and how to tap into Soulforce by facing life's challenges from a place of wholeness, aliveness, and connection, rather than the fragmentation, force, and alienation that currently pervades our society's way of life.

There remained some serious challenges before I could fulfill this purpose, however. Firstly, even though it was clear to me that Soulforce provides tangible answers to the challenges I just described, I was still unclear on the details. What were the methods by which artists could empower themselves to effectively address their creative, physical, emotional, financial, and spiritual challenges? In exactly what way could a work of art make a positive contribution to a world in turmoil? Moreover, was there truly a satisfying justification for spending precious time and resources on creativity, love, and play while the world is on a collision course with disaster?

This book is my attempt to answer these questions, and I invite you to come along with me.

Together, we'll embark on a journey whose destination is an artistic life full of Soulforce. The first step on our journey together is to examine our society's dismissal of the arts and discover the root cause of the everyday challenges artists face. In addition, we need crystal clarity on the reason for the destruction and strife all around us. As it turns out, our creative and societal challenges all have a single source, one that goes to the very roots of our civilization and whose antidote reveals the true purpose, meaning, and value of the arts in a world gone mad.

IT WASN'T SUPPOSED TO BE THIS WAY!

"You're wasting your SAT scores!"

— PIANIST AND DIRECTOR OF MUSIC AT ITHACA COLLEGE KARL PAULNACK'S MOTHER, UPON HEARING HIS DECISION TO BECOME A MUSICIAN[3]

Many artists have a secret fear: that our art doesn't really matter, that it isn't practical enough to make a tangible contribution to a world in need. As I already mentioned, this is because, despite the attention given to celebrity musicians and the like, our modern society regards the arts as essentially frivolous; something "nice to have," but in the end nothing more than a self-indulgent hobby. In this view, a work of art is a commodity valued only in terms of its role as an item of entertainment, luxury, or political influence.

This view stands in stark contrast with the knowledge carried by every artist and art-lover—the knowledge of the true value, function, and purpose of the arts. It is this knowledge that leads us to become artists in the first place, and what inspires us to courageously face the many challenges and sacrifices that accompany the mastery of an art form. It is also what leads audiences to seek out the arts as an oasis amid their busy lives. To those of us who carry this knowledge, art can seem like the one truly good thing that humanity has ever created. This can make its societal dismissal a source of confusion and pain.

The fear that our art doesn't really matter nags at nearly every artist, a constant drain on our creative energy and motivation. Everywhere we go, our decision to be an artist is questioned. The arts are the first things to be cut from school budgets. Our parents tell us we should go into a more financially secure career. Artists are rarely invited to the table when important political decisions are made. We are applauded when our art serves our financial gain or social status but ignored for our more authentic creations that fail to pay the bills. Everything around us seems to say that we've somehow made the wrong choice, that our love and creativity are unimportant flukes in a world driven by cold, hard facts.

Seeking respite from these painful societal messages, many artists look to the arts world itself for solace and guidance. However, the arts world can present us with its own challenges, which in turn serve up even more evidence of art's supposed impotence. Such challenges include the physical ailments that accompany rigorous artistic training, like repetitive strain injuries, nerve damage, back pain, excess muscular tension, and fatigue. Opportunities to share our work come with emotional challenges like performance anxiety, impostor syndrome, burnout, and an overactive inner critic. Learning environments can lean too heavily on mind-numbing practice methods, leading to creative plateaus, a lack of inspiration, and a reliance on technique over authenticity. Working conditions can present financial challenges, first and foremost, the inability to meet our basic needs through arts-based income, but also the difficulty of consistently cultivating appreciative, supportive audiences and the fear of "selling out." There is also a psychosocial context to artistic identity that can leave us with spiritual challenges like the loss of a larger purpose, meaning, and connection with community and other living beings.

Where do we turn when even our arts communities and institutions seem to drain the life out of our art?

All these challenges seem to carry the same message: that art, love, creativity, play, innocence, pleasure, aliveness, and a sense of the sacred have no place in our world. Yet, at the very same time, there is a place inside us all that rebels against this message, silently screaming, *It wasn't supposed to be this way!*

Despite the tidal force of society, institutions, and our own doubts, our hearts simply know that the arts have a deep and profound meaning. The source of our difficulty is not that art is meaningless or trite, but rather that society has lost touch with the true purpose of the arts. As a result, we as artists lack the intellectual and spiritual framework to properly articulate the purpose and power of our art. Without this framework, we are often at a loss as to how to justify the practical benefit of our art, and as a result we wonder if it really matters, after all.

When we consider the magnitude of what we are facing, is it any wonder that so many of us carry this secret fear?

ART IN A DEAD UNIVERSE

"Among the beneficial effects of art and religion at their best are to keep us from wandering aimlessly in this deserted landscape."

— IAIN MCGILCHRIST, *THE MATTER WITH THINGS*

If you secretly fear that your art doesn't matter or have any of the artistic challenges I just outlined, it's not actually your fault. It's not that you're not good enough or that you haven't tried hard enough. There's nothing wrong with your body, your emotions, your creative spirit, your art, or even the arts institutions of which you've been a part. This fear and these challenges have a deeper source, one that is larger than any individual's actions.

As it turns out, addressing this source is the answer to your artistic challenges and, as we shall see, it is also the key to stepping into your vital role in healing a world in turmoil.

Take a moment and read through the examples of artistic challenges in the previous section and ask yourself what might be common to all of them. Recall the ways any of them might have shown up in your own life. See if you can at least discern a certain feeling or energy that they all have in common.

What you might discover is that all physical, emotional, spiritual, or financial challenges faced by artists share a certain origin story about what the universe is, how it works, and our place within it. This story says that the universe is made up of countless tiny particles that bounce around without purpose or direction in a vast void of space, and that life itself is some kind of freak accident in an otherwise lifeless universe. In this narrative, the universe is more a *thing* than a *being*, a resource to be manipulated and from which value can be extracted. This story says that each person is an isolated individual in a world of "others," and that humans are the sole possessors of agency, sentience, and intelligence. It says that the universe is basically meaningless, and so we must create our own meaning by expanding the tiny, fragile light of human consciousness in a never-ending battle against the vast, impersonal forces of nature. Biologist Richard Dawkins summed it up well: "The universe we observe has precisely the properties we should expect if there is, at bottom, no design, no purpose, no evil, and no good—nothing but blind, pitiless indifference."[4]

This story is more than just a story. It's a whole worldview, a way of being, the source code of our civilization. It deeply influences how we think, what we do, and where we believe ourselves to be going. Author Charles Eisenstein calls it the "Story of Separation," and in many ways, it forms the entire basis for our global industrialized society's worldview about the universe and our place within it.

> The **Story of Separation** says that every person is an isolated individual in a world of "others;" that the universe is more a thing than a being; that life, at root, has no meaning or purpose; that humans are the sole possessors of consciousness; and that meaning can only be found in gaining ever greater control over ourselves and our surroundings.

Examine any of humanity's chronic crises—ecological destruction, political strife, inequality, the diseases of modernity, war, the hollowing out of communities everywhere—and you will find the fingerprints of the Story of Separation. In this worldview, we, as individuals, see ourselves as somehow separate from the world around us. We see nations as separate from other nations, humanity as separate from nature, our minds as separate from our bodies, and spirit as separate from matter. Separation thinking opens the door to all the destruction we now see all around us. If we knew that the Earth was our larger body, could we pollute it? If we knew that all of humanity was our larger family, could we wage war? If we knew that our creativity was a sacred gift, could we commoditize it? If we knew that matter was spirit made flesh, could we treat our bodies with so little reverence?

The Story of Separation also forms the root of all our artistic challenges, whether physical, emotional, creative, financial, or spiritual. For example, the injuries I sustained studying violin in music school were, at some level, the result of an unconscious belief that my body was a kind of machine subject to my bidding; a belief in accord with the strand of the Story of Separation that says that the world is made up more of things than beings. Because I believed my body to be a machine, I treated it like one. However, because my body is not actually a machine, it started to break down under the stress of the mechanical application of force and control that pervaded my violin practice sessions at the time. To make matters worse, many of the remedies I encountered in my years-long search for relief also inhabited the same mechanical story, which is why they offered little in the way of real healing. It wasn't until I stepped into a new story, the one that forms the basis for this book, that I found the relief I had been seeking.

The Story of Separation is also the basis for the fear that our art doesn't matter. In the Story of Separation, *nothing* really matters except the accumulation of wealth, fame, and power. Our society is now so accustomed to these priorities that many of us—even arts advocates—unconsciously take them for granted. However, art does little to further these priorities, and so, many arts advocates seek other justifications for the pursuit of art. All too often, these justifications backfire because they, too, are based in the Story of Separation and so entirely miss the point. For example, many well-meaning arts advocates tell us the arts are of central importance to humanity, but because their arguments fail to articulate the true purpose of the arts, their messages take on a Pollyanna-ish, hand-waving quality and lack the precision and insight necessary to fully convince us of their claims. Similarly, those who say that art exists for arts' sake, far from illuminating the arts' greatest contribution to society, only succeed in highlighting their irrelevance to tangible concerns. Even appeals to science miss the point. Yes, art is good for the brain—but is that really the fundamental motivation behind the greatest creations? The truth is that the arts *do* have a very clear purpose, value, and function. However, as we explore in this and later chapters, this purpose is inherently misaligned with the dominant worldview of our society. This is why our society so often dismisses the power and importance of the arts; like a dissonant chord in an ordered progression, art causes discomfort to those who have bought into the Story of Separation because its true purpose just doesn't fit.

The first step to counteract this dismissal, and thereby reclaim the rightful, empowered role of the arts in our global society, is to put words to the intuition our hearts carry about the true purpose of the arts.

THE TRUE PURPOSE OF THE ARTS

> *"Art is a means of playing upon human faculties in such a way as to provoke a consciousness of superhuman realities—of the realm beyond the senses. In every great ancient civilization, art has been used to further understanding, to lead men and women to a higher experience of reality than they might be able to achieve individually left to their own devices. Art is not meant to be 'enjoyed,' it is meant to illuminate."*
>
> – JOHN ANTHONY WEST, *SERPENT IN THE SKY*

The purpose of art is to bring us alive; to connect us with something bigger than our individual selves; to inspire, heal, and foster community. These are universal human needs whose fulfillment provides a necessary sense of meaning, purpose, and belonging. Without them, life becomes a dry, dusty bone. The greatness of a work of art is in direct proportion to the degree it serves this higher purpose; the more it does so, the more it enriches the lives of those who behold it. By the same token, without the guiding light of this higher purpose, a work of art can become vulnerable to financial, social, technological, or political influences, and thereby risk losing its essential transformative power.

For example, we love many of the well-known masterpieces of antiquity precisely because they instill in us a feeling of awe and timeless beauty. This is why Johann Sebastian Bach's solo cello suites, Ma Yuan's "one corner" paintings, and the megalithic walls of Machu Picchu each have an enduring popularity; each of them masterfully fulfills the true purpose of the arts.

This begs the question: what is the relationship between popularity and artistic greatness? Clearly, popularity doesn't necessarily signify transcendence. Much of what floods popular culture at any given time has little or no transformative power and is only widely known because of commercial influences. Meanwhile, countless works of potentially great power languish in obscurity simply because no one knows about them yet.

The relationship between popularity and a work's ultimate impact is complex. For example, one of the reasons Bach's music matters, beyond its transcendent qualities, is the simple fact that it has now been heard and enjoyed by millions upon millions of people. However, when popularity is not merely a product of financial interests, it often comes down to the accidents of history. It's chilling to think of how many world-renowned masterpieces were almost lost to accidental house fires or chance encounters. Furthermore, we may never know the more silent, indirect types of impact our creations have. Is bringing joy to your closest acquaintances truly less meaningful than pleasing faceless millions? In addition, given the serendipity possible over a long enough time scale, who can say that a composition rarely heard in a composer's lifetime will have a smaller impact than a top forty hit? Given these unknowns, it is unwise to actively pursue global renown because doing so distorts the creative impulse and rarely leads to works of enduring value. The best way forward is instead to create in alignment with the arts' true purpose—transcendence, aliveness, and connection—and to let go of the ultimate outcome.

Chapter 1 | DOES YOUR ART REALLY MATTER?

Understanding the purpose in this way also sheds new light on the use, function, and practical benefit of the arts. For instance, what is useful to you depends entirely on your larger aims in life. If your larger aims are money, fame, and power, then what is useful to you is an airport, a factory, or a stock exchange. In contrast, if your larger aims are to contribute to life and beauty on Earth and to delight in the magnificence of the universe, then what is useful to you is a Temple of Luxor or a Mirabai poem or a Botticelli painting, because it is these, and not the airport or factory, that can reliably produce the aliveness, inspiration, healing, and connection necessary to fulfill this larger aim.

Consider the Ancient Egyptians, who so strikingly expressed the ideals of their civilization in the form of sculpture and architecture. They understood their art to be more than mere objects of self-expression, social commentary, political influence, or even a means of aesthetic pleasure. As independent Egyptologist John Anthony West wrote in *Serpent in the Sky*, their art was "not meant to be 'enjoyed,' it [was] meant to illuminate."[5] In other words, their art had the explicit intention of inducing an altered state of consciousness, one that gave the viewer a mystical sense of connection with the forces of nature.

Even thousands of years later, their art still produces a powerful effect on visitors—and this isn't an accident. It isn't as though the Ancient Egyptians were actually involved with something else in life, and then just happened to produce countless works of transcendent architecture. The experience of transcendence was essential to the fabric of their civilization. It was what they were about, and they made this known through their art.

The Ancient Egyptians were not alone in their illuminative, transcendent use of art. As Joseph Epes Brown wrote in *Teaching Spirits*, many Native Americans, along with nearly all other indigenous peoples worldwide, "thought of the whole act of living in harmony with nature as their art."[6] Just as with the Egyptians, their worldview influenced the forms of art they created as well as the impact their art continues to have. Instead of the separation that characterizes modern society's worldview, many indigenous societies took (and still take) for granted the interconnectedness of all life. As a result, their art blurs the line between artist, audience, and environment, allowing all involved to become participants in the larger forces of nature.[7]

In other words, a worldview of interconnection gives rise to a purpose to life that goes beyond the individual ego, and to the extent that a work of art fulfills this larger purpose, that work can gain its fullest meaning, value, and importance.

From this vantage point, it becomes obvious that the reason our own society has lost touch with the purpose of the arts is that we have also lost touch with the purpose and interconnectedness of life itself. As is, we inhabit a story that tells us that the universe is essentially dead, with no meaning, no purpose, and no direction. It's no wonder, then, that we find ourselves in a world of chaos, destruction, and nihilistic despair; any action taken within a story of a dead universe can't help but further propagate its deadening effect. Within such a worldview, no aspect of life, not even art, can possibly fulfill its true purpose; and as a result, we suffer.

THE STORY OF INTERBEING

> *"A tree is alive, and thus it is always more than you can see ...*
> *It is every fly and bee and beetle that uses it for shelter or food,*
> *every bird that nests in its branches. Every one an individual,*
> *and yet every one part of the tree, and the tree part of every one."*
>
> **— ELIZABETH MOON, *OATH OF FEALTY***

If the cause of humanity's challenges is the story which we inhabit, then the solution is to step into a new story of the world, one which offers a more life-giving purpose and meaning to existence.

This is the **Story of Interbeing**, and as we shall explore throughout this book, it offers a fundamental antidote to the Story of Separation.

In the Story of Interbeing, the purpose of art is revealed to be in perfect alignment with the purpose of life itself, which is to celebrate, participate in, and propagate yet more life. According to the Story of Interbeing, we live in a holographic universe in which every part is a microcosm of the whole, and in which every seemingly separate *thing* is discovered to be a *being*, seamlessly integrated with everything else. Any action taken within the Story of Interbeing heals the wounds of separation in that its purpose, and result, is to bring forth greater aliveness, wholeness, healing, and connection.

It is from within the Story of Interbeing that we, as artists, can finally set our minds at rest about the "mattering" of our art. By creating from within the Story of Interbeing, instead of adding to the destruction and alienation characterized by the Story of Separation, we can bring about the healing our hearts, minds, bodies, communities, and ecosystems currently need. In an echo of the ancient Hermetic principle, "As above, so below," the Story of Interbeing offers reassurance that the smallest act, carried out with the proper intention, can have an untold life-giving influence on individuals, communities, and the world at large.

In this way, the Story of Interbeing can provide a new sense of hope and empowerment to any individual concerned about the state of the world. For artists in particular, it reveals that our art carries a previously hidden potential, one with transformative capabilities far beyond what is typically acknowledged in our society.

Many people, seeing the ongoing madness of our way of life, assume that solutions to the world's problems must not yet exist. The truth, however, is that solutions abound, many of which could provide quick and lasting relief to our challenges. It's just that we are simply so divided, and so entrenched in our fearful, atavistic mindsets, that we're unable to coordinate our efforts and take effective action.

The arts have an answer to this conundrum. After all, what else but the arts can so consistently reach beyond political or religious divides? What other than the arts can so deftly touch the vulnerability underneath our emotional armor? What other than the arts can leave us feeling uplifted and renewed in the face of life's stressors and struggles?

> We, as artists, are among the few in our world today perfectly positioned to heal the wounds of separation and usher in a more peaceful, vital, and beautiful world. Far from being well-meaning dreamers who waste our time and energy on frivolous pursuits, we are the architects and heralds of the **Story of Interbeing**.

Countless people around the world turn to the arts to provide the solace, connection, healing, and inspiration that are otherwise lacking in the rat race of modern life. Who else could effectively meet these needs but artists—we who have been born with an amplified proclivity for sensitivity, love, and creativity, and who have undergone the extensive training necessary to properly give these life-giving qualities form? The truth is that we, as artists, are among the few in our world today perfectly positioned to heal the wounds of separation and thereby usher in a more peaceful, vital, and beautiful world. Far from being well-meaning dreamers who waste our time and energy on frivolous pursuits, we are the architects and heralds of the Story of Interbeing.

HOW TO CREATE ART THAT DOESN'T MATTER

"It is no measure of health to be well-adjusted to a profoundly sick society."

— JIDDU KRISHNAMURTI, *COMMENTARIES ON LIVING: THIRD SERIES*

Despite the transcendent potential of the arts, and despite the knowledge of the true purpose of the arts that we, as artists and art lovers, hold in our hearts, the unfortunate reality is that the Story of Separation has infiltrated the arts world to an extent that many find difficult to believe. It governs the way we create; it controls the way we learn and teach; it rules how we inhabit our bodies, minds, and souls; and it dictates the ways we share our art and make a living.

This is, of course, to the great detriment of our art and our lives as artists, and, by extension, to the well-being of our audiences. For artists, the result is a life often filled with needless effort, disconnection, meaninglessness, pain, and struggle. Moreover, since our creations reflect our life overall, the result is that our art sometimes falls flat, feels inauthentic, or simply doesn't fulfill its transformative potential. The result for our audiences is that the consumption of such art fails to satisfy their longings for inspiration, healing, and connection.

Despite our best efforts to nonetheless follow the guidance of our creative souls, the Story of Separation can now be felt in nearly every aspect of artistic life. It can be felt in the daily grind of artistic careers that regard our creative spirit as a resource to be extracted rather than a gift to be honored. It can be felt in the anxiety that comes from trying to put on a perfect technical performance rather than one that features the authentic channeling of our soul. It can be felt in the chronic injuries that come from regarding our body as a machine to be corrected through constant vigilance and effort. It can also be felt in the perverse attitudes artists carry toward money, either in hungrily regarding our art as a commodity and our audiences as a source of income or in the disdain for money and selling that prevents us from sustaining ourselves financially.

If we continue to create in this way, the result will be creative death. Our bodies will break down with chronic injuries, our creativity will dry up, our souls will throb with anxiety and self-doubt, and we will struggle to find satisfying and sustainable opportunities to share our gifts. While our creations may carry a certain power through their technical prowess, popular appeal, or monetary benefit, deep down we will know that our artistic life contradicts everything we love and value about the arts.

These kinds of experiences are both the cause and result of our society's view of the frivolity and impotence of the arts. Even though these experiences contradict our heart's knowledge, they carry real cultural weight because, in a strange way, they point to something true: when we create from within the Story of Separation, the arts become devoid of everything that makes them meaningful and enlivening. Art created in agreement with the story of a lifeless universe is likewise lifeless. It is art without its transformative potential—its Soulforce—and without Soulforce, does it matter?

Of course, the answer is not just to prevent creative death but also to foster creative flourishing. Doing so will benefit every area of our lives. Our lives as artists will be full of flow, meaning, and pleasure; our resultant art will be full of life and transformative potential; and our audiences will be endlessly grateful for our creations. In other words, our lives and our art will be in alignment with what our hearts have known and felt all along. Best of all, simply by coming more alive in ourselves and our art, we will be fulfilling our most vital societal role: to be the vanguard of culture, leading humanity out of our current turmoil into a new and more harmonious way of being. Art thus created answers the question, "Does my art really matter?" with a resounding "YES!" that we can feel in our bones.

MORE THAN A BAND-AID

"You cannot solve a problem from the level of thinking that created it."

— ALBERT EINSTEIN

Even though the Story of Separation now seems to pervade the arts at every level, it doesn't have to be this way. It is still possible—even simple—to reconnect to the true purpose of the arts and thus enable yourself to create with Soulforce, the transformative creative energy that so characterizes the greatest art.

Now that you understand something of the true purpose of the arts, as well as what supports that purpose, you may be thinking, *Reconnecting with the true purpose of the arts sounds great, but how do I do it? How do I learn to channel my Soulforce in my artistic life today?*

While answering these questions is, indeed, the point of this book, these questions also carry a hidden danger. Jumping into the "how to" without a proper foundation may only result in more of the same, just under a different banner. After all, if you're unconsciously creating from a place of separation, then you may still bring the residue of separation to any new method of creating. Given how deeply entrenched and unconscious are the many manifestations of the Story of Separation in the arts and elsewhere, our next step is to first develop a deeper understanding of this story, its ramifications, and its antidote.

What's needed to address our current challenges goes well beyond the Band-Aid style—superficial solutions that are so familiar in our society. I won't promise you that you'll "find your Soulforce in thirty days," or that "if you do this one simple thing, your entire artistic experience will change." To reverse the effects of the Story of Separation, we need to dig deep enough to unearth and extract the root cause of the insanity. Only then can we begin to rebuild.

So, before we get to the solutions—by which I mean, the practical applications of the Soulforce Arts Approach—we must take a little detour.

We'll begin with a descent into madness.

"Hollywood is a place where they'll pay you a thousand dollars for a kiss and fifty cents for your soul."

– MARILYN MONROE, *MY STORY*

CHAPTER 2

THE ARTS IN A WORLD GONE MAD

Almost invariably, when I meet someone new and they find out I'm a professional violinist, they exclaim with joy about how lucky I am to be doing something with my life that I must truly enjoy. However, instead of feeling the unmitigated gratitude they seem to expect, my reaction during such conversations is often mixed.

On the one hand, I recognize that I truly am fortunate: I can comfortably support myself with something creative; I have a certain amount of freedom in how I spend my time; and what I do seems to have a genuinely positive impact on my audiences and students. At the same time, their joyful exclamations also land in a sore place within me. Being an artist has not shielded me from the painful effects of separation that these people presumably experience in their own "less creative" careers. On the contrary, my experience has been that my life as an artist in our society has all the same potential for dreariness, drudgery, and disenchantment as does any nine-to-five desk job; the main difference being that I sit on a stage rather than in a cubicle.

This reality often surprises people who work outside the arts, but the artists I know understand it with a world-weary cynicism. This world-weariness is the natural result of living within a society whose values repeatedly betray the knowledge our hearts carry about what the arts are for and what being an artist is supposed to be like.

The values of our society are not the values of life but of machines. Instead of our economic activities producing a more abundant, verdant, and beautiful world, we get one in which everything that is beautiful and good is transformed into a commodity, chewed up and spit out on the altar of infinite economic growth. As a result, we are constantly faced with the terrible choice between our love and our survival. Given that we need to survive in order to love, the machine in which we live forces us to relentlessly betray the knowledge our hearts carry, which is that we also need to love to survive, and that love is what makes survival worthwhile. The result for many artists is a state of disillusionment and despair, wherein we ask, "Is this *really* why I got into the arts?"

I have heard countless variations of this betrayal during conversations with my colleagues and students. Here are a handful of examples that vividly illustrate this point.

Emory, a painter, described her disappointing experiences in art school where she recalled butting up against a culture of contrivance, inauthenticity, and cliquishness. She told me, "I felt frustrated that I didn't get to have any female studio art professors and that my style of art was not appreciated by my male professors. I wanted to make something beautiful, but they wanted me to make something edgy. It felt invalidating, and I wanted to see more opportunities for the valuing of more styles of art, including things that are beautiful and not just edgy."

Tom, a singer-songwriter, described a similarly dispiriting experience in his attempt to improve his musicianship after music school: "I felt myself industrializing my own music into an assembly line, like a production. That pressure, exploitation, and perfectionism was destroying my relationship with music, and I think that's what led to me going into hiatus. It fed that little voice that says I'm not good enough. I got too much into my head, and then I grew to fear the arts."

Maddie, a young actor, suffered not from physical or creative injuries, but of the deep sadness she felt when recognizing the disenchanting realities of developing her nascent acting career: "In order to be an actor, you have to climb the ladder and you have to do shitty parts that don't feed your soul at all in very tiny gigs that you don't get paid for at all. And then, while you're not getting paid, you do side jobs that you don't particularly like."

Similarly, Nadia, a fashion designer, described her less-than-inspiring experiences in the fashion industry: "I was sending work into a black hole with no feedback and no appreciation and no real measure of the effort or elegance that's been put into it.... I also felt like I was just a hamster on a wheel to create these cost-effective productions and there was no real art and no real creativity, just using somebody else's idea rather than actually creating from the heart ... it felt robotic. I was sort of like a cheap intermediary, like I was being wrung out for all I have."

Finally, Debbie, a sculptor, described her fears about the world's widespread political turmoil and her perceived inability to make a positive impact: "When I think about what's coming down the road, I want to hold a higher vision than destruction and division, but I honestly feel hopeless. I want to be a part of the solution, I want to be of service more, but can I really do all that if I'm in my little hobbit cabin creating art?"

What strikes me about these conversations is not just the fact that being an artist in our society can be painful; it's how our hearts' knowledge of what the arts are for and what being an artist is supposed to be like is universal. This inborn knowledge forms the implicit and unspoken backdrop of our artistic challenges, without which we could not even tell that something is wrong with the machine-like way our society now guides us to create.

The essential mission of Soulforce arts is to illuminate our hearts' knowledge and put it back in its rightful place at the core of how we create, practice, perform, teach, and make a living in the arts. Soulforce arts says that, while we will always face certain challenges as artists, they are the result not so much of something inherent to the arts, but rather of the arts exposed to the almost total influence of the Story of Separation.

As mentioned previously, learning to create within a new story requires a personal transformation. Our next step toward that transformation is an underworld journey, one that will show us what we've lost under the guidance of the Story of Separation. However, just as every blues artist knows, the point of such a journey is not to leave us feeling down in the dumps, but to show us those cracks where the light shines through.

THE LESSER GODS

"Insanity is a perfectly rational adjustment to an insane world."
— R. D. LAING, *THE POLITICS OF EXPERIENCE*

If the knowledge of the purpose of the arts resides so inherently within us, how is it possible that we forgot it in the first place? Answers come from a deeper understanding of the Story of Separation, the wound it creates, and the "lesser gods" it has spawned that now so deeply inform the ways we live and create.

At the core of the Story of Separation is the belief that matter is separate from spirit. To those of us who have grown up in this story, it just seems obvious that there is the world, our bodies, and stuff in general on the one hand, and mind, sentience, and the sacred on the other. This belief pervades nearly every aspect of life and is, unexpectedly, an area of agreement between Western religions and science. Our religions paint a dualistic picture, telling us that what is worldly is profane, and that salvation is to be found in ascending to a separate, ethereal spiritual realm. Our science more or less agrees, saying that the world is "just" matter, but making the further move of dismissing consciousness, love, life, and the sacred from the realm of reality altogether.

Chapter 2 | THE ARTS IN A WORLD GONE MAD

Whatever the source, this story leaves little room for the arts. Recall that the true purpose of the arts is to induce a shift in consciousness, one that brings us into a felt connection with something bigger or which brings us more alive. In the Story of Separation, however, there is nothing bigger to connect to. In this story, even if spirit exists in some ethereal plane, the universe that we find before us is nothing more than a bunch of rocks and giant balls of flaming gas that whirl randomly in an infinite void.

Within the assumption of a lifeless universe, consciousness itself is regarded as highly suspect; feelings, inspiration, connection, and anything else that can't be readily measured sit low on the pecking order of "realness." As a result of this assumption, anything that relies on a transformation of consciousness for its essential functioning—like art—sits similarly low on the pecking order. This is why artists never get a seat at the table when the big kid decisions are being made; in a society suffused by the Story of Separation, art just doesn't seem all that *real*.

What do seem more real are money, status, technology, and power. These are the **lesser gods** of the Story of Separation, the underlying values and goals it best comprehends. Simply put, the Story of Separation perceives *things* (matter devoid of spirit) more easily than *beings* (matter as expression of spirit), and the lesser gods just fit more easily in the thing category than the being category. The arts, on the other hand, fit better in the being category, and are thus something of an enigma to the Story of Separation.

> The **lesser gods** of the Story of Separation are money, status, technology, and power.

However, it's not as though the arts don't have a place within the Story of Separation. They do. It's just that in a universe stripped of spirit, their true purpose doesn't really compute. The result for both artists and audiences is an experience that is correspondingly dispiriting.

The aspects of the arts that do fit within the Story of Separation are any that align with the lesser gods. For example, how much money to exchange for a poem—that computes. Figuring out and repeating the mechanics of a certain technique—that computes. Using technology to increase the efficiency and monetary return of your creative process—that computes. Using your creative talents to win competitions, followers, accolades, or political influence—that computes. Any use of the arts that can be measured, instrumentalized, objectified, mechanized, manipulated, forced, or controlled—all of that computes. But a movement of the soul that leads to an ineffable feeling of awe?

(Cue computer voice.) *Does. Not. Compute.*

Thus, it is the undue dominance of "thingness" over "beingness" that we now find our cities choked with drab, boxy buildings, parking lots, and billboards; that our most popular music is vacuous and coarse; that the walls of our hotels and airports are covered with art chosen for its sheer banality; that technology is increasingly used to compensate for a lack of artistic skill; that our most popular films utterly lack satisfying plot lines; that an artist's celebrity is valued over their creative power; that our communities are disintegrating in part due to a lack of shared artistic experiences; and that we, as artists, are treated like cogs in a machine. The cheap, ugly, superficial art that now pervades our cultural landscape, and the concomitant suffering of artists, are a perfect reflection of the belief in a dead universe.

Not just confined to the arts, the belief in the separation of matter and spirit also has dire consequences for our society at large. It is precisely this belief that has led to the madness we now see all around us. The nihilism, despair, addiction, and rage that now suffuse our society are the perfectly understandable response to living within a story of a dead universe. This is because we are, in fact, wired for connection, beauty, and aliveness. As author Brené Brown puts so powerfully in *Daring Greatly*, "Connection is why we're here. We are hardwired to connect with others, it's what gives purpose and meaning to our lives,

Chapter 2 | THE ARTS IN A WORLD GONE MAD

and without it there is suffering."[1] Any being wired for connection, beauty, and aliveness living in a story that results in disconnection, ugliness, and lifelessness is bound to go more than a bit mad.

The Story of Separation contradicts who and what we are at a fundamental level. Its ubiquity thus leaves a huge, gaping hole in our hearts—the wound of separation. In a sense, all the madness of the world can be regarded as a poorly guided attempt to heal this wound and regain our lost wholeness. However, our society lacks even any clarity on what has been lost, much less the effective means to regain it. So, we thrash around, grasping for anything that will, however temporarily, staunch the wound. This is why we now find ourselves mired in addictions: to drugs, alcohol, violence, consumerism, fossil fuels, oppression, and fame—all variations on the theme of the lesser gods.

It hasn't always been this way. From time immemorial, the saints and sages of all cultures have proclaimed that there is a deeper unity and interconnectedness underlying the seeming separateness we find around us. Their universal and timeless message has revealed a profound purpose to life: to gain conscious awareness of this unity (otherwise known as Buddha nature, God, the Universe, the Ground of Being, Brahman, Nature, or Life) and to thereby realize who and what we truly are.

Because of the inadequacy of concepts to bring about such an awareness, other means have often been used to convey its reality; namely, the arts. Why else would the Taj Mahal, Basho's haikus, or Michelangelo's "Pieta" have such timeless appeal? These, among countless other great works of art, speak to us because, as Joseph Campbell wrote, they "render ... the 'radiance' of all things, as an epiphany or showing forth of their truth."[2] In other words, we love these works of art because they put the lie to the Story of Separation. They reveal the underlying unity of all things, remind us of our inherent connectedness and aliveness, and thereby heal the wound of separation.

By and large, guided as they are by the Story of Separation, the arts within our society today fail to fulfill this profound purpose. No amount of Walmart superstores can ever fulfill our need for Chartres Cathedrals. It's not that sacred art is better than secular. It's rather that art worthy of the name obviates the difference by illuminating the divine in the mundane and the mundane in the divine. When we instead deny the possibility of something bigger to which we can connect, when we dismiss consciousness and aliveness as impotent side effects of a reality that consists of nothing but the concrete, then there is no possibility of healing the madness caused by the wound of separation. Ultimately, art created within this story only makes things worse. People, longing for beauty and connection, but receiving only the superficial, mass-produced trash our society churns out, will be gradually driven insane.

Ugly in, ugly out.

> It's not that sacred art is better than secular. It's rather that **art worthy of the name obviates the difference** by illuminating the divine in the mundane and the mundane in the divine.

Deflected from its true purpose by the hollow promises of the lesser gods, a work of art loses all its transformative power. Really, it isn't art at all, truly becoming nothing more than an item of luxury or entertainment. Artists, then, become nothing more than self-indulgent hobbyists and navel-gazers. The arts then deserve their position at the kids' table of our cultural hierarchy. Created upon the altar of the lesser gods, our creations lack the Soulforce necessary to address the madness all around us, and so we find ourselves playing a sick game of make-believe in which we can only pretend that the artistic baubles we play with can come alive.

Chapter 2 | THE ARTS IN A WORLD GONE MAD

THE ALMIGHTY DOLLAR

"Writing is like sex. First you do it for love, then you do it for your friends, and then you do it for money."

— ANONYMOUS

Everywhere we look, the arts are for sale. Music downloads, concert tickets, prints, paintings, dance classes, university arts degrees, home décor ... The list goes on and on. The exchange of money for art is now so ubiquitous that it might almost seem like a natural part of the artistic process. Still, money and the arts have always had an uneasy relationship. After all, how much is a transcendent artistic experience worth? That's a lot like asking how much a sunrise is worth. What makes something true art simply cannot be quantified in terms of money.

And yet, quantify we must, because we live in an economic system that requires money for our survival. Few landlords or grocers, for example, will accept a poem or a dance in exchange for rent or ramen. This forces artists to turn art into a commodity so that it can be exchanged for money, which can then be used to buy life's necessities. This exchange, however, can challenge the integrity of art. Our economic system is one that requires endless growth to survive, incentivizing the creation of generic replications that can then be produced at scale, rather than those created with the authenticity, time, and attention required for genuine art. The commodification and mass-production necessary to survive in this system benefits artists in some ways because it does allow for the widespread propagation of our work. However, this benefit comes at a great cost. As author Lewis Hyde wrote in *The Gift*, it is "possible to destroy a work of art by converting it into a commodity."[3]

The drive to make money from art often distorts and cheapens it. For instance, the whole pop music industry seems less focused on creations of beauty and more on the bottom line. This focus has cheapened every step in the creation and propagation of pop music: songs are composed via formulas designed to maximize catchiness, edited with pitch-correcting software that masks a singer's lack of vocal technique, and brought in front of focus groups before release to ensure marketability and sales.[4],[5] The results, while ear-catching, are often shallow and unsatisfying.

Similarly, IKEA brands itself as a place where ordinary people can buy artistic items, but there is simply no comparison between one of their factory-made chairs and a hand-crafted Shaker antique. One looks chic from a distance but breaks as soon as you sit in it. The other exhibits an astonishing level of craftsmanship and aesthetic beauty and will last for more than three hundred years of regular use.[6] What accounts for the difference in quality? IKEA makes their chairs in search of profit, but the Shakers made theirs to serve God. Different intentions, different output.

Even in art and music schools the bottom line is king. Economic pressures motivate schools to become like factories for churning out art students, the result of which is that many graduates are saddled with injuries, burnout, and crippling debt. What's happened is a sort of mission drift, where the original mission of the school—to support the flourishing of young artists—has slowly shifted over time to a new mission: keeping the doors of the school open at all costs. Animated by this new mission, a school no longer really serves the arts but rather the bureaucracy that runs it, as well as the personal and professional interests of the faculty and staff. The result is that bureaucratic thinking infects the learning environment such that being a student or a teacher in one of these schools often feels more like checking off items on a to-do list or trying to keep up with a too-fast conveyor belt of tasks rather than an opportunity for creativity to flower in its own time.

Clearly, none of this serves the flourishing of students, teachers, society, or the arts. So, why does it keep happening? It's because our society has placed the almighty dollar above all else, and when art is created in the service of economics, the very thing that makes it art is lost.

Chapter 2 | THE ARTS IN A WORLD GONE MAD

WE USED TO SING TOGETHER

"Without music, life would be a mistake."

— FRIEDRICH NIETZSCHE, *TWILIGHT OF THE IDOLS*

The cheapening of the arts is also partly due to the increasing prominence of technology. Even though technology has improved our lives in countless ways, it also carries a hidden cost. In the arts, it has led to the loss of creativity and connection. A clear example of this is recorded music and its effect on community ties. On the one hand, recorded music has brought incredible benefits to society, including the ability for audiences to hear music from faraway places and for artists to share their music more widely. However, recorded music is now so ubiquitous and inexpensive that, for example, many people throwing a party now choose to just plug in an iPod rather than deal with the hassle of a live band.

This trend, writ large, has led to a massive decline of live music in our society, especially that created by nonprofessional musicians in community settings. The result is that, even though many of us still love live music, many more of us are now so accustomed to canned music that we no longer really realize what we're missing.

Another hidden cost of recorded music technology is a decline in our creative abilities. The power and ease-of-use of recording technology is now such that anybody can program a beat with just a few clicks of a computer mouse. The upside is that we can make a decent-sounding beat without going through the laborious, years-long process of becoming an accomplished drummer. However, skipping this hands-on learning process has a hidden consequence: it robs us of the full richness of the creative experience. While programming beats on a computer does have its appropriate uses, the real-world process of becoming an accomplished drummer grants access to a deeper experience of creativity, mastery, and accomplishment than is otherwise possible. The result of the ever-increasing use of recording technology is that fewer and fewer of us have a felt sense of being a truly creative person.

A further cost of recorded music can be seen in the disintegration of community in our society. Not that long ago, our Saturday evenings would have been filled by gathering around a piano in someone's parlor and singing our favorite tunes. This would bring people together and affirm a sense of belonging. However, the ever-increasing predominance of recorded music has undermined this source of human connection. Nowadays, the vast majority of music is passively consumed, usually in isolation and while staring at a screen with headphones on. All too often, technological advance, in the arts and elsewhere, comes at the cost of the full experience of creativity and connection otherwise possible.

MAKE SURE YOU GET MY GOOD SIDE

> *"Fame! You'll be famous as famous can be, with the whole wide world watching you win on TV. Except when they don't. Because, sometimes, they won't. I'm afraid that sometimes you'll play lonely games too. Games you can't win 'cause you'll play against you."*
>
> — DR. SEUSS, *OH, THE PLACES YOU'LL GO!*

In ancient times, monarchs were often considered to be incarnations of the gods and were thus treated with worshipful adoration by their subjects. Of course, things are no different today. Just look at the way we treat our most famous musicians. These are modern-day gods incarnate. But do they really deserve our worshipful adoration? Or are they mere mortals—talented musicians who have simply benefited from having an army of image consultants, a mountain of advertising dollars, and the right marketing strategy? Whatever you think of the current chart-topping pop stars, it is often obvious that the pursuit of celebrity is not necessarily synonymous with transcendent artistic output. Indeed, it often gets in the way.

For example, among musicians, what often gets the most attention from audiences and colleagues is flashy technique. This attention can bring tangible benefits. Musicians who attain the highest levels of technical virtuosity and perfection often reap greater fame and fortune than those with more modest abilities. For some, however, the attempt to reach celebrity status via flashy technique comes at the expense of musical depth. One historical example is violinist Niccolo Paganini, who rose to meteoric fame in nineteenth-century Europe. The key to his success? He focused on developing his technique to an extent never seen before. However, in achieving all this, he left something important behind. Although his many compositions are indeed masterpieces of violinistic virtuosity, a common critique is that they also lack a certain depth of soul. Did he sacrifice that depth in pursuit of celebrity status? Only Paganini knows. Nonetheless, he was not the only one who has apparently made this trade-off. Many modern musicians have also found celebrity through displays of mind-bending technique. For some, their desire for celebrity status outweighs deeper musical considerations. The result are performances that wow many audience members—and just as often leave others feeling emotionally unsatisfied.

Another example comes from the world of avant-garde art, wherein the pursuit of social status has now become so all-consuming that it has stunted the further evolution of the arts. Postmodern ideas about the deconstruction of all previous modes of thought have led artists to the curious, if depressing, attempt at deconstructing their own art. For example, a colleague of mine who taught for twenty-five years at a prestigious fine art program described listening in horror to a group of students and colleagues debate whether six people standing in line counts as a drawing. While such inquiries can lead to new perspectives and techniques necessary to art's collective evolution, more often than not they reflect a priority on social, rather than artistic, advancement. The result is that much contemporary art can only be understood by a tiny clique within an elite avant-garde for whom authenticity and beauty are regarded as painfully gauche. Dismissing authenticity and beauty, all they are left with is a contest in shock value, ironic self-critique, trendiness, virtue signaling, social posturing, and in-group popularity contests. The manifestations of this dynamic now fill many modern art museums to head-scratching effect. However, there's no one to blame here. This is simply what art looks like when connection to a deeper source of creativity is supplanted by the desire for social status.

I'LL TELL YOU WHAT ART IS

"It's a beautiful thing, the destruction of words."
— GEORGE ORWELL, *1984*

It has long been known that the arts have an incredible ability to move us. This has tempted many leaders throughout history to use the arts as an instrument of political power, with mixed results. Sometimes this use has had an uplifting effect on art, artists, and society. For example, European monarchs and church leaders often commissioned works from the greatest artists of their times as a demonstration of their own piety and divine right to rule. The results are some of what we now consider to be the greatest works of European art, including Mozart's music, the palace of Versailles, and the frescoes in the Sistine Chapel. At other times, however, the use of art as an instrument of power has coincided with efforts to dominate, control, and oppress. In these cases, art, artists, and society have only suffered.

For example, the Russian and Chinese communist parties regularly used art as a tool of propaganda. The countless frescoes, statues, songs, and illustrations they commissioned were designed to inspire,

Chapter 2 | THE ARTS IN A WORLD GONE MAD

and frighten, their populations into supporting the communist cause. These works, while emotionally provocative, portray only a false sense of transcendence. Underneath their pseudo-inspiring exterior, they leave the viewer with an empty feeling in the gut and the sense that only a dupe could wholeheartedly believe in the message displayed. This is not an accident; these works of art were a form of Orwellian domination. They said to the viewer: "Set aside your real feelings and make yourself believe in the party—or else." That the societies that produced these works were also home to the Gulag Archipelago and the purges of the Great Leap Forward is not a coincidence. A society's art perfectly reflects its worldview.

Not all acts of domination in the arts world are so overt. Some are an unspoken part of our most prestigious arts institutions. For example, when Carnegie Hall or the Metropolitan Museum of Art puts on a show, they are not just sharing works they enjoy. Institutional heavyweights like these have such wealth and prestige that when they share something, they are, in effect, saying, "This is what art is." On the one hand, this is useful because we do need institutions to uphold treasured traditions and put forward what's new in the arts. On the other, institutional authorities can also become unmindful of their own biases, stuck in ideological ruts, beholden to financial or political interests, or reflexively dismissive of new ideas or people. Clearly, none of these downsides serve the arts or society.

An attitude of domination, force, and control can even be found in the artistic process itself. Think of an overbearing orchestra conductor trying to *make* his orchestra follow him, or an eager dancer trying to *make* her body form a gesture. While such efforts can seem to work well outwardly and in the short term, they always carry a hidden cost. A conductor who gestures too forcefully sends an unconscious message of forceful musicality to his orchestra. A dancer who forces her body into a tight position cuts off the flow, grace, and poise that her audience craves to experience. These are examples of a subtle use of coercive power, one many of us may be so familiar with that we might not be fully aware of its impact on our lives. The truth is that the subtle use of coercive power is the root cause of many of the challenges we face, artistically and societally. Its familiarity belies an important truth, however: the desire for power undermines the very search for transcendence it purports to ensure.

FINDING OUR WAY BACK HOME

"You can't be saved alone because you aren't alone; you are the whole cosmos."

— ALAN WATTS, FROM A LECTURE ON THE MIDDLE WAY

The arts in our society have lost their way. Instead of helping guide us into an experience of aliveness and connection, our art all too often leaves us feeling hollow and disconnected. This is because, perhaps to a greater extent than in any other society throughout history, our art is created in service of the lesser gods of money, technology, status, and power. Art created in this way not only fails to uplift and connect us but is actually an integral piece of the madness we see in the world today.

Of course, there are many exceptions to this. Rock concerts and electronic dance music festivals are wildly popular because they offer an immersive, cathartic experience that gives people a needed sense of flow and connection that's otherwise nearly impossible to find in mainstream secular society. In addition, there are countless authors, musicians, designers, architects, filmmakers, and others whose work inspires millions to new ways of thinking, feeling, and being. There are also many more lesser-known artists who bring their heart and soul to their art, despite the pervasive influence of the economic and societal disincentives described in this chapter. The issue isn't that there aren't enough soulful and vibrant artists in the world today; it's that our soulfulness and vibrancy happen in spite of the system we inhabit, not because of it.

Despite the best efforts of countless artists and art lovers, the underlying forces that cause the wrongness we see in the arts today continue apace. More and more "art" is created in distant factories, in ways that hurt people, communities, and our planet. More and more aspiring artists go through their artistic training and enter the marketplace, only to become injured, burnt out, and broke in the process. More and more people reach for their smartphone for the connection and inspiration that can only truly be found in a shared artistic experience.

No artist involved in this process consciously seeks the cheapening of the arts. Nor are these problems the fault of particular individuals or institutions. Rather, they are the natural result of inhabiting a story of separation, force, and control. The answer, then, is to step into a new story, one that rests upon the truth of who and what we are as described by the world's saints and sages. One in which the universe is regarded as alive, interconnected, and whole. One that will allow you to simultaneously create the most transformative art, support your greatest well-being, and allow you to be deeply of service to a world in need.

While learning about the extent to which the Story of Separation may infuse your artistic life can be uncomfortable, it is a necessary precondition to make space for a new story. This is why it's so important to spend a little more time in our underworld journey before moving on; it's hard to fit new food in your belly without fully digesting the old. Use the following guided meditation to digest the remnants of the Story of Separation as they now appear in your artistic life.

SOULFORCE INQUIRY 2.1
FULLY DIGESTING THE STORY OF SEPARATION

The Story of Separation can create many wounds within your body, mind, and soul. The key to unraveling these wounds is not to try to change them or even to seek improvement of some kind because many of the ways you currently seek change may themselves be part of the problem.

The answer is instead to fully digest the emotions and memories related to the wounds of separation. This will release any stuck places in your body, mind, and soul, granting you relief, a newfound wholeness, and many useful insights.

To begin, go back over this and the previous chapter to identify the stories, phrases, or ideas that brought up an emotional charge of some kind, whether positive or negative. Spend a minute with each section, reading through it and noticing the emotions that come up. Bathe your reactions in your awareness without trying to change them at all. If memories arise, simply notice these memories. If painful emotions arise, simply notice these, too. Let it all arise and be exactly as it is for at least two minutes.

In a society whose mode of operation generally rests on force and control, attention and allowing can seem at first like weak sauce. However, the simple act of giving your wounds spacious attention has unexpected power: by itself, it initiates the healing process and is the secret to bypassing more problematic ways of seeking change.

The process of stepping into a new story and then letting it guide your artistic life begins with a personal transformation, but it doesn't end there. The vision of Soulforce arts is the creation of a global movement to reconnect the arts to their true purpose, one that will lead to the widespread creation of transformative art and the healing of our bodies, minds, and souls, thereby ushering in a more beautiful, life-giving world.

Participating in this vision presents four main challenges. The first has to do with your sense of self. Like it or not, the Story of Separation has probably become entrenched in certain parts of your personality and artistic practices. Making space for a new story will require letting go of some of the ways you've come to know yourself thus far, a process that can, at times, be uncomfortable. How much you'll have to let go of depends on how deeply you've learned the ways of separation. You get to decide how far down the rabbit hole you want to go.

The second challenge has to do with social pressure. As your personal transformation progresses, there will be times, from the perspective of those around you who are still deep in the Story of Separation, when *you* will be the one who seems to have gone mad. When they see how differently you create, practice, perform, teach, and make a living in the arts, they may not understand your actions and may even try to get you to come back to your old ways of being and creating. The answer to this challenge is to find the intellectual, spiritual, and social support necessary to allow the new story to become fully integrated into who you are.

Finding this support is the third challenge. This book provides the intellectual and spiritual basis for the personal and societal transformations you may now seek. You can find the social support you will need along the way by actively engaging friends and colleagues in your process, as well as with other resources listed in the back of this book.

The fourth and final challenge is to address the question of how individuals without gobs of money, fame, technology, and political power can affect change on a large enough scale to make a tangible difference. It is with this question in mind that we now turn to the next chapter.

"A human being is a spatially and temporally limited piece of the whole, what we call the 'Universe.' He experiences himself and his feelings as separate from the rest, an optical illusion of his consciousness. The quest for liberation from this bondage [or illusion] is the only object of true religion. Not nurturing the illusion but only overcoming it gives us the attainable measure of inner peace."

— ALBERT EINSTEIN, IN A LETTER
TO ROBERT S. MARCUS

CHAPTER 3

THE FOUNDATIONS OF SOULFORCE

I'm not doing that again, I thought to myself as I returned home after a show, exhausted, tense, and drained. I had just performed with a well-known regional orchestra, and I knew that, at least on paper, it was a great opportunity. As a budding violinist, I should have felt very fortunate to play with a group where I was paid well, where I could put my all into my playing, where I was appreciated by the other musicians, and where there was a good chance that I could officially join the group and thereby enjoy a future of greater financial security. However, despite the seeming benefits, I found the music deathly boring, the conductor exasperating, and the marathon rehearsals an exercise in painful endurance. Was the professional advancement on offer worth the lack of creative fulfillment and the emotional and physical strain?

As I unpacked my things and slumped on my sofa to rest, this question rolled through my mind, prompting me to reflect on other less-than-inspiring musical experiences I'd recently had. I was reminded of how, despite the intense effort and focus I had brought to my performances in music school, my sense of creative fulfillment had only lessened with time. I also reflected on my more recent professional performances and felt a growing sense of sadness and anxiety as I realized how few of these brought the artistic impact I desired. *Is this really how it's going to be?* I wondered. Facing a future where my art all too often felt like meaningless drudgery filled me with despair and led me into a deepening existential crisis. If my music couldn't bring me the creative fulfillment and artistic impact I desired, then what could? Did my life as a violinist even matter? Did anything matter?

I then began what became a years-long search for satisfying answers to these questions. For a long time, I found none and often struggled with the despair and emptiness I felt as a result. However, a turning point came when, instead of continuing to seek fulfillment through professional advancement alone, I began to question the assumptions underlying my existential and creative challenges. Examining these challenges closely, I repeatedly found the following assumptions: that I was separate from the world around me; that having and doing were more important than being; and that my self-worth was measured in how much I strove for monetary and professional advancement.

With further exploration, I came to understand these assumptions as the hallmarks of the Story of Separation. As I learned more about them, I discovered two surprising connections. The first was that, contrary to its very name, the Story of Separation was what *connected* all my artistic challenges, whether physical, creative, emotional, or financial. The second was that the very same forces that made my artistic life needlessly challenging were also those that contributed to the societal chaos I saw around me.

A new sense of empowerment dawned as I realized I now had the answer to my existential crisis. The answer lay in discovering the deeper connection and aliveness hidden under what at first seemed to be separate, fragmentary, or inert—in other words, to step into the Story of Interbeing. I realized in a flash that doing so would effectively address all my artistic challenges, and furthermore, that an artistic life founded on such deeper connections was exactly what the world needed from me as an artist.

Chapter 3 | THE FOUNDATIONS OF SOULFORCE

Following these realizations, I saw that my own artistic purpose—my greatest creative potential and my unique contribution to the world—was not limited to what I could achieve with the violin alone. Rather, my purpose was to discover all the ways in which we, as artists, could step into the Story of Interbeing in our artistic lives and enjoy the creative fulfillment and impact our hearts knew we were meant for.

This act transformed my life in countless ways. For one, it led to the development of Soulforce arts and the writing of this book. It also transformed my whole approach to playing violin, allowing greater enjoyment, ease, and depth of expression. Furthermore, it helped me find fulfillment when performing in less-than-ideal circumstances. Now, even when I'm getting paid next to nothing for playing background music for a crowd who doesn't even seem to be listening, I know that the aliveness I yet bring to my playing is at some level healing the wounds of separation in myself and the others present. I can relax and take the pressure off this or any gig to provide the fulfillment I desire because I know how to take at least a small step toward my artistic purpose in any circumstance.

Practicing, performing, composing, and teaching have all become opportunities to tap into my creative aliveness. Thus enlivened, each creative act becomes like a positive glitch in the matrix, an anomalous data point of wholeness and connection that is itself an instantiation of what Charles Eisenstein calls "the more beautiful world our hearts know is possible." The result is that I now trust that even the smallest creative act has the potential to, through unknown and circuitous means, catalyze this more beautiful world on a larger scale.

Your own journey into the Story of Interbeing will, of course, look different than mine. The connections you unearth, the wounds you heal, and the artistic purpose you discover will be unique to you. What will be similar, however, is the overall effect stepping into this story will have on all areas of your artistic life. Where before your body felt tense and awkward, your body will now feel effortless and free. Where before you suffered from performance anxiety or impostor syndrome, you will instead find a new sense of confidence and self-trust. Where before you struggled with the fear of selling out, you will be empowered to create new opportunities for sharing your art that honor your creative soul. And where before you doubted your creative worth and hid your light, you will instead let the creative aliveness within you, your Soulforce, suffuse your art to transformative, transportive effect.

Your journey into the Story of Interbeing has already begun with your introduction to the Story of Separation and its presence in your life. We now deepen this journey by exploring examples of the Story of Interbeing in the arts, learning how this leads to Soulforce, and discovering the precise way in which your unique artistic contributions can bring forth a more harmonious, peaceful, and beautiful world.

ART IN A LIVING UNIVERSE

"Nothing ever exists entirely alone; everything is in relation to everything else."

— BUKKYO DENDO KYOKAI, *THE TEACHINGS OF BUDDHA*

The **Story of Interbeing** is a worldview that says that all things are so deeply interconnected that they are one, while still retaining their individuality. The term *interbeing* was coined by Buddhist monk Thich Nhat Hanh, who defined it this way: "In one sheet of paper, we see everything else, the cloud, the forest, the logger. I am, therefore you are. You are, therefore I am. That is the meaning of the word 'interbeing.' We interare."[1]

> The **Story of Interbeing** says that all things are so deeply interconnected that they are one, while still retaining their individuality; that the universe is more a being than a thing; that life has an inherent purposiveness; that the universe is a conscious, living, unified whole; and that meaning is best

> found in aligning yourself with the evolutionary unfolding of the universe, whose voice is your innermost truths and desires.

The Story of Interbeing has profound implications for the purpose and meaning of life and, as we shall see, of the arts. As you'll recall, the Story of Separation says that the purpose of life is to expand the realm of human control ever outward by commandeering resources from a lifeless universe. In contrast, the Story of Interbeing says that, since all things are interconnected, then consciousness, intelligence, and aliveness must be inherent features of the universe at large. Therefore, the purpose of life, and what makes for a meaningful life, is to participate in and with that larger aliveness in an ongoing flow of giving and receiving.

The Story of Interbeing says a meaningful life is to be found in the giving and receiving of gifts. So, half of what makes for a meaningful life is to develop your gifts fully and to give them well to those who can best receive them. To give well means to honor the truths and desires that are core to your being as well as bring forth what you were born to express. It includes everything else you could do to make the world more beautiful, vibrant, and alive.

The other half of a meaningful life, then, is to be found in fully receiving the gifts around you. It is to view the totality of creation as a gift: the sun, the earth, your birth, the food you eat, the art you behold. Fully receiving these gifts means being enchanted by them, being fully present in your enjoyment, playing and having fun, and otherwise basking in the glory of the universe. You know you're receiving well when you can look back over your life and say with satisfaction, as did the Creator in Genesis, "It was very good."[2]

In the Story of Interbeing, the purpose of the arts is the same as life overall: to illuminate and embody the truth of who and what we are. What is this truth? It is that your self is not bounded by the limit of your skin nor defined by any label, concept, or story you might carry.

Rather, you are the entire universe experiencing itself through your particular body, mind, and soul. However, even putting it in words this way cannot capture the fullness of the truth because, as it says in the *Tao Te Ching*, "The Tao that can be told is not the universal Tao."[3] The truth is really the felt experience of Divine Presence itself—the source of conscious awareness—timeless, unbounded, and utterly interconnected with all that is.

In other words, the Story of Interbeing is a story of a living universe, and the purpose of the arts within that story is to illuminate and celebrate that reality. Art can thus be defined as anything that heals, makes whole, enlivens, connects, and otherwise draws both audience and artist into the apprehension of the numinous. This is both the end goal of a work of art as well as the defining feature of a creative process capable of accomplishing that goal. To make these ideas more tangible, here are some real-life examples.

> In the Story of Interbeing, art can be defined as **anything that heals, makes whole, enlivens, connects,** and otherwise draws both audience and artist into the apprehension of the numinous.

Henry, a professor of violin at a university, came to me for help releasing the excess muscular tension in his arms that made playing violin for long periods feel awkward and tiring. What we discovered together was that he was aware only of his arms and hands while playing, an overly narrow focus based on the subconscious belief that his body comprised a collection of separate parts. I then explained that the muscles and bones of his body were, in fact, integrated aspects of a seamless web, and helped him expand his body awareness so he could experience how the unconsciously held tension in other, seemingly distant parts of his body was affecting his arms. Supported by this new, more holistic body awareness, Henry was then able to better release tension throughout his whole body. After putting this awareness to use in his daily life, he later told me, "Playing violin is feeling significantly better now, and when I'm teaching, I can demonstrate the kind of ease I want my students to have." Whole body, whole music.

Francis, a young cellist who attended one of my workshops, told me she wanted help with a tricky passage in one of her pieces. After she demonstrated this passage, I asked her what she noticed about herself and she reported that her body got tight, and that she was mainly thinking about getting the notes right. I then asked her to play the passage again, this time thinking to herself, *I'm at ease with myself and I have plenty of time.* The result was immediate. With this one little change in thought, she reported that she felt much more relaxed and that her sound improved. I then asked the other participants what they noticed in themselves as she played, and they all said that they, too, felt more relaxed and enjoyed her music more. I then shared the deeper lesson with everyone present: "The truth is that, while getting the notes right is important, it's not really what your audiences want most from you. They want to feel more relaxed and uplifted, and you can offer that to them by thinking in a way that lets your body be more relaxed and uplifted as you play." The lesson we learned that day? When you create from a place of unity between the mind and body, as well as that of artist and audience, a more life-giving creative energy spontaneously pours forth.

Reese, a gifted illustrator, told me of the creative malaise she recently had been experiencing. In our conversation, we discovered the source: in pursuing what had become a comfortable career doing corporate illustration, she had lost connection with a larger purpose. She said, "I'm tired of trying to sell myself; I want my art to be for something bigger than just paying the bills. I want to be of service." I then invited her to make a sketch with her desire to be of service in mind. She reported that she came more alive when she drew, that her body relaxed, and that she had had more fun. I could see and feel the results of this shift when I looked at her sketch. We then spoke of the implications of this experience for her artistic life overall. Drawing her own conclusions, Reese said, "I really need to remember to remain open to the magic. Art is a spiritual process. By honoring myself as a vessel for a creativity that is both of me and beyond me, I can now see a way that my art can serve something larger than myself and help make the world a better place." The moral of the story? Connection with that which is alive inside you is necessary to create art that is alive. Moreover, doing so is vital to your role in societal and planetary healing.

The Story of Interbeing contains the answers to many of our most pressing and perplexing challenges. As mentioned, discovering these answers requires an understanding of interbeing that goes beyond the level of concepts and instead rests on a lived reality. Use the following practices to build familiarity with the Story of Interbeing by bringing its perspectives into your daily life.

SOULFORCE INQUIRY 3.1
INTERBEING AND THE PURPOSE OF THE ARTS

Take a moment now to review the statements above about the purpose and meaning of life within the Story of Interbeing. Notice how your body feels as a result. Then consider what your heart and soul already know about the purpose of the arts. Can you feel how the Story of Interbeing naturally aligns with and supports the true purpose of the arts better than does the Story of Separation and its lesser gods?

SOULFORCE INQUIRY 3.2
EXPERIENCING INTERBEING

This is an exploration designed to give you a felt sense of interbeing. This practice is adapted from the work of Amanda Krichbaum, teacher of The Heart of Now. If desired, do this exploration with a friend or as you interact with other people throughout your day.

Look into someone's eyes and say to yourself, either aloud or inwardly: *You are me, seeing the world through a different set of eyes.* Repeat it several times until a new experience of yourself emerges. You may begin to feel the boundaries of yourself dissolving such that you really do see that this other person *is* yourself, just in a different body and with different life experiences.

You are me, seeing the world through a different set of eyes.

Repeat this phrase many times over the next week as you interact with people and non-human beings. How does it change how you view yourself? It's especially useful and instructive to say this during moments of difficulty or stress—how does it change how you view the "other" in a conflict?

THE GATEWAY TO SOULFORCE

"Again and again, we must rise to the majestic heights of meeting physical force with soul force."

— MARTIN LUTHER KING, JR., FROM HIS 1963
"I HAVE A DREAM" SPEECH

Take a moment to reflect on the shift each of my three students experienced in the previous stories. What was common among them was that, instead of responding to their creative challenges from a place of fragmentation, force, and control, as is so common in our society, they learned to respond with a greater wholeness, healing, and purpose. In other words, their response came from a place of interbeing, with the result that they spontaneously gained access to a creative energy that benefited their art, well-being, and ability to be of service to a world in need. The name of this energy? Soulforce.

As discussed in Chapter 1, **Soulforce** is the transformative creative energy that comes from facing life's challenges, whether creative or otherwise, from a place of wholeness, aliveness, and connection. It is what spontaneously shines forth when you relinquish the fragmentary outlook and rigid control so common in our society and instead act from your deepest, most authentic truths and desires. Soulforce is an energy, a felt experience, and a state of participation with life. The term *soul force* was coined by Mahatma Gandhi in describing his philosophy of nonviolence. This idea guided his campaign to free India from British colonial rule and is a translation of the Sanskrit term *satyagraha*, which also means "love insistence" or "firmness in the pursuit of truth."

> **Soulforce** is the transformative creative energy that comes from facing life's challenges, creative or otherwise, from a place of wholeness, aliveness, and connection. Soulforce relies on the power of resonance to create change.

Gandhi's critical insight was that the British-run Indian government couldn't be overthrown by force, because to do so would only invite inevitable violent retaliation from their superior military. Knowing that change had to happen nonviolently, he instead tapped into the latent potency of Indian society by speaking and acting from his deepest truth, that India should rule itself. Others also held this as a deep truth, and the resonance with his message galvanized Indian society. Ultimately, his strategy led to an India free from British rule. It also later inspired the anti-apartheid movement in South Africa and the civil rights movement in the United States, among others.

Given its impressive track record, it's clear to see that Soulforce has an immense power for transformation. However, its transformative power works in a very different way than what our society is currently used to. Our conventional ideas of power come from the Story of Separation and involve creating change using force and control; think of domineering, trying hard, or *making* something happen. In contrast, what gives Soulforce its unique ability to create seeming miracles, such as the end of the British colonial rule of India, is the release of force and control in a moment that otherwise might seem to call for it. Far from being a sign of weakness, naïveté, or capitulation, this release allows access to the power of resonance: the latent potential for transformation that exists within us all.

This is as true in the arts as it is for movements for social change. A creative process that leads to Soulforce is one that surrenders the methods of separation—force and control—and instead embraces the methods of interbeing—attention and allowing—to create effective change. Surrender is the gateway, a necessary condition to clearing away what's not working anymore and making space for new and creative solutions to arise. Soulforce is the gift you receive in return, one characterized by the spontaneous pouring forth of the wisdom, love, and compassion essential to who you are and that potentiates the same in those who receive it.

I have seen the transformative effect of Soulforce countless times in my experiences as an Alexander Technique teacher working with artists of all kinds and experience levels. For example, students often come to me with various issues related to excess muscular tension in their music-making. Without fail, when I help them release this tension, not only do they enjoy a feeling of relief from their discomfort, but also a new, luminous, expressive power spontaneously comes through in their playing. After we both marvel at the shift in their music-making, I often ask my students whether they now believe that all their usual tension helps their playing. The answer is always "no." I then ask my students why they might have been holding all that tension in the first place, and they universally reply with some variation of, "I was trying too hard to get it right" or "It was about control." In other words, the tension reflected the methods of creating change within the Story of Separation. As soon as they released those methods, they were able to access a deeper source of authentic expression—their Soulforce—and were then able to enjoy the aliveness and connection they had been seeking all along.

The transformative effect of my students' Soulforce is not limited to their own subjective experience of the creative act; it also works upon me as a listener. I am often deeply touched, sometimes even brought to the point of tears. In those moments, I am reminded of why I love music, and I reflect on how beautiful life can be. I discover much-needed perspective on my typical daily aggravations, and I leave lessons like these feeling uplifted, joyful, and connected to my heart. In other words, I undergo a tangible transformation in consciousness. My students' Soulforce, coming from a connection with something bigger than their individual selves, resonates with the potential for a corresponding connection in myself. The result for each of us is a shift from the usual egoic self to a felt sense of the numinous. Given that transformations like these are the point of art, it's plain to see that Soulforce is essential to the creative act.

Gaining access to this power requires surrendering the methods of force and control, and this often takes an act of courage. For those of us steeped in the Story of Separation, these are the methods we rely on to ensure our safety and survival. Surrendering them reveals our vulnerability, sometimes a dangerous move in a society where so many relationships are characterized by games of power and dominance. In relying on such games, what our society fails to realize is that vulnerability has power, too. In the right circumstances, seeing someone's vulnerability pierces through our own emotional armoring and touches the forgotten vulnerability within. Given the way acting from our emotional armoring is the source of so much misunderstanding and violence, bringing our forgotten vulnerability back into the conversation is utterly essential to returning to a place of sanity and healing.

In reality, the surrender required to promote sanity and healing only takes courage when you believe that there are no viable alternatives to force and control. When you're clinging for dear life high up on a ladder, however problematic that ladder may be, you won't feel safe stepping off until you're sure a new support can properly hold you. So, we next strengthen that new support with a deeper understanding of what it means to initiate beneficial change in an interconnected world.

SANITY, INSANITY, AND THE SECRET TO EFFECTIVE CHANGE

"The end justifies the means. But what if there never is an end? All we have is means."

— URSULA K. LE GUIN, *THE LATHE OF HEAVEN*

The Story of Interbeing and the Soulforce it brings forth are more than a pair of nice ideas. They comprise the answer to the insanity that increasingly permeates our society, as well as the most effective means of bringing about needed artistic and societal sanity. Harnessing this potential requires letting go of familiar, limited notions of how to create change and adopting new ones that better fit the deeper, more expansive truth of who and what you are.

What is insanity? It is to ignore anything that's true. Let's say you're practicing a technique and making the same mistake over and over. In response to the mistake, you try harder and harder to get it right. Finally, you get it right—but then you notice how tense and drained you feel.

What you have just engaged in is not so much a step toward true artistic mastery, but a step into insanity. Why? The ultimate point of any technique is to better channel the fullness of your Soulforce, but this can't happen when you try hard because trying hard constricts your body and emotions. When you try hard, you focus on a narrow definition of what is right and ignore the impact your body and emotions have on the flow of Soulforce. Obviously, with your body compromised with effort and tension, you cannot fulfill the ultimate point of the techniques you practice. Thus, trying hard is a form of insanity because it ignores the ways that your quality of effort determines your artistic output.

When you try to create change through force and control, you are, in essence, optimizing a part at the expense of the whole. But there are no parts separate from the whole. The universe, your body, the planet, a work of art—all of these are wholes that both comprise smaller wholes and are aspects of yet larger wholes. They are also seamless, with no fixed beginnings nor ends. In the Story of Interbeing, all we have are means and wholes.

If insanity is ignoring anything that's true, then sanity is taking account of that which has been ignored. For a musician, sanity is sensing how a flourish of their fingers is a movement not limited to the hand alone but involves their whole body. Sanity is practicing in a way that leaves them feeling open and free, knowing that how they practice becomes how they perform. Sanity is working toward artistic excellence and, at the same time, letting go of rigid control over the outcome of any creative act. Knowing that the quality of the means creates the quality of the end, the sane answer to trying hard is trying easy.

> Insanity is ignoring anything that's true. Sanity is taking account of that which has been ignored.

Sanity is also the answer to the age-old question of how an individual's actions can direct societal change. In the Story of Separation, big societal changes can only happen through the application of an even bigger force, and thus are only available to those with lots of money and influence. The Story of Interbeing, however, shows that this is not the whole truth.

The truth ignored by the Story of Separation is that your individual actions are already a part of the larger flow of things. Just as an improvement in the health of one of your body's organs improves your overall health, so it is that your individual flourishing improves the well-being of society. Your actions, however seemingly small and insignificant, always matter because they are embedded in the larger flow of the whole world. Everything you do already makes a difference—the only question is, what kind of difference do you want to make? Rather than imposing your limited will and resources upon the world, effectively creating societal-level change is more like snowflakes collecting on a hillside. Every avalanche is initiated by just one snowflake at the right spot.

Activism sometimes gets a bad reputation in our society precisely because it employs force and control in attempting to make the world a better place. Any activist cause that does so is itself a form of insanity. Environmentalists who demonize polluters, anti-abortionists who bomb reproductive health clinics, and social justice warriors who cancel those whom they deem racist all ignore the same truth: more fighting only leads to more fighting. While fighting can lead to individual victories, such victories are hollow because they come at the expense of the trust needed to cooperate to handle larger systemic problems. Without this cooperation, we are like those too busy with a fist fight to quench our burning building. It doesn't matter how good the stated goal is; when victory over the enemy takes precedence over actual long-term healing, everybody loses.

In a way, Soulforce arts is a form of activism; but it is a sacred activism, one based on the fundamental reality that the flourishing of the whole world requires the flourishing of every part, without exception. Based on this reality, Soulforce arts contains the secret to effective change. It says that to make the world a more enlivened and beautiful place, you as an artist don't need to have vast wealth, political influence, or millions of followers. You don't need to rage against the machine. All you need to do is to open yourself to the larger interconnectedness in which you are already embedded. Having reverence for this interconnectedness, you can relax and allow yourself to enjoy, play, and create, trusting that your creative aliveness is giving birth to a more beautiful world.

PRACTICAL MIRACLES

"Miracles are not contrary to nature, but only contrary to what we know about nature."

— AUGUSTINE OF HIPPO, *THE COMPLETE WORKS OF ST. AUGUSTINE OF HIPPO*

From within the Story of Separation, our global situation is hopeless. The forces of destruction are so monumental, and the hour is so late. Those with sufficient money and power to shift the needle are too mired in the system as it is to be motivated to take corrective action. Countless other well-intentioned activists further ingrain the system by creating change through force and control. What can any person do other than despair?

Despair and hopelessness, far from being a painful dead end, are the fertile ground of the answers we seek. By letting yourself fully process these emotions, you open yourself to new, creative answers capable of resolving issues that once seemed utterly intractable.

When they come, these answers can seem like miracles. They arise out of nowhere and carry a potency beyond that offered by more familiar solutions. Not confined to the province of fairy tales and wishful thinkers, a miracle is simply something that exists outside your current paradigm. It operates according to a deeper truth, one that resolves existing problems by making obsolete the paradigm that created them. In a world whose dire challenges are caused by our current paradigm, the only practical step is to adopt a new one. Having done so, we will gain powers and possibilities previously unimagined. As Arthur C. Clarke wrote in *Hazards of Prophecy*, "Any technology sufficiently advanced will seem like magic," and so it will be with our art.

The Soulforce Arts Approach, described in the following chapter, is just such a technology. It is the next step in the evolution of arts pedagogy in that its explicit goal is to help you cultivate the miracle of Soulforce. The works of art that result from following this approach will have a miraculous power. They will bring the inspiration, healing, and connection that are the answer to the fundamental challenges our world now faces. The Soulforce Arts Approach is the answer to the fear that our art doesn't matter. It says that to suffuse your artistic life with this energy and have fun while doing so is the most practical step you can take as an artist today.

"Don't ask what the world needs. Ask what makes you come alive and go do that, because what the world needs is people who have come alive."

— **HOWARD THURMAN, CIVIL RIGHTS LEADER**

CHAPTER 4

THE SOULFORCE ARTS APPROACH

Dana, a cellist, composer, and music teacher in her mid-thirties, came to me for advice regarding the physical, creative, and motivational issues her students had recently been struggling with.

"When they play, they're just kind of stiff. I can't get them to play with real emotion. And while some of my students practice regularly, others can't seem to keep it up. I really want my students to love playing cello. What can I do to help them?" she asked.

As Dana spoke, I immediately saw the thread connecting the various issues her students were having. Their physical, creative, and motivational issues all had the same source: disconnection from their creative aliveness, their Soulforce. Without connection with their Soulforce, no matter how hard Dana tried to instill a love of cello, nor how many times she told them to relax, nor which pieces or techniques her students learned, they would never find the ease, enjoyment, and connection that had originally inspired them to pick up the cello.

I then offered Dana a new perspective from which to teach her students: "What if the point of teaching wasn't so much to get your students to learn certain things, but to help them come more alive?

How would centering Soulforce change your approach to teaching?" Considering this, Dana realized that she had unconsciously been teaching from a somewhat mechanical place. Despite the love for music she so clearly held in her heart, her focus in lessons had primarily been on helping her students get certain techniques—even expressive ones—"right." As a result, while her students did make technical progress, both she and her students ended up feeling somewhat less connected from their love of music. Thus disconnected, they had to resort to the excess use of effort to play cello and motivate themselves to practice. I explained that all her students' challenges would disappear once they reconnected with their own aliveness as they played, and that the first step toward helping them do so was to connect with her own aliveness while she taught.

This new perspective sparked something for Dana, and she later told me that she and her students were now getting a lot more out of their lessons together. She was no longer relying solely on repetition to instill technique, which both she and her students found boring and tiring. Instead, she focused on her own ease and heart connection as she taught, an awareness that allowed her to more sensitively guide her students to channel their own creative Soulforce. Dana reported that she was very pleased to see that she could still hold her students to a high standard with this new approach, whereas she initially feared that a certain relaxation might lead to a lapse of standards. To the contrary, she was surprised to discover that her students now made faster progress with their pieces!

Gratified by these results, Dana felt motivated to apply this same approach to other areas of her creative life. Over the course of our lessons together, Dana discovered that a focus on aliveness led to new methods for addressing her artistic challenges as well as new reasons for doing so. In addition, Dana realized that her creativity was a product of her whole self, her whole life, and wasn't limited to what happened in her studio or on stage. In the end, what had started as a simple question about physical tension and creative blocks led to a wholesale transformation of her artistic life.

The new approach Dana now follows is one also shared by many of my other students. I call it the Soulforce Arts Approach, and it centers the transformative power of Soulforce into every area of artistic life. The Soulforce Arts Approach answers many of our most confounding artistic challenges, turning tension into ease, anxiety into excitement, boredom into inspiration, and helplessness into empowerment. Through it, your artistic life will take on a whole new significance. You'll discover a deeper artistic purpose, enjoy new levels of well-being and ease, be able to make art that you and your audiences love, and know that you're making a positive contribution to our world. In this chapter, we will explore the Soulforce Arts Approach in detail, outlining its purpose, components, and unique perspectives on the creative process, as well as how it can help you create the art you were meant for.

ART THAT MAKES YOU COME ALIVE

> *"Art is technically and literally magic. There is 'black' art, 'white' art, sacred art and secular art, but all achieve their effect—if they achieve it—by magical means, by a summons to an innate human capacity to respond to harmony."*
>
> – JOHN ANTHONY WEST, *SERPENT IN THE SKY*

The **Soulforce Arts Approach** is a comprehensive, holistic arts pedagogy whose ultimate goal is no less than the transformation of our society's entire way of being: away from the Story of Separation and into the Story of Interbeing. It achieves this by helping you as an artist cultivate Soulforce in every area of your artistic life, including how you create, practice, perform, teach, and make a living.

The Soulforce Arts Approach is based on the idea that the arts carry a transformative power—Soulforce—and that the true purpose of the arts is to harness this power for needed personal, creative, and societal change. This approach is based on a radically holistic perspective, one that takes for granted that your art reflects the whole of your being: body, mind, soul, society, and planet. Further, it considers that your whole being finds reflection in every creative act. Because it takes account of areas of life that other arts pedagogies sometimes miss, the Soulforce Arts Approach allows for unforeseen levels of creative power, personal well-being, and societal impact.

The Soulforce Arts Approach is based on the idea that the full potential of your Soulforce already lies within you, and that if you aren't experiencing as much of it as you would like, there may be certain restrictions or limitations at work. These restrictions are almost always a reflection of the Story of Separation, the antidote to which is the healing and growth made possible by the Story of Interbeing. Thus, your fullest potential of Soulforce is made accessible not through the application of yet more effort and toil. That may only serve to further entrench your restrictions. Rather, your Soulforce will effortlessly pour forth when you align your creative process with the greater wholeness, aliveness, and connection essential to who and what you are.

The Soulforce Arts Approach addresses the following areas of concern:

- Creative blocks
- A sense of not having met your full potential as an artist
- Disconnection from a sense of meaning or purpose
- Physical tension and painful conditions such as carpal tunnel syndrome, tendinitis, back pain, and other musculoskeletal issues
- Emotional challenges such as performance anxiety or an overactive inner critic

- Difficulty making a living in the arts
- Uncertainty in how to make a positive contribution to the society and planet

> The **Soulforce Arts Approach** is a comprehensive, holistic arts pedagogy whose ultimate goal is no less than the transformation of our society's entire way of being: away from the Story of Separation and into the Story of Interbeing. It achieves this by helping you as an artist cultivate Soulforce in every area of your artistic life, including how you create, practice, perform, teach, and make a living.

The Soulforce Arts Approach comprises several overarching features. First, it is founded on the idea that the transformation our society needs will come from two distinct, yet interconnected, shifts in consciousness. The first shift, **soulfulness**, is something we've already touched on in this book. It is the experience of something bigger, a feeling of connection with Nature, the Universe, God, Love, or other larger forces. The second shift occurs with **holistic values development**, which is the process of evolution toward greater personal and societal maturation, sophistication, competence, and inclusivity. The cultivation of each of these shifts in consciousness is what grants greater access to Soulforce.

The felt experiences and values inherent to both soulfulness and holistic values development form the experiential and pedagogical foundation for the Soulforce Arts Approach. They can be cultivated in yourself and your art via the Seven Elements of the Soulforce Arts Approach. The Seven Elements are the specific areas of development and training that support your ability to access and give form to Soulforce in your artistic life.

With concurrent development of each of the Seven Elements, you will be able to access greater soulfulness and more holistic values within yourself. This, in turn, will allow you to convey a richer, more potent transmission of your Soulforce through your art. The full flowering of this potential is the fulfillment of the Soulforce Arts Approach.

THE SEVEN ELEMENTS OF THE SOULFORCE ARTS APPROACH

"The chief beneficiary of art is the artist. He can put into his work only as much as he understands. In the exercise of his art, he develops his understanding."

— JOHN ANTHONY WEST, *SERPENT IN THE SKY*

The **Seven Elements of the Soulforce Arts Approach** are the specific areas of development that allow for your greatest connection with Soulforce. The Seven Elements take for granted that your art is connected to every aspect of your life, and so they are concerned not just with what happens in the art studio or up on stage, but also with your health, mindset, and desired contribution to the world. By taking this interconnectedness into account, you will be able to fine-tune your creative life at a whole new level. The result will enliven you, your art, and your audiences in unexpected and powerful ways.

When you begin to engage in the Seven Elements, on an outward level your artistic life might at first look very much the same as what you're already used to. If you already paint, you'll still be painting. If you already make a living as an artist, you're still going to make a living. But on the inside, things will feel very different. This is due to how the Seven Elements redefine the things you normally do as an artist, helping you orient these activities toward greater soulfulness and more holistic values. Within this new orientation, much of what has felt disconnected or challenging will find new meaning and ease—a shift that may very well lead to some very big outward transformations!

Chapter 4 | THE SOULFORCE ARTS APPROACH

The Seven Elements of the Soulforce Arts Approach are:

1. Discovering Your Artistic Purpose
2. Effortlessness and Embodiment
3. Playing from the Heart
4. The Yoga of Art
5. The Spirit of the Gift
6. Growing Up the Spiral
7. Soulforce Livelihood

Each of these Seven Elements work in synergy with the others; each one affects all the others so that when one is particularly strong or weak, the others are likewise strengthened or weakened. While the Seven Elements are best developed concurrently, your early engagement with the Soulforce Arts Approach will be best supported by following the sequence outlined here.

DISCOVERING YOUR ARTISTIC PURPOSE

Your artistic purpose is the transformation you were born to bring forth through your creative activities and talents. It is an inherent part of who you are, the larger "why" that resonates with your soul. Once discovered, your artistic purpose allows you to let go of the inauthentic modes of creating you may have inherited, providing instead a reason for creating that you genuinely care about that reaches beyond the imperatives of the lesser gods. You will discover your own artistic purpose in Chapter 5.

EFFORTLESSNESS AND EMBODIMENT

Your body is the gateway to your Soulforce, the primary instrument through which your creative impulses take form. Connecting with your body and learning to move with effortlessness are essential to a creative process that allows your light to shine through. Effortlessness and Embodiment are also necessary to a sustainable, injury-free artistic life. In addition, these elements provide the experiential grounding necessary to turn the concepts in this book into lived experiences. You will experience greater effortlessness and embodiment through the Mind-Body Interludes between each chapter.

PLAYING FROM THE HEART

Playing from the Heart is a process of tapping into your inner aliveness that turns the individual parts of a work of art into a cohesive, living, flowing whole. It is the "X factor" that transforms, for example, a collection of notes into real music. Commonly thought to occur only by chance or in the lives of a lucky few superstars, Playing from the Heart is a process that can be easily and effectively learned by beginners and experts alike. It will help you go beyond the traps of mechanical technique or mere self-expression and instead tap into a genuine source of creative aliveness. You will learn how to play from the heart in Chapter 6.

THE YOGA OF ART

Mastering an art form, or even gaining a moderate competence, takes diligence, time, and effort. However, the kind of effort used also matters. All too many artists try to address their creative challenges with an excess of willpower that reflects a split between the part of them that wants to do something and the part of them that doesn't. Creating from this split causes more problems than it solves. The solution is to reunify the self, and this is the purpose of a yoga. The Yoga of Art helps you unlearn the reflexive use of willpower and instead seek a deeper soul-level motivation to access the key to a sustainable, joyful, and vital artistic life. You will learn to unwind the fallacy of willpower in Chapter 7.

THE SPIRIT OF THE GIFT

Intuitively, we know that genuine creativity is more than the product of technique, calculation, and effort alone. If unforced, an authentic creative impulse is, in fact, a gift; it arises spontaneously from a deeper source that is both within you and beyond you. Understanding the nature of gifts and more fully inhabiting their spirit brings new life, trust, and freshness to the creative act. You will learn to inhabit the Spirit of the Gift in Chapter 8.

GROWING UP THE SPIRAL

Psychological and sociological research reveals that, to meet an ever-changing environment, individuals and societies can evolve through a predictable series of developmental stages. Each stage builds on the previous, spiraling up with a new, higher-order competence, maturity, and inclusivity. Much of what seems limited and outmoded in both the arts world and society at large is the result of certain earlier stages of development retaining undue influence. As an artist, your greatest art, and your greatest contribution toward societal sanity, rests on a foundation of your own personal development up the spiral. You will learn how to catapult your own growth up the spiral in Chapters 9 and 10.

SOULFORCE LIVELIHOOD

Many artists struggle with the contrast between the need to make money to survive and the fear of selling out. Answers come in the form of two new approaches. The first is to create new artistic "products and services" that align with the true purpose of the arts. The second is to connect your livelihood with something larger than your individual self. Combined, these approaches resolve much of the "ick" you may feel around money, while at the same time bringing in new sources of abundance that allow you to not just survive but thrive as an artist. You will learn how to align your artistic livelihood with your deepest values in Chapter 12.

SOULFORCE INQUIRY 4.1
YOUR CURRENT MODEL OF ARTISTRY

Reflect on your current beliefs about artistry, what it means to be an artist, how to gain skill, and how to share your artistic gifts. Get out your journal and complete the following prompts with three to five unique answers each:

- "An artist (or musician, dancer, etc.) is ..."
- "An artist does ..."
- "An artist feels ..."
- "An artist has ..."
- "An artist values ..."

Now, take stock of what you've written. What do your answers say about your current beliefs about artistry? Compare what you've written with what's included in the Seven Elements. Are there areas of overlap? Are there areas of difference? There are no right or wrong answers; this is simply an opportunity to become aware of your mindset regarding artistry.

Combined, the Seven Elements of the Soulforce Arts Approach form the basis for a new kind of creative life; one that may feel at times intangible or unfamiliar, and at others will affirm what your heart has known all along. The process of incorporating the Seven Elements into your creative life will provide many insights into what's been driving your personal and artistic challenges. Some insights might be painful and involve recognizing the ways you've been living in the Story of Separation. Others might be joyful and involve healing old wounds or rediscovering a sense of wonder and play. Regardless of its valence, every insight affords the opportunity to redefine the art you make and how you make it in more life-giving terms.

There are several other important concepts to explore before we continue with the rest of the book. These are concepts and perspectives that naturally result from regarding the arts through the lens of interbeing. They redefine and clarify the function of the arts, the path to artistic mastery, and the channels through which your unique artistic contributions affect the world around you. Unlike the Seven Elements, they don't follow a progressive sequence, but are rather ideas to which we will refer at various times throughout this book.

One of the primary questions raised by this book is how to attain artistic mastery (in whatever form) without unnecessary stress, tension, and disconnection. Different ideas of mastery lead to very different outcomes in terms of the quality of your art and life. Indeed, many of the challenges artists commonly face are a direct result of embodying certain limited ideas of mastery, ones that have been passed down through the generations, often without much thought. Continuing to hold such ideas will only lead to more of the same old challenges. What's needed, then, is a new idea of mastery, one that allows for artistic greatness and your full potential for Soulforce, but without the drawbacks of the old ways of getting there. This is Soulforce Mastery.

THE THREE STRANDS OF SOULFORCE MASTERY

"If you're an open channel when you're onstage, if you're just a vessel, things are going to come out that are stored away deep in your DNA."

— LESLIE ODOM, JR., ACTOR

The Soulforce Arts Approach sheds new light on what it means to make progress in and master your artistic skills. Your Soulforce is not something external to you, something you need to reach for to achieve. It is inherent to who you are, just waiting to be given form and released. So, you begin by recognizing that your greatest expressive power, your Soulforce, is in some sense already fully formed inside you.

This stands in contrast to conventional approaches to mastery in the arts. A hidden assumption within these approaches is that the path to mastery is a combination of pure luck (you were either born with a special creative talent or you weren't), sufficient hard work (as in Malcolm Gladwell's famous 10,000-hour rule), and technique (the more virtuosic the better). Obviously, luck, hard work, and technique all have their roles to play in the path to mastery. However, they are not the whole story. Relying on luck is deeply disempowering; after all, what do you do if you're not one of the lucky few? It's also possible to work hard and exert great effort without ever tapping into genuine creativity. In addition, it's possible to display the most virtuosic technique without any connection to your soul.

The Soulforce Arts Approach recognizes these shortcomings and instead defines mastery in terms of what will allow for your greatest connection with Soulforce. **Soulforce Mastery** comprises three strands: technique, effortlessness, and the knowledge of the soul. Soulforce Mastery happens when you're in connection with your knowledge of the soul, when you have sufficient technique to give form to whatever is inside your soul, and when you can move your body freely enough to become an open channel for whatever wants to come through you. You know you have reached Soulforce Mastery when you feel like you've become a vessel for your art.

Each of the three strands of Soulforce Mastery are necessary, and none is sufficient by itself. Each one depends on the others for its fulfillment; when one is lacking, the others will fail to meet their full potential. Soulforce Mastery suggests that true artistic mastery, wherein you create art or music that transforms yourself and the world around you, is only possible when you have developed all three strands to a high degree.

THE THREE STRANDS OF SOULFORCE MASTERY

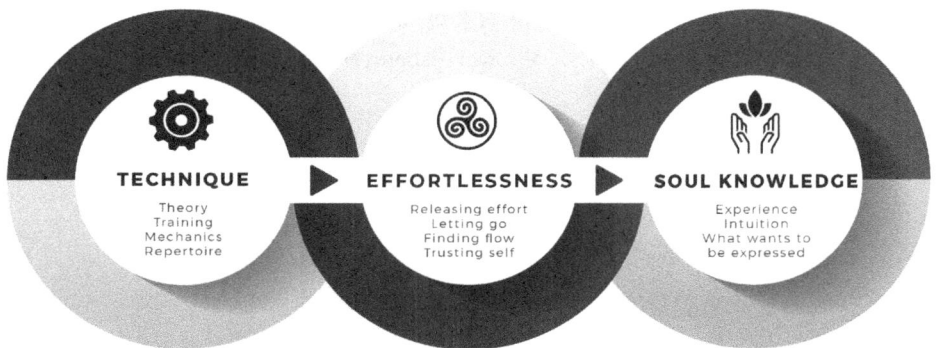

TECHNIQUE

The first strand, technique, involves all the things that trained artists already know how to do well: taking lessons, developing the mechanics of your art, learning repertoire, copying the masters, learning how to collaborate, learning how to create in various contexts and formats, gaining experience as a professional artist, learning theory, and more. Technique is necessary for giving form to your creative ideas. When developed alongside effortlessness and the knowledge of the soul, having virtuosic technique is wonderful because it allows you the quickest, richest, and most effortless translation of your ideas into a more concrete form. Without a sufficient level of technique, you will likely be frustrated by your inability to express what's inside you. This is a gap that no degree of effortlessness or knowledge of the soul can bridge on their own.

The development of technique comes with a word of caution. Among the three strands of Soulforce Mastery, technique is the most easily understood and co-opted by the Story of Separation. One result is that, in our society, technique tends to be the primary focus in art and music education, even to the point that emotional expression itself is often taught as a technique to be acquired and reproduced at will.

Without the knowledge of the soul, the development of technique leads to an empty, stale, soulless virtuosity, where you have the how but not the why. Without effortlessness, the development of technique leads to the buildup of muscular tension, physical discomfort, and even injuries.

EFFORTLESSNESS

The development of effortless bodily movements is essential for all artists. On one level, effortlessness skills are necessary to relieve the tension that is the underlying cause of physical discomfort, as well as injuries like back pain and tendinitis. Learning such skills will help you feel more at ease, comfortable, and confident during your creative processes. Your effortlessness is also a big part of what your audiences want to experience from you and your art. Many people seek out artistic experiences to feel refreshed and relaxed, and the best way to offer that to them is for you to be at ease in yourself, even during the most challenging artistic moments.

Effortlessness complements the development of both technique and the knowledge of the soul. For example, effortlessness is essential for emotional expression in the arts; it is how you open a channel within so that your knowledge of the soul can shine through. Effortlessness is also the key for making swift progress in developing technique; oftentimes, when a technique feels awkward or just isn't working, it's because you're using too much effort. And while the conventional approach—practicing more—can, with time, bring a degree of ease to the material at hand, it also ignores a vital truth: how you practice becomes how you perform. In other words, practicing with tension creates performances with tension. However, having a toolbox of effortlessness skills will prevent you from ever-more-deeply ingraining excess effort into your creative practices. When you first experience how a single moment of effortlessness can propel you toward greater technical achievement than might otherwise have occurred through several months of diligent practice, you will naturally be motivated to infuse your entire approach to learning technique with a healthy dose of effortlessness. Indeed, many highly trained musicians and artists don't really need more technical training; they have done enough hard work and can discover much greater gains through letting go.

Effortlessness is essential even for artists who don't think of their body as an important part of the creative act. Many writers, photographers, designers, and others often don't realize the profound role their body actually plays in their creative process. It helps to consider that having tight muscles is not just a physical issue. It affects every part of your being, including your imagination and emotions. These essential creative faculties have their root in the body, and any muscular tension you hold dampens your connection with them.

Unfortunately, effortlessness is much neglected in conventional arts and music education beyond the admonition to "just relax." However, unless you have actual training in effortlessness, this advice is worse than useless. When you don't know how to relax in moments of creative challenge, the attempt to do so can become just another thing to get stressed out about. Thus, effortlessness should be an integral component of your path to artistic mastery. After all, can you really say you've mastered something if it isn't effortless?

THE KNOWLEDGE OF THE SOUL

The knowledge of the soul is what's inside you that wants to be expressed. It is the core of who and what you are, the essential energy that you radiate without even trying. It is the source of authentic emotional expression and genuinely creative insights.

The knowledge of the soul has a somewhat paradoxical nature in that it has both personal and impersonal aspects. On the one hand, it is uniquely yours in that it reflects the sum total of your life's experiences, artistic and otherwise. On the other hand, it may hold things that you, as your ego, may find surprising or that may connect you to a feeling of something bigger than your individual self.

Ultimately, your knowledge of the soul, given form by excellent technique and freely expressed through your effortlessness, is your greatest gift to the world around you. It is the core of your "system update," the transformative potential of which increases in direct proportion to your degree of connection and development of your knowledge of the soul. It is the why for your art, without which the development of effortlessness and technique have no real purpose.

While the importance of the knowledge of the soul may be intuitive and obvious to many, like effortlessness, it doesn't really get the attention it deserves in many art and music education settings. This may be due to the simple fact that it's easier to talk about a technique than an ineffable feeling. However, your knowledge of the soul can be developed and deepened, and doing so actually improves your technique and effortlessness. The process of deepening the knowledge of the soul is one of increasing self-awareness, and with such awareness comes a confidence and ease that will be reflected in your physical movements. Furthermore, when you know yourself better, you'll know what you want to give form to. This will free you from trying to improve your technique through tedious exercises because the development of your technique will be tied to something you actually care about, and so will become fun and fulfilling.

Thus, instead of merely maximizing virtuosic technique, when you develop all three strands of Soulforce Mastery together, you give yourself what you need to enjoy a balanced and fulfilling artistic practice. This holds true whether you're a seasoned professional or a hobbyist with no intentions of fully mastering an art form. No matter your ambitions, you will more quickly and completely reach your full potential as an artist with all three strands of Soulforce Mastery.

Chapter 4 | THE SOULFORCE ARTS APPROACH

THE MOMENT OF TRUTH

"Great art grabs you, against your will, and then suspends your will. You are ushered into a quiet clearing, free of desire, free of grasping, free of ego, free of the self-contraction. And through that opening or clearing in your own awareness may come flashing higher truths, subtler revelations, profound connections. For a moment you might even touch eternity; who can say otherwise, when time itself is suspended in the clearing that great art creates in your awareness?"
– KEN WILBER, *THE EYE OF SPIRIT: AN INTEGRAL VISION FOR A WORLD GONE SLIGHTLY MAD*

Imagine you're going to a musical concert. It's by one of your favorite artists, and you're looking forward to the performance with great anticipation. You sit down in your seat and then the music begins. As the music washes over you, you can feel your daily worries floating away. Your body relaxes. You drop into the music even more, and then something unexpected happens. The intense beauty of the music touches something deep inside you and you feel a pang of grief, relief, and awe. All the tension you've been holding around your heart without even realizing it suddenly releases and you feel blasted wide open. When the concert is over, you leave the venue half in a daze. Stepping outside, you look up at the starry night sky and then around at all the other concertgoers on their way home, and then you suddenly realize that the whole universe is alive with music. A sense of connection with all there is fills every atom of your being. Somehow this new sense of connection allows you to trust that you're going to be okay, no matter what happens. You've just experienced a moment of truth.

A **moment of truth** is a shift in consciousness that puts you in touch with something bigger. It is a discrete moment of transformation in which something new is recognized, something old is reintegrated, or a boundary softens to include a larger picture. The initiation of a moment of truth is the essential function of a work of art and is what marks the difference between one that is truly great and one that is more pedestrian.

> A **moment of truth** is a shift in consciousness that puts you in touch with something bigger.

Moments of truth work along two different axes: toward greater soulfulness or more holistic values. Both are essential for your evolution, growth, and healing as an artist or audience member. The story about experiencing live music is an example of a moment of truth that moves you into an experience of greater soulfulness. Moments like these are well-known in the arts world, and are essential for the healing, inspiration, and togetherness that are what make certain works of art truly great.

Less well-known, but every bit as important, are moments of truth that can lead you to more holistic values. Adopting more holistic values is a vital part of the growth and development of every person and society. The wisest and most compassionate people and societies tend to be those who have adopted the widest, most holistic view of things. Likewise, the most destructive people and societies are often those who have failed to do so.

Art and artists have had a vital role in helping both individuals and societies grow into more holistic values. We can see evidence for this in how the role and forms of art have changed to match different historical periods. For example, neolithic art is different from that of the time of the Agricultural Revolution, the Scientific Revolution, or that of our own Information Revolution. At each transition point in history, artists have reflected their society's values, states of mind, and ways of being, and have helped their society dream new possibilities into existence. This is a truly vital role because without the help of artists, who

Chapter 4 | THE SOULFORCE ARTS APPROACH

are often at the vanguard of culture, humanity would have a harder time adopting the new ways of being, thinking, and acting that are required to overcome the challenges of each era.

A wonderful example of this comes from the art of fifteenth-century Europe. This era marked the beginning of the use of perspective in visual art where, for the first time, painters developed the means of creating an image on a flat surface that looked truly three-dimensional. This artistic development was an integral part of the newly emerging Scientific Revolution, and its use in art both exemplified and further promoted the values of that revolution.

For example, the Scientific Revolution valued objectivity over symbolism and religious dogma. What does an objective painting look like? It's one that's going to look like the three-dimensional world we see with our eyes, not the flattened, symbolic world commonly depicted in paintings before this time. Three-dimensional perspective and the values of the Scientific Revolution went hand in hand.

More than providing a reflection of the newly emerging values of this era, the use of perspective also hastened the widespread adoption of these values. Imagine for a moment that you're from fifteenth-century Europe and you've only ever seen paintings with a flattened aspect, like in many early Christian depictions of the Last Supper. Then you come across the one painted by Leonardo da Vinci in 1498, which displays the same scene, but with perfect three-dimensional perspective. What effect might this have on your mind? What might this touch inside you? What new possibilities might suddenly become available to you as a result?

At the time, seeing a painting like this must have been like undergoing a spontaneous initiation into the Scientific Revolution. Such a painting was like a message from the future, a clarion call beckoning people into the new modern age. As the use of perspective spread, more and more people saw paintings that exemplified the new values of that era. Each viewing initiated a moment of truth, one that may have deepened the viewer's trust and familiarity with the values of the Scientific

Revolution. With greater trust, its values would have felt more and more tangible and less like a far-off fantasy, as is so often the case when encountering newly emerging values. Thus, we can see that the arts were an integral part of a huge leap forward for European society, one that led not only to the development of objectivity, but also to the scientific method, democracy, and universal human rights.

This is not to say that the point of the arts, as a whole, is to propagate the values of the Scientific Revolution. Far from it. While the Scientific Revolution was an important, necessary step in humanity's cultural evolution, it was also just a product of its time. It was not humanity's first major cultural revolution, and it was certainly not the last. Before it were the Neolithic and Agricultural Revolutions, and since then have been the Industrial and Information Revolutions. No matter the era, the role of the arts has remained the same: to act as midwife, leading and inspiring humanity into embracing the values of each newly emerging era.

Our own society is currently undergoing a transition every bit as radical as any of these revolutions—perhaps even more so. Even though many can glimpse a new way of being on the horizon, there is no guarantee we'll get there. What we need are people who are ahead of the curve, and who can help guide the rest of us through the madness that accompanies every such transition. You, as an artist, have a special role to play in this transition, which you can begin to fulfill by first embodying the values of the coming era in yourself. We will explore this possibility further in Section III: Evolution.

To enable more and better moments of truth for your audiences, your creative process must reflect the cutting edge of soulfulness and holistic values. Neither mindless traditionalism, empty virtuosity, bland self-expression, shock value, commercial gain, nor even the dismantling of outdated power structures now comprise the cutting-edge of artistic expression. These are tired games that neglect entire realms of artistic expression in their pursuit of narrow aims. By itself, technique has no meaning, shock value becomes tedious, and self-expression fails to transport. None of these historical artistic aims can bring forth the aliveness and vision needed to navigate our current challenges.

What you need instead is an artistic approach that takes account of all aspects of artistic mastery. It is only a holistic approach that can induce the greatest expression of soulfulness. When you bring together all three strands of Soulforce Mastery, for example, your technique goes beyond the correct replication of certain mechanics to the lattice through which your knowledge of the soul effortlessly flows through you. A creative process supported by the latter will produce art that has the same revolutionary effect as did da Vinci's perspective. Only, instead of helping us move beyond the strictures of religious dogma, it will help us navigate current issues like ecological destruction, authoritarianism, and the diseases of despair.

Both soulfulness and more holistic values bring necessary sanity and new insights to our current challenges. Through a process of personal development, you can expand along these axes to the benefit of your personal well-being and artistic mastery. Supported by this expansion, your creativity will more easily initiate needed moments of truth in your audiences. In this way, you can fulfill your most vital role as an artist in today's world.

SOULFORCE INQUIRY 4.2
YOUR MOMENTS OF TRUTH

What have been the most important moments of truth in your own life? Take a few minutes to reflect on moments when you've been genuinely touched such that your life changed in important ways. Find three examples from your life outside the arts and three from your life within the arts, and write them down in your journal.

THE THREE CELEBRATIONS

"Life itself is a magical recreation of the genesis of the universe, and by celebrating in certain ways humans are reliving the cosmic process of the universe and can thereby access the divinity that is responsible for us being here."

— JOHN ANTHONY WEST[1]

Art is essentially a celebration of the mystery of life. All throughout history and across the globe, humans have found ways of celebrating the universe and their place within it, the results of which have been some of the greatest works of art ever made. Understanding the traditional forms these celebrations have taken can greatly aid your ability to contribute to this essential human activity.

While such celebrations have taken countless specific forms across cultures and time periods, the Sacred Design Lab of the Harvard Divinity School has discovered three essential avenues for celebration common among all societies and time periods: beyond, becoming, and belonging.[2] The Ancient Greeks had their own terms for these: ecstasis, catharsis, and communitas. In plain English, these are inspiration, healing, and connection. These are the **Three Celebrations**—the essential ingredients for human flourishing and the specific avenues through which moments of truth take place.

> The **Three Celebrations** are the specific avenues through which moments of truth take place. They are inspiration, healing, and connection.

Each of the Three Celebrations has an essential role in the arts. Together, they create an opportunity for moments of truth and transcendence to occur.

Chapter 4 | THE SOULFORCE ARTS APPROACH

THE THREE CELEBRATIONS

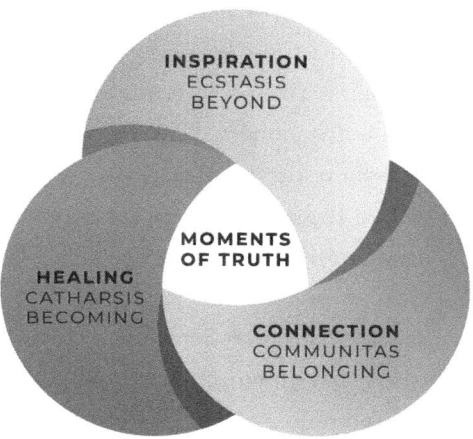

INSPIRATION

Inspiration is an experience of awe, enchantment, or fulfillment. It is an answer to the monotonous grind of daily life and the feeling of the meaninglessness of life's inevitable suffering. Inspiration is a moment of connection with something bigger than yourself that puts things in perspective and gives you a reason to go on.

Inspiration is a peak state, a temporary yet intense feeling of flow or being in the zone. This state is so powerful and pleasurable that people throughout history, from spiritual seekers to high-performance athletes, have gone to extreme lengths to experience it again and again. Flow researcher and University of Chicago professor Mihaly Csikszentmihalyi put it this way: "There are moments that stand out from the chaos of everyday life like shining beacons. In many ways, one might say that the whole effort of humankind through millennia of history has been to capture these fleeting moments of fulfillment and make them a part of everyday existence."[3]

Inspiration is central to what makes a great work of art. When you step into the hush of a cathedral and feel a connection with something sacred, when the swelling of an orchestra threatens to sweep you away, or when you get so lost in a film that you don't even remember to breathe—this is inspiration. Inspiration also defines a meaningful creative act. When you are immersed in the rush of a performance, when a new creative insight hits you like a lightning bolt, or when you put down your pen and realize that hours have gone by without you noticing—this is inspiration, too.

In *The Rise of Superman: Decoding the Science of Ultimate Human Performance*, author and flow expert Steven Kotler writes that there are three main benefits to cultivating inspiration, all of which are relevant for artists.[4] Firstly, inspiration provides powerful intrinsic motivation; when you reach a state of flow in your creative process, you'll be so immersed in enjoying what you're doing that you won't want to stop. Secondly, inspiration actually speeds up your learning processes to such a degree that it can cut the path to mastery in half. Thirdly, it just feels great! According to Kotler, the people who experience the most inspiration are among the happiest on earth.

SOULFORCE INQUIRY 3.4
ATTUNING TO INSPIRATION

Call to mind any memorable experiences of awe, inspiration, or fulfillment in your artistic life. What are the times you've experienced inspiration as an audience member? Or while in the creative process yourself? Write a few sentences in your journal about what you felt, did, and thought during those moments. Then, keep these memories in mind as you go about your creative activities this week so that you can become more and more attuned to inspiration.

HEALING

Healing is a moment of unburdening or regaining your wholeness. It is an answer to Shakespeare's "slings and arrows of outrageous fortune";[5] a profound relief from traumas of all kinds, ranging from the chronic stress endemic to our society all the way up to full-blown PTSD.

From relaxing sound baths to the medicinal use of the Aboriginal didgeridoo to the participation in a trance dance that leaves you feeling at once emptied out and full again, the healing power of music and the arts has long allowed us to transform our suffering into something profound.

To illustrate the kind of healing that is possible, here is an account from a woman who attended one of my musical concerts:

> *It was the quality of perfection that I heard in your music that felt like it "slayed" me in some way and left me feeling completely hollowed out. It was so devastating that I even felt anger toward you both [the performers] for a while that this had happened to me, but mostly I just felt intense grief ... At the intermission, I left and went back to my room, where the process of healing continued, and when I woke up the next morning I felt like a new person.*
>
> *It has now been a couple weeks since that night, and I wanted to share with you where I am now. For starters, the insomnia that has plagued me for many, many years is now almost completely gone. It's like that night gave me a reset to my whole nervous system because I feel calm and peaceful now even in the face of things that used to unsettle me. This is what happens when trauma heals in the body, and that is what happened to me from my experience at that performance. It also feels like my ego went through a transformation where it is now more*

> *aligned with the goals of my soul, because I do not find myself "taking the bait" anymore when people act in a way that would normally really trigger me. My husband has noticed this change, as well as other close family members, so I am getting affirmation from outside myself, as well.*

This is catharsis, the power of the arts to heal.

SOULFORCE INQUIRY 4.4
ATTUNING TO HEALING

Call to mind any memorable experiences of healing, unburdening, or regaining your wholeness in your artistic life. What are the times you've experienced healing as an audience member? Or while in the creative process yourself? Write a few sentences in your journal about what you felt, did, and thought during those moments. Then, keep these memories in mind as you go about your creative activities this week so that you can become more and more attuned to healing.

CONNECTION

Connection is a feeling of togetherness, belonging, or group flow. It is the answer to the fragmentation of our communities and the experience of isolation and loneliness that is so widespread in our society.[6] Connection is the sense that other people have your back, that you're loved and wanted, and that we're all in this together.

Connection provides a necessary sense of togetherness for audiences. For example, it is what draws tens of thousands of people to rock concerts and electronic dance music festivals every year. These events are wildly popular precisely because they offer an immersive, cathartic experience that gives people a rich sense of flow and connection. Keith Sawyer at the University of North Carolina at Chapel Hill calls this experience "group flow," and says that it is so pleasurable and powerful that it is up to three times as rewarding as an isolated peak experience.[7]

Connection is also a vital part of what makes for meaningful experiences as an artist. Group flow happens when you work toward a worthy goal alongside others. You experience connection when your own individual creativity and decision-making merges with a collective intelligence; in other words, when you feel that the whole is more than the sum of the parts.

For example, imagine that you're taking part in a theater production. You and the other cast and crew members have been working closely together for several weeks now. You've made it through "hell week" together, and the jitters of opening night are behind you. As the play begins, you can feel that you're really hitting your stride now, and there is an effortless flow on stage. You and the other cast members seem to be able to read each other's minds. At the end of the performance, during the final bows, you look around and your heart swells, feeling a delicious and timeless sense of camaraderie and closeness with all your peers. This is connection.

SOULFORCE INQUIRY 4.5
ATTUNING TO CONNECTION

Call to mind any memorable experiences of togetherness, belonging, or group flow in your artistic life. What are the times you've experienced connection as an audience member? Or while in the creative process yourself? Write a few sentences in your journal about what you felt, did, and thought during those moments. Then, keep

> these memories in mind as you go about your creative activities this week so that you can become more and more attuned to connection.

Author Frederick Buechner said that your life's purpose is "the place where your deep gladness and the world's deep hunger meet."[8] The three celebrations are the direct path to that very place. When you cultivate inspiration, healing, and connection, you will simultaneously be reaching the place where your greatest well-being, joy, creative fulfillment, and artistic mastery meet the deep hunger your audiences have for these very qualities.

There are countless ways to reach this magical place. As always, this process begins with you. The first step to cultivating the three celebrations in your art is to notice your own needs for inspiration, healing, and connection. Where are these needs being met, or not? The more you become sensitized to your own needs, the more you'll be able to make informed artistic choices; choices that will allow you and your art to become a medium by which powerful experiences of inspiration, healing, and togetherness can occur for both you and your audiences.

The Soulforce Arts Approach provides the intellectual and spiritual framework necessary to give Soulforce its rightful place at the center of the creative process. This we have laid out in the previous chapters. The rest of this book offers practices and perspectives designed to turn this framework into an embodied reality.

Your next step to embodying the Soulforce Arts Approach is to discover your artistic purpose, the deeper "why" whose fulfillment will bring new clarity, meaning, and energy to every area of your artistic life.

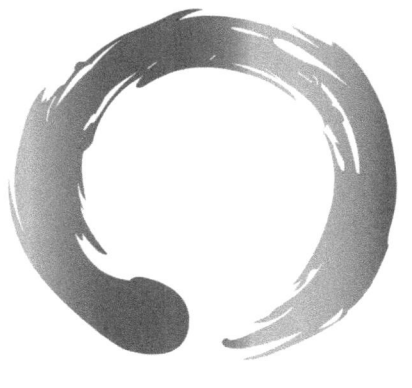

SECTION II

PRACTICE

"Those who have a 'why' to live, can bear with almost any 'how.'"

– VIKTOR FRANKL, *MAN'S SEARCH FOR MEANING*

CHAPTER 5

YOUR ARTISTIC PURPOSE

Cynthia, a gifted operatic singer, initially came to me for help with several challenges related to breath support. She told me that while practicing at home, she often felt short of breath, her back felt tight, and she had a habit of leaning to one side at the end of each phrase. In addition, while singing during church services, she felt a heightened sense of anxiety that only made these other symptoms worse. During an early lesson together, we made a surprising discovery. While we initially thought she had a breath support problem, it turned out that the real issue was one of artistic purpose. Here's what happened.

In the lesson, I asked her to sing one of her pieces so I could see and hear her breath support issues firsthand. Responding to the excess tension she reported and which I also saw, I decided to support her with some Alexander Technique hands-on guidance. As an Alexander Technique teacher, I have been trained to use my hands to give a gentle yet unmistakable signal of muscular release to my student's body. Cynthia was already familiar with this practice, so I stepped up to her, gently placed my hands on her neck and then her ribs, and guided her body into a state of ease. I then asked her to sing her piece again, only this time while continuing to follow my hands.

While she sang, my hands on her ribs gave me a very clear sense of what was happening in her body. With every out breath she squeezed her ribs tight, a needless application of muscular effort that interfered with her body's natural breath support. At the same time, I could also sense that she was, to an extent, following the easeful guidance of my hands such that her whole body was freer than it had been the first time she sang. When she finished singing, we each shared what we noticed. Cynthia said that her back had felt more comfortable and that she felt like she had more air for each breath. So far, so good.

I intuited that even more freedom of movement and a deeper musical expression were possible and so, knowing of the mind-body connection, I asked her what she was thinking about when she sang. She replied, "Mostly, I'm thinking about how to get in all the notes in each phrase without running out of air. I'm also focused on following the breath technique my singing coach has suggested." In response, I cautioned that focusing too narrowly on technique could create so much muscular tension as to interfere with the technique itself. A new focus was needed, one that would allow her to sing with the physical, emotional, and mental freedom she desired.

So, I asked her, "Why do you love singing? Is getting the technique or notes right really why you sing? What's your ultimate aim?" Cynthia thought about this for a moment, then replied, "I love connecting with people through music. Even though I'm not religious, I love the idea of helping the congregation I sing for connect with spirit through my music." She went on to tell me of the inspiration she felt in music lessons with her first singing teacher and her desire to spread a similar inspiration through her current performances.

I replied, "Wonderful. It sounds like your artistic purpose might be to connect with spirit and to provide that connection through your music to inspirational effect." Cynthia nodded in agreement with my summary. I went on, "The best way to share connection and inspiration is to feel their presence in yourself as you sing. So, sing your passage again, only this time remembering your artistic purpose as you do so."

The results were deeply moving. Her sound had a new, haunting quality, and her body seemed to float as she stood and sang, her ribs moving effortlessly. My own body shivered and tingled as she sang, resonating with the deeper emotional connection now shining forth from her music. "Wow!" Cynthia exclaimed when she finished the passage. "That was so different! Everything flowed, I had plenty of breath, and I didn't even think about technique. I felt much more engrossed in the meaning of the music, more connected with my heart. That was fun!" Cynthia later told me that her subsequent performances felt more effortless and calm. She also received outside confirmation of her inner shift. After her performances, her congregation shared new kinds of compliments, telling her that her music had a healing quality and a new depth of emotion.

My takeaway from that lesson with Cynthia was that many of the challenges artists face are but symptoms of a deeper issue: disconnection from their artistic purpose. Disconnected from your purpose, the creative act will feel effortful, mechanical, or hollow. Connection with your purpose resolves these issues by providing a why that energizes your Soulforce. Thus energized, your creative juices will flow, your body will relax, and your art will be filled with life. Fulfilling your artistic purpose improves everything you could care about in the creative process. So, what is artistic purpose and how can you discover your own?

THE PLACE WHERE YOUR ART, WELL-BEING, AND THE WORLD'S HUNGER MEET

> *"The purpose of art is to raise people to a higher level of awareness than they would otherwise attain on their own."*
>
> **— BRASSAÏ**

Your **artistic purpose** is the deeper why that motivates your artistic life. It is an expression of who and what you are, the soul-level impulse that brought you to the arts in the first place. It is the source of your greatest artistic inspiration whose results are your most life-giving gifts to the world. I'll share again the words of Frederick Buechner from his classic *Wishful Thinking:* your artistic purpose is "the place where your art, well-being, and the world's hunger meet."[1]

Your artistic purpose is ineffable, meaning that words can never capture it entirely. Rather, purpose is an expression of your very being, beyond all concepts and labels. In addition, discovering your purpose is not a one-time affair. The life moving within and around you is always changing and flowing, so what might have been your purpose at one point in life may no longer fit at another. Purpose discovery, then, is an ongoing process of the revelation of your deepest truths and desires. Connection with these truths and desires is the essence of creativity.

> Your **artistic purpose** is the deeper why that motivates your artistic life.

Your artistic purpose connects you to something larger than your individual ego. It is a response to the needs of the world around you, the act of service which is your unique way of feeding the world's hunger. As such, your artistic purpose goes beyond the level of the imperatives of the lesser gods. Neither the pursuit of money, professional advancement, technical achievements, nor fame constitute your artistic purpose. Nor does a mere hobby; your artistic purpose must align with where your greatest gifts and skills lie. While egoic and personal desires have their place in everyone's life, none carries sufficient Soulforce to truly bring you, your art, and thus your world, more alive.

Your artistic purpose is the transformation you were born to enact through your creative activities. When connected with your purpose, your art becomes a beacon or a catalyst, taking your audiences on a journey from meaninglessness, sickness, and alienation to inspiration, healing, and connection. The most powerful transformations you can enact for your audiences are a mirror to the ones you have successfully navigated in your own life.

For example, you may have experienced certain childhood wounds. Though painful, undergoing these wounds is often a necessary precondition to having a worthy purpose. The struggle these wounds entail is what provides the motivation to dig deep inside yourself and thereby gain valuable self-awareness, insights, and healing knowledge. These are the gold in the dragon's lair, your greatest assets in helping others heal from similar wounds. Witnessing your art have this kind of transformative effect is the very definition of a fulfilling creative life.

SOULFORCE INQUIRY 5.1
INKLING YOUR ARTISTIC PURPOSE

A good first step toward discovering your artistic purpose is a life review. Use the following prompts to glean clues to your purpose from formative life experiences.

- What are the most formative experiences in your childhood? Who have you become as a result?
- What are your earliest memories of falling in love with the arts? What transformation did these experiences evoke within you?
- What are the themes that come up in your art, again and again?
- What do people most often ask you for help with?
- What do you find yourself doing, no matter where you go?
- What are those causes or events that, perhaps inexplicably, call to you at a visceral level?

INHERITED PURPOSE AND SHALLOW EXPRESSIVITY

> *"Our patient has no grasp of the whole, he sees only isolated parts and gets nowhere. In developing his plan, he relies purely on his powers of cerebration, since instinct, as he says, has gone missing. Speaking of music one day, he declares that for him it is no more than a succession of sounds: 'I don't know how to feel—everything has to go through my brain.'"*

— CLINICAL REPORT BY PSYCHIATRIST FRANÇOISE MINKOWSKA

From one perspective, all the creative, physical, emotional, and spiritual challenges described in this book share a common root cause: disconnection from your artistic purpose. However, the presence of these challenges is not a sign of utter purposelessness. Instead, they are a sign that what's motivating your creative process are the purposes that you have inherited from the Story of Separation and its lesser gods. Reconnection with a more soul-led artistic purpose is greatly aided by exploring the presence of these inherited purposes in your life.

An **inherited purpose** is the attempt to discover a more fulfilling creative process through insufficient means, such as technical, academic, social, or financial advancement. It is the natural result of creating from within the Story of Separation, in which creativity is viewed as a thing to be manipulated. This view results in a creative process disconnected from the true source of creativity within. An inherited purpose is a coping strategy for this disconnection, an ultimately misguided attempt to requite your soul's longing for something juicy and alive.

An inherited purpose inevitably leads to shallow forms of creative expression. Disconnected from a reason to create that goes beyond the lesser gods, your only recourse is to try to manufacture something artificially. The result is art devoid of real creativity, of Soulforce, and so feels stale, forced, empty, or robotic. Unfortunately, many of our arts pedagogies and institutions fail to adequately articulate a more fulfilling artistic purpose, with the result that many artists are left with a giant hole in our hearts. We have the feeling that we're "meant for more than this," that something vital, yet indefinable, is missing. The tragedy is that, lacking the framework to understand our predicament, many of us resign ourselves to an artistic life that can never fulfill the greatness our hearts know is possible.

> An **inherited purpose** is the attempt to discover a more fulfilling creative process through insufficient means, such as technical, academic, social, or financial advancement. While these may have a role in anyone's life, they do not constitute your true artistic purpose.

You know you're creating from an inherited purpose when:

- Your creations rely too heavily on shock value, fads, trends, technical virtuosity, or tradition to achieve their effect.
- You experience creative plateaus, burnout, writer's block, boredom, procrastination, or other signs of a lack of creative inspiration.
- You experience performance anxiety, perfectionism, impostor syndrome, an overactive inner critic, competitiveness, or other signs of a creative process focused on the avoidance of ostracization and shame.
- You rely on effort to get you through, resulting in muscular tension, overuse injuries, and exhaustion.
- You find yourself creating solely for money, academic accolades, or prizes.
- You fear selling out to such an extent that you inadvertently curtail your full potential.

Which forms of inherited purpose show up in your own life depends on your life circumstances, such as your familial and societal values, inherited emotional baggage, and early artistic training. While your overall aim should be to rely less on inherited purposes, there's no need to feel anxious or ashamed when you find yourself caught in them. After all, inherited purpose is something congenital, and it is not your fault that you were once too little to know better. At a deeper level, an inherited purpose belies what's underneath: the life-giving wish to give fully of your gifts. Spend some time getting clear on how inherited purposes show up in your life. Doing so is a necessary step to clearing the way for your more soulful gifts to shine through.

SOULFORCE INQUIRY 5.2
YOUR INHERITED ARTISTIC PURPOSE

Look back over the list above and notice which modes of inherited purpose stand out to you. Do any of them seem familiar? Which one is easiest to relate to, and why? Which one do you least want associated with yourself, and why?

Now, consider how these approaches may have developed in your life. When did they first begin? What were the formative events that led to their development?

Later, when you next engage in your creative practice, pause for a moment and bring awareness to any forms of inherited purpose that might be present. Simply make note of what shows up, for example saying to yourself, *Ah, there's my "fear of criticism" habit. How about that!*

Bring some curiosity to how this habit shows up in your bodily sensations, thoughts, emotions, and scope of attention. (Not to worry: I'll show you how in Mind-Body Interlude #1.) If you notice frustration, anxiety, or shame at the mere appearance of this habit, notice that too, reminding yourself that it's okay to have "bad" habits.

Finally, and most importantly, identify the life-giving wish underneath your unique forms of inherited purpose. What positive goal are you reaching toward?

Make some notes in your journal about your go-to habits of inherited purpose. The more awareness you bring to them, the greater the freedom you'll have from them.

Even if you have long felt lost and artistically unfulfilled, you have never been in any danger of falling completely prey to inherited forms of artistic purpose. You are wired for purpose, and, despite any appearances to the contrary, your soul has known all along what your true artistic purpose is. Thus, the anxiety, meaninglessness, or tension you may have experienced along the way are not so much a sign that you're fundamentally lost. Rather, they are forms of protest from your soul, messages designed to grab your attention so you can get back on track. In this light, far from being obstacles to your creative growth and healing, you can regard even the most challenging artistic issues as trailheads pointing the way home.

PURPOSE DISCOVERY

"The loss of the way you've known yourself is the price you pay for the journey of the Soul."

— JONATHAN GUSTIN, PURPOSE GUIDES INSTITUTE

Purpose discovery is the ongoing revelation of your deepest truths and desires. It is the process of bringing these truths and desires to conscious attention and giving them form in the world. Purpose discovery is a universal and ancient human practice; there is evidence of its central role in indigenous wisdom traditions around the world.[2] Inspired by these ancient roots and disillusioned by contemporary society's outdated notions of progress, many are now looking to purpose discovery in their search for a more meaningful and vibrant life.

Purpose discovery is essential to a creative process suffused with Soulforce because the seat of purpose and that of creativity are one and the same. When you discover the deepest why that motivates your life, you naturally want to give it form through creative activities. The form it takes, being a spontaneous and authentic expression of the whole of your being, is unique and alive, with no trace of contrivance or manipulation. It is thus the very definition of creativity, a movement of life that finds expression through your body, mind, soul, and world.

Your artistic purpose comprises three related facets: vision, essence, and action. Your vision includes the kind of world you want to create; your essence includes your core values, radiant energy, soul-level powers, and message; and your actions include your genius, mission, and vocation. Use the following prompts to flesh out your artistic purpose.

> Your artistic purpose comprises three related facets: **vision, essence,** and **action.**

SOULFORCE INQUIRY 5.3
THE THREE FACETS OF ARTISTIC PURPOSE

- **Vision.** Your artistic purpose is guided by your vision. Vividly describe the big picture view of the kind of world you want to create. Example: "I envision a world of reverence for life, where everybody effortlessly works toward the larger good."

- **Essence.** Your essence includes the qualities inherent to your artistic purpose, comprising your values, powers, energy, and message. What are your deepest-held *values*? Examples: compassion, justice, kindness, truth. What are your unique, soul-level *powers*, the skills and proclivities you were born with? Examples: musicality, problem solving, listening, empathizing. What *energy* or "vibe" do you radiate, even when doing nothing in particular? Examples: depth, love, joy, illumination. What is your *message*, the single truth you were meant to proclaim, described in a pithy statement. Example: the Buddha's message was that awakening to the true self is possible and can be accessed when no longer clinging to anything as me or mine.

- **Action.** Your purpose-driven actions comprise your genius, mission, and vocation. What is your *genius*, the specific activity you employ to transform those around you; your unique gift to the world. Examples: motivating, helping birth the true self, confronting power, speaking truth. What is your *mission*, the tangible goal or assignment that moves you toward your vision? Example: the mission of Soulforce arts is to reconnect artists with their Soulforce so they can create a more beautiful, harmonious world. What is your *vocation*, the specific job, channel, career, product, platform, or profession used to give form to your genius? Examples: dancer, producer, content creator, activist, therapist, books, film, compositions, and other media.

There are two main avenues for bringing your artistic purpose to conscious attention. The first is extrinsic. When you reflect on the patterns of your life, ask a friend for their impressions of you, or engage in journaling exercises, you are using **extrinsic methods** of purpose discovery. These are a great place to start because they are readily available to most people and can quickly give you a sense of your purpose. However, as mentioned, your true artistic purpose is an expression of your being that transcends all words or concepts. So, to get the whole picture, you also need **intrinsic methods** of purpose discovery, those that reveal your purpose at the level of the felt experience of the soul. These are the tried-and-true methods handed down to us by our ancestors. While they are sometimes more challenging, and often benefit from guidance by a trained facilitator, intrinsic methods of purpose discovery are what result in the most profound and lasting personal transformations.

The following Soulforce Inquiry is a list of common methods of purpose discovery, both extrinsic and intrinsic. Choose which ones you feel most comfortable with and use them as opportunities to reveal your soul's deepest truths and desires. Let yourself be surprised by what you discover. Be open to answers that come in the form of sensations, memories, bodily movements, symbols, colors, stories, archetypes, or even synchronicities and signs in nature. Don't rush to put words to your insights and discoveries; let them sink in at a felt level first. Then, if what you learn in a purpose discovery session fits into the three facets of artistic purpose, write it down in a purpose discovery document that you review and update regularly.

SOULFORCE INQUIRY 5.4
PURPOSE DISCOVERY SESSIONS

Use the following methods to discover your artistic purpose. Engage in purpose discovery sessions regularly for the next several weeks or months, and then again whenever your creative juices start drying up. Start with those that feel most comfortable. Seek expert guidance from trained facilitators for more advanced methods.

EXTRINSIC

- **Three Facets Journaling.** Go through the prompts for the three facets of artistic purpose in Soulforce Inquiry 5.3 and make notes based on what you already know about yourself.

- **Past Journaling.** Reflect on your childhood. What stands out most to you about your upbringing? What were the most pivotal experiences? What were your greatest accomplishments? What were the times when you stood up for something you valued? What causes or people were you most drawn to help? How did any of these experiences inform your artistic choices?

- **Future Journaling**. Imagine yourself ten years in the future. What have you accomplished? What have you created? What are you able to do now that you couldn't ten years ago? What have you stood up for along the way? What are the most surprising positive changes you've experienced? What communities have you served? In what ways have they been transformed because of your influence?

- **Ask Your Friends.** Ask trusted friends to fill out the three facets of artistic purpose prompts based on their impressions of you, either in writing or during an in-person conversation.

INTRINSIC

- **Dialogue with Nature.** Go to a favorite spot in nature, a spot that is as wild and secluded as you can find (even if that's your local dog park). Make yourself comfortable and engage in a dialogue with the non-human beings around you, using the three facets of artistic purpose prompts to get started. Open your mind to receive answers in the form of gusts of wind, the creaks of trees, and the calls of birds. What might each of these signify, symbolically, for your purpose?

- **Breathwork.** Connection with deeper layers of your soul can be facilitated by altered states of consciousness. Breathwork modalities such as Wim Hof's, shamanic breathing, and holotropic breathwork are safe and effective means of quieting the discursive mind and opening a space within. Engage in a breathwork session for about half an hour and then pause the breathwork to bring forth one of the three facets of artistic purpose prompts. Don't actively seek an answer; just let the prompt float in your newly opened consciousness like a petal on a pond. Let any answers arise spontaneously.

- **Fasting.** Extended fasting is an ancient practice known to elicit altered states of consciousness. Once you enter these states, investigate the three facets of artistic purpose prompts. Caution: fasting carries certain risks. Before you begin any fast, educate yourself thoroughly on proper fasting techniques and get medical clearance from your healthcare provider.

- **Psychedelics.** Psychedelics are a powerful means of purpose discovery. They have been used by countless people throughout history and across the world. Examples include the Amazon ayahuasca ceremony, the Ancient Greek Eleusinian Mysteries, and the Siberian shaman's use of the amanita muscaria mushroom.[3][4][5] You can quickly access transformative insights into your life purpose by bringing the three facets of artistic purpose prompts into a psychedelic session. As with fasting, psychedelics carry certain risks, legal, medical, and psychological. Before taking any psychedelics, check to see which substances are legal in your area, get medical clearance from your healthcare provider, and seek the guidance of a trained facilitator.

Some may object to the idea of engaging in purpose discovery practices that derive from indigenous societies unrelated to your own. Sometimes this caution is warranted. After all, without due respect for their origins, these practices and their lineages can become commoditized, cheapened, and sometimes destroyed altogether. However, the answer is not to chastise those who seek indigenous wisdom. We can learn a lot from indigenous peoples, both individually and at a societal level, and the best way to learn their lessons is to actively embody what they teach. To do otherwise would dishonor their precious teachings and leave us without the vital information necessary to transform our extractive way of life. If indigenous wisdom calls to you, actively seek out its sources, either in the form of books, vetted online content, or better yet by learning directly from living indigenous lineage holders.

GIVING PURPOSE FORM

"Chop wood, carry water."

— ZEN SAYING

Hopefully by now you've engaged in the purpose discovery practices and have gleaned some real insights into your artistic purpose. Whether you've had a small inkling or a full-blown mystical experience, the next step is always to integrate what you've learned into your daily life. Any revelation is momentary, and so purpose discovery is only effective when it extends these revelations into other areas of your life, especially those that seem most mundane. You can integrate your insights in three ways: by discovering your artistic soul name, developing a purpose statement, and bringing your newly discovered purpose into its rightful place at the center of your artistic activities.

ARTISTIC SOUL NAME

Your artistic soul name is the identity you were born with that reflects your artistic purpose. Here's a story of how one of my students discovered his artistic soul name and the positive effect it had on his creative life. Taylor is a classical guitarist who came to me for help with chronic muscular discomfort and tension he felt while playing, as well as the burnout he had begun to feel as a guitar teacher. During one lesson together, we discovered that both his tension and burnout stemmed from an outmoded artistic purpose. Like many musicians who receive high-level training, and despite his gentle personality, Taylor had inherited a forceful attitude toward his body and creativity. His term for this attitude was, "Gotta get it done." I asked him what name or identity might match that attitude. He replied, "Good Little Musician."

I explained that this attitude and its related identity comprised his inherited purpose, and that he might benefit from adopting a more soulful one. I suggested he go inside and ask his heart and soul for a name that might better match his true artistic purpose. After a few moments, he opened his eyes, smiled, and said, "Joyful Musician!" I invited Taylor to go on. He said that Joyful Musician had a purpose: to spread love and joy through music. I then asked him to play his guitar as Joyful Musician. The results were similar to those of the opera singer, Cynthia: a whole new level of relaxation, enjoyment, and emotional expression. I also asked him how bringing Joyful Musician into his teaching might change how he felt about lessons. He immediately saw how Good Little Musician's "gotta get it done" attitude had contributed to his burnout, and that Joyful Musician's purpose could provide a new source of energy and inspiration while he taught.

SOULFORCE INQUIRY 5.5
YOUR ARTISTIC SOUL NAME

You can discover your artistic soul name through the purpose discovery methods in the previous section. For example, sit under your favorite tree in a nearby park, make yourself comfortable, and close your eyes. Take a few calming breaths. Sense your body and let the sounds around you play with your ears. Then, when your system has settled somewhat, gently bring up the question, *What is my artistic soul name, the identity I was born with, and which reflects my artistic purpose?*

Don't grasp for answers. If a name arises, it will do so of its own accord. You will know you've found it when you get a whole body "yes!" Sometimes you might only get a vague feeling, a fuzzy image, or a partial name in response to your inquiries. If that's the case, keep coming back to this practice until you find one that truly fits. Remember: a true artistic soul name is an organic part of who you are and isn't a reflection of what other people have said you should be.

PURPOSE STATEMENT

A purpose statement is a one- or two-sentence statement that captures the essence of your artistic purpose. Sometimes it can come in the form of an image: "My artistic purpose is a river of honey that glows under misty mountains." Or a feeling: "I know I'm acting according to my artistic purpose when I feel lighthearted and free, like I'm a joyful, mischievous, wise fairy who re-enchants the world with her magic wand." Or an archetype: "My artistic purpose is to be a king who faces challenges with a lion's heart." Or an animal: "I'm a soaring eagle, bringing wild beauty and an untethered soul to my people." In addition to receiving such images, feelings, archetypes, or animal totems, you can also use the following Soulforce Inquiry to put words to your purpose. Once you develop your purpose statement, write it down and put it in a place where you will see it regularly.

SOULFORCE INQUIRY 5.6
PURPOSE STATEMENT

Use the following formula to develop your purpose statement: "I create a world of [your vision] by [your actions], supported by [your essence]."

For example, *"I create a world of magic, fun, and love by speaking my truth and helping others remember the magic within, supported by my depth, compassion, and divine nature."* The more time you spend refining your purpose statement, the more you will own your purpose and see its positive effects in your artistic life.

RECENTERING YOUR ARTISTIC PURPOSE

Many of the challenges in your artistic life are the result of having unconsciously defined how you create, perform, practice, teach, and make a living in terms of an inherited purpose. Placing your artistic purpose back at the center of these activities can yield immediate and transformative results.

SOULFORCE INQUIRY 5.7
RECENTERING YOUR ARTISTIC PURPOSE

Think of the artistic activity where you experience the most challenge, creatively, physically, spiritually, or even financially. Ask yourself: *If the pain or disconnect I feel surrounding this challenge could talk, what would it say? Is there a hidden, inherited purpose at work?* If so, put it into words and let its presence sink in, bringing this area of shadow into the light of consciousness.

Next, recall your artistic purpose, whether in the form of your soul name, purpose statement, or a resonant symbol. Get curious as to how remembering your artistic purpose, your deeper why, might change how you do this challenging activity. Take a moment to imagine letting your purpose lead. Then do this activity while holding your purpose in mind and see what changes.

Finally, ask yourself: *What would I have to let go of to truly embody my purpose during this activity?* The answer might be the same inherited purpose you first uncovered, or another. Bring an awareness of this old habit into your next creative session.

DIVINE SELFISHNESS

"I wish I could show you when you are lonely or in darkness the astonishing light of your own being."

— HAFIZ OF SHIRAZ, FOURTEENTH-CENTURY SUFI POET

Embracing your artistic purpose may be one of the most important steps you take in your artistic life. It is essential to the creative fulfillment, enjoyment, and impact that your soul may now long for. However, embracing your artistic purpose can, at times, bring up certain concerns. Some initially resist fully embracing their artistic purpose because of what it might mean for meeting their survival needs, how they collaborate with others, their path to artistic mastery, and their ultimate responsibility to the world around them.

Many of these concerns are understandable. For example, what role does following your artistic purpose have when you're playing a soulless gig to pay the bills? Or in collaborative projects when your own desires are not the only ones in play? Or when the highest standards of technical virtuosity are needed? Or in the long-haul discipline necessary for artistic mastery? Can you truly be of service to your world when you're in your little hobbit hole, creating to your heart's desire, or is following your artistic purpose inherently selfish? These are important questions. After all, if pursuing your artistic purpose meant slavishly following your whims, regardless of the consequences, or if creative constraints necessarily meant abandoning your purpose, then who in their right mind would want to embrace their artistic purpose?

Answering these questions starts with an understanding of the perspective they come from: the Story of Separation. Through this lens, your artistic purpose poses a threat to the concerns just discussed. It sees a threat to your livelihood because your artistic purpose requires, in many cases, letting go of the familiar values of the economic machine we live in and instead trusting in the generosity of others. It sees a threat to your ability to collaborate with others because it regards collaboration as a power struggle, a zero-sum battle of wills between isolated individuals. It sees a threat to your artistic mastery because of the narrow way the mind of separation defines mastery and the stringent self-denial it believes is necessary to reach it. In addition, it sees a threat to your artistic impact because what furthers your artistic purpose and what brings you the most money or fame are often very different. To the mind of separation, artistic purpose is a luxury you probably can't afford.

Chapter 5 | YOUR ARTISTIC PURPOSE

There are certain grains of truth in the resistance that separation has toward artistic purpose, which is partly why such resistance can be difficult to counter. However, despite these grains of truth and the cultural weight they carry, the reality is that the Story of Separation has little to offer in the way of creative and satisfying solutions to concerns beyond a soulless, effortful self-denial.

This is where artistic purpose, founded in the Story of Interbeing, comes in. For example, following your artistic purpose will help your livelihood because what your audiences want from you, and are thus most willing to pay for, is your creative aliveness. It will help your collaborations because it allows you to regard your ideas and those from others with the same "yes, and ..." mindset so essential to genuine creativity. It will help you achieve greater artistic mastery because it gives a deeper, juicier why to necessary technical advancements. In addition, it will help your art have a greater impact on our world because it will orient you to serving and connecting with those who most need your creative gifts.

When you see the real-world benefits of following your artistic purpose, any fear that doing so is selfish or irresponsible will fall away. You will recognize that the self to which you are being selfish is actually much grander and interconnected than you previously thought. You will be living from the Story of Interbeing, able to recognize how your creative impulses and those of the beings around you all come from a single, larger, divine self.

It is the Story of Separation and its attitude of puritanical self-denial that is the real problem because, in the end, it ruins the very things it purports to protect. The antidote for such self-denial is more connection with your deepest truths and desires, not less. When you "selfishly" recover the desires and feelings that have gotten squashed in your attempt to fit into our society's inhumane way of life, you are taking a necessary step toward your artistic purpose. Your resultant art will transfix with a breathtaking wildness.

Ultimately, there is never any conflict between areas of creative constraint and your artistic purpose. Rather, your artistic purpose is better understood as a set of values and goals that can bring needed perspective and direction to times of stress, confusion, and challenge. This is why artistic purpose is so central to channeling your Soulforce; it helps you face your creative challenges from a place of aliveness, wholeness, and connection. In this, Soulforce entails an attitude of empowered acceptance in the spirit of the saying, "When life hands you lemons, make lemonade."

In other words, your life is the way it is right now, and certain challenges are inevitable. There are always going to be crummy gigs, difficult colleagues, and creative plateaus. While we can certainly work toward a better future, trying to escape the "lemons" that come your way or wishing things to be otherwise paradoxically only leads to more suffering. Thus, the only real question is how you respond to challenges. When you include your artistic purpose in the conversation, you lose nothing and gain a new and more life-giving set of choices that were previously unknown and whose fulfillment may have seemed impossible.

SYSTEM UPDATES

> *"Evolution, I realized, is not an impersonal force.*
> *You and I are participating in it at this very moment.*
> *You and I are the butterflies, flapping our wings,*
> *only dimly aware of the hurricanes we're setting in*
> *motion. And not one of us is insignificant."*
>
> — PATRICK FARLEY, *CHRYSALIS COLOSSUS*[6]

When you discover and then give form to your artistic purpose, your art begins to matter in a new way. Purpose-driven art allows you to have the kind of impact on your world your heart knows you were meant for. However, the exact nature of this impact may, at first, seem unfamiliar.

Chapter 5 | YOUR ARTISTIC PURPOSE

Contrary to our society's familiar linear and effortful means of creating change, your greatest artistic impact will not happen through an exertion of your creative will upon the world, as is so common with agitprop or "art with a cause." Such activist art often leads to a creative dead-end because its political agenda completely disenchants the creative process. All too often, the result is art without Soulforce—and can that truly be what the world needs from you?

No, the key to your greatest artistic impact is, paradoxically, to let go of trying to impress your individual values and goals and to instead recognize that your values, goals, and creative impulses don't fully belong to you as an individual. Rather, you are the channel through which creative impulses flow. Which impulses flow through you are a perfect reflection of your unique place within the larger system of society and planet.

From the perspective of the Soulforce Arts Approach, your art matters when it helps this larger system heal and evolve. Just as with all living systems, healing and evolution are an inherent, organic function of our society and planet. For that function to best take place, this system needs to update itself in the same way that a brain develops through new and more robust neural connections. You are like a neuron in the brain of our society and planet; your actions, feelings, perceptions, and creations, far from being solely the product of your separate ego self, are how your surrounding system updates itself. Given your inextricable embeddedness in this system, your most life-giving impact happens when you open yourself to the ongoing flow of information in and around you, and then let that information guide how and what you create.

What kind of information might this include, and what kinds of updates does your surrounding system need? As we saw previously, sanity and healing begin when anything that has been repressed or ignored is integrated. Do you feel heartsick because yet another wilderness area near you has been paved over to make a parking lot? Instead of stuffing those feelings away or demonizing the people who did it, you can let your grief and anger inform how and what you next create.

A **system update** is the individual act of communication by which the ongoing survival and evolution of a community of individuals takes place. Each system update is a response to the individual's own state of being within its environment and has a potentially transformative effect on all community members.

Let's say you're acting in a play, and upon feeling the grief of seeing this new parking lot, you decide to participate in a system update by bringing your grief into your next performance. Even though you don't mention the parking lot or your grief while on stage, the raw emotion you channel during your performance nonetheless impacts your audience. Though they may not realize what's happening, they are touched by the new energy in your performance. They may even experience a moment of truth that connects them with their own unprocessed emotions. Any action they subsequently take may then carry the healing effect of your cathartic expression, thus propagating its life-giving impact through the mysterious pathways of our interconnected world. A system update has just happened.

> A **system update** is the individual act of communication by which the ongoing survival and evolution of a community of individuals takes place. Each system update is a response to the individual's own state of being within its environment and has a potentially transformative effect on all community members.

You only believe that your art doesn't matter when you see yourself as a separate individual. The truth is that you are a node in a larger system. Your grief is not just your grief, after all; it is the planet grieving through you. You can aid our collective grieving process by creating from the raw aliveness of these feelings and then sharing your creations with those around you.

Your artistic purpose, being the place where your art, well-being, and the world's hunger meet, comprises the ideal system update. It necessarily involves clearing out or more fully integrating what has been stuck in your inner and outer system. This is the essential function of the arts and a description of your most vital role as an artist in a world in turmoil. Your greatest artistic impact will best be fulfilled when it acts as a necessary update for the well-being of the larger system.

What does this updating function look like in practice? Let's further illustrate its workings with an example from the natural world.

It is well-known that birds call to one another to attract mates, announce their presence in their territory, warn each other of predators, and, it seems, to express the sheer joy of being alive. People who grow up close to forests and are closely attuned to their environment often speak of a sort of "wood wide web," a communication network among birds that spans miles in all directions. This web appears to allow the community of birds to know exactly where the nearest hawk or fox is, when the weather might change, and what's happening with their avian neighbors over the next hill.

This communication network exists in a state of dynamic equilibrium in which there is a continuous hum of vocalization even in times of relative calm. The continuity of this hum allows birds to respond quickly and appropriately to changes in the environment so that the community as a whole can survive and thrive. This means that each individual bird has a particular responsibility: when it notices something new in the environment, its most important job at that moment is to broadcast a system update to the wider community so that all members can adapt to the change as appropriate.

The system in this example is a community of birds, and the update is a particular bird's song that is sung in response to certain changes in the environment. When a hawk flies over, the song will change to help others avoid the predator; when the angle of the sun signals evening feeding time, the song will change again to reflect this need. Both help the community to survive threats and to thrive.

Each bird carries its own unique style of system updates, in its own uniquely recognizable voice. Each bird also responds to the events that it is most attuned to, which might well be different to those of other birds. Over time, every change in the surrounding forest gets reflected in the content and subtleties of the community's songs.

When all the birds are healthy, well-attuned to their environments, and in communication with their community members, this system works exceedingly well. However, this finely tuned system could easily break down if some of or all of the members lose their ability to sing, hear each other, or see things in their environment. If this were to happen, the community of birds would disintegrate, leaving each individual vulnerable to all kinds of danger. Thus, the greatest threat to any community of birds isn't actually a specific danger in their environment—it's a lack of timely, accurate, and appropriate system updates.

The impact of these system updates is not limited to the community of birds. They are, after all, deeply interconnected with all other living beings in the forest. It is well known that other animals respond to predator calls from birds, thus making birds the eyes and ears of the whole forest. Directly or indirectly, birdsong plays a vital role in the health of every living being in the forest.

Artists play a similar role in human society as birds do in a forest. Artists produce system updates in the form of works of art, performances, literature, new ideas, and fresh perspectives. Each creative act is a system update that originates in response to the artist's own state of being within their environment and has a potentially transformative effect on audiences. Artists can be regarded as the eyes and ears of society; artists who remain alert to changes in their cultural environment can communicate these changes and participate in their evolution through their works of art. Each artist's system updates are uniquely shaped by their past experiences, present life circumstances, and what they are naturally most attuned to.

Sometimes a specific work of art can be considered an artist's system update; for example, Beethoven's Ninth Symphony. At other times, an artist's system update might be a new technique or perspective like the cubism developed by Pablo Picasso and others. For performers, their system update might come in their unique interpretation of a specific piece of music or style of dance. Importantly, system updates reflect the artist's life as a whole, including their mental, emotional, and physical state, as well as what's happening in society around them, either directly or indirectly.

Your system updates perfectly reflect what's going on inside and around you. If you as an artist or the society that you are part of is unwell, your system updates will tend to reflect that. If you are concerned with preserving the past or with advancing the cutting edge of culture, your system updates will tend to reflect that. If you are full of aliveness as you sing, dance, or paint, or if you are just going through the motions, your system updates will reflect that also. When you hear a piece of news, when you heal a wound, when you lose a friend, when you learn a technique, when you travel to new places, when you start a new diet—every experience finds some form in your system updates.

As the truth of this interconnectedness sinks in, you may find yourself naturally taking greater responsibility for your system updates, especially if you are concerned with addressing societal ills. Since so many of our social and environmental problems are themselves symptoms of the Story of Separation, then you'll want to make sure that your system updates are not also transmitting more of this separation signal. Instead, aligning your creative process with the Story of Interbeing ensures that your system updates transmit a new signal, one that imparts a felt understanding of interbeing. As you transmit this signal, you'll be supporting others to become attuned to this new understanding, just as a bird sends signals to its community members. The more our society gains this understanding, the more readily these challenges will be resolved.

> Align your creative process with the Story of Interbeing to ensure that your system updates transmit a new signal,

> one that imparts a felt understanding of interbeing. As you transmit this signal, you'll be supporting others to become attuned to this new understanding, just as a bird sends signals to its community members.

Thus, your greatest contribution to both society and humanity's relationship with our planet can, despite societal messages to the contrary, come through your art via the same inner workings found in nature. Indeed, the true value of the arts is not that they are uniquely human, but rather that they reflect the same forces that guide the shining of the sun, the folding of DNA, and the nurturing of cubs by their mothers.

What this means is that your artistic purpose and the Soulforce it brings forth are actually that of the universe as a whole, and as such, they have an inherently life-giving quality. In this way, discovering and fulfilling your artistic purpose is far from a self-indulgent or frivolous act. Rather, it is precisely what allows for your greatest and most positive impact in these times of change. When you transmit your unique system updates via your artistic purpose, you ineluctably support the health and thriving of our world.

INITIATION AND PARADOX

> *"The kingdom of heaven is within you; and whosoever shall know himself shall find it."*
>
> —THE GOSPEL OF THOMAS: ANNOTATED AND EXPLAINED, STEVAN L. DAVIES (EDITOR)

Discovering your artistic purpose is an act of initiation. It is the revelation that there is something larger than your individual self in which you deeply desire to participate. It is a rite of passage that leads you from an unconscious, immature mode of creating to one that is radiant and empowered.

Chapter 5 | YOUR ARTISTIC PURPOSE

Initiation into your artistic purpose is a necessary precondition to the creation of art with Soulforce. Driven by outmoded and inherited purposes, your art will never be truly alive, only ever a simulacrum. In contrast, when energized by your artistic purpose, your art will take on a whole new level of transformative potential. It will go well beyond what is either nice or shocking, the technically advanced or merely self-expressive. Instead, guided by your own healing and growth, it will contain the seeds for the healing and growth of those around you. When you create guided by your purpose, you will finally find the source of the creative Soulforce you've been seeking all along. It was right where it's always been: at the place where your art, well-being, and the world's hunger meet.

After identifying your artistic purpose, the next step is to embody it in every creative act. Embodying your artistic purpose contains a paradox, however. On the one hand, it better enables you to take life-giving action in the world. On the other, it is not, in fact, something that you can *do*. It is more something that you *are*, something you can channel as you create. Indeed, the ultimate creative act is one in which you become a vessel, simply witnessing impulses of unknown origin taking miraculous form through your actions. While this beatific state is known and sought-after by artists, many believe that it can only be accessed by a lucky few, or in rare moments. This is not true.

Anyone can easily learn to become a vessel for their art. All it takes is to pay attention to the creative aliveness within—also known as Playing from the Heart.

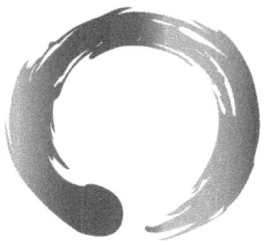

MIND-BODY INTERLUDE #1

SPACIOUS AWARENESS

"Develop a mind that is vast like space, where experiences both pleasant and unpleasant can appear and disappear without conflict, struggle, or harm. Rest in a mind like vast sky."

— THE BUDDHA, *MAJJHIMA NIKAYA*

"**T**unnel vision" is a response to creative challenge that plagues many artists. It happens when your focus becomes tight and narrow, and the amount of space you're aware of becomes very small. When you're in tunnel vision mode, your mind and body become tight. Thus tightened, your creative juices dwindle as your Soulforce tries to flow through your now constricted being. To make matters worse, your attention, now hyper-focused, prevents you from even noticing the source of this constriction. So, you try harder and harder to make the flow happen to no avail. This is a vicious cycle that leads to creative death.

The answer to tunnel vision is spacious awareness. Spacious awareness connects you with the space beyond the tunnel. It is a response to creative challenge that balances your habitual hyper-focused attention with an enhanced peripheral awareness. The relaxation and flow it affords make it the ideal state of consciousness for the creative act. Spacious awareness can be cultivated deliberately, as with the following Soulforce Inquiry. It is also the natural result of acting in alignment with your artistic purpose.

The first step to experiencing spacious awareness is to clarify what is meant by attention and awareness. Often used interchangeably, these terms refer to two distinct aspects of consciousness. *Attention* is the focal point of consciousness. It can move around either at will or spontaneously and can include a smaller or bigger area of space. Attention is like the fovea of the eye, the focal point of vision that has the most clarity and detail. *Awareness*, in contrast, is the larger background of consciousness, the field in which attention plays. Awareness is the unchanging ground for the ever-changing details of your sensory experience. It is like the totality of your visual field, which includes both the fovea and your peripheral vision.

Do the following Soulforce Inquiry to start bringing the benefits of spacious awareness to your next creative session.

THE NEEDLE AND THREAD

Pretend that you have a needle and thread in your hands in front of you. Now pretend to thread the needle, guiding the thread into the tiny hole at the tip of the needle. Oops! You missed. Try again!

Pause and notice yourself. What is happening to your sense of space: is it getting bigger or smaller? What is happening to your quality of movement: is your body getting tighter or freer? What commonly happens is that your sense of space becomes very small, and your body gets tighter. This is tunnel vision; your world shrinks to a narrow focus of attention and your peripheral awareness gets excluded entirely.

Now, connect with your peripheral awareness by taking in a big sense of space. Look above, to either side, below, and behind you. Remember that you're in a whole neighborhood with the sky above and the ground below.

What do you notice now? Is your sense of space getting bigger or smaller? Is your quality of movement getting tighter or freer? What you might notice is that your sense of space becomes very large, and your body gets freer. This is what happens when you include your peripheral awareness and have a larger focus of attention.

Mind-Body Interlude #1 | SPACIOUS AWARENESS

> Finally, practice spacious awareness by balancing attention and awareness during an activity. Take up your needle and thread again, this time remembering that you still have space all around you as you try to thread the needle.
>
> Remember that the tiny space inside the needle hole is continuous with the space that includes the sky above you and the ground below you.
>
> What do you notice now? Are you able to balance attention and awareness? What happens to how you feel and function as a result?

There are two main ways to practice spacious awareness. The first is during times of ease, such as during seated meditation, walking, or creating for pleasure. The second is to bring it into moments of creative challenge, such as those involving technical issues, time pressure, intense emotional expression, physical pain, or when you need to hear, see, sense, or move something small and precise. Simply notice when you're in tunnel vision, pause, remember the larger sense of space around you, and then bring your spacious awareness into your activity.

"If you attempt to see in the way prescribed by any mechanical system of drawing, old or new, you will lose the understanding of the fundamental impulse. Your drawing becomes a meaningless diagram and the time so spent is wasted."

— **KIMON NICOLAÏDES,** *THE NATURAL WAY TO DRAW*

CHAPTER 6

PLAYING FROM THE HEART

I still remember the day when I discovered the key to creative aliveness. It happened during what started as an ordinary lesson with my young violin student, Sara. I remember sighing inwardly with boredom as she dutifully played her current piece, a minuet by Johann Sebastian Bach. On the surface, there was nothing wrong with her playing; it just didn't have any *juice*.

What happened next took me by surprise. Sara, who was twelve at the time, asked, "Why does my music sound so robotic?" What a great question! What self-awareness! This was the first indication I'd had from her that she was interested in a deeper expressive power. The stage was now set for discovering what to do about it.

Clearly, what was missing from Sara's music was the sense of emotional expression, the flow, the inner meaning, the magic spark that turns mere sounds into vibrant music. Like many experienced musicians, I intuitively knew how to make the music come alive in my own playing, but how could I impart this skill to my young student?

Here I faced a dilemma: I could easily ask her to play with more varied dynamics, articulations, or even to play while thinking of a story or image that the song evoked. Experience told me, however, that asking her to do so would be tantamount to asking her to apply more effort to her playing. I had seen, time and again, that while such conventional means of musical expression would probably bring a certain degree of interest to her music, it was just as likely that she could end up using each of these techniques in a way that still sounded mechanical or forced. To tap into the magic she was seeking, I needed to guide her to a fundamentally different source of musical expression.

My first step was to better understand what was going on for my student when she played. So, I asked her what she had been paying attention to while she played. She thought for a moment and then replied, "I guess I was just trying to get the notes right." Aha! This made perfect sense. Her attention was on getting the notes right, and this was exactly how her performance had sounded.

What if she could pay attention to something else? Would she get a different result?

I paused for a moment to think of some of the ways we commonly talk about music that's really alive: "heartfelt," "with real feeling," "soulful." These terms all imply some kind of emotional connection. So, I asked if she had felt any emotions while she played, and she said, "No." That explained it! Without her emotional involvement, there's no way she could bring the music alive.

Here again, however, I saw the same dilemma as before. Yes, I wanted her to be more emotionally involved in her playing, but I was wary of trying to get her to feel something in particular because this might lead her to inadvertently force her own emotional response. That would never do. I needed to instead lead her to the source of her own emotional response to the music she played.

So, I asked her, "When you listen to a piece of music that you like, how do you know that you like it? What in your experience tells you that you like it?" She thought for a moment and replied, "It makes me feel good, warm, like I want to dance."

Excited, I replied, "Exactly! There's a pleasant emotional response

Chapter 6 | PLAYING FROM THE HEART

in your body when you hear music you like. What about music you don't like? How do you know you don't like it?" I asked.

She said, "I don't feel good. I feel nothing—closed off."

"That's right!" I replied. "There's an unpleasant emotional response in your body when you hear music you don't like."

I explained further. "That pleasant or unpleasant feeling in your heart, head, or gut when you listen to music are messages from your 'Inner Audience Member.' Your Inner Audience Member listens to all the music that you hear, even the music you play on your violin, and expresses her opinion via these feelings in your body. What if you were to play this piece again and, for every note that you play, you noticed your Inner Audience Member's feelings in your heart and gut?"

The results were stunning. This time, as she played the piece again, instead of hearing a mere sequence of sounds, I heard *her* coming through her playing. It's as if her essence, the core of her being, was flowing through her sound. Her body was more relaxed, the music flowed freely, and there was a sense of the music being truly alive. Even though she was playing a relatively simple song, and one that I had heard her play countless times, I was really touched by her performance and wanted to hear more.

I told her what I had noticed and asked her to share her experience, too. She said, "I enjoyed that! It felt good. I really felt the music. It was more fun, and it even felt easier to get the notes right." Amazing! Not only did her technique and sound quality improve, but it felt more effortless, she had more fun, and she was able to suffuse her music with the aliveness inside her that was just waiting to be expressed.

Sara and I made a profound discovery together that day. We discovered a method for reproducing the X factor, the transfixing creative aliveness that all artists and audiences seek. Many believe that the X factor is a matter of luck; that you either have it or you don't, and that it certainly can't be taught. What we discovered, however, is that the source of the X factor exists within everyone, and that beginners and masters alike can easily learn to access it. I call the method for doing so Playing from the Heart.

Playing from the Heart is the process of channeling your inner aliveness during the creative act. By Playing from the Heart, you can turn a collection of notes, movements, brushstrokes, or words into art that has real life and breath. Whatever you are "playing"—an instrument, a canvas, a stage, or a page—Playing from the Heart is a simple, powerful balm for creative challenges of all kinds. Playing from the Heart can help you interpret your art in an original, fresh, lively, and inspired way; bring more fun into your creative life; consistently create in a way that moves and transports your audiences; become a vessel for a deeper creative expression; effortlessly collaborate with others; perform with confidence; and find your unique voice as an artist. Because of these benefits, Playing from the Heart is a core practice of the Soulforce Arts Approach.

> **Playing from the Heart** is the process of channeling your creative aliveness during the creative act.

Before we get to the "how to" of Playing from the Heart, we need to explore the source of creative aliveness within, explaining what it is and what it isn't.

We start by getting to know your Inner Audience Member.

GETTING TO KNOW YOUR INNER AUDIENCE MEMBER

Dan Rather: "When you pray to God, what do you say?"

Mother Teresa: "Why, I don't say anything. I just listen."

Dan Rather: "Okay ... then what does God say to you?"

Chapter 6 | PLAYING FROM THE HEART

> *Mother Teresa: "He doesn't say anything either. He just listens. And if you don't understand that, I can't explain it to you."*
>
> — MOTHER TERESA, *A SIMPLE PATH*

Your **Inner Audience Member** is the felt experience of the creative aliveness within you. Also called your heart (as an emotional center), soul, intuition, the felt sense, gut instinct, or your inner compass, your Inner Audience Member comprises the dynamic flow of emotions and other energies that arise in your body during a given situation, creative or otherwise. Your Inner Audience Member is the seat of your knowledge of the soul, and, just like Sara, you can channel its creative energy by paying attention to it during the creative act. Doing so is like opening a window to your soul, allowing that which is alive inside you to pour out into your art. Paying attention to your Inner Audience Member is the central act of Playing from the Heart.

> Your **Inner Audience Member** is the felt experience of the creative aliveness within you. It comprises the dynamic flow of emotions that arise in your body during a given situation, whether artistic or otherwise.

The Inner Audience Member is your sacred inner self, and when you tap into it, the essence core to who you are will pour through your creative acts. This sacred self has long been known and revealed by wisdom traditions the world over. Some call it the Atman, the Observer, Spirit, the Ground of Being, or the Godhead. It is who you truly are, hidden under the layers of the egoic personality. Calling it the **Inner Audience Member** reflects this ancient knowledge; it is the same I AM that the saints and sages have long revered.

Another example of the Inner Audience Member's sacred nature comes from Ancient Greek mythology. For the Greeks, the source of creative inspiration was personified in the deities called the muses, a term from which the words *music* and *museum* are derived. The Greeks believed that by coming into the proper relationship with the muses, you could gain certain boons, such as new creative ideas and energy.[1] By the same token, ignoring the muses or treating them poorly was a sure way for your creativity to dry up.

Your Inner Audience Member is just such a muse. At the same time that it is the most intimate and personal aspect of your creative life, it is also a source of creative impulses that seem to come from an intelligence other than your own. Your Inner Audience Member's creative impulses are like gifts from a muse. You can best assure their continued arrival in your life by honoring these gifts with the reverence they deserve. Manufacturing creative impulses through willpower, assembling empty technical masterpieces, or disregarding technique in favor of bland self-expression dishonors these gifts by either ignoring them entirely or failing to fully actualize them. In contrast, sensitizing yourself to your muse's subtle messages and developing them to their fullest potential tells your muse that you care. In response, your muse will provide you with a rich source of creative energy and ideas that can propel you through even the most stagnant creative plateau.

The Inner Audience Member is often experienced as sensations in the body. You might feel it as emotions (like joy or sadness), in the felt sense (like a feeling of openness or a desire for closeness), or in bodily movements (like involuntary nodding or dancing to the beat of a song). The easiest places to identify your Inner Audience Member's sensations are in the primary emotional centers of your heart, gut, head, neck, or groin.

Your Inner Audience Member may speak to you in various ways:

- You might feel more open or more closed.
- The feelings might be more pleasant or unpleasant.
- You might feel more tense or freer.

- You might have more of a desire to move or to stay still.
- You might feel various emotions or moods, like joy, fear, or sadness.
- The feelings might be widely distributed throughout your body or located in just one area.
- The feelings might change rapidly or slowly.
- Your attention might be more entranced or more disengaged.
- You may feel something or nothing at all.

It's important to note that none of these feelings are good or bad. They are simply information, almost like the speedometer in your car. They are forms of feedback that can help you make appropriate decisions as you create. For example, while your ultimate aim in the creative act might be to feel more open, noticing when you're feeling more closed helps you know when you're getting off track. Similarly, while pleasant feelings are great, unpleasant feelings often provide vital contrast and energy to a creative process that might otherwise be only pleasant to the point of tedium. Sometimes you may notice no particular feelings at all, just a space or silence within—and that's okay! An absence of discernible feelings is no more a sign of failure than is a rest between two notes. What matters most is that you're closely listening to the feedback your Inner Audience Member is sending your way. All feedback is useful feedback.

As you get to know your Inner Audience Member more, you will find that it has two different kinds of messages: *responses* and *wishes*. Responses are more retrospective, arising as a reply to what has just been created. Wishes are more prospective, arising as the felt desire for how to shape what comes next. When you create something, your Inner Audience Member might first produce a felt response about what you just created.

Following that, your Inner Audience Member may then produce a wish for how best to shape what comes next. The ongoing feedback loop of creation, responses, and wishes is what comprises the creative act.

Whether you're taking in your own creations or someone else's, your Inner Audience Member is always talking to you, conveying vital information about every aspect of your creative process. The more time you spend building your connection with your Inner Audience Member, the deeper and livelier your artistry will be. The next two exercises are a first step to greater familiarity and trust of your Inner Audience Member.

SOULFORCE INQUIRY 6.1
EMBODIED ART APPRECIATION

Recall the question I asked Sara: "When you hear a piece of music that you like, *how do you know you like it?*" It's the same with any art form. In response to a painting or a sculpture, for example, you open to it when you like it, and you close and contract away from it when you don't. Use this exploration to find the answer to this question by becoming more familiar with your Inner Audience Member.

Come to a work of art you enjoy, whether a piece of music, visual art, or even the next meal you eat. Before you take it in, spend a minute sensing your whole body. Then bring some curiosity to your heart and gut as you take in the work of art.

How does your Inner Audience Member respond to what you see or hear? What emotions and feelings come up in your body? Use the list of Inner Audience Member responses to help identify what you notice.

Don't place value judgments on what you hear or what you feel; just make note of the physical sensations of the feelings and emotions that arise in your body in response to the work of art. Remember: you may or may not experience discernible feelings, and that's okay, too. It's the act of listening to your Inner Audience Member that counts here.

Do this practice every day for a week to gain an embodied understanding of your Inner Audience Member.

SOULFORCE INQUIRY 6.2
COMING INTO RIGHT RELATIONSHIP WITH YOUR INNER MUSE

Consider your Inner Audience Member, your I AM, your creative muse. What kind of relationship do you now have with it? Do you listen to it during daily life and at times of creative expression? How often do you follow its hints and intuitions, its responses and wishes? How do you feel when you do or don't follow its messages?

Take a moment now to listen closely to your Inner Audience Member. How does it feel toward you as an artist? Does it feel that you've honored its messages? If not, what does it want you to do to repair your relationship? Does it have any other messages for you now?

Write anything you notice in your journal and make a point to include any new insights or messages in your next creative session.

HEALING THE INNER CRITIC

> *"When you get curious about a part, you naturally gain clarity regarding what it's all about, which typically results in a newfound compassion for all it's been through and is trying to do."*
>
> — RICHARD SCHWARTZ, *INTERNAL FAMILY SYSTEMS*

One of the most common questions I get when teaching people about the Inner Audience Member is how it differs from the inner critic. The **inner critic** is a part of you that carries unobtainable standards of success and berates other parts of you for failing to reach them. For some, the inner critic has such a powerful presence in their internal world that it can seem to drown out their Inner Audience Member. When this is the case, the sheer intensity of the negative messages coming from the inner critic can make it hard to connect with the more life-giving qualities of the Inner Audience Member.

The first thing to know is that your inner critic is not the same thing as your Inner Audience Member. Your inner critic is an aspect of your inherited expressivity, being an emotional wound that you internalized from others early in life. When your inner critic is active, your creative process becomes more a compensation for the pain within than an expression of your creative aliveness. You may find yourself prioritizing other peoples' creative ideas and approaches over what feels true for you. In contrast, your Inner Audience Member is the source of authentic creativity. Creating with your Inner Audience Member in the lead allows you to regard other ideas as potentially useful suggestions in a process that results in an ever-deeper connection with your innate truths and desires. You know you're letting your inner critic lead when creating leaves you feeling anxious, tense, and small. In contrast, you know you're letting your Inner Audience Member lead when creating leaves you feeling fulfilled, at ease, and expanded.

Chapter 6 | PLAYING FROM THE HEART

> The **inner critic** is a part of you that carries unobtainable standards of success and berates other parts of you for failing to reach them. It is not the same thing as your Inner Audience Member.

An overly developed inner critic comes into being through repeated exposure to situations where you, during important moments in your youth, were harshly criticized to the point that you were afraid for your well-being. This is a survival situation that stimulates the imperative to regain a sense of self-worth and connection with your community—even if that means seeking connection with the ones who just criticized you.[2] Your inner critic forms when, instead of rightly seeing that you don't deserve such treatment, you blame yourself for having caused such a painful interaction. This new habit of self-blame becomes the inner critic.

On the one hand, the inner critic can play an important role in your life, protecting you from re-experiencing certain painful interactions. However, what protects can also confine; if your inner critic becomes too dominant, it can severely restrict your quality of life, artistic or otherwise. Many artists view this restriction as a necessary evil because they appreciate how their inner critic contributes to their artistic excellence. For them, the inner critic becomes a sort of inner taskmaster, driving a perfectionism that leaves no room for mediocrity. However, such perfectionism is, in the end, exhausting and unsatisfying because its pursuit is founded on a felt sense of unworthiness and fear. Unless your underlying sense of unworthiness is healed, no amount of artistic perfection can ever sate the otherwise unending hunger of the inner critic.

The presumed connection between excellence and the inner critic gives rise to a common objection to trying to heal its associated wound: will such healing take away your edge, your creative drive? To some, the very idea of healing the inner critic brings up real fear, with a voice that says that any kindness or compassion for yourself is self-indulgent and naïve. What this perspective ignores, however, is that your inner critic is an enormous drain on your life force energy, and that healing your inner critic is necessary to your fullest creative energy and inspiration. Your inner critic expends a great deal of your energy just trying to keep you safe. When you heal the inner critic, you unburden yourself of this energetic drain. Thus unburdened, you regain the creative energy and other qualities that were otherwise previously occupied. The result will be a new sense of vitality, playfulness, and creative insight.

SOULFORCE INQUIRY 6.3
HEALING THE INNER CRITIC

The following meditation is inspired by Internal Family Systems, a form of psychotherapy developed by psychologist Richard Schwartz. Internal Family Systems is based on the idea that you have many "parts" inside you, kind of like an inner family that you can get to know and unburden (heal) through self-dialogue. This meditation can prove challenging, especially if you're new to Internal Family Systems-style inner dialogues. If this is the case for you, simply spend time getting to know the parts of you that aren't yet ready to let you get close to the inner critic.

Sit in a comfortable posture and close your eyes. Bring to mind your inner critic, the part of you that is trying to protect you by being overly critical of your behavior. As you focus on that part, notice where it shows up in or around your body, and while you focus on that place, notice how you feel toward this part. Most people with an overdeveloped inner critic will have some strained feelings toward it. Say a welcome to your inner critic and thank it for showing itself to you, then notice how it reacts.

Chapter 6 | PLAYING FROM THE HEART

Imagine placing your inner critic part in a comfortable room where it can't escape, perhaps with some nice snacks and a place to sit. Be sure to include a window in this room through which you can see your inner critic. Let any other parts of yourself, like the ones that have strained feelings toward the inner critic, know that the inner critic is going to stay in that room for the duration of this meditation. See if they're willing to relax and make some space inside so you can get to the point of having at least a little curiosity toward the inner critic.

If they're not willing to separate and make space, that's okay. Just spend the rest of your time getting to know their fears about the inner critic or the issues they have with it. If you can get to the point of any kind of curiosity or openness, then let it know that and ask what it wants you to know while it stays contained. See if you can communicate with it through the window. What does it want you to know about itself? What is it afraid will happen if it stepped out of its role?

If it answers these questions, see if it's possible to extend some appreciation toward it for at least trying to protect you. Ask how old it thinks you are. If it's a different age than you actually are, then update it and see how it reacts.

Now ask your inner critic some version of the following question: "If you could change or heal what you're protecting so that it wasn't an issue anymore and you were freed from the responsibility of protection and could do something else instead, what would you like to do?" After it answers that question, see what it would like from you in the future.

Finally, check in with your other parts and notice how they're reacting to this process. Thank all your parts for showing themselves to you and let them know this won't be your last visit. Take a deep breath and gradually open your eyes. Write down any reflections in your journal.

Almost invariably, when unburdened from its protective and rigid role, the inner critic turns into a life-giving, joyful, and playful inner child part. It often reveals keen insights and creative energy that are a great resource to your life as an artist. In addition, its healing resolves any conflict you may feel between the inner critic and the Inner Audience Member. Some feel that the painful messages of the inner critic couldn't truly coexist with the more life-giving messages of the Inner Audience Member. What you may discover instead is that, when unburdened, the inner critic's newly regained positive qualities, such as a finer intuitive sense, reveals that the inner critic was an essential aspect of your Inner Audience Member all along.

HOW TO PLAY FROM THE HEART

"Attention is a creative act, and creation is really about the induction of a highly attentive state. It is like an ear that is listening and receptive, without actually having anything at all clear yet to hear ... It involves remaining open, and yet being able to receive something which is, in the end, quite specific and particular. In this, it is somewhat like prayer."

— IAIN MCGILCHRIST, *THE MATTER WITH THINGS*

Playing from the Heart is a central practice of the Soulforce Arts Approach because it is what brings your art alive. It does this by including that which is alive inside you, your Inner Audience Member, in the creative act. To Play from the Heart, simply pay attention to your Inner Audience Member during the creative act.

Playing from the Heart rests on the notion that attention itself is a creative act; your creative output always reflects where and how you pay attention. When you pay attention in a way that regards your creativity as a thing to be manipulated, your art will take on a forced quality. On the other hand, when you pay attention as though your creativity is a being to be honored, your art will resound with authentic heart and soul. In this, Playing from the Heart takes inspiration from Hebrew and Japanese; in both languages, the word for *paying attention* can be translated as "putting heart."

> To Play from the Heart, simply pay attention to your Inner Audience Member during the creative act.

Playing from the Heart can make a radical shift in how the creative act feels. In the Story of Separation, the creative act feels like a one-way street, from inside your brain out into the world around you. The truth is more in alignment with the Story of Interbeing, which reveals that creativity is a feedback loop. A feedback loop describes any system in which there is an ongoing flow of activity or energy that regulates itself in a responsive, dynamic way. When you regard the creative act as a feedback loop, you no longer need to effortfully manufacture creative impulses or guess where the next one may come from. Instead, you simply pay attention to your Inner Audience Member and let its creative energy flow through you.

The feedback loop of the creative act has four interconnected phases:

1. The creative impulse (your Inner Audience Member's wishes) leads to
2. Bodily movement, which then leads to
3. Artistic output, which is then assessed via
4. Emotional impact (your Inner Audience Member's responses), which in turn leads to a new creative impulse, and so on.

THE FEEDBACK LOOP OF THE CREATIVE ACT

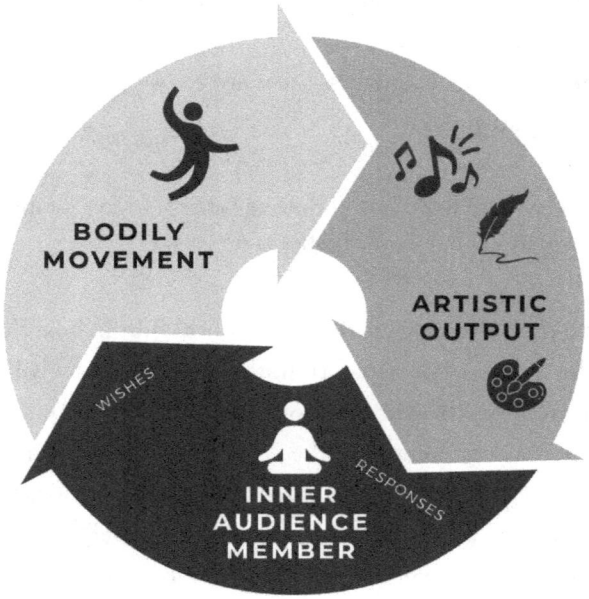

Playing from the Heart is a root cause solution to all forms of inherited expressivity, the most common of which is "trying to get it right." Trying to get it right is a vicious cycle that ultimately fails to produce satisfying art. Remember, the place from which you express always finds perfect reflection in your artistic output. When you try to get it right, your expressive focus is a mere mental representation. A mental representation is an abstract entity, one devoid of life and flow, and as such, it inevitably produces a lifeless expressive effect. Attempting to overcome this lifelessness, either through sheer effort or ever-more sophisticated mental representations, only serves to further disconnect you from the source of creative aliveness within.

In this way, trying to get it right is like trying to count to infinity; no matter how high you go, you'll never reach the ultimate destination. No matter how deeply ingrained your habits of inherited expressivity are, the creative aliveness offered by Playing from the Heart is only ever a thought away. When you notice your inherited expressivity, don't fight against it; just get to know it. Once you have acknowledged and felt its presence, simply shift your attention to what you now know is a better source of creativity: the Inner Audience Member.

SOULFORCE INQUIRY 6.4
PLAYING FROM THE HEART

Over the years of teaching Playing from the Heart, I have found that different students need different ways of thinking about this process. So, here are several variations on the basic instructions of Playing from the Heart:

- **Basic instructions.** Simply notice the ongoing flow of emotional energy in your heart and gut as you play. Let this energy arise and pass away of its own accord, letting it be exactly as it is.

- **Variation #1: More open or more closed?** When you like something, your Inner Audience Member will tend to be more open, and when you don't like something, your Inner Audience Member will tend to be more closed. To begin with, simply notice when your Inner Audience Member is more open or closed as you create. When you feel ready, take it a step further by creating in such a way that your Inner Audience Member opens up.

- **Variation #2: The wishing well.** Imagine that your Inner Audience Member is a wishing well. For each sound or gesture that you make, imagine that you're tossing a coin into the wishing well. Notice what comes up in your Inner Audience Member after each sound or gesture. You will know your wishes have been granted by the pleasure and creativity you may enjoy as a result.

- **Variation #3: The crystal ball.** Imagine that you are a mystic, peering into a beautiful crystal ball (your Inner Audience Member). What comes up from the depths of this crystal ball as you play? What mysterious messages make themselves known? Follow these messages as you play and see where they take you.

- **Variation #4: The inner opinion.** Think of your emotional response to each creative act as your Inner Audience Member's opinion of what you're playing, just like what you might have for someone else's performance. Make sure that you're listening to the impression coming from your heart and gut, not your inner critic.

- **Variation #5: Creating for pleasure.** Whatever you're creating, do it for the sole purpose of pleasing your Inner Audience Member. Set aside any notions of what you "should" do, and simply create in such a way that your Inner Audience Member feels good. What gives you real pleasure? What feels more unpleasant?

How do you know if you're on the right track with Playing from the Heart (or with any of the other practices in this book)? Reflect on your felt experience of the creative act and ask yourself the following questions:

- Does my body get tighter or freer?
- How does the emotional content of my playing change?
- Are there times when my Inner Audience Member is happier and more open? Or more dissatisfied and closed? What's common among those moments?
- How much fun am I having overall when I create?

Chapter 6 | PLAYING FROM THE HEART

- How much trust or mistrust do I have in my Inner Audience Member? What's the message underneath my trust or mistrust?

In the end, what's most important when Playing from the Heart is the simple act of listening. Here, listening refers to a quality of attention including, but not limited to, the aural sense. It is the experience of deep absorption, even enchantment, and this can occur in response to any artistic form, whether a written word, a painting, or the body in movement. It's commonly thought that notes, images, shapes, words, and movements are what comprise a performance or other work of art. However, without the silence and spaciousness of the act of listening, these are all meaningless. Street sounds are not considered music, for example, as they are just a collection of sounds. Those very same street sounds would be transformed into music, however, if those who made the sounds were simultaneously listening to the effect their own sounds and the sounds of others were having on their inner audience members.

> Authentic expression is more an act of listening than something you do or make happen.

Thus, listening is essential to what brings art alive. The quality of your listening determines the quality of your art such that the deeper your listening, the more alive your art will be. Indeed, the apogee of Playing from the Heart is listening so deeply that people will be captivated by your presence even when you're not doing anything in particular. To some, it might at first seem impossible that listening, which is more of a non-doing than a doing, could achieve so much by itself. But as Alexander Technique teacher Marjorie Barstow was known for saying, "Sometimes, all it takes is a little bit of nothing."

A TECHNOLOGY OF INTERBEING

> *"There is a vitality, a life force ... that is translated through you into action, and because there is only one of you in all of time, this expression is unique. And if you block it, it will never exist through any other medium and it will be lost. The world will not have it. It is not your business to determine how good it is nor how valuable nor how it compares with other expressions. It is your business to keep it yours clearly and directly, to keep the channel open!"*
>
> — MARTHA GRAHAM, *MARTHA: THE LIFE AND WORK OF MARTHA GRAHAM*

Playing from the Heart is a technology of interbeing. Its purpose is to bring forth a transcendent expressive power that goes beyond what technique, self-expression, or effort can offer alone. It achieves this aim by addressing imbalances among the three strands of Soulforce Mastery—technique, effortlessness, and the knowledge of the soul. When the three strands are out of balance, the creative act can feel empty and effortful. When in balance, the creative act can feel enchanting, alive, and whole. The following are lessons garnered from the practice of Playing from the Heart that bring the three strands of Soulforce Mastery into greater balance and which thereby transform the creative act into a bridge to interbeing.

TECHNIQUE-BUILDING FROM THE HEART

The default way to learn technique in the Story of Separation is as a piecemeal, mechanical exercise, divorced from authentic emotional expression. While you might gain some benefit developing your technique in this way, in the end, such an approach ingrains a mechanical way of creating, devoid of the human feeling that gave rise to the technique in the first place. While some respond to this reality by eschewing technique altogether, Playing from the Heart reveals that it is possible to develop your technique in a way that brings you and your art alive—but how?

You simply include that which is alive inside you, your Inner Audience Member, as you develop your technique. For example, if you're a dancer practicing pliés, make the goal to notice how your Inner Audience Member feels when your limbs are perfectly arranged. If you're a sculptor honing your chisels, ask how your Inner Audience Member wants to guide each of your strokes over the sharpening stone. If you're a painter making the thousands of tiny dots needed for a pointillist painting, listen to your Inner Audience Member so each dot is made with life. This approach can even benefit the cognitive aspects of your art (like artistic theory). As you learn a theoretical notion, don't treat it merely as an item of information; instead, make it an embodied experience by noticing how it impacts your Inner Audience Member.

Technique and theory, devoid of human feeling, are worse than useless because they create the false impression of making progress toward your artistic goals. Addressing this lack is easy, however. When you're left wondering why you're using a particular technique or idea, simply reconnect with your Inner Audience Member and receive its more meaningful impressions. In the end, Playing from the Heart doesn't mean giving up cherished artistic techniques or methods; it's more about feeding what you already do through a different place in yourself.

CHANGING WHAT IT MEANS TO "GET IT RIGHT"

Trying to "get it right" is one of the most common blocks to Playing from the Heart. What does it really mean to get it right? Is it what happens to accord with tradition or please an authority figure? Is it what allows you to achieve technical mastery, or does it happen when you eschew the idea of getting it right altogether? Or do you truly get it right when what you create carries a certain authenticity or self-transcendence?

Each of these takes on getting it right have their place in the creative process. For example, you know that the task of assembling the basic building blocks of a piece, while necessary, is no more an act of authentic creative expression than filing your taxes (although that may also depend on which accountant you hire). In general, the Soulforce Arts Approach puts forth more authentic and transcendent measures of getting it right.

To illustrate these, let's take a cue from Duke Ellington, the great jazz bandleader, who was known for saying, "If it sounds good, it is good." Knowing that music, for example, is as much a somatic experience as an aural one, I like to instead say, "If it *feels* good, it is good." Such a perspective enables you to shift your metric of artistic success from an external source ("I got it right because teacher said so") to an internal one ("I got it right because it makes me feel more alive"). Such a shift doesn't imply abandoning what a given teacher says. Rather, the invitation is to judge what your teacher says via the authentic response of your Inner Audience Member. When you do this, the lessons you learn from others serve to take you deeper into your creative aliveness.

"GUITAR FACE" VS. EFFORTLESS EXPRESSION

Among many artists, there is a confusion between expressive tension and muscular tension. This confusion often takes form in a subconscious belief that more effort will yield more expression. The result is sometimes called "guitar face," because of the scrunched faces and contorted postures of artists who look like they're "really feeling it." However, trying hard, really feeling it, and even trying to be creative aren't actually the same thing as authentic emotional expression. In an echo of the adage, "If at first you don't succeed, try, try again," it's almost as if the message many of us get about expression is, "If it's not

Chapter 6 | PLAYING FROM THE HEART

expressive enough, just put more effort into it!"

The key to unraveling this confusion lies in an awareness of the body. Trying hard or putting more effort into expression creates bodily tension, which in turn interferes with your expressive potential. Emotion is a kind of energy, and expression of emotion requires the movement of that energy, like the flow of water through a hose. But when you try hard, tension builds in the body and acts like a kink in that hose. The result, instead of having the hoped-for emotional power, has only the characteristics of excess effort and ends up feeling strained, mechanical, or superficial.

It is obvious to many artists that this is counterproductive—but if it's so obvious, why do so many of us still get tense during the creative act? It's often a byproduct of childhood coping strategies.

In his Bio-Emotive Framework, clinical psychologist Douglas Tataryn describes how, as young children, our main strategy for coping with overwhelming and painful emotions is muscular tension. Muscular tension temporarily dampens or numbs the sensations of painful emotions, but it also prevents the emotions from dissipating fully, effectively "locking" the emotions in place. As we grow accustomed to finding relief from emotional pain in this way, the disconnection from our emotions becomes habituated, as does our excess muscular tension. What at first helped now only interferes.

There are countless methods for releasing muscular and emotional tension, including psychotherapy, meditation, Alexander Technique, and yoga. Using these methods to work through the "issues in your tissues" helps you regain access to the full spectrum of your emotions and is a vital part of accessing a richer, more vibrant expressive power. However, you don't need to spend years in therapy before regaining this power. You can, today, access more of this power than you might realize, more effortlessly than you might think possible, through the simple act of Playing from the Heart.

PLAYING FROM THE HEART IS DECEPTIVELY EFFORTLESS

Truly Playing from the Heart doesn't feel like you're *doing* anything at all to be expressive. The source of the Inner Audience Member's feelings and wishes is, at the level of experience, utterly mysterious. Many of us who have grown up in the Story of Separation may, at first, feel uncomfortable with this sense of mystery. You might even say to yourself, *Surely, it must take more effort than this to be truly expressive!* However, true expressivity is not a matter of effort, but of connection.

To illustrate this point, I will paraphrase Lao Tzu in the *Tao Te Ching*: To the fool, the Inner Audience Member is ignored. To the reasonably wise, the Inner Audience Member is listened to and acted upon. To the master, the Inner Audience Member plays *you*. The full flowering of Playing from the Heart feels exactly like this, like you've become a vessel for your art.

PLAYING FROM THE HEART IN HIGH- AND LOW-TRUST RELATIONSHIPS

It's easy to Play from the Heart when you're all on your own, but what do you do when you're working with or under others? It all depends on the kind of relationship you have. For example, let's say you're a graphic designer and your client gives you precise instructions to follow for an upcoming campaign. If you have a good relationship with this person and communication is working well, then you'll both feel that it is easy for your inner audience members to come out to play. This will allow the two of you to effectively work together to provide creative solutions that exceed the minimum requirements of the job with flair.

Things can feel very different in low-trust situations, however. When your client is disrespectful, uncommunicative, or authoritarian, you may feel tempted to shut away your Inner Audience Member and instead try to manufacture what they're asking for. While this might work temporarily, it will have predictable consequences: your body will get tighter, you'll have less fun, and your creations will suffer as a result. What to do?

The key lies in remaining connected with your Inner Audience Member, even in times of stress. For example, when a client's poor communication leaves you confused about what they want, focus instead on understanding the *feeling* they are going for. Often, what people ask for and what they're really looking for are two different things. So, if you can, when a client asks you for something, ask them in turn about what feeling they're going for. Perhaps they can demonstrate the feeling they want while you pay close attention to your Inner Audience Member. (If asking about the feeling isn't appropriate, then do your best to intuit what that feeling might be.) When you have a better sense of the feeling they want, craft your design in a way that elicits that feeling in your Inner Audience Member.

While you can never have control over your clients' reactions, you can at least enjoy the satisfaction that you Played from the Heart when the going got tough. Ultimately, staying true to your Inner Audience Member is about more than meeting the demands of any individual gig. It can also provide the self-trust necessary for recognizing which opportunities are no longer working for you and which are more worthy of your Soulforce.

MORE THAN MERE SELF-EXPRESSION

Many people believe that art is about self-expression—and in a superficial way it is, because the creative process often involves giving form to something within you. However, while self-expression has its place, its artistic results often lack the Soulforce necessary to invoke the shift in consciousness so characteristic to great art. In fact, self-expression is often a form of inherited expressivity, more a counter-reaction to overly strict artistic pedagogies than a genuine form of creativity. This is what author John Anthony West meant when he wrote in *Serpent in the*

Sky, "Self-expression is not a necessary aspect of creativity."[3] Without the technique and effortlessness necessary to give proper form to your knowledge of the soul, your art simply can't come fully alive. So, what's the alternative?

Let's consider the Ancient Egyptian monuments again. The Ancient Egyptians crafted their magnificent statues and temples with a deliberate use of harmonic proportions and mathematical principles, such as the golden ratio. Indeed, the transcendent effect their creations have on us was only made possible by a rigid adherence to these proportions and principles. In other words, the Ancient Egyptians did not practice whimsical self-expression in their art, and their art was all the better without it. Instead, at every level of their construction, through their expression of the harmonic proportions that govern the natural world, their megalithic constructions were able to "provide insights into the wisdom of the temple" to not only visitors, but upon everyone who was involved in their creation, too, including "the humblest quarryman to the master sculptor."[4]

Thus, true creativity is about service to a deeper source within, to something bigger than your individual self, just like genuine beauty or what brings you the most alive. Beauty and aliveness are universal experiences that can never be captured by any expression of yourself as an individual ego. In kind, true creativity requires a healthy dose of humility and the willingness to let go of the reactionary ideas and impulses that form your inherited expressivity. Only this will allow you to have the proper relationship to beauty and aliveness so that they can then bestow their gifts upon you. At the deepest levels, this is what it means to Play from the Heart.

WHAT IF MY INNER AUDIENCE MEMBER ISN'T "GOOD ENOUGH"?

This is a natural question if you've grown up in a society like ours where authenticity and vulnerability are sometimes discouraged or even punished. Having grown up in such an environment, you might naturally question the worthiness of your Inner Audience Member.

If you feel this way, first consider that you, as a human being, are a part of an unbroken chain of living beings that extends back 3.5 billion years. Given that each of your ancestors survived and thrived in large part because of their connection to their inner guidance, it is safe to say that you have 3.5 billion years of wisdom inside you. The truth is that this life-giving wisdom is what your audiences most want to experience from you and your art. Your Inner Audience Member is definitely good enough.

If regaining confidence in your inner worthiness seems like a far-off possibility, please know that trust in your Inner Audience Member can be rebuilt. The practices in this chapter are a great start to this process. Do the practices. Be gentle with yourself. Rebuilding trust with your Inner Audience Member can take time, but it may be one of the most important things you do in your whole life, so have courage and get to it!

THE PINOCCHIO EFFECT

"Art enables us to find ourselves and lose ourselves at the same time."

— THOMAS MERTON, *NO MAN IS AN ISLAND*

Pinocchio is a well-known character from Carlo Collodi's nineteenth-century classic *The Adventures of Pinocchio*. In this story, Pinocchio starts out as a boy carved from wood and then, at the end of his adventures, becomes a real boy made of flesh and blood. What led to his remarkable transformation? Upon hearing that his guardian fairy was ill and needed help, he made an offering, giving all his pennies toward her recovery. His transformation into a real boy was her token of gratitude for his heartfelt sacrifice.

A similar transformation is possible for you and your art. You can take the carved wood of your art form—the techniques, notes, gestures, words, and materials—and transform them into real music, real paintings, or real dance. Just as with Pinocchio, your own transformation will happen when you make an offering in service of the well-being of your own guardian fairy or muse: your Inner Audience Member. What does your Inner Audience Member need from you? Instead of pennies, it needs your time, attention, and trust, which you can offer your Inner Audience Member by Playing from the Heart. The more you do so, the more it will reward you with art that is truly alive.

One of the greatest hindrances to gaining this reward is the reliance on willpower to get yourself through moments of creative challenge. This is what is known as trying hard. When you try hard, it can feel like you've been split into two: the strident part of you that wants to do something and the lazy part that doesn't. Thus divided, your Soulforce will never find its fullest expression.

We will now explore the underlying reasons for this division and how you can bring a new sense of unity and fulfillment to the creative act.

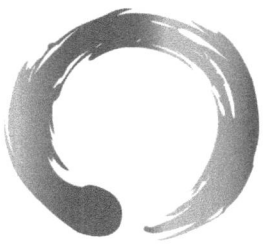

MIND-BODY INTERLUDE #2

TWO PERCENT EASIER

"It is not the degree of 'willing' or 'trying,' but the way in which the energy is directed, that is going to make the 'willing' or 'trying' effective."

— FREDERICK MATTHIAS ALEXANDER, ORIGINATOR OF THE ALEXANDER TECHNIQUE

There was once a competitive rowing team in Boston that sought to improve their racing times with more efficient body movements. So, they brought in an Alexander Technique teacher to watch them row along the Charles River and give them some pointers.

While watching the team row in their usual way, this teacher noticed that the rowers were straining as hard as they could, tensing their necks and backs. Knowing that excess effort and tension is counterproductive to performance, he suggested that they instead use two percent less effort as they rowed.

The results were surprising. On their next pass down the river, instead of going slower, they actually went faster—even though they were using less effort overall! [1] These results were so counterintuitive to the rowing team that their coach balked at allowing them this seeming luxury, saying that, despite the evidence of his own eyes, he didn't want them to slack off.

The truth about effort is that more is not always better. In fact, how you direct your effort matters as much, if not more, than the amount you use. Many are tempted to use maximal effort because, at a felt level, it seems to carry the promise of greater effectiveness. However, since maximal effort inevitably entails so much misdirected energy in the form of muscular tension, it ultimately backfires. Think about opening a stuck jar. Does squinting your face, tightening your neck, and scrunching your feet really help?

A great example of well-directed effort comes, again, from the world of athletics. Jesse Owens achieved athletic greatness when he set a world record for the hundred-meter dash in the 1936 Olympics. If you watch a video of this race, you can very clearly see that while most of the runners are heaving their bodies with great effort, Owens floats out in front of the pack and glides in for his famous victory. It's not that he wasn't using effort—it's that his effort was guided only where it was needed, and nowhere else.

What worked for Owens can also work for you in your artistic activities. In moments of challenge, you may be tempted to maximally exert yourself, to push, pull, strain, or give it your all. When this happens, ask yourself if such excess effort is truly necessary. Does it help your performance? Does it feel good? Does it help your Soulforce flow? Probably not. Instead, use two percent less effort and trust that you'll still be able to do what you need to do. You may be surprised with how little effort you need to meet even the most challenging artistic demands.

TWO PERCENT EASIER

Pick a challenging creative activity in which your body becomes tighter than you'd like. Try it as you normally would, noticing your body as you do so.

Now, do the same activity and try harder! What happens with that extra energy? Does it flow effortlessly into the activity, or does it get stuck in your neck and shoulders as excess tension?

Finally, do the same activity again, this time thinking "two percent easier" or "two percent less effort" as you do the activity. What do you notice? Did your body get tighter or freer? Was it more or less fun? Was your sense of space bigger or smaller? Did you feel more or less rushed? What happened to the quality of your creative output?

Mind-Body Interlude #2 | TWO PERCENT EASIER

What is the optimal amount of effort? Is the answer always to strive for two percent less? As with anything, it depends. Most people in our society reflexively use too much effort, so the optimal amount of effort will only be found by remembering, time and again, to stop pushing so hard. There are other people who use too little effort and so they need a different medicine. For them, what's needed is to focus more clearly on what they want so they can more effectively channel their energy.

How do you know what's right for you? It's when your technique, degree of effort, and creative expression are in balance. Simply ask yourself: *Am I able to do the thing correctly and cleanly? Am I getting freer when doing so? Am I connected with my Inner Audience Member or to a satisfying artistic purpose*? When the answer to all three is "yes," you know you're on the right track.

There is a final stumbling block to watch out for. It's possible for your attempt to find ease to be co-opted by effort. This has happened for you when you find yourself trying hard to relax, which is, of course, a contradiction. So, watch out for the belief that "If a little ease is good, then more must be better," because that's the same kind of thinking that caused all the trouble in the first place! Remember that every journey takes place as a series of little steps in the right direction. Ninety-eight percent of the time, two percent less effort is usually enough.

Principal Skinner: "Oh, licking envelopes can be fun! All you have to do is make a game of it."

Bart Simpson: "What kind of game?"

Skinner: "Well, for example, you could see how many you could lick in an hour, then try to break that record."

Bart: "Sounds like a pretty crappy game to me."

Skinner: "Yes, well ... get started."

— **THE SIMPSONS, SEASON 3, EPISODE 4**

CHAPTER 7

THE YOGA OF ART

"Sometimes, you just have to sit your butt down and *will* the words to come out," Brenda told me. She was describing one of her biggest challenges as a professional ghostwriter and book editor: that because her projects were so massive and the deadlines so frequent, she often worked beyond the point when her brain and body were done. Eager for her business to thrive, and confident in her writing skills and work ethic, she regularly set ambitious deadlines. Sometimes what this meant was that she overestimated the number of creative writing hours she could reasonably clock each week.

Here is where she got herself into trouble: to meet her ambitious deadlines, she sometimes forced herself to work beyond the point of exhaustion. Her main concern was that when she was caught in this cycle, she couldn't always deliver the highest quality product for her clients. She told me, "Delivery by force gets you eighty percent quality—and that's just not where I want to be with my creativity and business."

Annie, a professional modern dancer, told me a similar story of delivery by force. For her, instead of a decline in quality, she noticed a steep toll on her body. "At one point I was taking forty-eight dance classes a month plus performances. To pay the bills, I had to find a job that didn't interfere with my rehearsal and performance schedule. The only one I could find was a night shift making empanadas from midnight to eight a.m. Within a few weeks, I sprained my ankle, not due to a misplaced step, but out of sheer exhaustion."

Delivery by force can lead to creative blocks, as well. Christine, a singer-songwriter, told me of a recent creative plateau. "I knew I wanted to get to the next level with my guitar-playing and songwriting, but the only way I knew how to do that was through playing scales and musical exercises. I practiced and practiced, but even though I made some progress in my technique, quite frankly I was bored. I knew I was missing something important, the heart and soul of things, but I couldn't put my finger on what it was and how to get there. I ended up feeling stuck, unmotivated, and wondering if there was something wrong with me."

These stories are no doubt familiar to many artists and others. However, when you find yourself struggling with issues like these, it's not a sign that there's something wrong with you. Rather, these are perfectly natural responses to living in a society that incentivizes us to sacrifice our love, creativity, and well-being to fit into the system and survive. In this system, those who deliver by force are rewarded, regardless of the cost to their well-being. These incentives are so widespread and insidious that it is the rare person in our society who still has their love, creativity, and well-being fully intact.

Despite how pervasive and ingrained these incentives are, freedom from their grasp is possible. What's required is to understand what's going on under the surface and to seek a greater wholeness as you encounter areas of challenge.

Why wholeness? It's because when you sacrifice your love, creativity, and well-being to fit into the system, you must split yourself in two: the conscious part of you pushing forward toward a goal and the unconscious part of you unwilling or unable to comply.

Governed by such a split, it's like you're a horse rider who is both urging your horse forward while simultaneously pulling on the reins to slow down. The conscious rider, not aware of the unconscious reasons for the horse's resistance, can only resort to trying harder and harder to get the horse moving. However, relying on trying harder nearly always backfires because the rider only has so much willpower to surmount the horse's growing distress and confusion. You know that you're operating from such a split in your artistic life when you chronically experience stress, burnout, tension-related injuries, procrastination, and creative blocks.

The answer to such issues is to heal the split between the conscious and unconscious parts of yourself by connecting with your deepest truths and desires via the creative act. This I call the Yoga of Art. While the practice of yoga is generally known as a movement-based workout, the term *yoga* is a Sanskrit term that means to "yoke," "bind together," or "reunify." The **Yoga of Art** is a practice that reveals the underlying unity between anything you previously thought to be separate, such as mind and body, technique and expression, or the part of you that wants to do something and the part of you that doesn't.

When you practice the Yoga of Art, you no longer try to overcome your artistic challenges through sheer force of will. Instead, you regard your challenges as opportunities to listen more deeply to what wants to be born through you. By taking account of the feelings, needs, desires, or truths that you've previously ignored, you will experience a new feeling of wholeness, pleasure, purpose, and inspiration. In this way, the Yoga of Art is a primary path to the Soulforce that can best guide and energize your artistic life.

> The **Yoga of Art** uses your creative activities to connect with your deepest truths and desires, heal the splits within, and thereby access your Soulforce.

Your journey in the Yoga of Art has already begun; discovering your artistic purpose, Playing from the Heart, and the Mind-Body

Interludes comprise practices that reunify your technique, physical movements, emotions, and your soul-level purpose into a more seamless experience of creation.

We now deepen this journey by untangling the fallacy of willpower and learning the core practices that can help you tap into your deepest truths and desires and thereby enjoy an artistic life full of creative inspiration, freedom, pleasure, and life force energy.

THE WAR AGAINST THE SELF AND THE FALLACY OF WILLPOWER

> *"If a factory is torn down but the rationality that produced it is left standing, then that rationality will simply produce another factory. If a revolution destroys a government but the patterns of thought that produced the government are left intact, then those patterns will repeat themselves."*
>
> — ROBERT PIRSIG, *ZEN AND THE ART OF MOTORCYCLE MAINTENANCE*

For many creatives, art can feel like the one area of our lives that is entirely intrinsically motivated. Unlike the drudgery that so often characterizes chores or the more thankless aspects of our work, we turn to the arts for the sheer pleasure, fun, and love of the creative act. Things can change, however, when we try to advance our artistic skills within many of our society's methods of arts education—especially those found at high pressure, elite arts institutions. Steeped in the Story of Separation, these methods often rely less on developing the students' intrinsic motivation than on instilling extrinsic motivation in the form of "shoulds" and manipulation via grades, punishment, and rewards.

The result is a culture of self-denial and excessive willpower that eventually destroys everything that makes art matter. Within this culture, the fun and pleasure that brought us to the arts in the first place disappears. It is replaced by the constant pressure to set aside such "selfish and childish" concerns and instead achieve the narrow form of excellence defined by the system. Striving to succeed and survive within such a culture, you can even come to regard self-denial as a point of pride, with those who work themselves to the bone in service of their art seeming to occupy a rarefied and coveted place in the social hierarchy. Your artistic practices become something that is "good for you," as opposed to an expression of a larger interconnectedness. You even learn to fear that your art, and by extension yourself, are unworthy if your creative process feels too pleasurable or effortless. The result is a creative process focused more on the attempt to prove your self-worth than bringing yourself and your art more alive.

Not everyone is attracted to the culture of self-denial. Aware that a rigid work ethic feels terrible and, in addition, often fails to produce the transformative art it purports to ensure, many artists instead choose a more relaxed, free-flowing approach. These artists are motivated more by the drive for self-expression or even the deconstruction of any previous ideas of beauty, technique, or art form. In adopting a more *laissez-faire* approach, however, they sometimes make a mistake as serious as the one they attempt to escape. Without a considerable dose of discipline, sacrifice, and humility, they may never develop the artistic competence necessary to create something truly great, and so resort to more superficial forms of expression that are transformative only in name.

Clearly, the form of motivation you choose has a powerful impact on your life as an artist and on the quality of your art. As we've seen, both the rigid application of willpower and its reflexive dismissal have their downsides. Neither can grant access to the creation of art with Soulforce; one constricts too much and the other fails to provide necessary structure. So, what's the alternative? A deeper form of motivation can be found by examining what these two seeming opposites have in common: the war against the self.

The **war against the self** comprises a battle of wills between the part of you that wants to do something and another part that doesn't. It's when you *make* yourself do something without considering the ultimate consequences of doing so. Its most recognizable forms in our society are the overuse of willpower and the puritanical work ethic. Though less recognizable as such, the deconstructive approaches are equally a manifestation of the war against the self. Sometimes, self-expression can be more a means of escaping certain painful truths than a means to art with Soulforce.

> The **war against the self** is an inner conflict between the part of you that wants to do something and another part that doesn't. It says that your body and innate desires are somehow bad and in need of constant vigilance and correction.

The war against the self is a natural outgrowth of the Story of Separation; it rests on the same split between body and mind, matter and spirit, that we explored in Chapter 1. It is a profound form of self-rejection that says that your body and its feelings are somehow base, unruly, untrustworthy, and in need of constant vigilance and correction. In this, it makes a critical error. The truth is that the body is spirit made flesh, and so disconnection from your body is likewise disconnection from your artistic purpose, your inner aliveness.

The war against the self naturally leads to the excess use of willpower. After all, without connection with purpose and aliveness, what other means do you have of pursuing your goals than to impose your will onto yourself and the world around you? A willpower-driven approach can even seem to work well in the short-term, but in the long-term its limitations become more and more difficult to ignore. This isn't to say that willpower is bad or has no place in your artistic life. Willpower does have a useful function, which is to help you stay connected to your deeper truths and desires in times of imperfect clarity. It's just that willpower is

Chapter 7 | THE YOGA OF ART

a finite resource, one that is quickly drained by injudicious use.

The overuse of willpower is implicated in many of the challenges that artists commonly face, such as physical tension, emotional strain, creative ruts, and burnout. What's vital to realize is that, if these are the challenges that currently hinder progress in your creative life, then your progress will only be further hindered using yet more willpower. Indeed, for many highly trained musicians and other artists, your greatest creative gains will only be made possible by finding an alternative to willpower. As familiar as it might be, the overuse of willpower is part of a vicious cycle that causes the very problems it's trying to solve.

Unraveling the war against the self and its attendant overuse of willpower can bring up strong objections. Some ask, "Wait—wouldn't it be the case that giving up willpower and listening to my body would lead to a life of drunken debauchery? Wouldn't I turn into a lazy bum, sitting on my sofa all day, every day, eating doughnuts and watching reruns of *The Golden Girls*?"

Notice here the underlying assumption that your innate desires are somehow bad and unworthy. Sure, it's true that if you're used to a life of self-denial and stringent self-control that if you give yourself a break you may end up catching up on some much-needed rest, relaxation, and enjoyment. But that rest period wouldn't last forever. Maybe you'd lay around for a day or two, but eventually you'd get tired of being in bed, and you'd want to eat something other than doughnuts. So, you'd get up and do something else, perhaps engaging in a creative project, spending time with friends, or doing other things that truly nourish your body, mind, and soul. For many, the road back to Soulforce begins with a healthy dose of such nourishment.

The Yoga of Art is founded on the idea that there is an innate intelligence inside you, one that tells you when to rest, when to act, and what to do. With practice, what you may discover is that acting upon this intelligence consistently brings you more alive. At the very same time, this practice will also show you any old habits, beliefs, or behaviors that reflect areas of disconnection in your life. When you notice these, remember that they are simply your inheritance from a society that consistently serves the jealous lesser gods. Seen from their vantage point of disconnection, anything that brings you more alive is regarded with suspicion. Keep this in mind when you practice the Yoga of Art; be aware of any harsh judgments that come up because the parts of you that still serve the lesser gods may tell you that following what brings you alive is selfish, stupid, irresponsible, lazy, childish, or even insane.

In the long run, the Yoga of Art reveals that the real insanity is ignoring the consequences of acting in service of the lesser gods. The lesser gods promise success through force and control, but the truth is that acting in service of the lesser gods does nothing to guarantee your desired results. Indeed, the excess use of willpower the lesser gods invite only creates mind-body blockages that impede your creativity and well-being. Such blockages disconnect you from what is alive inside you, leaving you feeling contracted, heavy, and uninspired.

Again, feeling this way is not a sign that something's wrong with you—far from it! It makes perfect sense, for example, to procrastinate when your only idea of hard work involves drudgery. In fact, such procrastination is often a sign of your innate intelligence at work! So, when you're feeling unmotivated, the real question is not how to manipulate or force yourself into following some preconceived plan (which is just the war against the self), but instead to ask where your motivation is coming from.

In the end, the real problem behind a lack of motivation isn't an insufficient use of willpower; it's that you're not connected to what truly brings you alive. If you were connected to this, you would have no problems with motivation at all. In fact, the opposite would be the case; if you were in touch with what brought you truly alive, wild horses couldn't keep you from your creative practice. The real answer, then, is to get back in touch with what brings you alive and to learn how to let that lead your every artistic decision.

> SOULFORCE INQUIRY 5.1
> THE ROLE OF WILLPOWER IN YOUR LIFE
>
> Consider the role of willpower in your life. What are the times when you most often force yourself to do things you don't really want to? What motivates those decisions?
>
> Reflect on moments of physical tension, emotional stress, slow progress, creative ruts, or burnout. What's the role of willpower in each of these situations?
>
> What stories or feelings come up for you when you consider letting go of willpower and doing what feels good instead? What fears or judgments might you have about yourself or someone else who did this? Spend a few minutes with your journal reflecting on these questions.

CONNECTING WITH WHAT BRINGS YOU ALIVE

"You only have to let the soft animal of your body love what it loves."

— MARY OLIVER, "WILD GEESE"

The answer to the war against the self is the Yoga of Art. The Yoga of Art is the practice of encountering your artistic challenges guided by your inner aliveness. As we already explored, the war against the self incentivizes sacrificing your creativity and well-being in service of a contained, narrow goal, such as getting the mechanics right or meeting certain financial requirements. In contrast, the Yoga of Art helps you meet those same goals while in connection with something more open-ended, mysterious, and life-giving: your deepest truths and desires.

The Yoga of Art has three main advantages. Firstly, it helps you connect with a genuine source of creativity and frees you from effortful and inherited forms of expression. Secondly, it enhances your well-being, rather than diminishing it. These, in turn, lead to the third advantage, which is that it helps you find new, creative solutions to your artistic challenges that leave you feeling uplifted and inspired and that make the necessary hard work feel more worthwhile. The delightful result of the Yoga of Art is that it often yields unexpected creative fruit that simply cannot be otherwise found through effort and toil.

The following is the core practice of the Yoga of Art. It will help you connect with what is alive inside you during any creative choice, such as deciding what to practice next, how best to teach something to a student, or whether to take a certain gig. You will find it a useful companion practice to discovering your artistic purpose and Playing from the Heart.

SOULFORCE INQUIRY 5.2
THE YOGA OF ART

Use the following practice to help you navigate your artistic choices. Begin with briefly checking in with yourself to notice your body, your overall attitude, and any emotions or thoughts that are present. With your attention on your Inner Audience Member, ask a question related to what you're about to do next, such as:

- What would bring me alive today?
- What do I want to do right now?
- What do I want to create, practice, or learn today, and in what way should I go about that?

- What would be a fun way to do this?
- When should I create or practice today?
- Should I take a break now, and for how long?
- What kinds of warm-ups or other exercises should I start with?
- Should I take this or that work opportunity?
- Should I work with this or that collaborator or student?
- Should I wear the blue shirt or the black shirt for tonight's performance?
- How can I best help this student right now?

You can even ask your Inner Audience Member about other areas of your life, such as "What food do I want right now?" or "Should drive or take public transit?"

Simply notice what your Inner Audience Member tells you. The answer may come in a variety of forms, such as an intuition, bodily movements, emotions, images, symbols, messages, or shifts in attention.

Be sure to notice if other parts of you want to jump in and try to manage, cover up, rationalize, or otherwise obscure or change the message you got directly from your Inner Audience Member. These other parts may have important messages or roles in your inner system, but they may also interfere with your ability to know your deepest, truest, authentic self. Just get to know this whole family of inner voices so you can then make appropriate choices.

Finally, you get to decide what to do with the answer! Maybe you'll get a clear answer, and you will feel good about going with whatever that is. If you get an unfamiliar answer, maybe you will feel willing to experiment and try something new. There are no right or wrong answers here; simply be aware of the choices you're making.

> **SOULFORCE INQUIRY 5.3**
> **WHAT AM I SAYING "YES" TO?**
>
> If you ever feel uncertain about the messages you get from inside, ask yourself, *In making this choice, what am I saying "yes" to?* For example, if the way you're creating feels rushed and makes your body tight, then every time you create in this way you're saying "yes" to a future with more rushing and tightness.
>
> When you notice you've been making this choice, check in with yourself and ask what you would want to say "yes" to in this same situation instead. For example, "I want an artistic life of self-mastery and ease." Then, find a way to bring this deeper truth into your next creative choice.

Ultimately, the Yoga of Art is about reclaiming the sense of pleasure, play, magic, wonder, and fun that brought you to the arts in the first place. These comprise the juice that gives art its transformative power, without which your artistic activities can instead feel like work.

What is the relationship between art and work, for that matter? While work is a necessary part of reaching worthwhile goals, the drudgery that often accompanies it needn't be. Moreover, an artistic life with too much drudgery will be unlikely to lead to art with Soulforce.

A path out of drudgery can be found by realizing that much of what we call work is simply a degraded form of art, one devoid of breath and life. Flipping burgers only becomes drudgery when you consign yourself to doing so, day after day, on an assembly line to feed hundreds of anonymous customers for minimum wage. Reclaiming the art of burger flipping begins with inviting your Inner Audience Member into the picture.

For instance, instead of relying solely on a timer to let you know when the burger is done, and instead of flipping the burger with a rote, mechanical motion, you let your gut tell you when the burger is done and ask yourself, *How does my heart want to flip this burger?* Let the answer arise from your Inner Audience Member and directly inform your body's movements in flipping. The benefit of doing so is to ground your time at the grill in a richer, more flowing, and connected sensory experience. Further, it may help sensitize you to the longing for more meaningful work that may otherwise go unnoticed in the daily grind. Thus sensitized, you may find yourself taking action to upgrade your cooking skills and to find a more life-giving venue for your culinary gifts. This is the kind of process by which the Yoga of Art breathes new life into anything that now feels like work and accomplishes the reunification of your art and that which is alive inside you.

WHEN YOU HAVE TO, BUT DON'T WANT TO

> *"The preparation of a feast should be as enjoyable as the feast itself, and you can tell in the taste of peoples' food whether they enjoyed preparing it or not."*
>
> — ALAN WATTS, LECTURE ON THE WAY OF TEA[1]

The Yoga of Art applies even to those life circumstances in which you choose to deliver by force. After all, a practice that is only relevant in ideal life circumstances is of little use to anybody. So, when you don't want to do something but force yourself to anyway for survival reasons, it's okay. It's all part of the process.

What's helpful in such circumstances is to reclaim a sense of conscious agency so you don't feel helpless. This you can do by first taking the "have to" out of the equation. When you take a commission because otherwise you won't make rent, you're still making a choice. Taking responsibility for that choice is the first step to cultivating more life-giving circumstances.

Secondly, realize that, even when it feels like you don't have a choice about what to do, you always have a choice in how you do it. When deciding how to do something you dislike, what's helpful is to engage in a compassionate negotiation between the part of you that's choosing to do it and the other part of you that doesn't want to. For example, let's say that you're preparing for an art exhibit with a looming deadline and an overwhelming amount to do. When you think about all the work ahead of you, you feel a heavy sensation in your gut and a desire to distract yourself with cat videos. Instead of bulldozing through your overwhelm or letting yourself get distracted, you can negotiate with the part of you that is overwhelmed.

You might say to that part of yourself, *I see you're feeling overwhelmed. I get it. There's a ton to do and you're worried about getting exhausted and not delivering the highest quality product. What do you need from me so we can take at least a small step toward finishing some of this work today?*

Listen to the overwhelmed part of you as it replies. Then let its reply sink in and allow it to inform how you proceed. Perhaps you decide to start with just one little task while letting go of an attachment to getting the project done all at once. Maybe you agree to intersperse fun mini breaks throughout your artistic activities. Or maybe you firmly promise to take a refreshing spa day after the exhibition is over. Whatever it is, make sure that you truly are willing to make this change in your approach. The difference between self-negotiation and self-manipulation lies solely in the honesty of your willingness.

Negotiating with yourself in this way has ramifications beyond simply getting the job done. It can transform your entire approach to the creative act. For instance, if your heart tightens when you think about practicing a dance, instead of simply ignoring it and pushing through to your practice session, you could first enter a negotiation with the tightness in your heart.

Listening closely to its emotions and messages, you might discover that the real issue is not the simple fact that you're about to practice, but rather the way you practice. The tightness in your heart may, in fact, be a rebellion against the commonly taught idea that to practice is to inculcate the correct procedure until it becomes sufficiently ingrained. Inquiring further, you discover a hidden truth: that this familiar approach to practicing has been making your body tighter and cutting you off from the very creativity and aliveness you want in your performances.

Realizing the futility of practicing in this way, you begin to explore other ways of practicing that better align with the kind of performances you wish to give. You realize that what will bring you the results you want would be to let go of inculcation and instead to further develop your effortlessness and knowledge of the soul. Your purpose in practicing then shifts from the mechanical development of your physique to the facilitation and channeling of your Soulforce. You then enjoy a whole new world of desires and creative inspiration that was previously suppressed.

In this way, the Yoga of Art is like jujitsu, the martial art known for turning an opponent's attack into useful energy. It takes what, at first, seems like an obstacle ("Ugh, I have to practice") and turns it into an advantage ("How can I use this practice session to connect with something more life-giving?"). It accomplishes this by helping you take account of your hidden truths and then bringing them to bear on your current challenges. The result is a more fulfilling creative process whose results exceed what can be accomplished through willpower alone. This is an act of true artistry.

BUT WILL IT WORK?

"Note that the conscious mind thinks it knows best, despite its lack of understanding."

— IAIN MCGILCHRIST, *THE MATTER WITH THINGS*

One of the most common objections many have when first encountering the Yoga of Art has to do with trust. Can you trust your inner guidance to get you to where you want to go? Can an awareness of what brings you more alive truly help you successfully navigate the very real challenges you face, artistically and otherwise?

In other words, *will it work?*

The first question, as always, is to ask what assumptions lie hidden under these objections. In this case, what's assumed is that your survival depends on your ability to control yourself and your world, and that the best means to do so is through the lesser gods. Their imperatives are where the cold, hard facts of life are soberly faced, and anything else is mere frippery. To the lesser gods, the wild aliveness that art, at its best, brings forth is only useful as an instrument of attaining a limited set of survival needs such as financial or social gain.

For its part, the wild aliveness within couldn't care less about the pursuits of the lesser gods; all it wants is to bring more life and wildness into the world. To the aliveness within, money, technology, fame, and power are tedious distractions from the all-important cosmic play of life. Its view is that survival without art and play is meaningless.

At first, these two takes on life and art can seem mutually incompatible, but the Yoga of Art reveals otherwise. It shows that both have something useful to share, and that the real mistake is to ignore one in favor of the other. For example, some artists, inclined to a serious attitude toward life, tend to sacrifice their creative aliveness in favor of meeting their survival needs within the system of the lesser gods. Others, inclined to a more carefree attitude, tend to sacrifice their survival needs and eschew the lesser gods in favor of their creative aliveness.

What both approaches fail to realize is that the lesser gods are not the only means to survival. Whether to cling to their imperatives or dismiss them entirely is the wrong question. For instance, your continued survival doesn't only occur through your acts of will, but also comes about through grace, play, pleasure, and happy coincidences. Furthermore, seeking survival through money and other utilitarian concerns can stimulate your creative aliveness as much as anything else. Gandhi knew this well during his campaign to free India from British colonial rule; the Soulforce that energized his movement only became available by bringing its members' aliveness to their practical challenges.

There are other steps you can take to learn to trust the guidance your inner aliveness brings forth. You can also explore what happened in your early life that led you to mistrust your inner guidance in the first place (see the following Soulforce Inquiry). You were not born this way, after all; when you were very young, you were a creature of instinct and only wanted to play and have fun. You were born wired for aliveness, and thus any disconnection from that is something that you learned later in life.

Unfortunately, few in our society escape childhood with their wildness still intact. Our education system, even in the arts, tends to stamp it out wherever possible. As a result, artists and others learn from a very young age that success comes from self-denial and toiling. "You'd rather go and play than sit still and practice for five hours? You'll never reach the top that way! No pain, no gain!" Such an approach is ultimately futile. When reaching the top requires disconnection from your inner guidance, your resultant creations lose everything that makes them art.

Similarly, you can consider the kind of impact you want your art to make. Is your ideal impact going to come from ignoring your aliveness or treating your art like an effortful chore? Is that really what's going to get your Soulforce flowing? Is such an artistic process even sustainable for your well-being in the long term? Is art with a system update of self-denial, self-flagellation, and even self-hatred—all hallmarks of the war against the self common to many artists—really what you want to be putting out there in the world?

Your art always reflects your being. To create from the war against the self is to create art that doesn't matter because it doesn't bring you and your audiences more alive. Art that matters is art that inspires, heals, and connects, and this is only possible when you're in service of what brings you alive during the creative act. If a certain way of making art means that you cannot honor the life that is inside and around you, then it's probably not the kind of art you want to be creating, anyway. What's more important is the larger vision of what wants to be born inside you, our society, and our planet. How do you know when you're in service to that larger vision? It's whenever you feel more alive.

> If a certain way of making art means that you cannot honor the life that is inside and around you, then it's probably not the kind of art you want to be creating, anyway.

For many, learning to navigate by what brings you alive brings up deep survival fears. Will you really be prepared for that audition if you take it easy today? Will you be able to pay your rent or feed your kids if you say "no" to the opportunity that pays well but you know will leave you feeling drained? Will you really nail that technique if you don't exert maximum effort? Or even: will being honest with yourself reveal that the pursuit of your art form is no longer for you?

There are no easy answers to these questions. However, a good first step to finding any answers is a period of being okay with not knowing. It's not that there aren't good answers; it's just that the first step is to acknowledge that the old, familiar answers may not be working for you, and so you need to make space for the intelligence of your aliveness to generate new answers. The great news is that these new answers often turn out to work much, much better than the old ones.

SOULFORCE INQUIRY 5.4
FINDING YOUR WAY BACK TO SELF-TRUST

If you find trusting your inner guidance challenging, you may benefit from reflecting on how that trust was first broken. Find a comfortable place to sit, preferably in nature, and explore the following guided meditation.

Check in with your body and find the feeling of mistrust inside. First, notice any features of this feeling: its size, location, shape, color, image, or movements. As you do so, take a few deep breaths, letting them out very slowly. What do you notice about the feeling of mistrust now?

Now engage in an inner dialogue with this feeling: What does it want you to know about itself? How did it get to be this way? What does it want from you as your wise, mature, adult self? What beliefs did it take in about yourself or the world? Be patient, curious, and kind, openly accepting whatever comes up.

If this part of you shows you a scene or a memory from your past, step into that scene as your adult self and take your younger self into a new one, either where you are presently or a safe imaginary place. Hold your younger self, saying to them, "I'm so sorry you went through this and took in all these feelings and beliefs. It's all over now. I'm here to take care of you. I'm here to heal this. You're my number one. You're safe now." Repeat this as many times as is necessary to feel some relief inside.

Next, take a moment to view your younger self as a wise inner guru. Ask this guru, "If it's not true that [your old belief about yourself or the world], then what is true?" A response may come back like, "I'm great!" or "I'm a survivor" or "Life is supposed to be good." You'll know it's a genuine piece of wisdom from your inner guru when the message arrives with a feeling of deep truth.

Now, repeat this new truth to yourself many times until the feeling of truth and relief floods your body. Repeat it to yourself in this way every day for at least a week so that this new belief and feeling find firm footing in your body. If you want, write the new truth down in a place where you'll see it every day as an extra reminder. Finally, reflect on how this new belief affects your relationship with your willpower and make some notes in your journal.

PRACTICAL REUNION

"Stay close to anything that makes you glad you are alive."
— HAFIZ OF SHIRAZ, FOURTEENTH-CENTURY SUFI POET

Here are several real-life examples of the principles of the Yoga of Art providing new and better solutions to some of the most common challenges artists face. (Note: A common reason for the excessive use of willpower among artists has to do with fears about not being able to earn enough money. We will explore this topic in Chapter 12.)

WHEN YOUR STUDENTS DON'T PRACTICE

If you're an arts teacher, you've probably experienced how some students are easy—they practice every day and come to every lesson well-prepared. And other students are more frustrating—they rarely practice, if ever, and only seem to come to lessons because their parents tell them to. What can you do to get the latter kind of students to practice more beyond explaining the importance of daily practice?

One choice is an authoritarian approach in which you manipulate your students through bribes ("If you practice every day this week you can get an extra sticker for your practice chart!") and threats ("I'm going to be very unhappy with you if you don't practice more!"). The trouble with this approach is that once you rely on these methods, you must continue resorting to them whenever the student fails to practice. Ultimately, what students inadvertently learn from this approach is that they must manipulate themselves into practicing—and is this really the lesson you want them to take away?

A common remedy put forward is a permissive approach. In this approach, young students are put in a leadership role ("We can do whatever you want.") and standards are lowered to avoid the pain of failure ("Everybody gets a gold star."). The trouble with this approach

Chapter 7 | THE YOGA OF ART

is that students, especially the young ones, need firm rules, boundaries, and expectations to thrive. Without these guardrails, they can feel lost and anxious, and are deprived of the vital experience of seeing that they can overcome their challenges. Clearly, neither approach, in its extreme, can cultivate the intrinsic motivation necessary for students to thrive and enjoy practicing.

The answer comes in several layers and combines the best of both worlds. Firstly, check in with the student to ensure that what you have to offer is, indeed, what they genuinely want to learn. If it is, explore what underlying goals and desires are motivating them to learn from you in the first place. What you may discover is that what they want, for the most part, is to have fun, to learn things they enjoy, and to copy their peers and idols.

Next, consistently connect your rules, boundaries, and expectations to their underlying desires. When they discover that the structure you provide helps them move toward something they care about, they will trust more in the process and become naturally motivated to make progress. Further, ensure that your lessons focus on all three strands of Soulforce Mastery: technique, effortlessness, and the knowledge of the soul. Balancing all three is necessary for lessons that are fun and productive. Finally, remember that you are a role model for your students; when you connect with what brings you alive in teaching, you demonstrate the path to art with Soulforce better than any admonition or gold star.

THE SUPERSTITION OF HURRYING

I once gave a masterclass on the Magic Pause (see Mind-Body Interlude #7) to a college chorus, where I pointed out that one of the most common moments of unnecessary tension for singers was just before the onset of sound. I explained how it was at this moment when many singers would become the tensest. Just before they started singing they would push their shoulders down onto their ribs, almost as if they thought of their ribs as a fireplace bellows that they could use to power their sound.

So, to help the singers in this chorus prevent this same kind of unnecessary tension, I asked them to sing a song, this time while doing a Magic Pause right after each in-breath and before they began their next phrase. When they were done, I asked them what they noticed. One singer said he felt much more ease in his body, another said she noticed that the whole chorus sang more cohesively, and another said she noticed that she felt like she had so much more time and felt less rushed.

In responding to this last singer, I explained how one of the most common reasons for physical tension is needless hurrying and rushing, and that one of the deeper lessons of the Alexander Technique is that of regaining your personal sovereignty. When you're rushing across the room to get your coffee cup or hurrying to respond to the baton of the orchestra conductor, you are, in a way, a slave to old fears and other people's expectations of you. The trouble is that when you give into these fears, the resultant tension and stress compromises your well-being, which then negatively affects the quality of your art.

The unfortunate truth is that, despite how bad it is for our body, mind, and art, the habit of hurrying is endemic to our society. It's almost as if we believe that hurrying and the tension are like a superstition or magic charm: "If I rush and get tense, then I'll be successful, then I'll be worthy, then I'll be safe!" However, rushing and tension can't provide any of these things—only regaining your personal sovereignty can. This you can do with the simple act of taking a pause before you respond to something; and in doing so you regain your ability to make appropriate choices. This will almost always leave you feeling and functioning better, so why choose otherwise?

THE FALLACY OF DOING IT THE "RIGHT" WAY

Susan is a professional violist who came for some lessons with me to help with the stiffness and fatigue she often noticed while playing. During

Chapter 7 | THE YOGA OF ART

one of our lessons, she became curious about how to improve her bow-hold, since she noticed a great deal of tension in her right arm as she gripped the bow. So, Susan asked me, "What is the *right* bow-hold?"

I laughed out loud when I heard this because I knew from experience how people can make their bodies very stiff while trying to get the "right" technique. I knew that even if she put her fingers in the right places on the bow, none of that would matter if her fingers were still tense. I explained that everybody's body is different, so everybody's technique will be different. Furthermore, a violist has to move her bow along the string in order to make music, which means that, unless she's holding her bow in an unchanging death grip, her bow-hold may, in fact, look very different from one moment to the next.

She seemed to consider this and then said, "Okay ... But what's the *right* bow-hold?"

I laughed again, and asked, "Who gets to decide what the right bow-hold is? Just because Itzhak Perlman's bow-hold worked for him doesn't mean it's going to work for you."

We then talked about how, in a certain sense, there is no such thing as the right bow-hold. It's all context dependent. The deeper truth is that a piecemeal approach to technique invites effort and tension that interferes with the technique itself.

Recognizing that, as the saying goes, "It's easier to act your way into a new way of thinking than it is to think your way into a new way of acting," I decided to give Susan a direct experience of what I was talking about. I used my Alexander Technique hands-on guidance to invite her body into an experience of ease while she set up her bow-hold and played again. The ease in her body gave her a new basis from which to shape her bow-hold. Instead of forming it according to an external metric, she shaped it from a place of inner ease. The result was a fresh, flexible bow-hold that was right for her body, allowing for a much more vibrant sound and emotional expression in her playing.

WORKING THROUGH LESS-THAN-IDEAL CIRCUMSTANCES

Ben is a wonderful jazz guitarist who took some lessons with me for help with occasional pain he had in his arms while playing. After a few lessons together, he told me he was in the middle of a very busy performance schedule: twenty days of performances in a row, with only one day off in the middle! He was glad to have plenty of work but was worried about exhausting himself and exacerbating his arm pain.

So, as usual, I asked him what was happening in his body during these performances. He told me that the shows that were most challenging for his body were not the ones that demanded the greatest virtuosity or endurance, but the ones where the audience wasn't listening, where he felt he was no more than auditory wallpaper. Sometimes when he saw his audiences' disregard, he would feel dispirited, and this would drag his body into an uncomfortable slump that made playing his jazz licks feel effortful and awkward. Then he would try to regain his audiences' attention by playing harder, which only made matters worse for his body.

I told Ben that there are three important elements to preserving well-being in less-than-ideal performance settings. The first is to understand that a performance is a relationship in which the quality of listening of each party invites that same quality in the other. The great thing about an audience that listens closely is that their close attention draws out the very best in the performer, who then benefits from a creative freedom and energy they might not have had access to alone. Of course, while an ideal performance setting includes an attentive audience, we can't control what our audience does. The first step to relieving our tension, then, is to acknowledge our relationship with the audience—whether good or bad—and to let go of the attachment to reaching everyone.

Doing so leads to the second element, which is to focus on the areas of enjoyment that are possible, regardless of audience attention.

For example, letting go of the attachment to reaching everyone in the audience relieves us of the burden of working so hard to connect with those who aren't listening. Thus relieved, we might be better able to enjoy the simple sensory experience of creating and allow ourselves an attitude of unrestrained play and experimentation. If the audience isn't listening anyway, then why not mess around and have fun? Another example is that, even when most of the audience doesn't seem to be listening, there's always at least one who is. Find that person and enjoy playing just for them.

The third element is to fully digest the pain of not having a fully attentive audience. Given that what makes life meaningful is to give our gifts well and have them be well-received, it makes sense to feel some pain at being ignored by an audience. What many fail to realize is that this pain is life calling us to our fullest potential and the more beautiful world we were meant to create. If we try to cover up this pain or resign ourselves to it, we may miss the clarion call that could inspire and energize us to seek, or create, more fulfilling performance opportunities. If we fully digest the pain, on the other hand, we can respond to this call and create the kinds of performances that can bring both us and our audiences more alive.

TRUSTING OUR FUNDAMENTAL INTERCONNECTEDNESS

As a violinist, I've had the opportunity to play under many orchestra conductors, some of whose direction I really enjoyed and others who made every moment of music-making an experience of effort and disconnection. What was the difference? Often, it came down to the conductor's nonverbal communication. Did the conductor embody a visceral, intuitive connection with the orchestra, or were they more disconnected and disembodied?

For example, one conductor I worked under had very poor nonverbal communication: his bodily movements were stagnant and disjointed, such that he looked almost like a slouching toy soldier, with his arms moving separately from the rest of his body. I remember having such a hard time following his conducting because I constantly had to guess what his stiff arm movements actually meant. In fact, interpreting his movements took so much effort that I and the other orchestra members often left rehearsals and concerts feeling drained and tense.

In addition, the impact of the conductor's poor nonverbal communication included needless strife during rehearsals. When the conductor made a disjointed gesture and we didn't match his timing, he would get angry and scold us for not following his baton. He would then redouble his effort to try to get us to follow more closely, but this often only made things worse. My overall impression of this conductor was that he had no visceral experience of our interconnectedness, and so all he had to rely on was his willpower to *make* us follow him.

In contrast, I remember working under another conductor who made full use of the interconnectedness that existed between her and the orchestra members. She was so at ease with herself that the flow of emotion in her Inner Audience Member was effortlessly translated into her movements. Her effortlessness and flow were infectious; her demeanor helped us relax and made receiving her direction equally effortless. The result was rehearsals characterized by an easy, engaging, and emotionally satisfying synchrony that brought out the best in everyone involved. The lesson I took away from these experiences was that the best foundation for leadership and collaboration is not willpower and control, but a trust of our fundamental interconnectedness.

Working under the latter kind of conductor obviously makes for a more desirable musical experience, but what do you do when you're stuck playing under someone whose direction leaves you feeling drained or frustrated? The most important thing is to let go of trying to conform perfectly to their direction, since doing so will only cause you grief. Instead, you can realize that, while this gig may be important for paying your bills, it is not your only source of well-being. A much greater source of well-being is the aliveness within you. You can reclaim a sense of freedom and fun by asking this aliveness (your Inner Audience Member), *How do I want to follow this conductor's directions today?* Let yourself be open to new ideas. Let your heart be your guide. You may discover that doing so takes the pressure off the situation and allows you to regain a sense of humor and creativity that makes the whole experience more worthwhile.

THE ARTS IN SERVICE TO LIFE

"Just sit there. Don't do a thing. Just rest. For this separation from God, from love, is the hardest work in the world."

— HAFIZ OF SHIRAZ, FOURTEENTH-CENTURY SUFI POET

When you first begin practicing the Yoga of Art, you may find yourself grappling with many of your old beliefs and habits. You may even find yourself secretly using the principles and practices of the Yoga of Art to manipulate yourself into feeling good about doing something you don't genuinely want to do. But that's the war against the self all over again, just in new clothes.

Ultimately, the Yoga of Art is about learning how to be more in service to life. It's about how to attune yourself to that which will add to the complexity, richness, and growth of the life within you and around you. Indeed, when your heart and gut say "no," it might be because what you're doing, or the way you're doing it, isn't in service to life. When this is the case, the "no" you feel is life speaking through you, guiding you away from anything that doesn't serve the well-being of yourself, your art, our society, or planet. It's up to you to decide how best to move forward in any situation, but as an experiment, whenever you're uncertain about a choice, whether artistic or otherwise, simply ask yourself, *Is this in service to life?*

The truth is that you won't ever have to force yourself to do something when what you're doing, and how you're doing it, is in service to life. It will naturally fill you up, motivate you, and guide you in the right direction. Indeed, when you're really connected to serving life, you may end up working harder than you ever have before; but this time, instead of getting physically tight and emotionally drained, you may instead feel deliciously tired. You will recover the sense of play, magic, fun, and wonder that probably brought you to the arts in the first place, and which is the natural result of the reunion of what you want to do and what you end up doing.

The road to this place of reunion and the fulfillment it provides is not always easy. There are many forces in our world that support the war against the self, permeating how we learn, communicate, create, teach, and make a living, often in surprising and hidden ways. However, this is not a problem. In fact, according to the Zen proverb, "The obstacle *is* the path."

> You won't ever have to force yourself to do something when what you're doing, and how you're doing it, is in service to life.

Without actively facing worthy obstacles, you will never access enough Soulforce to create something beautiful and life-giving enough to make an actual difference in our world.

Remember, you only gain access to your Soulforce when you face life's inevitable challenges while standing in a deeper truth.

How do you discover that deeper truth? Through a practice like the Yoga of Art, where you listen deeply to that which is alive inside you and let that guide your choices.

The Yoga of Art is a vital part of the shift to the Story of Interbeing. It, along with your artistic purpose and Playing from the Heart, embodies a new model of creativity. In this model, creativity is a process that deepens your relationship with something larger than your individual self. It requires the release of control over the ultimate outcome and enhances your personal sovereignty. In other words, in this model, creativity is a gift, and not something that can be willed or consigned to mere chance. When you step into the Spirit of the Gift in your creative life, you receive a gift in return, which is the magic and enchantment that is art's true purpose. We will now explore the Spirit of the Gift in the creative act via our next Mind-Body Interlude.

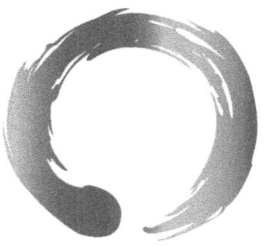

MIND-BODY INTERLUDE #3

EXACTLY AS IT IS

"Everyone is always teaching one what to do, leaving us still doing things we shouldn't do."

— FREDERICK MATTHIAS ALEXANDER, ORIGINATOR
OF THE ALEXANDER TECHNIQUE

Imagine you're bent over a drafting table, working on a challenging illustration. You want to get each line just right, with the shading and texture exact. Things go well for a while, but soon you notice that your neck and shoulders feel painfully tight, so you pause to stretch. You're worried about this tightness because it has become an increasing part of your time at the drafting table, and it threatens to reduce the number of hours you can draw each day. Today, the painful tightness is annoyingly persistent, resisting any attempt to stretch or find a better posture. As you get back to drawing, it constantly distracts you and prevents you from getting into the flow of creation. Frustrated and anxious, you wonder if you'll ever find a way out of your discomfort.

Chronic muscular tension, and the repetitive strain injuries it can eventually lead to, pose a serious issue for many artists. They can turn the creative process from an experience of play and flow into a constant attempt to escape pain, discomfort, and physical constraint. The trouble is that, while it generally makes sense to try to avoid pain, often the very attempt to do so only makes things worse. Unaware of the root cause of the issue, you may be tempted to fight against the pain. However, it doesn't matter how much you stretch it out, how straight you make your spine, or how often you massage the painful area; if your attempt to escape physical discomfort makes your body tighter, then you will never find complete relief.

If the unconscious attempt to escape pain only makes things worse, then the answer is to consciously stop escaping. Physical ease is solely the result of allowing your sensory experience to be exactly as it is. As soon as you resist any sensation, especially those that are painful, your body will become tighter, thus perpetuating the root cause of your discomfort.

The most amazing thing happens when you let your pain and discomfort be exactly as it is. Instead of deepening or perpetuating your pain, as you might fear, letting your pain be exactly as it is grants access to an unexpected source of joy and well-being. It's not that letting pain be "as it is" magically removes it from your life. Rather, it's that, as soon as you stop trying to escape your pain, you feel a lightness, joy, and relief that seems to come out of nowhere. You discover that joy and well-being are inherent to your primordial beingness and are not dependent on whether your outer circumstances are perfect.

So, instead of relating to pain as a problem to be fixed, you realize that even excruciating pain is no hindrance to the wholeness, aliveness, and connection you've been seeking your whole life. You have the surprising insight that the constant attempt to escape pain, instead of bringing the desired relief, has actually been a heavy burden. Ultimately, letting your pain be exactly as it is provides one of the most important realizations a person can have: that all experiences are equal pathways to the immense joy intrinsic to being.

EXACTLY AS IT IS

Pause for a moment and check in with your body. Allow an awareness of your whole body to arise in consciousness all at once. Notice which areas of your body feel pleasant and which feel unpleasant. Notice if there's any attempt to escape those that are unpleasant. If you find this resistance, see if you can instead, allow the unpleasant sensations to be exactly as they are.

Say to yourself, "*No escape, no escape.*" Or, "*Let the whole thing be exactly as it is.*" Or, "*Being with, being with.*"

> How does this change your relationship to discomfort and pain? What happens in your body as a result—do you get tighter or freer? Does your sense of space get smaller or bigger? Do you feel more emotionally connected or disengaged?
>
> If allowing certain painful sensations to be exactly as they are proves too challenging, then focus on your resistance to the pain and allow that to be exactly as it is. Any release of the attempt to escape sensory experience is a step into the peace and ease that is your birthright.

Two final notes. This practice does not mean that you shouldn't make every effort to protect yourself from physical or emotional harm. Quite the contrary! Letting your sensory experience be exactly as it is allows you to clearly see, perhaps for the first time, that some of your usual ways of protecting yourself result in a form of chronic suffering. It's the way you protect yourself that matters. In addition, even though this Mind-Body Interlude focuses on the pitfalls of unconsciously avoiding pain, it applies just as much to the equal issue of unconscious attachment to pleasure. The paradox, again, is that letting sensations of pleasure be exactly as they are, as opposed to immediately seeking more, brings forth a deeper pleasure than any quick fix could ever afford.

"The meaning of life is to find your gift.
The purpose of life is to give it away."

— PABLO PICASSO

CHAPTER 8

THE SPIRIT OF THE GIFT

Peter is a gifted violinist who came to me for help in relieving the chronic muscular tension that had recently made playing violin painful. Years earlier, he had gotten a degree in violin from a prestigious music school, and while he could clearly have made a career in the arts, the physical pain and emotional burnout he experienced in school led him to choose a different means of making a living. He still loved music, though, and wanted to remain connected to the violin, no matter what. Now, his increasing pain put even that possibility in jeopardy.

One day in a lesson, he asked me to help him relieve the tension he felt while practicing a challenging musical passage. So, I asked him to demonstrate how he practiced, and we both noticed how his body became tense and rigid while he repeated the passage. I asked him what he was thinking about that was making him so tight, and he said that it was about gaining maximum control: he was trying to make his body do what he wanted so that he could get the passage right. We both agreed he needed a new approach to practicing so that he could enjoy the freedom of movement and musical expression he sought after.

We started with a new body movement idea while he repeated the passage, so he would think, *soften my body* while he played. Instructions like this are common in the Alexander Technique, but in my experience, while sometimes helpful, thinking about being at ease while also doing something as challenging as playing a violin concerto can make it feel like you're doing two difficult things at once, instead of just one. My gut said to help him reframe how he thought about practicing instead.

So, I said to Peter, "You seem to be thinking about your body and your ability to learn as if you were some sort of machine. But what works well for a machine—repetition and control—is terrible for a human body. What if you were to stop trying to control the outcome of each repetition of the passage so tightly and instead *receive* what you play in a more spontaneous and uncoerced kind of way—in other words, to think of what you're playing as a gift?"

The results were immediate and palpable. His whole demeanor changed; he relaxed and sat back in himself. His movements became more fluid and less forceful. His sound opened up, becoming softer, rounder, and more resonant, and a new, lively musicality suddenly came through. When he was done playing, he told me how he felt much more at ease and that, while he still had made a few mistakes here and there, those slip-ups didn't bother him as much. He was able to just watch it all happen, and in so doing, paradoxically, he had gained much greater control over his violin playing! Peter later told me that this realization marked a noticeable shift in his overall approach to practicing. While he still experienced excess tension at times, regarding his music as a gift allowed a new, sustained level of ease in his subsequent practice sessions.

How did Peter gain access to these many benefits? He stepped into the Spirit of the Gift.

The **Spirit of the Gift** is a relationship to the creative act revealing that creativity is more a gift you receive than something solely the result of your personal efforts. It affords a creative power that isn't limited to what you can *make* happen, but one that instead relies on connection with a larger intelligence to provide the creative gains, energy, and inspiration you desire.

Chapter 8 | THE SPIRIT OF THE GIFT

> The **Spirit of the Gift** is a relationship to the creative act revealing that creativity is more a gift you receive than something solely the result of your personal efforts.

The Spirit of the Gift is a fundamental answer to all the challenges we've addressed so far in this book: creative blocks, burnout, performance anxiety, physical tension, and even difficulty making a living in the arts. When you experience any of these, it might be a sign that you've lost touch with an important truth: that creativity functions as a gift—and it's easy enough to forget this. Our society is like a great machine, and to survive within the machine, we must, in many ways, conform to its demands and act like machines. There is a price to be paid for doing so, however. Acting like a machine is dispiriting—literally, dis-spiriting. It strips the spirit (what is life-giving, human, and enchanting) out of almost everything it touches, including the arts.

For example, mastering ballet can be tremendously life-giving—except when you have to do it six hours or more a day to graduate from your elite arts school. Playing shows for audiences is a vital source of human connection—except when you have to do 250 shows a year just to cover your basic expenses. Collaborating with fellow artists can be joyful and fun—except when you realize that the survival pressures your collaborators face leads them to treat you as a means to an end. The result in every case is that art becomes more like work: just another factory job, sometimes devoid of the very things that make art powerful and enjoyable.

The answer is a process of re-spiriting all aspects of life, which you can do by stepping into the Spirit of the Gift. As you do so, you will regain access to your Soulforce through an experience of greater creative energy, effectiveness, and enchantment. The Spirit of the Gift will transform your relationship to your creative process, your body, your livelihood, and to our society and planet.

For many, the Spirit of the Gift feels like a balm for the soul because it brings relief from all the effortful striving of the war against the self, lends a new sense of meaning and significance to your creative work, provides answers to many of the deepest conundrums of artistic life, and opens you to a creative process that connects both you and your audiences with something larger than your individual selves.

So, what is a gift, and how can you incorporate the Spirit of the Gift into your artistic life?

WHAT IS A GIFT?

> *"Any release of control is a step into the gift."*
> — CHARLES EISENSTEIN, *LIVING IN THE GIFT*

More than a material exchange expected on birthdays and holidays, a gift is a whole mode of being. In examining its widespread use throughout history, we find that the gift is our primordial means of relating to ourselves, each other, and our universe. Many of us in the modern world, accustomed as we are to markets and transactions as a primary means of exchange, might not realize that gift-giving was the predominant means of meeting needs, building relationships, and finding meaning throughout most of human history.

Marcel Mauss, in his classic book *The Gift: The Form and Reason for Exchange in Archaic Societies*, makes abundantly clear that the customs of indigenous and traditional peoples around the world—from the Northwest Coast Native Americans to the Scandinavians to the Polynesians, among many others—was based on the Spirit of the Gift. He called the system of gift exchange a "total social phenomenon" that, up until the invention of market economies, guided humanity's entire way of life—how we ate, spoke, worshiped, celebrated, connected with others, dreamed, created, healed, and more.

Understanding the inner workings of gifts is the first step to reclaiming the creative power to which the Spirit of the Gift grants access. As Charles Eisenstein teaches in his work, gifts have three fundamental characteristics: sovereignty, release, and relationship.[1]

- ***Sovereignty*** means that a gift cannot be coerced, either by the giver or recipient. If I hold you up at gunpoint and demand your wallet, and you give it to me, it is not a gift. Similarly, if I dump a pile of my old furniture on your lawn, then you may not necessarily think of this furniture as a gift. Not all gifts are "pure"—many come with strings attached and obligations of various kinds—but the essence of giving and receiving is of free, uncoerced choice.

- ***Release*** refers to the release of control that defines a true gift. If I give you a thousand dollars but then demand that you sign a contract saying that you'll pay it back under penalty of legal action, then this is not a gift because I haven't released my control over what happens with the money. In his book *The Gift: Imagination and the Erotic Life of Property*, Lewis Hyde says that a true gift "goes around the corner." This means that the gift and its energy are released into the unknown and that some kind of faith is required to trust that it will come back to you in some form. For something to be a true gift, you must release any attempt to ensure the time or form that a gift will return to you.

- ***Relationship*** refers to how gifts strengthen connections among people, unlike transactions or even barter. If I play you a song that you've paid for, we are in a transactional relationship. In a transaction, there is an inherent power difference between us, such that I, as the payee, am somewhat beholden to you as the payer. The result of such a power difference will likely be a feeling of distance between us because power differences often carry an implicit threat of the misuse of power. Gifts have a different outcome: if I play a song for you freely and without expectations, then you may receive it as a gift and be energized by it. You may then feel closer to me because of my gift, grateful to have received something beautiful, and you may then feel a natural impulse to give something in return, thus continuing a virtuous cycle of reciprocity and connection.

As we will explore further in Chapter 12, regarding your creations as gifts answers the age-old conflict between artistic purity versus selling out. Simply put, art is a gift and so is the money (or other resources) you receive in return. The great challenge is that our economic system incentivizes us to regard our art as a commodity, a shift that dis-spirits our creative process and its resultant art. However, you always have a choice in how you respond to these incentives. In ways both big and small, you can take steps into the Spirit of the Gift as you seek to support yourself with your art. The result is a creative process that preserves what is life-giving in your art even as you exchange it for money or other resources. Moreover, since what is life-giving is where your art's true value lies, and is also what people are most inspired to pay for, stepping into the Spirit of the Gift in your livelihood may even result in greater financial and material abundance.

SOULFORCE INQUIRY 8.1
EVERYTHING IS A GIFT

Sit comfortably in a quiet place, preferably in nature. Take a few deep breaths and connect with your body and surroundings. Bring the following contemplations to mind, one by one, and let yourself steep in each one for a minute or two.

Chapter 8 | THE SPIRIT OF THE GIFT

Consider the possibility that everything in life is a gift. Did you earn the sun, moon, or the earth? Or were these gifts? Do trees offer their fruits as transactions or as gifts? Did you earn your body, family, friends, consciousness, desires, or natural proclivities? Or were these gifts? Did you earn the thoughts that pop into your mind, the feelings that arise in your body, or the longings you carry, deep in your soul? Or are all these gifts, too?

Now think of a time you were given a gift that made a positive difference for you. It could be as simple as a hug or cup of tea when you needed one, a performance or work of art that changed your life, or it could be the simple gift of having been born. Pick something or someone that readily comes to mind, and which has some emotional energy to it.

Notice that this gift was a *gift*, and not something that you had to earn or prove that you deserved to receive. Notice the impact it made in your life. Notice that whoever gave this to you—whether it's someone you know, someone long dead, or not even a person at all—didn't have to give it. They freely chose to give to you.

What feelings come up as you contemplate all of this? What state of being is evoked? How does it change how you feel about yourself and our world? If desired, make some notes in your journal.

THE MANY FORMS OF GIFTS IN THE ARTS

"It is when gifts stir us that we are brought close, and what moves us, beyond the gift itself, is the promise (or the fact) of transformation, friendship, and love."

— LEWIS HYDE, *THE GIFT*

The Spirit of the Gift pervades the arts from top to bottom. Your natural talents and proclivities are gifts. The elements of your childhood environment (parents, teachers, schools, friends, socioeconomic background, access to artistic resources, access to beautiful experiences, and more) that allowed you to develop your talents were gifts. Your cultural heritage is a gift. Any moments of creative inspiration are gifts. Your ability to work hard is a gift. Your ability to relax into creative flow is a gift. Your audiences are a gift, your students are a gift, and you are a gift to your audiences and students. The extent to which you're able to go beyond the mere mechanics of what you're creating is a gift. Freedom of movement arrives as a gift. It's even the case that every improvement in any skill you practice also comes as a gift.

The Spirit of the Gift is also what makes a work of art different from a mere commodity. On the one hand, a commodity is interchangeable, impersonal, and made for the primary purpose of being exchanged for money. No more effort goes into creating a commodity than could be justified for the money received. True art, on the other hand, is unique to a time, place, and set of people, its primary purpose is a devotion to beauty. The creation of art, by definition, requires the investment of more time, care, and beauty than can be justified for the exchange of money (an exchange which, of course, might very well still happen). As Lewis Hyde wrote in *The Gift*, "If where there is no gift, there is no art, then it may be possible to destroy a work of art by converting it into a commodity."

The Spirit of the Gift is inherent to who we are. Its implicit presence in our souls explains the icky feelings many of us have around selling ourselves and our art; there's simply a place inside us that longs to be deeply moved and knows that no commodity carries the Soulforce necessary to do so. In this way, art is like nature, which has the power to transfix us through the sheer generosity of its beauty. A great work of art draws on this same source of power precisely because it is far more beautiful than it needs to be for the grade, paycheck, or social status it could garner. This "extra" beauty is the gift that a work of art shares. The more generously a work of art shares its beauty, the greater its power to hold our attention and move our souls.

Chapter 8 | THE SPIRIT OF THE GIFT

**SOULFORCE INQUIRY 8.2
I ALREADY LIVE IN THE GIFT**

Pause for a moment and check in with your body. Take a deep breath and let it go slowly.

Think to yourself, *I already live in the gift*.

Let this idea sink in. Contemplate your life and be curious about how this might already be the case. Look around you, thinking, *I already live in the gift*. Contemplate your environment, both built and natural, and just try it on for size: *I already live in the gift*.

Contemplate your artistic life with the same idea. In what ways are your artistic endeavors already examples of the Spirit of the Gift? How does it feel to let this idea sink in?

Here's a story that illustrates the Spirit of the Gift in a musical setting. Becca is an aspiring singer-songwriter who attended one of my classes because she wanted to feel more at ease while singing for her audiences. When I asked what had been happening for her recently, she told me how her shoulders would get tight when performing, how sometimes her hands didn't seem to do what she wanted while playing her ukulele, and how her throat would become strained when she sang.

I intuited that Playing from the Heart might be the key to unlocking all of this, so I invited her to notice her Inner Audience Member as she played and sang one of her songs. The result was deeply moving. There was a new resonance, flow, and depth of musical expression that poured from her. Becca then told me how she felt more relaxed and less rushed, and that she enjoyed herself more. I also shared my own experience; that while listening to her, my own body had relaxed, I had involuntarily taken a deep breath, and that my own Inner Audience Member had been touched by this new quality in her music.

This seemed to strike a chord in Becca, so I reinforced her experience by pointing out that all these benefits hadn't been the result of going home and practicing for six hours a day. Her newfound ease and musicality were gifts from her Inner Audience Member, ones she could tap into any time she wanted.

Becca then told me that this touched a source of grief and strain deep inside her that had come from trying so hard to compensate for a feeling of unworthiness she had carried since childhood, and that that feeling was what was behind all the effort and strain she had felt recently.

So, wanting to help release her from that old feeling, I said to her, "The greatest gift you can give your audiences isn't some kind of perfect performance, but *you*, your essence. *You* are the gift your audiences have been looking for. What a relief! You no longer have to try to prove anything—it doesn't even matter if you make a million mistakes up on stage. Your Inner Audience Member is connected to a deeper source of creativity and expression than you might realize. Just tap into your Inner Audience Member, and whatever flows through you will carry the greatest gift you can offer—the mystery that is your true self."

IT'S NOT YOUR CREATIVITY

"The artist appeals to that part of our being ... which is a gift and not an acquisition—and is therefore more permanently enduring."

— JOSEPH CONRAD, *THE CHILDREN OF THE SEA: A TALE OF THE FORECASTLE*

The Spirit of the Gift reveals that true creativity is a function more of the Being Mode than the Thing Mode. The **Thing Mode** is a byproduct of the Story of Separation in which you regard yourself, your art, and your world as things to be manipulated. The **Being Mode**, in contrast,

Chapter 8 | THE SPIRIT OF THE GIFT

is a byproduct of the Story of Interbeing in which you regard yourself, your art, and your world as beings to be honored. In the Thing Mode, creativity is largely a plodding effort, the result of an assembly line process, mere mimicry, randomness, or otherwise a product of willpower. In the Being Mode, creativity is a gift that arises by entering a relationship with something larger than, and yet not separate from, your individual self, and which is essentially a mystery. (See Mind-Body Interlude 4 for a guided experience of the Thing Mode and the Being Mode.)

While the Being Mode, in the end, is a better source for life-giving art, this doesn't mean that the Thing Mode has no place in the creative process. The Thing Mode can play an important role in making pragmatic choices about the creative inspiration you receive. However, its grasping, mechanical, and almost predatory manner makes it oblivious to the strokes of insight that characterize true creativity. This is why, for true creativity to take place, the Thing Mode and the Being Mode must exist in a hierarchy with the Being Mode as the dominant influence. As author Ian McGilchrist wrote in *The Matter With Things*, "The less we leave things to fortune, the less likely we are to make a fortunate find."

> Creativity is a gift that arises by entering a relationship with something larger than, and yet not separate from, your individual self, and which is essentially a mystery.

The Being Mode allows for the fact that the fruits of creativity almost always come from the fringes of consciousness, and that any attempt to categorize or control the outcome of what you're creating too early may destroy what is coming into being. The Being Mode answers this concern by allowing you to listen to the voice of being itself with an attitude of humility, custodianship, and care for what is received. The result of relying primarily on the Being Mode is everything that makes for a truly generative creative process: one where you feel you have a greater breadth of vision, tolerance for ambiguity, willingness to change according to circumstances, and ability to forge distant connections. Writing of this receptive attitude toward creativity, McGilchrist again writes that, "We can't make creativity happen, but we can certainly do our best to stand in its way."

You know you're engaging in true creativity when the fruits of your labor arise whole and unbidden as flashes of insight. It's as though a veil has been lifted and you can suddenly understand, see, or do things that were previously inaccessible to you. There can even be a feeling that these flashes have an intelligence or will of their own. Think about it: when a completely new idea pops into your mind, where did it come from? Why did it choose that moment to arise? Can you really say that you, as your individual self, fashioned this new idea of your own devices? Or is it more accurate to say that the fruits of your creative processes arrive as *gifts* from some source to which you have access but whose inner workings are hidden from view?

If the latter is true, then what is this mysterious source? Where do these gifts come from? The answer depends on what story of the world you inhabit. From within the Story of Separation, all creative ideas and improvements in ability come from within the confines of your individual self. However, this model is unsustainable and insufficient for true creativity. As Lewis Hyde writes: "We are lightened when our gifts rise from pools we cannot fathom. Then we know they are not a solitary egotism and they are inexhaustible. Anything contained within a boundary must contain as well its own exhaustion."

In other words, living from too narrow a sense of self inevitably results in the exhaustion of your creative energy. The Story of Interbeing answers this by saying that who and what you are is not limited to what you think of as your individual self. Instead, you are connected, fractal-like, with the whole universe; as philosopher Maurice Merleau-Ponty wrote, "The body-mind is an open circuit, completed by the world."

Chapter 8 | THE SPIRIT OF THE GIFT

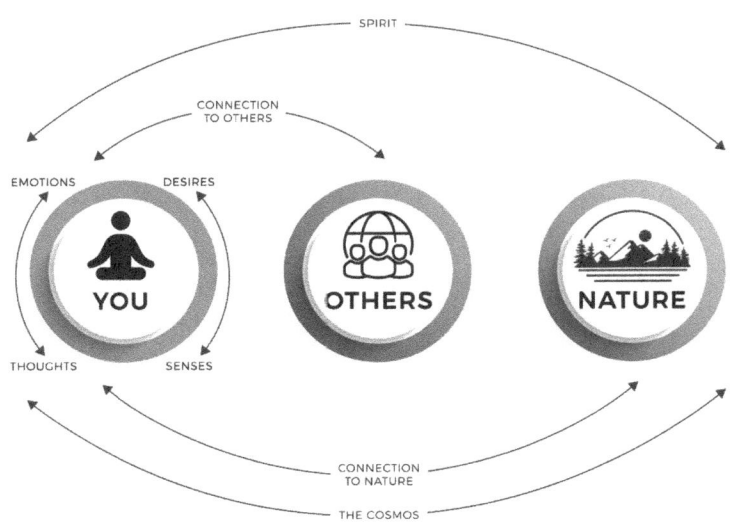

In other words, you are not an isolated individual in a world of "other." Rather, you are a "mind-body-world" comprising many nested feedback loops. These feedback loops include the parts of your body, the beings around you, our society and planet, and even the universe as a whole. What this means, ultimately, is that your creativity doesn't belong to what philosopher Alan Watts called "the skin-encapsulated ego." Rather, it's more accurate to say that the creative impulses to which you have access come as a result of your relationship with the many feedback loops that comprise yourself as a mind-body-world. It is this larger self that is the true source of creativity.

SOULFORCE INQUIRY 8.3
WHO AM I IN THE SPIRIT OF THE GIFT?

Spend some time responding to these prompts in your journal, preferably while sitting in a place of natural beauty.

Review your relationship to your artistic practices. What are your greatest gifts as an artist, teacher, performer, creator, and student? What gifts feel best for you to give?

Now recall examples of other people's art you love the most. What is the essence of the gift you receive when in contact with these works?

Then, let yourself steep in the acknowledgment of all these gifts, and ask yourself, *If these truly are gifts and not acquisitions, then who am I? What am I?* As you sit with this question, notice any shifts in your body, mind, and perception of the world around you.

Finally, see if an affirmation, image, or symbol comes up that might capture or represent the essence of who you are in the Spirit of the Gift. Write this down and keep it in a place where you'll see it daily. Bring it to mind regularly to let it sink into your system.

THE GIFTS OF THE FIVE PHASES OF THE CREATIVE PROCESS

"During the period of offering, solutions often spontaneously arise. When the mind is no longer grasping for an answer, space opens. [There is] room for a Divine plan, even in impossible messes."

— TOSHA SILVER, *OUTRAGEOUS OPENNESS*

When you no longer view your skin-encapsulated ego as the sole source of creative inspiration, you open yourself to unexpected gifts in each of the **five phases of the creative process**. As Iain McGilchrist teaches in his work, these five phases include trying, failing, relaxing, receiving inspiration, and then succeeding. It is only when you honor the gifts of each phase that you can access the real magic of the creative process.[2]

Chapter 8 | THE SPIRIT OF THE GIFT

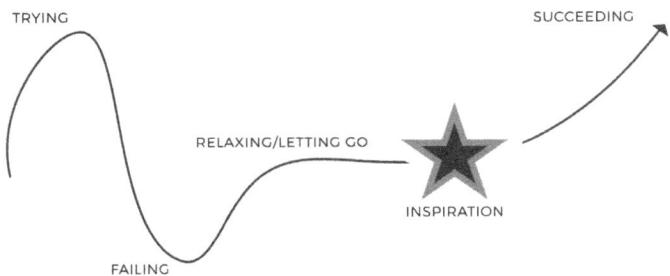

The **trying phase** is what many of us are most familiar with. It includes the time spent in the practice room or with a loaf of dough in hand, doing the hard work necessary for creative gains. While such hard work is, indeed, necessary to the creative process, many in our society mistakenly believe that the trying phase alone is where the "real" action happens. The result of this mistaken belief is an overemphasis of the trying phase, in which your creative process becomes a matter of drudgery and tightening your control over the outcome. I hope it's obvious to you by now that this may only drain your creative energy.

In contrast, the Spirit of the Gift says that your hard work, careful assessment, and planning are like an offering you make as a sign of your earnest and sincere devotion to whatever aims you are in service to at that moment. When you view the trying phase as an offering, you naturally receive a return gift: freedom of all the pressure that comes from trying to "get it right." Any tension or anxiety you normally feel drains away, and you finally feel free to *play* at your art, rather than toil.

> When you regard the trying phase as an offering, you are finally free of all the pressure that comes from trying to "get it right."

Many are surprised to learn that the following **failing phase** also bestows useful gifts. When you reach the limit of what you know how to do, and when nothing seems to be working, you may be tempted to take this as a sign that there's something going wrong in your creative life. It turns out, however, that failure has a crucial role to play in your eventual success.

Failure simply means that you've come to the natural limit of your energy and abilities. When you allow this to happen without worry, the result is yet another return gift: the boundaries of who you are and what you think is possible soften to create space for new possibilities. Philosopher and mathematician Jacques Hadamard knew well the importance of the failing phase when he wrote, "It is as though it were necessary for the conscious self to be weakened in order that unconscious ideas may break through."

The following **relaxing phase** has its gifts, too. This phase comprises time taken away from your creative labors when you engage in rest or other nonproductive activities. Many who are used to overemphasizing the trying phase often dismiss the relaxing phase, but in doing so they miss the invaluable behind-the-scenes processing of creative ideas that happens during a period of relaxation. For example, one of the greatest painters of the twentieth century, Salvador Dali, used the power of the relaxing phase to his distinct advantage. In between stints at the canvas, he would take naps with his keys held in one hand over a dinner plate he had set on the floor beside his sofa. Then, when he had relaxed deeply enough into sleep to start dreaming, his grip on his keys would loosen, causing them to fall on the plate and make a clink loud enough to awaken him. Upon awakening, he would recall the images from his dreams and then use them in his brilliant and surreal paintings.

The relaxing phase offers two return gifts. Firstly, it lets you recharge your batteries; Dali himself believed that "the brief moment spent between wake and sleep would revive your physical and psychic being." Secondly, to quote McGilchrist again, the relaxing phase allows for a period of incubation, during which any knowledge acquired during the previous phases "gets a chance to sink in, be reorganized and combined with other (seemingly irrelevant) ideas by the unconscious brain."

Next up, the **inspiration phase** is when the fruits of the incubation offered by the relaxing phase come to awareness. It consists of "aha!" moments, unexpected progress in ability, new perspectives, or a sense of physical relaxation. These are gifts from the mysterious source of creativity, ones that, if acted upon, have the potential to become great works of art. Importantly, what keeps these precious gifts alive is exactly the sense of mystery about their origin and meaning. As the painter and sculptor Georges Braque said, "In art there is only one thing that matters: what cannot be explained."

The final **succeeding phase** happens when you honor all the gifts you have received in your creative process thus far by using them well. You know you have used them well when you feel refreshed and at ease, when you or your audiences have been transformed in some way, and when your creative process leaves you feeling connected with something bigger than your individual self. In sum, learning how to frame your creative process as a series of gifts and offerings allows you to reliably access the creative magic of the universe.

SOULFORCE INQUIRY 8.4
FIVE PHASES INVENTORY

Spend a few minutes contemplating each of the five phases of the creative process. Which ones are you most or least familiar with? Which ones get the most or least attention and time in your own life?

Choose the phase that you give the least time and attention to and come up with a simple action step you can take this week to truly honor it. For instance, when you notice any failures in your creative practice, just pause a moment and ask yourself what that failure might be softening within you. Or plan to rest for a few minutes within a given practice session. Choose what feels good to you and notice what happens as a result.

ESTABLISHING A RELATIONSHIP WITH THE MYSTERIOUS SOURCE OF CREATIVITY

"The passage into the mystery always refreshes. If, when we work, we can look once a day upon the Mystery, then our labor satisfies."

— LEWIS HYDE, *THE GIFT*

Through the Spirit of the Gift, art is best understood as the product of a living relationship between you and the mysterious source of creativity. As you just read about, this source is not actually distinct from who you are or even from the world around you. It is both fundamentally intrinsic to your being, and yet, at times, it can also somehow seem like something outside of you. It can take form through your body, mind, and soul, but also has a generative capacity beyond what your skin-encapsulated ego can manufacture. Its fruits may puzzle your intellect and yet carry deep resonance in your body and soul. It goes by many names; some call it God, Brahman, Source, the Divine Beloved, Love, the Universe, Nature, or the Mystery. Importantly, establishing a relationship with this mysterious source is essential to opening yourself to receive the creative gifts that are your birthright.

The following practice will help you establish just such a relationship by drawing on some of the most ancient elements of human culture: offerings, sacrifice, and devotion. Even though these elements of culture evolved in religious settings, you don't need to subscribe to any religious beliefs to gain benefit from the following practice. All you need is an attitude of openness, humility, and curiosity.

SOULFORCE INQUIRY 8.5
MAKING AN OFFERING TO THE MYSTERY

Use the following meditation to receive creative inspiration, healing, or help with other challenges.

Chapter 8 | THE SPIRIT OF THE GIFT

You can use it for just about any kind of challenge you're facing, whether emotional, physical, relational, artistic, or financial. Just try it and see what happens!

- **Identify the problem**. Get clear on what you want help with. What exactly do you want, or no longer want? For example: "I want relief from performance anxiety" or "I need more money because I'm tired of scraping by."

- **Get in touch with the Mystery.** Sit quietly with eyes closed and allow your body and mind to relax. Notice the space around you and listen to the silence that contains all the sounds you hear. Think to yourself, *Intelligence runs through it, intelligence runs through it*. Ideally, you'll have a sense that, as you listen to the space and silence around you, it is listening back to you.

- **What are you in service to?** Very often, the challenges we face are caused by being in service to a lesser purpose. So, the next step in making your offering is to get clear on what you're in service to as an artist at the very highest or deepest levels. Ask the Mystery the following: *What vision of the world does my heart most desire? What secret desires do I have for my artistic life?*

- **Wait for an answer.** Staying in touch with the experience of the Mystery, focus on the questions above, one at a time, and with genuine curiosity. Then, just wait for any answers to arise. Answers can come in all sorts of forms, from sensations, thoughts, memories, inner words, emotions, images, or bodily movements. Be patient. You may not get an answer right away, and if not, you might check to see if you have any hidden agendas or if you've formulated your question properly. You'll know you have a proper answer when you get an "aha!" moment and there's a truth response in your body (usually some kind of muscular release, emotional response, or deep breath). Examples of answers might include: "I want to be able to pour my heart out in front of a rapt audience," "I want to create a more loving and beautiful world through my art," or "I just want to be me!"

- **What are you willing to sacrifice?** To make space for new possibilities in your life, you need to make a sacrifice of some kind, one that will help you move closer to what you're in service to. Here's a basic question you could ask yourself: *What do I need (or need to sacrifice) for [the problem] to be healed/resolved?* For example, "What do I need to sacrifice to feel more at ease and confident on stage?" or "What do I need to let go of to make space for better paying gigs in my life?" Make sure the question truly lands at an emotional level for you, and that what comes up is something you're genuinely ready to let go of, and not something your inner critic thinks you should let go of.

- **Take action.** Thank the Mystery for any answers that have arisen so far. Then, ask the Mystery for an idea for a small, easy-to-achieve action step related to the answers you just received. Again, stay in touch with the Mystery and simply wait for an idea to arise. You could ask, for example: "What's one small step I can take today (or this week) to nurture my inner child?" or "What's one small step I can take today (or this week) to show myself I am worth getting the kinds of gigs I'd really love to play?"

- **Make the offering and stay open to receive any return gifts.** When an action step arises that feels doable and is related to your initial question, then thank the Mystery again and make an agreement with yourself to complete the action step at a specific time. For example: "I will spend five minutes right now simply noticing the feeling of my inner child inside my body," or "I will talk with my friend about my ideal gigs tomorrow when we meet for lunch." When you do this action step, keep in mind that you're making an offering to something you care about, and stay open for any return gifts that may come. Return gifts might come immediately or some time from now, in an obvious way or in a more diffuse way. They might come in the form of "aha!" moments, emotional or muscular releases, or even synchronicities (strange coincidences that seem connected to your initial question). Just stay open to receive what comes.

THE GIFT OF ARTISTIC MASTERY

"My concern is for the gift we long for, the gift that, when it comes, speaks commandingly to the soul and irresistibly moves us."

— LEWIS HYDE, *THE GIFT*

One of the biggest advantages of stepping into the Spirit of the Gift is the way it re-enchants the journey to artistic mastery. All too often, the approach to mastery is characterized by either self-denial and slogging through, or the deconstruction of the idea of mastery altogether. Both these approaches disenchant the creative process and block access to Soulforce.

To re-enchant the creative process and craft your unique approach to artistic mastery, you need to take account of what each of these more familiar approaches ignore: that the learning process takes place as a sequence of gifts.

Imagine coming to your art and trying something you've been practicing recently and finding that you can do it better than you ever have in any previous practice session. Where did that extra bit of improvement and skill come from? Think about it—as you're practicing, you discover that you have new and unexpected capabilities. You have never done this thing so well and now you're nailing what has previously been shaky. How does that happen?

The merely mechanical model of "practice it enough times perfectly and then you'll perform it perfectly" simply doesn't explain this extra bit of skill and ability. After all, if you program a machine to do activity X, it will just do X until it breaks—it doesn't get better! In contrast, you, having practiced something imperfectly many times previously, do get better. Where does that improvement come from? If, as we've seen, it doesn't come solely from the toil of your individual self, then it must be a gift that comes back to you from the mysterious source of creativity. If you pay close attention to this process, it begins to feel a lot like magic.

SOULFORCE INQUIRY 8.6
LEARNING IS A GIFT

> The process of developing a skill benefits greatly from regarding your progress as a series of gifts. The following is an exploration that will guide you through the five steps of the creative process so that you can have an embodied experience of the Spirit of the Gift as you learn something.

Chapter 8 | THE SPIRIT OF THE GIFT

Get ready to learn something related to your art form, for example honing a new technique. Before you begin, take a moment to reflect on what you're in service to as you practice this technique—for example, beauty, life, authenticity, or other aspects of your artistic purpose. Spend a moment dedicating your practice session to this higher purpose.

Proceed with one small step in the technique, and then pause. Notice how it went. Did you succeed or fail? Did your body get tighter or freer? Did your sense of space get smaller or bigger? What emotions came up?

Repeat this several times, receiving the outcome of what you're doing as a return gift from the mysterious source of creativity. Don't try to force the outcome; just keep in mind your overall purpose or values and notice what comes up each time. If you begin to get tired, take a break by lying down, going outside, or taking a walk. Only come back to your practice when you feel refreshed. Are there any improvements that occur after the break?

As you continue to practice, ask yourself what phase of the creative process you might be in, and do your best to give it the time and attention it deserves.

Then, answer these questions in your journal:

- Overall, what difference did this approach make to your process of learning?
- Did it feel familiar or unfamiliar?
- Were you still able to learn what you needed to?
- What happened in your body, mind, and soul because of this approach?

As you experiment with relating to your creative practices as gifts, you may notice that a new sense of play, wonder, and surprise emerges.

Things that seemed mundane or boring suddenly take on a new life. You may even find yourself being surprised by what happens in your practice sessions, rather than being bored by the same old, same old.

A sense of surprise and wonder is vital to transmitting your Soulforce when you create. As we've previously explored, there exists an immediate, visceral connection between you and your audiences, such that what you feel during the creative act will be transmitted to and felt by your audiences. So, when you view the creative act as a gift, and are subsequently surprised and delighted by what comes up as a result, your audiences will be surprised and delighted by what you're creating, too. This sets up the perfect conditions for moments of truth to occur.

Here's another real-life story of the Spirit of the Gift in the creative act. Jane is a professional violinist and violin teacher who, among other reasons, came to see me about her intense performance anxiety. During one of our lessons, she told me that while she was totally at ease playing violin for herself and her students, as soon as she even thought about going on stage her body tightened up, her heart started racing, and she felt intense anxiety in her gut. She was now getting tired of how stressful her performances had become.

Experience told me that performance anxiety is a sign of being in service to a lesser purpose, so I knew that our first step was to discover what that was. I asked her, "What would you have to let go of to feel more at ease up on stage?"

Jane thought for a moment and then replied, "I want their approval. When I'm performing, I want the audience to like me. I'm terrified of making a mistake and then looking bad."

I then said, "Ah! It sounds like there's something big at stake here for you. Is it possible that your performances are currently being made on the altar of protecting your self-worth? If you believe that making mistakes will put your self-worth in jeopardy, then of course you're going to feel afraid up on stage." Jane took this in for a moment, and then I went on.

"Now, is avoiding shame and judgment the point of music? Is that the real reason you play the violin? If not, is there something bigger you're in service to? Something that would make getting up in front of people worth all the trouble?" After another pause, Jane told me how she thought that music is a form of medicine, and that she loved the idea of her music healing her audiences.

I replied, "That's beautiful. What if you were to make 'music as medicine' your primary purpose in playing, and make the first recipient of that medicine the part of you that's scared to play in front of others? Altering your purpose this way will help you feel less afraid."

During our next lesson, I inquired if this shift in her purpose had brought any return gifts. Jane told me about a performance where she made an offering of her fear and thought of her music as a gift of medicine to her audience. She reported that, while it didn't make her performance anxiety completely disappear, it made enough of a difference for her so that she began to feel at ease and have fun again on stage.

THE MUD AND THE LOTUS

> *"You never change things by fighting the existing reality. To change something, build a new model that makes the existing model obsolete."*
>
> — BUCKMINSTER FULLER, ARCHITECT AND FUTURIST

Just as with the Yoga of Art, the Spirit of the Gift can raise certain concerns and objections for some. You might ask, "What if it doesn't work? What if I don't get the creative inspiration I want and need?"

Firstly, it's important to remember that the point of the Spirit of the Gift isn't to force the mysterious source of creativity to give you something. Rather, it's about establishing a relationship with this source. Just like in any relationship, seeing it flourish takes time and the proper attitude. If you're not used to relating with the source of creativity in this way, it may take some time for its creative energy to begin to flow. Treat the process like you would in befriending a wild animal; honor its needs as much as your own.

Ultimately, it's not a problem when things don't seem to go well. Even when you try the practices in this chapter and you don't get answers right away, or you don't get the answers that some part of you secretly wants, or you get answers that don't even make sense, it's not a problem. It's all just part of the process. If the practices in this chapter don't work right away for you and you feel worried, ask yourself where that worry is coming from. You might discover that it's coming from an attempt to fit yourself into other people's expectations or the demands of our machine-like economy and educational system.

Of course, meeting the demands of others and the machine we live in is sometimes necessary for your survival, and when this is the case, experiment with letting these concerns be part of what you bring to the Mystery. After all, it won't do to try to ignore the practical and often trying circumstances that you and so many others face daily. The good news is that the Mystery, an inherent part of who you are, is the primordial source of creativity itself. When you make the proper offerings, it may bestow upon you unexpected new ideas for progress through challenging times. Almost invariably, the power that these new ideas have will help you achieve the limited goals of the machine even better than before. But it's vital to remember that that's not their true purpose; their true purpose is to serve life and create a more beautiful world.

The truth is that any such ideas, and any art based on such ideas, are pure gold because the answer to the survival pressures of the machine we live in are not to be found in the same kind of thinking that now feeds the machine. What's needed, just as Buckminster Fuller said, is to find new ways of thriving and flourishing that make the machine obsolete. Just like how a lotus can only grow in muck and mud, you will only find such answers by standing in a deeper truth as you fully face your current challenges. This, of course, is the essence of Soulforce.

Chapter 8 | THE SPIRIT OF THE GIFT

A MEDICINE FOR OUR TIMES

"And still, after all this time, the sun never says to the earth, 'You owe Me.' Look at what happens with a love like that—it lights the whole sky."

— HAFIZ OF SHIRAZ, FOURTEENTH-CENTURY SUFI POET

This book was written to help guide artists from an old story of the world into a new one. The old story, as we've seen, is largely responsible for the sense that something vital is missing from our mainstream ways of creating, performing, teaching, learning, and making a living as an artist. Even though being an artist in such conditions can sometimes be painful, in the end, such pain can be a gift, too, in that it may spur you to find a more life-giving way of being.

The search for a new way of being can often feel lonely because few of the conventional resources available to us are adequate to help us in the growth process necessary for the full resolution of our challenges. However, even the most hopeless and futile search is only seemingly so. Once you inhabit the new story, it becomes obvious that the search was itself an offering whose very hopelessness invited in the help that was needed.

The Spirit of the Gift is a vital part of this new story in that it serves as an induction into the experience of a living universe. For example, when you view your every creative act as a gift, you will begin to feel that the universe is alive and responsive to your thoughts, feelings, and actions, and that your creative energy comes from a bigger, deeper source than you've previously known. Not only will this experience help you feel and create better, but by making art in this way, you also invite your audiences into the experience of a living universe. Indeed, such art—whatever the form, whether seen by many or by few, whether appreciated or reviled, whether lucrative or profitless—may be the most important medicine we, as artists, can offer for the ills of our times.

Discovering your artistic purpose, Playing from the Heart, the Yoga of Art, and the Spirit of the Gift form the heart and soul of the Soulforce Arts Approach. Now that you are familiar with them and have hopefully begun implementing them into your artistic life, we enter Section III to explore how more holistic values can benefit your life, art, and the world around you.

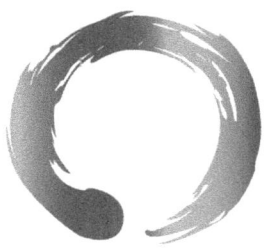

MIND-BODY INTERLUDE #4

THE THING MODE AND THE BEING MODE

"The Church says: the body is a sin.
Science says: the body is a machine.
Advertising says: the body is a business.
The Body says: I am a fiesta!"

— EDUARDO GALEANO, JOURNALIST

The Stories of Separation and Interbeing give rise to modes of operating that profoundly shape how you create, feel, function, and impact your world. In the Story of Separation, you regard yourself, your art, and the world around you as things to be manipulated. In the Story of Interbeing, you regard yourself, your art, and the world around you as beings to be honored. Each has predictable consequences on your well-being, the quality of your art, and the system update your art carries.

When you regard yourself and your world as a thing to be manipulated, life becomes a dreary slog. Your body becomes tight, your creativity dries up, you feel anxious and frustrated, and you may even wonder if your resultant creations matter. On the other hand, when you regard yourself, your art, and your world as beings to be honored, life becomes a fiesta. Your body relaxes, your creative juices flow, you feel able to meet life's challenges with a sense of the basic goodness of all things, and you feel free to create what matters most to you.

In a sense, shifting from the Thing Mode to the Being Mode is the fundamental answer to the challenges raised in this book. The Being Mode is a smoothly paved road to your artistic purpose, well-being, and the creation of art with Soulforce. You can travel easily down this road at any time and in any activity. Explore what it's like to pick up your paintbrush, talk with your student, or receive money for your art while in Being Mode. How does this change how you feel and the outcome of your activities? The great benefit of Being Mode is that it releases you from the toil associated with the lesser gods and organically brings forth the life-giving qualities inherent to the greatest art. Use the following experiment to become acquainted with the Being Mode and to learn to shift into it when desired.

THE THING MODE AND THE BEING MODE

While inhabiting the Thing Mode, bring your hands up in front of your chest with palms facing one another. Tap the tips of your thumbs together, then your forefingers, and then your other fingers in turn. Tap in this sequence, back and forth, several times while regarding your hands as things to be manipulated.

What do you notice? Did your body get tighter or freer? Did you have more fun or less? Did your sense of space get bigger or smaller? Did you experience the movements as more fluid or disjointed?

Now do the same movement, this time inhabiting the Being Mode. Tap the finger sequence again while regarding your hands as beings to be honored.

What do you notice this time? Did your body get tighter or freer? Did you have more fun or less? Did your sense of space get bigger or smaller? Did you experience the movements as more fluid or disjointed?

Experiment with the Being Mode whenever possible in your daily activities, relationships, and creative time. How does it change your experience of yourself in the creative act? How does it inform your artistic purpose? How does it change the quality of your art? Simply make note of what happens and enjoy the Soulforce that results.

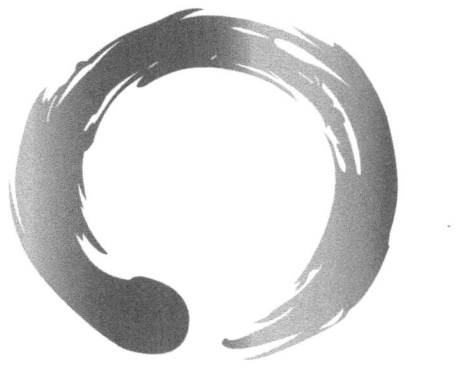

SECTION III

EVOLUTION

"The role of the artist is exactly the same as the role of the lover. If I love you, I have to make you conscious of the things you don't see."

— JAMES BALDWIN, *CONVERSATIONS WITH JAMES BALDWIN (1961 TO 1988)*

CHAPTER 9

SPIRAL DYNAMICS AND THE ARTS

As a young boy, I often struggled to make sense of the world and my place within it. There were simply so many perspectives on life, art, relationships, and everything else. What made this so confusing and difficult was that the people in my life from whom I sought guidance—parents, teachers, friends, favorite authors, political figures, and others—spoke so compellingly and with great confidence, as though they held the one truth about what was most important in life. The trouble was that, despite their confidence, the perspectives they espoused often contradicted what others said, and so were a source of conflict. Inhabiting this complex and confusing landscape, I sometimes felt like a helpless billiard ball, bouncing from one perspective to another as I sought to make sense of it all.

One example of this confusion came from my artistic training. What did it mean to be a good artist? Did it mean doing what my parents and teachers said or relying more on my own judgment? Did it mean looking good in the eyes of my peers or expressing my authentic self, regardless of what others thought? Did it mean trying hard to achieve milestones or learning to relax and go with the flow? Did it mean making lots of money as an artist or eschewing money matters to pursue artistic purity? Where was I to land among these varying perspectives? Which was the *right* one?

Answers finally came when, as a young adult, I began to read works by authors like Ken Wilber, Don Beck, and Robert Kegan. These are researchers and theorists in the fields of developmental psychology, human potential, Spiral Dynamics, and Integral Theory. What they, along with other innovators, offered was a "Theory of Everything," a map of human growth and potential that gave a unified account of the multiplicity of perspectives that now crowd our globalized information landscape.

This Theory of Everything maps all aspects of human experience as well as all the ways humans can grow. It states that all phenomena have subjective and objective, as well as individual and collective, characteristics. It reveals the multiple lines of development that we can grow along and shows the complex relationships among those lines. Understanding this Theory of Everything provides the means to placing yourself on the map of human potential, and stimulates the growth needed to reach that potential. Learning this Theory of Everything initiated a moment of truth for me. It gave meaning, context, and direction to situations I previously found perplexing. The essence of this theory is that every perspective has its grain of truth, but it's only partial. In addition, there exists a developmental sequence to human thought and culture that has a place for every perspective, value, and creation we encounter. I felt empowered by this theory because it helped me make sense of our societal conflicts and artistic challenges and provided tangible solutions that were previously hidden from view.

Coming back to my previous example, this theory provided a larger context in which I could better make sense of what it means to be a good artist. Instead of being faced with a miasma of competing values and goals, the Theory of Everything I learned revealed an orderly sequence that honored each of the perspectives on offer. For example, for someone just starting out, being a good artist means learning certain rules and roles handed down from authority figures and tradition.

Chapter 9 | SPIRAL DYNAMICS AND THE ARTS

When those rules and roles are mastered, good artistry then comes to mean going beyond obedience to include achievements and gaining acceptance from peers. When such achievements lose their luster, good artistry then comes to mean questioning traditions, finding flow, and creating through authentic self-expression. Then, when even self-expression seems too limiting, being a good artist comes to mean combining the best of all the previous stages for a deeper, more nuanced, and mature approach. In other words, being and becoming a good artist involves not reaching a fixed end point, but rather a process of development that spirals to include wider and deeper skills and perspectives.

Integrating this theory transformed my life. As an artist, I was better able to understand why certain approaches to mastery worked, or didn't, and why. As a teacher, I was better able to understand how to appropriately shape what I taught to match my students' perspectives. As a worker, I was better able to understand how to avoid the pitfalls of our extractive economic system and make a living in the arts aligned with my values. As a citizen of the world, I was better able to understand our current societal divisions and what I could do to heal them.

In every situation, I navigated previously confounding challenges through adopting a wider, more holistic, and capable set of values. Combined with the soulfulness I developed through practices like Playing from the Heart, these more holistic values enabled me to truly become a Soulforce artist, one who can navigate our complex cultural landscape with ease and who can translate the lessons learned along the way into the most transformative art.

In this and the following chapter, you will learn about Spiral Dynamics, which is one component of the Theory of Everything I found so helpful. You will learn what Spiral Dynamics is, what it means for your life as an artist, and how to put its lessons into practice to make uniquely transformative art. You will learn how it helps you fulfill your artistic purpose and create more freely and skillfully. In addition, you will learn how Spiral Dynamics helps you create art that, as James Baldwin noted, makes your audiences conscious of the things they don't yet see, and which therefore matters to how we navigate our world's current tumult and transitions.

We begin with one of the areas of greatest need and greatest confusion for many artists and our society at large: the crisis of meaninglessness that now threatens to undermine our art and rip our world apart.

ART AND THE MEANINGLESSNESS CRISIS

> *"[Postmodernism] deconstructs every single truth and value you find .... which rapidly leads to nihilism and ... narcissism."*
>
> — KEN WILBER, *TRUMP AND A POST-TRUTH WORLD*

In a sense, the greatest challenge of our times is not climate change, political strife, or inequality. The rancor and polarization around these and other issues belies the fact that effective solutions do already exist and could be implemented immediately. What keeps us from doing so is not a lack of solutions, but a lack of coherence and cooperation. It's like we're all on a big rowboat together out in the middle of a stormy ocean, and instead of rowing together toward a safe harbor—any harbor—we're spending all our time and energy arguing and whacking each other with the oars.

What underlies this lack of cooperation is not so much that different people have different perspectives; this will always be the case among humans. Rather, the issue is that, possibly more than any other time in history, the predominant culture actively denies that truth, meaning, and purpose can, in principle, exist. This denial is founded on the two most dominant worldviews of our contemporary era: modernism and postmodernism.

Modernism's contribution to this denial rests on its embrace of scientific materialism, a facet of the Story of Separation. In essence, modernism says that the universe is inherently without meaning and that it's our job to impose order on its inherent randomness. Postmodernism also denies truth, meaning, and purpose, but for different reasons. It says that all truths are merely social constructions, and that anything that purports to be good, true, or beautiful is, at root, merely a cynical ploy to gain power.

The result of this one-two punch to truth, meaning, and purpose is the meaninglessness crisis. The **meaninglessness crisis** is a cultural fragmentation that results from the denial of truth, meaning, and purpose. It is the fragmentation of the story of who we believe we are and what we're here to do, and it leads to a pervasive existential dread, anxiety, and despair. The fruits of the meaninglessness crisis are plain to see all around us. It's what underlies the narcissism and nihilism that eat at our souls. It's why we're destroying the earth and fighting senseless wars. It's what's behind the alarming rise of the diseases of despair, including substance abuse, alcohol dependency, and suicide.[1] It's also why we have such a hard time not just agreeing on what effective solutions to our collective challenges look like, but whether these challenges actually exist in the first place.

Navigating the crowded landscape of competing truths is one of the great challenges of our times. Doing so effectively is central to surviving and thriving in the coming decades. However, rather than face this complexity with humility and openness, many instead choose to either cling to outmoded ways of being handed down from authorities or to cynically claim that all truths are power grabs in disguise. Neither approach satisfies.

Many of the outmoded ways of being are themselves the root cause of our problems, in that when we deny truth, meaning, and purpose, chaos reigns. Without humility and openness about our favored approach, those who disagree with us lose trust in our ability to include them in our vision of the world. The result is a culture of mistrust, conflict, othering, and epistemological overwhelm that leads many to throw up their hands and deny that finding a collective way forward is even possible. This is the meaninglessness crisis in action.

> The **meaninglessness crisis** is a cultural fragmentation that results from the denial that truth, meaning, and purpose can, in principle, exist.

The meaninglessness crisis driving our global challenges exists in the arts as well—and much to their detriment. Since about 1950, the leading edge of arts and culture has been postmodernism, whose central project is to dismantle nearly everything that came before.[2] This project started from a healthy impulse: the strictures of traditionalism and the emptiness of modernist ideas of progress were no longer serving the arts and society.

However, there are signs that this project, which now dominates arts institutions of all kinds, has since outlived its usefulness. Instead of leading us out of confusion and fragmentation, postmodernism seems now to only generate more. For example, once you've deconstructed every artistic technique, idea, and movement—even the notion of beauty itself—what is there left to create? If you believe, as many postmodern artists do, that technique and beauty are culturally constructed artifacts of an oppressive power hierarchy, where does that leave your authentic creative impulses?

These are not merely philosophical questions—they have profound implications for artists, audiences, and society. For example, many postmodern composers of music believe that to create pleasant-sounding harmonies and melodies is hopelessly naïve. Instead, serious music consists mainly of pitilessly dissonant strains. Similarly, postmodern visual artists believe that beautiful, coherent images are a relic of the past, and that a urinal or a haphazardly painted canvas has just as much artistic value as a Renoir or Michelangelo.[3]

While there is, of course, a place for questioning traditions and morays, the postmodern approach also has critical limitations. The main limitation is that, for an artist who totally embraces postmodernism, beauty, technique, and authenticity are essentially off the table, and so all that's left to do is to ironically critique their own attempts at creation. Ultimately, this is a situation that leaves such artists feeling unsatisfied and without a meaningful artistic purpose.

Audiences share this sense of dissatisfaction because art that deconstructs the very act of creation in this way has all the resonance of a cracked bell. For example, one result of postmodern dissonance in classical music is that many ordinary audience members no longer connect with classical music at all, which must, in part, explain declining attendance in concert halls.[4] Similarly, a common experience among contemporary art museum goers is not of awe, inspiration, and connection, but of bafflement, confusion, and disdain. Because of this, many audiences are now tired of the relentless irony, superficiality, cynicism, and narcissism that has come to characterize so much of the contemporary art on display. We long for something that speaks to our souls and brings us alive, and this is something that much postmodern art fails to accomplish.

At a larger level, what this failure suggests is that, far from continuing to fulfill its role in advancing the arts and helping our society grow and evolve, the postmodern movement is now holding us back. It's contributing to the meaninglessness crisis rather than resolving it. What our society actually needs from us now, as artists, is for us to grow past postmodernism and create art from a more mature and evolved way of being.

For us as artists, this more evolved way of being will allow us to enjoy a more authentic, soulful, and purposeful mode of creating. Our own evolution will be reflected in our art, which will then resonate more deeply with our audiences, initiating needed moments of truth and healing. Importantly, it is only art created from this more evolved way of being that can inspire society to grow out of the chaotic meaninglessness crisis and into something more beautiful and life-giving.

The question for us, as artists, is thus, "How do we help ourselves and others grow into this more evolved way of being? In what ways can we do this through our art?"

THE CONSCIOUSNESS ESCALATOR

> "It is often said that in today's modern and postmodern world that the forces of darkness are upon us. But I think not; in the Dark and the Deep there are truths that can always heal ... It is an exuberant and fearless shallowness that everywhere is the modern danger, the modern threat, and that everywhere nonetheless calls to us as savior."
>
> —KEN WILBER, *SEX, ECOLOGY, SPIRITUALITY*

The key to resolving the meaninglessness crisis lies in recognizing that the perspectives that largely gave rise to it—modernism and postmodernism—are themselves but individual stages in the ongoing development of human consciousness. In other words, there are stages that came before these, and there are stages that will come after. So, even though a modernist or postmodernist may, themselves, feel like the perspectives of their own stage carry some kind of ultimate truth, they are not the end-all-be-all.

The deeper truth here is that human consciousness has a developmental trajectory, and when you recognize that trajectory, you will no longer be caught in the limitations of any particular stage of development. The limitation of the modern and postmodern worldviews is that their logical endpoint leads to nihilism and despair. However, when you recognize that these worldviews are only steps on the escalator, you needn't take such nihilism so seriously. Instead, you trust that further personal development is possible and, as a result, life suddenly feels full of promise. You feel that there's somewhere truly worthwhile to move toward, and you're motivated to play a role in that movement.

Chapter 9 | SPIRAL DYNAMICS AND THE ARTS

This is the essence of **Holistic Values Development**, which, as we touched on in Chapter 4, comprises the growth of consciousness toward greater personal and societal maturity, evolution, sophistication, competence, and inclusivity. When your consciousness grows in this way, what is actually expanding is what you are conscious *of*. You become aware of a greater variety of phenomena in yourself and in the world at large, you expand your tolerance for complexity and nuance, and you increase the size of your sphere of concern by moving, for example, from egocentric to ethnocentric to world-centric stages of development, or even beyond.[5]

The growth of consciousness involves becoming aware of an ever-expanding sphere of concern, from an egocentric level involving concern only for the individual self, all the way up to—potentially—a holistic or cosmocentric level involving concern for all beings that may exist in the entire universe.

> **Holistic Values Development** comprises the growth of consciousness toward greater personal and societal maturity, evolution, sophistication, competence, and inclusivity.

At a societal level, Holistic Values Development is absolutely vital because so many of the challenges humanity now faces are all caused by clinging to outdated, immature, and narrow-minded ways of being. Specifically, what lies at the root of so many of our collective challenges is that what matters to most people doesn't even include all of humanity (a sociocentric stage), much less all of life on earth (a planet-centric stage). Why is this so important? People only care *for* the things they care *about*, and they only care *about* the things they are aware *of*.

This, for instance, explains what's behind the alarming degradation of the topsoil in our agricultural lands, whose robust health is utterly necessary for our survival. The farmers and policymakers who engage in soil-destroying practices are simply not aware that the topsoil is part of their larger body, and that its health is therefore of primary importance for life on earth. If they were aware of this, they would naturally seek out different farming practices because they would have a visceral sense that the soil is just as much a part of their beingness as are their own arms and legs. Thus, the destruction of our topsoil is not necessarily the effect of ill-intentioned individuals, but rather may be the natural result of not being fully aware of our interconnectedness with the earth and each other.

The fundamental solution, then, to a challenge like this is for enough individuals to decide to grow into a stage of development that includes a felt awareness of the value of all life on earth (planet-centric/post-postmodern/Integral).[6] When this happens, more and more of the decisions that impact life on earth will come from this more expansive awareness, and this will naturally result in choices that lead to greater harmony, truth, love, freedom, conscious evolution, and reverence for life.

A similar shift is possible for the arts world. Some of what gets in the way of our most fulfilling and masterful expressions of the human spirit—the strictures of traditional arts pedagogy, the emptiness and stress of the modern achievement orientation, and the nihilism of postmodern deconstructive modes of artistry—are all artifacts of the limitations of certain stages of human consciousness. The answer to each of these limitations, no matter what stage they come from, is the same: yet more growth in consciousness.

For example, the answer to strict traditionalism is the modernist freedom to explore and innovate. The answer to the emptiness and stress of modernity's overemphasis on achievement is the postmodern return to feeling and care. Similarly, the answer to postmodernity's nihilism is to see yourself, and your art, as a participant in the ongoing evolution of life and consciousness. No stage has the ultimate answers; every stage has its limitations, and the answer to those limitations is to keep growing.

Chapter 9 | SPIRAL DYNAMICS AND THE ARTS

Your direct, intentional, and ongoing participation in this evolution is utterly essential to the fulfillment of your role as an artist in creating a more beautiful world. When you evolve and grow as an individual, your own evolution will inevitably find expression in your art, which, in turn, will then transmit a system update to your audiences. Art that transmits such a system update can act as a kind of consciousness escalator, lifting others into the more evolved stages of consciousness that our society so desperately needs right now.

> When you evolve and grow as an individual, your evolution will inevitably find expression in your art, which, in turn, will then transmit a system update to your audiences.

To create the kind of art that answers the meaninglessness crisis, you must initiate your own growth and evolution as an individual. One of the very best means for inspiring such growth is Spiral Dynamics.

AN INTRODUCTION TO SPIRAL DYNAMICS

"Briefly, what I am proposing is that the psychology of the mature human being is an unfolding, emergent, oscillating, spiraling process marked by progressive subordination of older, lower-order behavior systems to newer, higher-order systems as man's existential problems change."

— CLARE GRAVES, PROFESSOR OF PSYCHOLOGY

Spiral Dynamics is a science-based model of human growth and development that comes from the world of developmental psychology and describes the various stages of evolution that humans go through both individually and collectively. It explains how the growth of consciousness affects all areas of life, including the arts. First developed by Dr. Clare Graves in the 1960s, it shows that each stage of development is characterized by a unique worldview or values system, one that builds on—but is no longer limited to—the previous stages of development.

While the developmental stages that children go through are widely understood, Spiral Dynamics tells us that there are stages of development that continue well into adulthood. In addition to reflecting individual development, these stages also describe societal evolution.

Here are the stages of Spiral Dynamics along with their core values, from least to most evolved.

- **Purple.** *Feeling at home, safety, ritual*
- **Red.** *Power, control, impulse*
- **Blue.** *Order, rules, traditions*
- **Orange.** *Achievement, success, strategy*
- **Green.** *Group focus, ideals, social connection*
- **Yellow.** *Visionary, systems thinking, synergy*
- **Turquoise.** *Holistic, wholeism, cosmic/collective consciousness*

Each subsequent stage is characterized by greater capabilities and a larger and more inclusive sphere of concern. Spiral Dynamics is a particularly powerful model of human development because it explains the ways people can understand or misunderstand each other; it allows insight into the ways in which we might be getting stuck; and it tells us the directions in which we are likely to grow. Each stage is indicated by a color (Purple, Red, Blue, Orange, etc.), which the developers of Spiral Dynamics picked somewhat arbitrarily, and which have no unique meaning in and of themselves.[7]

> **Spiral Dynamics** is a science-based model of human growth and development that comes from the world of developmental psychology and describes the various stages of evolution that humans go through both individually and collectively.

Chapter 9 | SPIRAL DYNAMICS AND THE ARTS

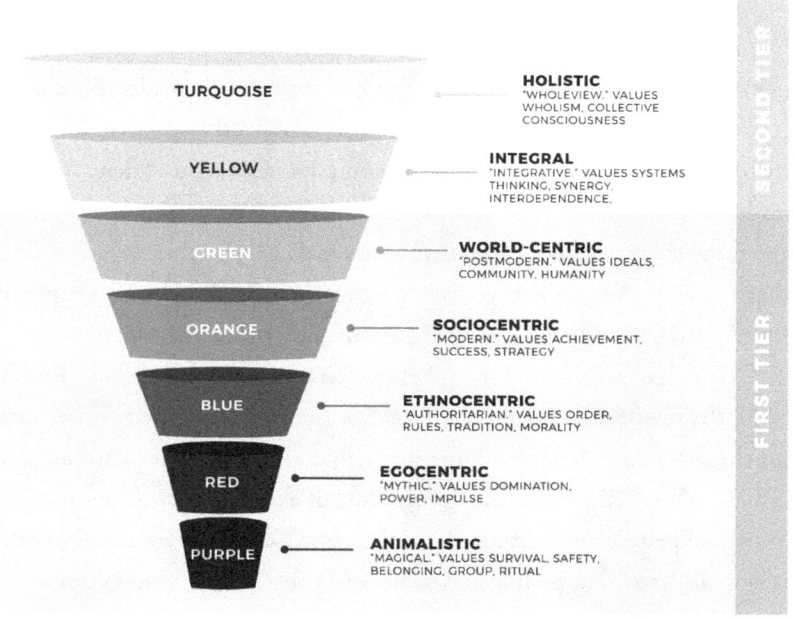

As you read about each stage, keep in mind that all stages are necessary to healthy development. To try to bypass or downplay certain stages will only lead to disaster; after all, a strong, healthy tree trunk is necessary for strong, healthy branches and leaves. The sequence of stages, then, has a clear chronological order: the stages further down the spiral are those that emerge earliest in a person's or society's life, and those that are further up the spiral are those that can only emerge later in life.

No stage, once embodied, is ever left behind. For example, a healthy person at Spiral Dynamics stage Orange will also have healthy Blue, Red, and Purple characteristics. Integral philosopher Ken Wilber famously described this dynamic with the phrase "transcend and include."[8] What he meant was that each stage builds on the last, but is no longer limited to it, just as running includes the bipedal motion of walking, but goes beyond it with greater speed.

This is especially important to keep in mind because all the Spiral Dynamics stages prior to Yellow and Turquoise tend to deny the validity of all the other stages. For example, people at the traditionalist Blue stage tend not to be able to understand the more advanced impulse to inclusivity of postmodern Green. Likewise, people at Green tend to deny that the traditional values or institutions encouraged by Blue could possibly have any more value. Indeed, Spiral Dynamics makes it possible to understand that much of the conflict we see in the world today is because people in Purple, Red, Blue, Orange, and Green just don't get each other.

This all changes with stage Yellow. Graves considered stage Yellow to be the beginning of a "second tier" of human consciousness because it's the first stage to fully acknowledge that all other stages have unique gifts to offer. Yellow sees things in terms of evolutionary development. While all people and societies have the same foundational moral worth, it's equally true that people and societies evolve and gain new complexity and competency over time. For example, someone in this second tier of consciousness may acknowledge the value of Blue's institutions while realizing that such institutions also need to be open to change to meet the needs of contemporary life.

Such a recognition grants Yellow and other second tier stages a power and capability unique among all the other stages. By accepting the evolutionary necessity of all the previous stages, Yellow gains access to the benefits of each of the previous stages while avoiding many of their pitfalls. This ability allows someone at stage Yellow a far greater sense of well-being, creativity, functionality, competence, self-actualization, and vision than is otherwise possible. This is why Graves called stage Yellow "a momentous leap" in human consciousness.[9] An excellent example of Yellow thinking itself, the Spiral Dynamics model is also a tool that you can use to grow into stage Yellow and beyond.

Chapter 9 | SPIRAL DYNAMICS AND THE ARTS

COMMON MISCONCEPTIONS

"I have one major rule: Everybody is right. More specifically, everybody ... has some important pieces of truth, and all of those pieces need to be honored, cherished, and included in a more gracious, spacious, and compassionate embrace."

— KEN WILBER, *COLLECTED WORKS OF KEN WILBER*

When first learning about Spiral Dynamics, many people have certain misconceptions about what this model implies. So, before diving into the following Spiral Dynamics analysis of the arts, let's first address these misconceptions.

What are these stages and what are they not? The stages describe commonalities among values sets; they are useful abstractions, cultural memes discovered through a rigorous scientific process. The stages do not—and cannot—describe the totality of any person or society. They are generalizations of psychological data and are not meant, in any way, to pigeonhole, demean, disempower, or categorize people. As a study, Spiral Dynamics is firmly grounded in the reality that people and societies are living beings whose value and essence can never be reduced to numbers, colors, or concepts.

One of the most common objections to developmental models like Spiral Dynamics is that, historically speaking, notions of progress or hierarchy have been used to destroy our environment and oppress marginalized peoples. The concern is that since Spiral Dynamics seems to have a hierarchical structure, it too may be used to justify destruction and oppression—but this is not the case.

The fear that a model like Spiral Dynamics may be used to oppress others misses three critical insights. The first and most important is that hidden behind this fear is yet another hierarchy: that of preferring non-hierarchy over hierarchy. More than a philosophical quibble, it's vital to take account of this hidden contradiction to end some of the most intractable confusions of our current culture wars. As a societal trend, a hatred of hierarchy, combined with a secret wish to impose non-hierarchical values on others, leads to the contradiction of intolerance in the name of tolerance. For example, when those who espouse inclusivity then cancel those with different opinions, their actions come from an unconscious hierarchy of inclusion over exclusion whose unintended result is oppression in the name of inclusion. As an artistic trend, a hatred of hierarchy also leads to the confusion between artists who are truly skilled and those who merely believe themselves to be so. For example, in some artistic circles, skill is regarded solely as a manifestation of oppressive power structures. In this view, skill itself becomes associated with oppression, such that those artists who eschew skill are regarded, paradoxically, as the most skillful. These are clearly cultural and philosophical dead-ends.

The second insight is that, while harm has, indeed, been done in the name of progress and hierarchy, forms of hierarchy and progression are foundational to life and reality as we know it. One hierarchy in nature is that of the great chain of being, which describes the structure of reality from atoms to molecules to organisms to ecosystems and beyond. Within this chain, despite its apparent hierarchy, no link oppresses any of the others; they all work synergistically to constitute reality as we know it.

The third insight is that progress is also a feature of nature and poses no inherent threat. For example, it is the very progress of human thought over the ages that allows us the perspective necessary to be concerned about oppression in the first place. Indeed, without the very considerable societal and philosophical progress our ancestors made—as imperfect as it was at times—our own survival conditions would still be so difficult that we wouldn't be able to enjoy the luxury of caring for others. (To wit, the very fact that you're reading this book in particular is a result of that progress!) The deeper truth available here is that more growth up the spiral is synonymous with a movement toward greater sanity, healing, and care.

Thus, the real problem at hand is not that Spiral Dynamics might be used to oppress or dominate people at earlier stages. Rather, it's that collective problems are the result of trying to meet the demands of our increasingly complex world with outdated modes of being—modes that are expressions of earlier stages. Because of this, trying to prevent yourself or others from growing up the spiral is not an act of protecting potential victims from harm; it actually dooms humanity to repeat the destructive patterns that caused all the harm to begin with. The ultimate lesson of Spiral Dynamics is that what humanity, the planet, and the arts all need right now is a period of intense growth up the spiral. Nothing less will help us navigate our turbulent times.

> Many fear that the seemingly hierarchical nature of Spiral Dynamics will lead to oppression. The truth is that the oppression they fear is the result of people at earlier stages not having evolved enough.

Here are some final preliminary notes. Firstly, nobody is ever at just one stage of development. You may inhabit one stage or another at various times in a single day, and your overall developmental center of gravity will almost certainly evolve and change over your lifetime. In addition, healthy growth means including all previous stages of development as already mentioned. Each subsequent stage, while certainly exhibiting greater capacities, is not necessarily better than the previous stages. Each represents an appropriate fittedness to the surrounding environment that first gave rise to it.

Finally, the path to growth begins with acceptance of the reality of where you are, an acceptance that, paradoxically, requires the relinquishment of the fantasy of already inhabiting "higher" Spiral Dynamics stages. Keep in mind that your greatest and quickest growth must begin with a sober assessment of your current stage of development, and is best energized by the thoughts, emotions, and actions you take that gradually change the reality of your developmental stage over time.

GETTING THE MOST FROM THIS ANALYSIS

*"You cannot have exterior development without
the interior development to hold it in place."*

— KEN WILBER, *NO BOUNDARY*

Learning about Spiral Dynamics is not just an intellectual exercise. It is about upgrading your whole worldview, your sense of who you are, what you care about, how you think and feel, how you inhabit your world, and how you approach your artistic life. With this in mind, treat reading the following section as an embodied exercise.

Notice which stages you feel especially drawn to or repelled by and be curious what these reactions might mean. The stages you feel drawn to are likely your current stage and perhaps the stage you're growing into. The stages you feel repelled from are likely ones you've repressed or denied. You know you have fully integrated any stage when you are able to both appreciate its gifts and acknowledge its limitations. Remember, healthy growth means health at all levels, and none of these are "wrong" or "bad" any more than dinosaurs were "wrong" and more evolutionarily recent mammals are "right."

As you become more familiar with the stages and their characteristics, you may start to notice that they become an integral part of how you see yourself and the world. This is a good thing! It means that you've started to move into stage Yellow. So, in addition to noticing your reactions to the stages, you can support your movement into stage Yellow by noticing what kinds of people, ideas, or art that you feel drawn to or repelled by.

You will feel drawn to the people, ideas, or art that are near your own stage of development. You will know you're encountering something at a less developed stage than your own when it seems immature or crass. Similarly, you know you're encountering something at a higher level than your own when it seems too lofty or abstract. Your developmental "elevation" determines your perspective.

Here are some further questions to ponder while you read:

- Where do I see myself in this progression? What about my students or colleagues?
- Which stages have I most denied, ignored, or tried to repress?
- Which stages are most attractive?
- Which include areas of desired growth?
- Which stages have worked well for me in the past?
- In which stages am I strongest or weakest?

SOULFORCE INQUIRY 9.1
EMBODIED READING OF SPIRAL DYNAMICS STAGES

As you read through the following descriptions, notice all reactions that come up, especially your embodied response. What sensations, feelings, and emotions arise as you read each stage? Are there any memories, people, places, symbols, or other connections that appear? How do your feelings change as you continue from one stage to the next? What thoughts or judgments do you have about particular stages? Make note of your reactions in your journal while you read.

A SPIRAL DYNAMICS ANALYSIS OF THE ARTS

"[Egyptian art] was ... a continuous exercise in the development of individual consciousness."

— JOHN ANTHONY WEST, *SERPENT IN THE SKY*

The following analysis of each stage of Spiral Dynamics includes:

- The basics of each stage, including an overview of its worldview and sphere of concern, core values, motto, and percentage of world population at this stage
- The role of the arts in a society at that stage
- That stage's approach to the arts
- How the stage views mistakes and success
- A list of examples of art forms at that stage

Please keep in mind that my descriptions below are the result of my own research (and, in some cases, educated guesses), and are in no way meant to be taken as exhaustive or authoritative. While I have framed these descriptions in terms of the arts, be open to any connections that arise about how each stage applies to other areas of life and society. These basics are drawn from the works of Ken Wilber, Leo Gura, Susanne Cook-Greuter, the Stichting Center for Human Emergence the Netherlands, Don Beck, Clare Graves, and others.[10]

Also worth noting: my purpose in including the comments on mistakes and success is to address the deep-seated fears so many artists feel around making mistakes. Unfortunately, much artistic training, especially at the highest levels, focuses on mistakes to an extent that many musicians and dancers, for example, create with a chronic sense of anxiety. What many don't realize is the degree to which the way you react to mistakes is a function of your stage of development. In many cases, freedom from this anxiety can be found by growing into the later stages of development.

PURPLE — "MAGIC"

Core Values: Feeling at home, safety, ritual

Motto: "In the name of the clan and existential reality, I sacrifice myself."

BASICS OF PURPLE

Purple is all about safety, tradition, and belongingness. Its worldview is that the world is frightening and mysterious, that spirits must be placated, and people must join together to survive. Morally, Purple is collectivist, and its circle of concern is limited to its immediate family members within the group (about one hundred people). The individual self is not differentiated from the group. Purple is at its best in creating a safe environment, participating in social-emotional bonding, offering loyalty, and using intuition and imagination. Purple is at its worst in its fixed adherence to rules, closed-mindedness, insistence on clinging to the past, and "us vs. them" mentality. Purple first developed approximately fifty thousand years ago and currently comprises ten percent of the world's population.

THE ROLE OF THE ARTS IN PURPLE SOCIETIES

In Purple societies, there isn't an idea of the arts, as such. Instead, the arts are integral to every aspect of society, showing up in traditional crafts and folkways that give form to the built environment and religious needs. Everyone in the community considers themselves to be an artist or craftsmen in some way. In Purple, the role of the arts is to affirm the togetherness and identity of the group, to pass on the group's traditions, and to participate in the sacred and mysterious workings of nature.

THE PURPLE APPROACH TO THE ARTS

In contemporary arts contexts, Purple shows up as:

- The sense of bonding with fellow group members
- Regarding the creative act as mystical communion with the larger forces of nature
- Keeping your body or your instrument safe
- The use of applause
- Belief in backstage superstitions (e.g., "break a leg!") or the use of lucky charms
- The establishment of basic routines
- The enjoyment of repetition and basic motor skills
- Learning from and honoring elders
- Passing down traditions
- The expectation that the student or apprentice will follow a teacher's directions
- The attitude: "If it was good enough for Grandad, it's good enough for me"
- The feeling of trust and connection between teachers, students, or colleagues
- The use of a special space for creating or teaching
- The advice to "Slow down and just do what I say"

MISTAKES AND SUCCESS ACCORDING TO PURPLE

To Purple, mistakes are a sign of disobedience to the all-powerful and mysterious authority/deity/parent and are worthy of punishment, whether the mistake was accidental or intentional. Success happens when the authority/deity/parent is happy. Someone at Purple, upon seeing a mistake, might say, "The gods will be angry!" The primary emotions around mistakes are fear and shame.

Chapter 9 | SPIRAL DYNAMICS AND THE ARTS

EXAMPLES OF PURPLE ART FORMS

- Indigenous forms of drumming, chanting, and dance
- Work songs
- Folk music
- Traditional handicrafts
- The use of weaving as an aid in remembering the group's history and legends
- Indigenous "porquoi" stories (like "How the Leopard Got His Spots")
- Australian Aboriginal songlines
- Folk dance forms like square dancing
- Injunctions against certain forms of music or art
- Any oral traditions that are passed down generation to generation

RED – "MYTHIC"

Core Values: Power, control, impulse

Motto: "I take command while disregarding others."

BASICS OF RED

Red is all about passion, power, courage, and assertiveness. Its worldview is that the whole world is a jungle and that only the strong will survive—an "eye for an eye" mentality. Morally, Red is individualistic, and its circle of concern is primarily egocentric but can also extend to the people in its immediate group or religion. Red is at its best in its ability to "just get it done" under pressure, make bold choices, muster energy, and courageously stand up for itself. Red is at its worst in its egotism, authoritarianism, exploitation, impatience, and rudeness. Red first developed about ten thousand years ago and currently comprises fifteen to twenty percent of the world's population.

THE ROLE OF THE ARTS IN RED SOCIETIES

Red societies have the beginnings of specialization in the arts (i.e., court musicians and other artisans). For Red, the point of the arts is the glorification of the individual self, political figures, or deities.

THE RED APPROACH TO THE ARTS

In contemporary arts contexts, Red shows up in:

- The reliance on gut instincts
- The use of authority to get one's way
- A "my way or the highway" attitude
- Egotistical displays of technical prowess
- The thrill of powerful creative experiences
- The ability to follow and develop your own creative impulses
- The drive to get things done
- The creation of a sense of urgency
- The desire for instant gratification
- The view of the teacher as an all-powerful and all-knowing master
- A "do it because I said so" attitude
- The setting of boundaries
- The ability to break with traditional ways

MISTAKES AND SUCCESS ACCORDING TO RED

Red generally views mistakes as flaws belonging to other people and objects and will tend to blame others to avoid punishment. Like Purple,

Red can't yet fully tell the difference between intentional and accidental mistakes, and so to Red, the primary concern when making mistakes is whether Red can get away with it. Someone at Red, upon seeing someone else's mistake, might say, "*You're* wrong." Success, on the other hand, happens when Red gets its way. The primary emotions around mistakes are fear and anger.

EXAMPLES OF RED ART FORMS

- Death metal
- Gangster rap
- Taiko drumming
- Russian squat dancing
- Sea shanties
- "Hell week" (the period of intense rehearsals before the opening of a play)
- The use of pyrotechnics
- Anything ostentatious
- A "great big bang" at the end of the piece
- Parades
- Fanfares
- Portraits of the rich and powerful
- Theater or stories that glorify powerful political figures or gods
- Wild rock stars
- The "bad guy" from many stories and movies
- Stories that feature the Hero's Journey (like *The Iliad* and *The Odyssey*)
- Capoeira
- Graffiti and street art

BLUE – "AUTHORITARIAN"

Core Values: Order, rules, traditions

Motto: "I sacrifice myself to a higher goal for a future reward."

BASICS OF BLUE

Blue is all about order, rules and roles, morality, and a higher purpose. Its worldview is that the world is divinely ordered, and that the "wrong" views are to be punished and the "right" views are to be rewarded. Morally, Blue is collectivist, and its circle of concern extends to all the people of its religion or country. Blue is at its best in its professionalism, dedication, honor, sense of fairness, and service to a good cause. Blue is at its worst in its cold, distant, moralistic attitudes; inflexibility; fundamentalism; anal-retentiveness; and sanctimoniousness. Blue first developed about five thousand years ago and currently comprises thirty-five to forty percent of the world's population.

THE ROLE OF THE ARTS IN BLUE SOCIETIES

Blue societies are where all our traditional arts institutions have been created. Theaters, arts schools, and artistry as a profession are all aspects of Blue societies, as are our recognizable formal roles of artist-audience and teacher-student.

THE BLUE APPROACH TO THE ARTS

In contemporary arts contexts, Blue shows up as:

- A professional, stable, meticulous, and dedicated approach
- The specialization and extensive training in one art form
- The reliance on institutional knowledge
- The rules of dress and etiquette

- The ability to show up on time and get the gig done properly
- Discipline
- Self-control
- The ability to follow directions
- The ability to sacrifice the present for future gain (for example, practicing a technique by repeating its individual steps before moving on)
- The use of a rational, logical, step-by-step approach to learning
- Perfectionism
- Persistence
- The fear of disappointing parents and teachers
- Making a distinction between the "right way" and the "wrong way"
- The clear communication and enforcement of rules and roles
- An emphasis on fairness and justice
- The beginnings of compassion for people outside the group
- A sense of duty or responsibility
- Teaching by example

MISTAKES AND SUCCESS ACCORDING TO BLUE

For Blue, these are viewed in terms of the rules handed down from authority, law, and tradition, and are viewed in black-and-white, right-or-wrong terms. Blue can, however, tell the difference between intentional and accidental errors, and can sometimes exercise forgiveness for accidental errors. Upon seeing a mistake, someone at Blue might say,

"You did it wrong." Success belongs to those who follow the rules. The primary emotions around mistakes are fear and guilt.

EXAMPLES OF BLUE ART FORMS

- Classical music
- Ballet
- Opera
- Cathedrals
- Literature
- Arts pedagogy as a study
- Theater as morality tale
- Musical notation
- Professional artistry in general
- The development of standardized methods for practice, performance, and teaching
- Schools that specialize in the arts
- The development of standard visual arts forms (portraiture, landscapes, still life, etc.)
- Emphasis on lineage
- The use of the arts in political ceremonies
- Religious frescoes
- Music composed for religious ceremonies
- Hymns
- Anything that glorifies God and country
- Color-by-numbers

ORANGE – "MODERN"

Core Values: Achievement, success, strategy

Motto: "I improve myself through clever calculation."

BASICS OF ORANGE

Orange is all about achievement, autonomy, and a focus on improvement. Its worldview is that the world is full of possibilities for improvement and making things better. Morally, Orange is individualistic, and because its circle of concern extends to all humans, it is the first stage to recognize universal human rights. Orange is at its best in its innovation, curiosity, autonomy, pragmatism, reliance on rationality over mindless dogma, and entrepreneurial spirit. Orange is at its worst in its lack of emotional connection, opportunism, self-promotion, and lack of concern for others or the environment. Orange first developed about three hundred years ago and currently comprises twenty-five to thirty percent of the world's population.

THE ROLE OF THE ARTS IN ORANGE SOCIETIES

Orange societies see the emergence of secular arts. Artists are regarded as individuals who are striving for success in their field, whether through seeking status, money, fame, or otherwise making their mark. Orange arts institutions are driven by the bottom line, and tend to focus on sales, technical advancements, and breaking with stuffy traditions.

THE ORANGE APPROACH TO THE ARTS

In contemporary arts contexts, Orange shows up as:

- A focus on individual achievement
- Enthusiasm
- A desire for success through innovation

- Competitions
- Desire for profit
- Showy repertoire
- Glitz and glamour
- Gaining social or professional status via technical virtuosity
- A focus on the monetary or legal aspects of the arts industry
- Self-development
- A focus on technique that more or less ignores the heart
- Science-based practice or warm-up methods
- The use of trial and error to achieve the best results
- Pragmatically achieving results to move ahead
- The development of talent
- Teaching as mentorship
- "SMART" goals (A goal-setting technique that emphasizes specific, measurable, achievable, relevant, and time-bound goals)
- A flexible and fun attitude
- Achievement awards
- The use of games in teaching to achieve results

MISTAKES AND SUCCESS ACCORDING TO ORANGE

To Orange, mistakes are irritating glitches on the road to self-improvement. Orange understands that mistakes happen, but also tends to denigrate people who make mistakes as "losers." Someone at Orange, upon seeing a mistake, might say, "I don't like the way you did that." For Orange, success belongs to those who take risks and who are self-reliant. Orange is very focused on success and achievement in general. The primary emotions around mistakes are fear and anger.

EXAMPLES OF ORANGE ART FORMS

- The modern recording industry
- The use of the arts in advertisements and other corporate contexts
- The notion of popular art and music
- The emergence of for-profit art
- The idea of arts as entertainment
- Artists as celebrities
- "The Flight of the Bumblebee"
- Concertos
- The use of perspective
- Anything science- or research-based
- The idea that the arts are "good for the brain"
- Competitions
- Anything high-tech
- Pointillism
- Techno
- Bebop
- Muzak
- Photorealism
- Technical drawings
- Copyright laws
- The question: "But will it sell?"
- Top 40 radio

- Electronic amplification
- A focus on an artist's image or brand
- The use of profanity in lyrics
- Comedy as a profession
- "Selling out"

GREEN — "POSTMODERN"

Core Values: Group focus, ideals, social connection

Motto: "I seek acceptance by the group by sacrificing myself."

BASICS OF GREEN

Green is all about peace, love, inclusivity, and sensitivity. Its worldview is that the world is a habitat where humanity can find love and purpose through connection, sharing, and caring. Morally, Green is collectivist, and its circle of concern extends to all living beings and the most marginalized people. Green is at its best in its sensitivity, compassion, multiculturalism, egalitarianism, idealism, and tolerance. Green is at its worst in its woolly-headedness, patronizing attitude, tendency toward ideological fervor, fear of setting boundaries, and—paradoxically—intolerance of intolerance. Green first developed about one hundred fifty years ago and currently comprises ten percent of the world's population.

THE ROLE OF THE ARTS IN GREEN SOCIETIES

Green postmodern societies view the arts as mediums of self-expression and tend to denigrate technique, tradition, and—especially—achievement. Green societies emphasize non-hierarchical and multicultural arts contexts, and elevate heart over technique (but not always, as is seen with post-tonal music or abstract art).

Chapter 9 | SPIRAL DYNAMICS AND THE ARTS

THE GREEN APPROACH TO THE ARTS

In contemporary arts contexts, Green shows up as:

- Expressing feelings
- Building consensus
- Shared experiences
- Breaking down barriers
- Deconstructing and problematizing all traditions
- A view that the development of skill is potentially oppressive and exclusionary
- A fear of appearing to show off
- A "Just feel it, man" attitude
- Practicing and creating as an opportunity for self-expression and an investment in the self
- An idealistic approach
- The idea of an artistic practice leading to personal growth and development
- A greater social awareness
- A focus on feeling good
- A preference for collaboration rather than competition
- A preference to engage in "explorations" instead of "exercises"
- Teaching as mutual understanding and discovery rather than a didactic, one-way transmission of knowledge (e.g., when the teacher says, "In every lesson, I learn just as much as my students")
- A sensitivity to different learning styles and abilities
- Inclusive of emotions as a part of the learning process

- Being a great listener
- An ability of the teacher to show vulnerability
- Putting things into perspective
- Participation awards
- Wellness-oriented pedagogy
- A heart-centered approach

MISTAKES AND SUCCESS ACCORDING TO GREEN

For Green, mistakes are viewed with ambivalence. On the one hand, Green can clearly tell when something is wrong according to traditional standards, but it also tends to overlook mistakes due to not wanting to hurt anybody's feelings. When seeing a mistake, someone at Green might say, "That's okay! Let's just try again." For Green, success happens when everyone feels good or has been included. Green is also the first stage to view mistakes as potentially creative opportunities. Green's primary emotions related to mistakes are fear, shame, and to some extent, curiosity.

EXAMPLES OF GREEN ART FORMS

- Drum or song circles
- Jam sessions
- Nonjudgmental improvisation classes
- Anything multicultural
- Atonal and post-tonal music
- John Cage
- Jackson Pollack
- Impressionism
- Free jazz

Chapter 9 | SPIRAL DYNAMICS AND THE ARTS

- The use of social media
- "Process-oriented" pedagogy such as Method Acting
- The whole genre of world music
- Abstract and impressionist painting
- Improv theater
- The play *Waiting for Godot*
- Authentic Movement
- Anything mindful
- Anything New Age
- Anything with spiritual trappings (incense, candles, robes, crystal singing bowls, etc.)
- Arts activism
- Civil rights-era music
- Electronic dance music
- Raves
- Burning Man
- Flash mobs
- Intuitive drawing
- Psychedelic art
- Phish
- The Beatles
- The album *Kind of Blue* by Miles Davis

YELLOW — "INTEGRAL"

Core Values: Visionary, systems thinking, synergy

Motto: "I actualize myself while taking others into account."

BASICS OF YELLOW

Yellow is all about systems thinking, seeing the bigger picture, and self-actualization. Yellow's worldview is that the world is a complex, self-organizing system and that humanity's role is to create integral solutions for our collective problems. Morally, Yellow is individualistic, and its circle of concern extends to the entire earth. It can see how its own point of view builds on those of the past and how the consequences of its actions extend deep into the future. Yellow is at its best in its creative innovation, visionary outlook, ability to set aside egoic concerns, ability to resolve paradoxes and polarities, non-judgmentalism, nuance, ability to discern what is relevant or irrelevant, and access to universal consciousness. Yellow is at its worst in its overemphasis on complicated intellectual systems and maps, perceived aloofness, and tendency to get lost in its compelling daydreams. Yellow first developed about fifty years ago and currently comprises about one to five percent of the world's population.

THE ROLE OF THE ARTS IN YELLOW SOCIETIES

Yellow societies view the arts as an emergent property of a society that is both a cause and effect of that society's evolution into greater levels of complexity and consciousness. In this view, artists are agents of individual and collective self-actualization, playing many vital integrating functions such as bringing people together and tapping into the self-healing power of the body. Yellow artists are the first to fully integrate what had previously seemed separate: head and heart, body and mind, and the personal and the collective.

Chapter 9 | SPIRAL DYNAMICS AND THE ARTS

THE YELLOW APPROACH TO THE ARTS

In contemporary arts contexts, Yellow shows up as:

- An act of the devotion to beauty that is an expression of the whole artist (body, mind, soul, and spirit)
- The full integration of emotion and technique
- The ability to continuously sense and monitor the body during the creative act
- The ability to include and adjust to the energy of the audience in real-time
- The creation of purpose-driven projects
- The use of multiple forms of technology to create an engrossing experience
- Valuing knowledge and competency over status or rank
- The disappearance of fear due to growing beyond approval-seeking
- The idea of practicing and creating as acts of self-actualization
- An approach to teaching that takes account of the students' developmental stage
- The pursuit of learning for its own sake
- An attitude of flexibility, spontaneity, and functionality
- The creation of new models and systems to help students better understand, practice, and grow
- The balance of well-being and excellence
- Open-mindedness and clarity

- The ability to resolve paradoxes (e.g., how to instill internal motivation in students without forcing them to practice)
- Constructive criticism
- The ability to make choices based on a larger context or transcendent vision

MISTAKES AND SUCCESS ACCORDING TO YELLOW
Yellow no longer views mistakes as problems to be avoided but as genuine learning opportunities. Albert Einstein's quote, "A person who never makes mistakes has never tried anything new," is highly characteristic of Yellow's open acceptance of mistakes as a part of a lifelong learning process, as is common advice among jazz musicians to "make it sound like you meant to do it." For Yellow, success belongs to the most competent artists who are rewarded for taking the right approach or process—not necessarily for getting the right answers. Yellow's primary emotions around mistakes are frustration and curiosity.

EXAMPLES OF YELLOW ART FORMS
Yellow is still fairly new, so there aren't many examples in the arts, but here are a few:

- The use of the Alexander Technique in the arts
- The use of the arts for eliciting certain states of mind
- El Sistema
- The Society for Artistic Research in Weimar
- David Lynch's film pedagogy
- *Free Play: Improvisation in Life and Art* by Stephen Nachmanovitch

- *Goedel, Escher, Bach: An Eternal Golden Braid* by Douglas Hofstadter
- The ability to draw on many styles for use at appropriate moments
- The full integration of internet-age technology into the creative process
- *Star Trek* (each race is based on a different Spiral Dynamics level)
- Gandalf the Grey from *The Lord of the Rings*
- The Soulforce Arts Approach

TURQUOISE – "HOLISTIC"

Core Values: Wholeview/wholeism, cosmic/collective consciousness

Motto: "I benefit existential reality by both actualizing and transcending my egoic self."

BASICS OF TURQUOISE

Turquoise is all about the interbeing of self and cosmos, reverence for all of life, transpersonal perspectives, and experiencing the wholeness of existence through mind and spirit. Its worldview is that the world is a single intricately balanced organism that is now in jeopardy in humanity's hands. Morally, Turquoise is collectivist, and its circle of concern extends to the entire universe. It is primarily concerned with participation in the harmony of all things through all time. Historically, Turquoise can be seen at the core of many of the great wisdom traditions and in the teachings of certain luminaries and sages, but as a matter of a more widespread phenomenon, it is emerging only now.

Turquoise is at its best in its focus on searching for pragmatic planetary solutions that serve all life on earth, its relentless compassion, its ability to see the world and cosmos as one, and its effortlessness. Turquoise is at its worst in its otherworldly qualities, when it gets stuck in spiritual consciousness, and when it is unable to become grounded in practical, day-to-day realities. It currently comprises one hundredth of one percent of the world's population.

THE ROLE OF THE ARTS IN TURQUOISE SOCIETIES

Turquoise societies are extremely rare, but those that exist view the arts as manifestations of spirit and vehicles for mystical union with all there is. Artists act as agents of healing and harmony by participating in the flow of life force energy that runs through them. Turquoise artists serve a greater cause, are energetically attuned to all life, are community-oriented, and can, as William Blake put it, "hold infinity in the palm of your hand and eternity in an hour, to see the world in a grain of sand, and the heavens in a wildflower."

THE TURQUOISE APPROACH TO THE ARTS

In contemporary arts contexts, Turquoise shows up as:

- The view that the creative act is a meditation, contemplation, or prayer (e.g., "praying music" more than "playing music")
- The use of art to elevate the consciousness of all humanity
- The transmission of the artists' state of consciousness to the audience
- A focus on the transcendent and the sublime
- Flow states and other altered states of consciousness
- Complete effortlessness

- Being a vessel for your art
- The view that art facilitates the evolution of the self
- The integration of instinctive, cognitive, emotional, energetic, and spiritual modes of learning
- Technical and expressive skill that verges on the miraculous
- The integration of scientific and spiritual approaches
- The Oliver Wendell Holmes' "freedom on the other side of complexity"
- The view of teaching as a process of guiding students into humanity's deepest wisdom
- The ability to call on the full potential of the healing power of the arts
- The ability to integrate and use information from any source
- The ability to bring the past alive and show students or audiences their place in the grand scheme of things
- A childlike playfulness
- An attitude of spontaneity, humility, and a light-heartedness that comes from deeply seeing the natural flow of things

MISTAKES AND SUCCESS ACCORDING TO TURQUOISE

To Turquoise, the framing of mistakes vs. success seems simplistic and naïve. That being said, Turquoise can clearly and penetratingly see what works, what doesn't work, and why, and has compassion for the pain of not reaching one's goals. Turquoise views mistakes as creative gifts from the universe, no longer assigning praise or blame to the separate self. Turquoise also can "jujitsu" any problems or challenges that come along, turning what at first seemed like a mistake into a success. Turquoise experiences feedback from the outer world as reflections of the inner world, and when seeing that things aren't going as desired, Turquoise will ask, "What is it in me that doesn't want to reach this goal?" Success for Turquoise goes beyond seeking the benefit of any one individual or society or any polarized worldview. It happens when individual or collective action is aligned with the enrichment of life itself. The primary emotions related to mistakes are curiosity, compassion, and the joy of discovery.

EXAMPLES OF TURQUOISE ART FORMS
Many of the most transcendent works of art, even those created hundreds or even thousands of years ago, exhibit Turquoise characteristics. Examples include:

- Chartres Cathedral
- The Temple of Luxor
- The Taj Mahal
- Bach's Mass in C minor
- The late Beethoven string quartets
- Ravi Shankar
- John Coltrane's album *A Love Supreme*
- Devotional art and music aimed at industrial-grade spiritual practice (as opposed to faddish, New-Agey pseudo-practices)
- *Music and the Soul: A Listener's Guide to Achieving Transcendent Musical Experiences* by Kurt Leland
- *The Mysticism of Sound and Music* by Hazrat Inayat Khan
- Alex Grey's paintings and his book *The Mission of Art*

- Cory Ench's digital art
- The film *Koyaanisqatsi*
- M. C. Escher
- Buckminster Fuller
- The great wisdom tradition texts that blend spirituality and art such as the *Tao Te Ching*, the *Bhagavad Gita*, and the poetry of Jalaluddin Rumi
- The Soulforce Arts Approach

THE SIMPLICITY ON THE OTHER SIDE OF COMPLEXITY

"For the simplicity on this side of complexity, I wouldn't give you a fig. But for the simplicity on the other side of complexity, for that I would give you anything I have."

— OLIVER WENDELL HOLMES, IN A LETTER TO SIR FREDERICK POLLOCK

The promise of Spiral Dynamics is that of a tangible means of meeting your artistic purpose and addressing your challenges from a new, higher-order stage of consciousness that can bring many benefits to your art and life. When you become intentional about growing your consciousness up the spiral, you may find that many of your most perplexing artistic or personal challenges suddenly feel trivially easy. When yet other challenges inevitably arise, you may experience a newfound sense of equanimity and confidence. In addition, the growth of your consciousness may help you discover creative avenues that may have been previously hidden from view.

With sufficient personal growth, you will be able to enjoy the surest sign of true mastery: "the simplicity on the other side of complexity." Practicing your musical instrument will no longer feel like a mechanical task of inculcating the right procedures but will become a holistic and embodied process of self-discovery, healing, and growth. Acting in a play will no longer feel like an effort to prove your self-worth through a perfect performance but will become an act of devotion to beauty that transmits your own quality of consciousness—your system update—to your audiences. Similarly, teaching your art will no longer feel like an effort to get your students to do what you want but will become a process of helping your students grow their own consciousness so they can eventually participate in the leading edge of human development that will be emerging in their own time.

When you approach your artistic life in this way, you will be fulfilling one of the highest potentials of the arts: to act as a catalyst for growth, healing, connection, wisdom, and love. After all, this is what the greatest artists and their works of art have offered humanity throughout the ages.

You can play your part in this potential by growing up the spiral as fully and quickly as possible so that your art carries a system update that will beckon others up the spiral. Art made in this way has the potential to be of tremendous benefit to your audiences and others, creating a more beautiful, harmonious world.

In the next chapter, we will explore this potential further with a vision of the arts from the second tier of human consciousness, a critique of traditional arts schooling, the specific methods of stimulating your own growth, and the means by which Yellow and Turquoise art can help resolve the meaninglessness crisis.

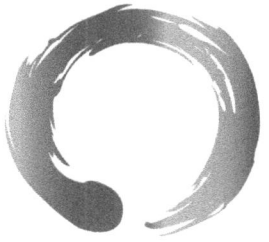

MIND-BODY INTERLUDE #5

FOUR THOUGHTS, FOUR BODIES

"You translate everything, whether physical, mental, or spiritual, into muscular tension."

— FREDERICK MATTHIAS ALEXANDER, ORIGINATOR OF THE ALEXANDER TECHNIQUE

Creation is an embodied act. Whether your art form is explicitly embodied, as with dance, or less obviously so, as with poetry, all your creative impulses, aesthetic judgments, and the movements that give them form are inescapably rooted in the body.

The trouble is that we live in a culture that has forgotten this and believes instead in the Cartesian split of mind from body. As a result, we tend to ignore our body, treating it like an inconvenient, needy vehicle whose main use is to escort our mind from place to place. Creating from this split is the source of many artists' common creative, physical, and emotional challenges. It's what's behind the belief that more effort and control lead to better artistic results, a lie that, in actuality, only leads to creative death.

In part, the belief that your mind is separate from your body is a product of growing through certain developmental stages. In Spiral Dynamics stage Purple, body, mind, and world are fused together. A process of differentiation then begins with stages Red and Blue and finds its apogee in Orange. Green sees a partial return to the body, but the full reintegration of mind and body only happens with stages Yellow and Turquoise.

For these second-tier stages, "mind" and "body" are regarded as mere words and conceptual categories that denote distinct, yet interrelated, aspects of an undivided whole. A creative process that takes full account of the underlying unity of mind and body is one whose artistic potential is undiminished by physical, emotional, or mental constraint, and so gives rise to the fullest expression of Soulforce.

You can reintegrate your experience of mind and body through a direct experience of the way thoughts and attention affect your quality of movement. Gaining awareness of the mind-body connection allows you to place your effort only where it is needed, saving you from unnecessary stress and tension. It also acts to catalyze your movement up the spiral through direct glimpses of second-tier ways of being. Use the following exploration to gain direct experience of the mind-body connection.

FOUR THOUGHTS, FOUR BODIES

Consider each of the following thoughts as you perform a simple movement, such as walking, speaking, writing, or getting in and out of a chair. Notice the effect each has on your mental state, emotional well-being, and quality of movement.

- "I have to do it right, and I have to do it fast!"
- "Oh no—I hope I don't mess up!"
- "I can't do it, and I give up."
- "I am at ease with myself, and I have plenty of time."

Many notice that the first thought leads to a tight body, a stressful attitude, an outward focus, and a sense of rushing. The second thought often leads to a similar tightness and stress, only with an inward focus and an uncomfortably slow sense of time. The third thought often leads to a sense of relaxation, at least in comparison to the first two; however, its relaxation is disempowered, has an overly inward focus, and lacks energy. The fourth thought has a very different effect from the others, inviting physical ease, a sense of pleasure and fun, and a focus that includes both the inner and outer worlds in a unified whole.

Mind-Body Interlude #5 | FOUR THOUGHTS, FOUR BODIES

> Bring an awareness of these four thoughts into your next creative session. Which thought is most prominent in times of creative challenge? What happens when you approach those same times from the fourth thought?

Ultimately, the purpose of art is to heal the splits and divisions that keep us from fully recognizing who we are and what we're here to do. One of the most prevalent and pernicious splits is that between mind and body; it lies behind much of our creative, educational, medical, relational, and existential confusion. You can heal this split by listening to, learning from, and honoring the living being that your body is. Doing so enables an experience of the unity of mind, body, and soul, and brings you closer to your true self. When you create from this unity, your art will carry a system update that calls others into a similar experience. This is one of the primary ways you can ensure your art brings forth the healing, inspiration, and connection our world now needs.

"We fear our highest possibilities. We are generally afraid to become that which we can glimpse in our most perfect moments, under conditions of great courage. We enjoy and even thrill to godlike possibilities we see in ourselves in such peak moments. And yet we simultaneously shiver with weakness, awe, and fear before these very same possibilities."

— **ABRAHAM MASLOW,**
MOTIVATION AND PERSONALITY

CHAPTER 10

SECOND-TIER ARTISTRY

"Why wasn't I taught this in school?" Sam asked with incredulity. We were in the middle of an Alexander Technique lesson in which she was practicing her lines for an upcoming play. She was taking lessons with me to help her stage presence, as well as the "clomping on stage" (heavy footfalls) her director advised her to address. I had just assisted her with some hands-on guidance to support her body to remain at ease as she recited and moved about the stage. The ease that resulted had astonished her and led her to reflect on why the effortlessness training she was now receiving wasn't more a part of her previous theater education.

"Seriously—what I'm learning here about the body and awareness, Alexander Technique, and Soulforce—I wish I had learned all this years ago. I could have saved myself a lot of grief!"

Sam's confusion about the gaps in her theater training hit home for me. It resonated with the similar gaps in my own musical training that led to the injuries I had experienced during music school. To help Sam make sense of the difference between her previous and current training, I shared this part of my own story.

My predominant experience at music school was that of physical and emotional stress. One of the primary reasons I ended up in such a sorry state was that the focus of my training almost entirely excluded my well-being. All my classes and activities were instead focused on the traditional aspects of musicianship: technique, practicing, ensembles, history, theory, and so on. While, on the one hand, my music school was right to focus on these aspects, the exclusive nature of that focus left out a vitally important truth: that my well-being was inextricably intertwined with my musicianship. Without acknowledging this truth, the training I received left me with no awareness or skills to help my body heal and relax. Without such awareness and skills, I had no way to address the intense stress and tension I felt at that time, a condition that eventually led to the arm pain that made playing violin almost impossible. Thus, because I was no longer able to make the kind of progress I wanted, the ultimate result of excluding my well-being from my music training was that my musicianship suffered.

It's clear that well-being and artistry are intimately linked. A violin won't play itself, nor will an actor's lines speak themselves, nor will a paintbrush move on its own. The body is your primary instrument; a tight body leads to diminished art, and a free body leads to Soulforce. Therefore, to create truly masterful art, you must take account of your body's well-being.

If it's so important, why isn't this body-centered approach taught more widely? It's because many of our arts institutions and pedagogies are stuck in the past. They come from a time when the way to survive as an artist was to subscribe to tradition or seek certain achievements, no matter the cost. Thankfully, our own survival conditions, for the most part, are easier than those of our ancestors, so we can afford to take account of our well-being and, by so doing, bring forth art that is even more transformative and alive. The trouble is that many of our institutions and pedagogies haven't yet caught up with this fact, so they often perpetuate outmoded approaches to the arts.

The answer isn't to throw away our institutions or traditions because it's much, much harder to build new ones than to midwife the current

Chapter 10 | SECOND-TIER ARTISTRY

ones into a more evolved place. The wiser choice is to appreciate what has worked in the past, while also seeking to bring forth something new. What does this something new look like? I don't have all the answers, but I know what it feels like. It feels like remembering the truths and desires you were born with, like laying down your effort and control and trusting beauty to guide your way, and like being okay with not having all the answers as you navigate complexity. Importantly, it feels like inhabiting a living universe, the gateway to which is honoring the being that you are, that your art is, and that our world is. You know you're creating from this more evolved place when the creative act, as well as your approach to artistic mastery, feels like a celebration of the dance of life.

As I finished relating these sentiments to Sam, I said, "Your job as an artist, then, goes beyond 'just' creating the greatest art you can. You can play an active role in bringing forth the kinds of art, arts institutions, and pedagogies that better fit our current world. This you can do by growing and evolving into the kind of individual who, for example, takes for granted the link between your well-being and artistic output. This process of evolution is necessary for the fullest expression of your Soulforce because it is only this that allows you to meet your artistic challenges from a higher-order, more comprehensive, and more nuanced understanding. The ultimate result of your own evolution is that you can create art that helps others grow and evolve as well, and this is something the world desperately needs right now."

I watched carefully as Sam took all this in. She told me that what I had just said helped her re-contextualize her previous challenges and current approach. As we continued that lesson and the following few, I noticed a marked shift in Sam's attitude and performances. Whereas before she was tentative and sometimes looked lost, she now had a deeper confidence and sense of purpose. She said she felt a new joy in our process of exploration and unlearning, and that she had a better sense of how to navigate her previously intractable challenges. She later told me that her initiation that day into a more evolutionary artistry brought many benefits. She felt grateful for how this approach improved her stage presence and quality of movement. She also told me there was more; Sam now had a new hope for our society and a sense of personal empowerment to create a more beautiful world through her art.

This chapter lays out a detailed overview of the two stages of artistic evolution that build upon those that are now widely available in many arts institutions and pedagogies. These are Spiral Dynamics stages Yellow and Turquoise. Your individual evolution into these stages will catapult your creative process into one whose artistic output has a greater sophistication, emotional impact, and transformative potential. What's more, your art will carry a system update that is necessary for the growth and evolution of your audiences. The result will be art that is truly relevant to a world in turmoil because its system update will be one that initiates your audiences into the higher-order perspectives necessary to meet our urgent and complex challenges.

The first step to your evolution into Yellow and Turquoise artistry has already begun with your introduction to Spiral Dynamics in the previous chapter. Our next step is to frame your current artistic challenges in terms of the limitations of certain Spiral Dynamics stages, and to explore what is possible when you grow beyond them.

STUCK IN THE PAST

"The only real battle in life is between hanging on and letting go."

— SHANNON L. ALDER, INSPIRATIONAL AUTHOR

Sam and I are not the only ones to have encountered the limitations of artistic training exclusively focused on the traditional and achievement-oriented aspects of artistry. I've had conversations with countless artists who share that, despite the high points of enchantment and excellence they sometimes experienced, their time in arts school was equally, or more often, stressful, painful, and even soul-crushing. This is why, in addition to their diploma, many graduates of fine arts programs also leave with creative burnout, repetitive strain injuries, performance anxiety, and the naïve assumption that they'll easily be able to make a living relying solely on their artistic talents.

For example, many performing arts students experience what are sometimes career-stopping musculoskeletal injuries. Studies show that this occurs for a significant proportion of performing arts students such that around eighty to ninety percent of those who become professional musicians also suffer injuries later in their careers.[1][2]

Other students are left with lingering emotional issues, such as performance anxiety, depression, and crippling perfectionism—and few, if any, tools to address them.[3] In addition, because mainstream arts training doesn't typically focus on practical career skills for the twenty-first century, many graduates also experience the considerable stress of entering the workforce with massive student loan debt and almost no viable means of making a living.[4]

The unfortunate truth is that, despite their best intentions, the worldview many mainstream arts schools inhabit only serves to contribute to these challenges. Instead of preparing young artists for the realities of our increasingly complex world, they generally prepare students for artistic careers relevant only to an earlier era, that few can realistically achieve, and that are rapidly disappearing. What's the role of fine portraiture in the era of twenty-eight mega-pixel smartphone cameras and AI-driven image generators? What's the value of a PhD in sculpture when the number of sculptors who can get tenured university positions or have their work sold in major galleries is vanishingly small? What options do highly trained classical musicians have when so many orchestras are going out of business?

Asking these questions is by no means meant to diminish the value of pursuing a fine arts education, nor to say that there's something wrong with learning the traditional aspects of artistry. There will always be people who are called to become fine artists, and formal training has been one of the foundational ways to do this. Rather, it's to say that artists are not well-served by arts institutions that haven't fully adapted to the twenty-first century.

From a developmental perspective, the real trouble with many mainstream arts institutions—even those considered the most elite—is that they are stuck in Spiral Dynamics stages Blue, Orange, and Green. You may have noticed the limitations of these stages in your own artistic training. For example, stage Blue pedagogy tends to be rigidly adherent to authority, rules, and roles, and it views sacrificing your well-being as a sometimes necessary step in achieving mastery. While stage Orange has a wider take on pedagogy than does Blue—for example, through its values of freedom, exploration, and innovation—Orange, too, has its own narrow-mindedness. When it becomes too focused on technical achievements, it can view time spent on well-being as an airy-fairy distraction from dominating your field.

Stage Green, in some ways, seems to answer the limitations of these earlier stages in that it marks the beginning of an important transition from the scarcity mentality of earlier stages to the abundance mentality of later ones. The shift into abundance naturally makes Green more inclined to value well-being and a more holistic approach overall. However, because Green often struggles to integrate what's valuable from the previous stages, Green can get lost in idealistic visions of the future that lack the rigor and practical-mindedness necessary to fully convince the more conservative elements of arts institutions to take considerations of well-being more seriously.

Make no mistake: Blue, Orange, and Green absolutely have their place in contemporary arts pedagogy. It's just that each of these stages has certain limitations that mean that any institution that doesn't grow beyond them risks remaining stuck in the past. The truth is that while each of these stages was a necessary and life-giving adaptation when it first appeared, the world has changed dramatically in the intervening years. The world is now so complex and interconnected that, while each of these earlier stages is necessary to the proper functioning of human life as a whole, none of them are sufficient on their own to meet the demands of contemporary life. Thus, any school that continues to teach solely from these stages risks failing to fulfill its primary mission: to create vibrant, productive artists who can truly flourish in the twenty-first century.

> While Spiral Dynamics stages Blue, Orange, and Green continue to have their place in contemporary arts pedagogy, any school that can't grow beyond them risks remaining stuck in the past.

The answer to this issue is to have an approach to the arts that includes a radically bigger picture of what it takes to become a masterful artist in the twenty-first century. One that takes into account individual well-being, the contemporary realities of building a career in the arts, and the urgent need to find new meaning and purpose in our society at large. This is what Spiral Dynamics stages Yellow and Turquoise have to offer.

One challenge in fleshing out this picture is that these stages are still relatively new, so we don't yet have a full picture of what Yellow and Turquoise artistry look and feel like. However, we can draw upon the existing literature about Spiral Dynamics and make certain inferences about the overall shape and characteristics of artistry at these stages. My hope is that this chapter will provide a general sense of what Yellow and Turquoise artistry look and feel like, the many ways these stages may shape your life as an artist, and how they can help all artists and arts institutions resolve the meaninglessness crisis and evolve into the twenty-first century.

A SECOND-TIER VISION AND PURPOSE

"A man who has a vision is not able to use the power of it until he has performed the vision on earth for people to see."

— BLACK ELK, OGLALA SIOUX SHAMAN,
THE DEATH AND RESURRECTION SHOW

The originator of Spiral Dynamics, Clare Graves, considered Yellow and Turquoise to belong to a second tier of human development (the first tier comprising all the previous stages). According to Graves, what characterizes the second tier is its ability to move through the spiral at will, healing, repairing, and unblocking each of the previous stages. In his own words, the second-tier stages link functions, people, and ideas into new, more natural flows that add precision, flexibility, rapid response, humanity, and fun to getting the work done. That is the power of new paradigm, "second-tier" thinking, to constantly survey the whole while tinkering expertly with the parts. Monitoring the full spiral is especially vital during periods of large-scale turbulence and change, like right now.[5]

Placed in the context of the arts, Graves' insights suggest that we need to take Yellow and Turquoise seriously because these stages are the only ones that can fully answer the needs of individual artists, arts institutions, and the society and planet we serve.

For example, as we've explored throughout this book, one of humanity's greatest needs right now is a new vision of the purpose of life, one that gives us a positive direction to move toward both individually and societally. Our current lack of such a direction is what is primarily responsible for the meaninglessness crisis. The second tier offers an awareness of the spiral and a desire to help others grow up it to the benefit of all life on earth. Its vision is that of a world of ever-increasing consciousness, healing, diversity of life, and wholeness. Its purpose is to bring this vision to life through personal development and systems change.

Chapter 10 | SECOND-TIER ARTISTRY

> We need to take Yellow and Turquoise seriously because these stages are the only ones that can fully answer the needs of individual artists, arts institutions, and the society and planet we serve.

The necessary context for understanding the second tier comes from appreciating the vision and purpose of artistry as seen from the first-tier stages. For example, Blue artists seek to create a world of order, security, and stability by honoring authority, professionalism, and a higher calling through their art. Orange artists seek to create a world of freedom, material abundance, and opportunity by achieving a high degree of technical mastery, professional advancement, and innovation in their medium. Green artists seek to create a world of peace, love, and harmony by connecting with audiences through a heart or feeling level, breaking down barriers to accessibility, and expressing a rich inner life.

Clearly, each stage has something valuable to offer artists. The only trouble is that each of the first-tier stages tends to deny the validity of all the others. For example, a Blue authoritarian may feel dismayed at Orange's disregard for tradition and fear the free-spiritedness of Green. An Orange achiever may scoff at the stuffiness of Blue's rules and roles and dismiss Green's sensitivity as woolly-headed. Likewise, a sensitive Green may abhor Blue's hierarchies and try to soften Orange's winners-and-losers attitude. The result of their inability to see the value of other stages is that the first-tier stages miss out on the opportunity to make good use of each of their unique gifts.

All this changes at the second tier. Both Yellow and Turquoise have the unique ability to integrate and call upon the gifts of any previous stage as appropriate. The result is an extraordinary power to fulfill the expanded vision and purpose available to you as an artist.

For example, Yellow artists seek to create a world of authenticity, self-actualization, and effective action through the integration of the head, heart, and gut. This is done via systems thinking and a desire to repair the damage done by the previous stages. Turquoise artists seek to create a world of healing, wholeness, and unity through a connection with the divine, the intention to create for the benefit of all beings, and by calling upon every aspect of their own being (cognition, energetics, emotions, and instincts) in the creative act. In other words, second-tier artists are visionaries who possess unforeseen abilities to initiate transformation, healing, and growth through their art.[6]

How do you manifest the abilities, vision, and purpose of second-tier artistry? First and foremost, it requires a process of ongoing personal development. You, as an individual, must grow into the second tier to become a fully integrated human being. Only then can you create art that reflects a more evolved stage of consciousness. As a second-tier artist, you can access deeper levels of creativity, artistic expression, technical mastery, and professional success. You can create art that inspires people to more expansive, inclusive, and mature ways of thinking, acting, and being. At a bigger level, you can play an active part in the individual, societal, and planetary healing that is needed right now.

Simply learning about developmental models like Spiral Dynamics catalyzes the necessary growth into Yellow and beyond. You can further strengthen and deepen this growth by immersing yourself in this and similar models.

SOULFORCE INQUIRY 10.1
CATALYZING THE SECOND TIER

The classic way to enter the second tier of human consciousness is to simply learn about developmental models. Spend at least fifteen minutes a day for the next week or more re-reading Chapter 9 or taking in other information on Spiral Dynamics. You can do this in the form of reading books, watching videos, or listening to podcasts. You'll find a good starting place in the Recommended Reading section at the back of this book.

Be open to any ways these ideas connect to your life. Where do you see yourself in the spiral? Into what Spiral Dynamics stage are you currently growing? What aspects of previous stages have you disowned? How does Spiral Dynamics inform your creative life? In addition, seek out friends who are also interested in this material; your own growth will be greatly enhanced by surrounding yourself with other growth-oriented people.

YELLOW ARTISTRY: WHOLE SELF, WHOLE ART

"Becoming a leader is the same as becoming a fully integrated human being."

— KEN WILBER, *INTEGRAL LIFE PRACTICE*

For Yellow, the purpose of life, and consequently the arts, is to participate in the evolution of consciousness by helping people grow up the spiral. As a Yellow artist, you achieve this through a focus on your own personal growth, an in-depth understanding of human development in general, and a commitment to authenticity through learning and real-world effectiveness.

Yellow understands that, while the world and the self are highly complex, they are also integrated wholes, and cannot be understood in terms of their individual parts alone. Yellow loves to try to understand the self and the world by making maps that show how all the pieces of a system fit together. Yellow is driven by a desire to break free of the group and to add to the well-being of the world through their own unique contribution.

Yellow first developed as a reaction to the pitfalls of Green, whose problem-solving methods (consensus, inclusion, and sharing) take a long time and don't always yield effective results. Yellow prefers, instead, to combine existing ideas in new ways and find hidden connections among them, and to take the select individual actions that will yield the biggest results. Yellow is largely free from fear because it takes responsibility for its own reactions to things and has the confidence to find its own way in the world.

One of its most vital contributions to human thought is to acknowledge that, while all perspectives and values have some truth, some have more truth than others. By this acknowledgment, Yellow resolves the sense of meaninglessness and confusion created by Green's overactive desire to make everything equal. Yellow also exercises a radical inclusivity by allowing a place at the table for all perspectives and values systems (an aim to which Green aspires, but, in the end, cannot fully accomplish; recall the intolerance of intolerance cited in Chapter 9).

What's most unique and powerful about Yellow is its developmental perspective. It shows us how art and culture evolve and gives us a larger context from which to understand where we came from and where we might be headed. In a sense, Yellow isn't so much a new stage, but rather consists of the ability to appreciate and integrate all previous stages. For instance:

- By including Purple's emphasis on intuition and lineage, Yellow puts you back in touch with your body and allows you to be grateful to your teachers and group—but without Purple's clinging to the past.

- By integrating Red's celebration of autonomy and power, Yellow gives you permission to forge your own path and to seek experiences of awe—while avoiding Red's impulsivity and narcissism.

Chapter 10 | SECOND-TIER ARTISTRY

- By honoring Blue's desire to preserve institutional knowledge, Yellow allows you to benefit from what has given order and structure to civilization—but without Blue's fear of systemic change.

- By harnessing Orange's desire for constant growth and improvement, Yellow gives you the drive and zest necessary to actualize and fulfill all your potentials—but without Orange's empty notions of progress.

- By embracing Green's heart, Yellow centers your artistry on a more soulful foundation—while avoiding Green's fluffy thinking and disregard for structure.

Because of its ability to appreciate the gifts of the whole spiral, Yellow no longer makes the mistake common to all the first-tier stages, which is to believe that their current perspectives on life and art are somehow pre-given and ultimately true. Instead, at Yellow, you understand that someone's perspectives on life and art depend entirely on their stage, which can change over time.

This understanding allows Yellow two unique abilities. Firstly, it allows Yellow to be able to initiate more, and more powerful, moments of truth because it can create or teach in ways that can be received by people in all developmental stages. Secondly, it allows Yellow the ability to create art with the specific intention of helping people grow up the spiral.

Yellow also offers a new appreciation for the interconnectedness of all the parts of a system. For example, as a Yellow artist, you recognize that your art is not just something you do on stage or in the studio, but is rather a reflection of your whole self and your whole life. You have a felt sense that every aspect of your being—inner and outer; personal and collective; body, mind, soul, and spirit; your developmental level, personality, and gifts—all find expression in your art, whether you're aware of their influence or not. This recognition allows a far greater ability to reach your highest potential because you can then exercise more agency over the things that were previously influencing your art without your awareness.

The main Yellow lesson for artists is that your stage of development, state of consciousness, which intelligences you draw upon, and so on, determine how you create and experience art. It also gives artistic mastery a new meaning. Instead of thinking that the path to mastery involves developing great skill in a few, narrow areas of life, Yellow says that you become a masterful artist by first becoming a fully self-actualized, integrated human.

You know you have achieved the Yellow vision of artistic mastery when you can effortlessly draw on every aspect of yourself, including the healthy aspects of all previous stages, during the creative act. You're able to recognize that taking care of every aspect of your life is essential to creating great art. The result for your art is that you're able to initiate moments of truth for more kinds of people, more deeply.

Becoming a Yellow artist is not easy. For some, it can take years of self-development work before they fully embody Yellow. Some may wonder if doing all this self-development work is even necessary. After all, many artists throughout history achieved greatness despite being sick, mentally ill, immature, or talented only in very narrow ways. In the end, whether you decide to grow into Yellow depends on your life circumstances.

If you're currently experiencing the kinds of creative challenges outlined in this book, if your well-being is compromised because of your artistic approach, or if you're simply wanting to get to the next level of artistic accomplishment, then embracing Yellow's holistic account of what is possible may be the necessary next step.

> **SOULFORCE INQUIRY 10.2**
> **CATALYZING STAGE YELLOW**
>
> The fastest way to grow into stage Yellow is to study maps and models of human development. Doing so goes beyond a merely intellectual exercise, and instead acts to catalyze the latent potential for Yellow within you.
>
> Begin with the resources in the Recommended Reading section at the back of this book. In addition, conduct internet searches for Spiral Dynamics, Integral Theory, and developmental psychology. Notice the effect learning about developmental models such as these has on your psyche. Locate yourself within these models and use them to direct areas of potential personal and artistic growth.

TURQUOISE ARTISTRY: PLAYING THE SONG OF BEING

"Out beyond ideas of wrongdoing and rightdoing there is a field. I'll meet you there."

— JALALUDDIN RUMI, *A GREAT WAGON*

For Turquoise, the purpose of life, and consequently the arts, is to participate in the divine order of the cosmos; or, in the words of Dr. Ervin László, to "evolve the consciousness of the cosmos by evolving our consciousness."[7] What emerges at stage Turquoise is a new, felt experience of the world and cosmos as an integrated whole—a perception that takes outward form as a desire to "explore, feel and pragmatically work together to solve [our] large complex problems [and thereby] serve humanity and the earth."[8]

A Turquoise artist is one who seeks to heal the collective, gets lost in the energetic flow of creation, and, in the words of visionary painter Alex Grey, "sings and shouts from the axis of truth to wake us up to who we are and where we are going."[9] As a result, Turquoise art functions to bring people "out beyond ideas of rightdoing and wrongdoing" and into a direct experience of their highest, most sacred potentials.

Essentially, a Turquoise artist achieves this function through a process of personal and spiritual development that fully resolves the Story of Separation and embodies the Story of Interbeing. For example, someone at Turquoise has the direct experience that there are no isolated parts anywhere in the universe; instead, what seems to be an isolated part is felt and understood to be a "holon," a whole within larger wholes comprising countless smaller wholes.[10] In this way, Turquoise art is both the result, and further catalyst of, the realization that all things flow within an immeasurable wholeness and irreducible beingness.

Even though the evolutionary timeline proposed by Spiral Dynamics postulates that Turquoise is not likely to have existed before our contemporary times, a glance through history reveals that Turquoise perspectives have long had an enormous impact on human society. For example, many of the great saints, sages, and mystics, despite having lived many hundreds or even thousands of years ago, espoused what are clearly Turquoise perspectives. Likewise, many of the greatest artists and works of art from antiquity—including the Chauvet Cave paintings, the pyramids of Giza, the cathedrals of early medieval Europe, the poetry of Rumi, and Mozart's Requiem—all display Turquoise characteristics. Ludwig van Beethoven's sentiments on the mission of art are classic Turquoise: "There is no loftier mission than to approach the Godhead nearer than other people, and to disseminate the divine rays among humanity."[11] Its appearance among the greatest luminaries of history doesn't mean that Turquoise is only ever reserved for the select few. What's unique about our own time is that Turquoise is now becoming a wider cultural phenomenon accessible to all.

Chapter 10 | SECOND-TIER ARTISTRY

Just as with all stages, Turquoise builds on the strengths of the previous stage—in this case, Yellow—and is also a response to its limitations. In the words of Spiral Dynamics researcher Don Beck:

> *While YELLOW attempts to stitch together particles, people, functions, and nodes into networks and stratified levels, TURQUOISE detects the energy fields that engulf, billow around, and flow throughout naturally. YELLOW connects the dots while TURQUOISE fleshes in the "art" of all of the colors and hues, and the picture comes alive. In terms of Spiral Dynamics, the YELLOW system gets its hands dirty dealing with the chaos. The TURQUOISE collective system steps back and creates the next form of order ... [Turquoise's] paradox construction and resolution is a good tool for tracking down the elegant, underlying order beneath YELLOW's chaos. Without doubt, TURQUOISE will show us how to use diversity in new ways since it is the first time people fathom the complexity of the Spiral in terms of the good of the super-group, Homo sapiens.* [Capitalizations in original][12]

As an artist, Turquoise allows you access to previously unfathomed abilities and insights. For example, for Yellow, models like Spiral Dynamics or Ken Wilber's Integral Theory are often experienced as an exciting intellectual exercise that potentially leads to new experiences and abilities. For Turquoise, on the other hand, the many facets of these models are experienced as a fully embodied reality. What this often means is that, as a Turquoise artist, you can draw upon your cognition, emotions, body, instincts, and energetic systems to achieve results that can seem superhuman to others.

One example is the way Turquoise fully integrates instinct and intuition into the creative process, holding them to be every bit as important as the intellect—and in certain ways, even more important. While it may be obvious to many that these faculties are vital to the creative process, instinct and intuition are often neglected or even repressed within the Blue and Orange approach to the arts. The Green approach gives instinct and intuition more importance, but also often fails to provide the structure necessary to give them proper form. A Yellow approach is the first to provide tangible tools to integrate instinct and intuition, but it's only in a Turquoise approach that the enormous creative potential and wisdom within intuition and instinct are deeply trusted and appreciated.

You know you have achieved the Turquoise vision of great artistry when your art has a higher significance, one that calls your audiences to their highest cosmic potential, their divinity. As a Turquoise artist, you may be drawn to such themes as a transcendent vision, the marriage of opposites, the recognition of the sacred in the mundane, or an awareness of the profound intelligence of the processes of nature. You know you've created a Turquoise work of art when it inspires both you and your audiences into a feeling of "awe [at] the cosmic order, [of] the creative forces that exist from the Big Bang to the smallest molecule."[13]

> You know you've created a Turquoise work of art when it inspires both you and your audiences into a feeling of "awe [at] the cosmic order [of] the creative forces that exist from the Big Bang to the smallest molecule."

ALTERED STATES AND THE PATHWAY TO TURQUOISE

Another realm of human experience often neglected by first-tier stages and subsequently reintegrated by Turquoise is that of altered states of consciousness. Altered states of consciousness, such as those experienced in meditation, on certain substances like psychedelics, or in other peak experiences, offer immense value to artists because of their ability to reveal distant connections, hidden meanings, and to dissolve

Chapter 10 | SECOND-TIER ARTISTRY

emotional, physical, or energetic blockages. In addition, altered states of consciousness provide a unique opportunity to become aware of transcendent realities—of a wholeness that we call an "altered" state only because the "normal" state that comprises much of waking life is so fragmented in comparison.

For many, entry into stage Turquoise itself only happens after years of industrial-strength spiritual practices that provide deep familiarity with altered states of consciousness. One result of such familiarity is the ability to draw upon your personal experiences of transcendent realities and to share them with others in ways that both illuminate and inspire.

In many ways, this ability is what is most unique about Turquoise artists. It is what allows Turquoise artists to transport their audiences to a deeply-felt emotional, energetic, or spiritual experience. For example, famed twentieth-century saxophonist John Coltrane used his own connection with transcendent realities to provide his music with incredible power. Coltrane was renowned for his mind-blowing technique and his ability to channel an irresistible musical force that entranced and inspired millions. How did Coltrane do it? When asked in an interview where his seemingly superhuman musical abilities came from, Coltrane replied with pure Turquoise:

> *My goal is to live the truly religious life, and express it in my music. If you live it, when you play there's no problem because the music is part of the whole thing. To be a musician is really something. It goes very, very deep. My music is the spiritual expression of what I am—my faith, my knowledge, my being ... When you begin to see the possibilities of music, you desire to do something really good for people, to help humanity free itself from its hang-ups ... I'd like to point out to people the divine in a musical language that transcends words ... I want to speak to their souls.*[14]

You can support your growth into Turquoise artistry in four main ways, three of which also contain Turquoise's answer to the meaninglessness crisis. These are:

1. Establish a firm foundation in Yellow
2. Understand interconnectedness
3. Explore altered states
4. Find a purpose-driven community

ESTABLISH A FIRM FOUNDATION IN YELLOW
Firstly, if you haven't yet fully embodied stage Yellow, don't spend your time and energy on trying to reach stage Turquoise. Instead, focus on growing and expanding ever more fully into Yellow because, in the end, your entry into Turquoise will only be as strong as your foundation in Yellow. All that being said, let yourself be curious about Turquoise and learn to recognize its unique flavor in the ideas and art you encounter.

UNDERSTAND INTERCONNECTEDNESS
Secondly, ground yourself in the core understanding of Turquoise: that you as an individual are utterly interconnected with the cosmos. Do this by actively seeking out examples of interconnectedness in your body, your relationships, and our society and planet. For example, notice how when your neck gets tight that your whole body stiffens, too. Or notice how something happening in a faraway place affects your life on a personal level.

It is through the embodied understanding of interconnectedness that Turquoise offers its first of three answers to the meaninglessness crisis. Turquoise teaches us that because all of reality is interconnected, that we don't need huge amounts of energy, force, or money to affect the whole. When we change, so does everything else. It is from this point of view that you become able to realize that your creative life has cosmic significance. For example, if you Play from the Heart, then you are inviting more heart energy and all its consequences into the world. In practicing, if you treat your body as a being to be honored, then you are inviting more reverence and all its consequences into the world. If you teach like everything you say matters to the fate of life on earth, then you may end up choosing words that heal any separation in your corner of the world, rather than inflict more. For Turquoise, there is no such thing as a meaningless act; everything you do matters because you are already inextricably embedded in the larger ecosystem of life. From this perspective, every action, whether in your art or otherwise, is like a prayer that says to the universe, "I want more of this."

EXPLORE ALTERED STATES

Thirdly, find ways of exploring altered states of consciousness, whether through meditation, breathwork, ecstatic dance, listening to transportive music, activities that put you into flow states, or even the thoughtful use of psychedelics. Practices that cultivate non-dual awareness are especially important because they reveal the true nature of reality, self, and consciousness. Here, the term "non-dual" refers to a conscious recognition that the felt duality of self versus world is just a feeling, and not ultimately true. A non-dual state of awareness is one in which the feeling of separation dissolves into an apprehension of the unity of all things.

It is through its connection with non-dual awareness that Turquoise offers its second answer to the meaninglessness crisis. A practice in non-dual awareness reveals that what we're all searching for, our primary goal, the "secret agenda" that underlies all our actions (and even the Story of Separation itself) is a desire to come home to ourselves, to feel our primordial oneness with all that is, to be bathed in the love of just being. The paradox is that we already are home in this place, but because we believe it to be otherwise, we spend our lives in a state of angst that leads to all kinds of destructive behaviors. The key to resolving this is to spend time doing things (like meditating on non-dual awareness) that show the feeling of separation to be the illusion that it is, thus opening the way to the embodied recognition of the oneness that has always been.

To begin exploring this territory, read books, listen to lectures, and watch videos about non-dual awareness and other altered states of consciousness to give yourself a sense of what's possible. Then, commit yourself to the practices that feel best to you. See the Recommended Reading list for more resources on this topic.

FIND A PURPOSE-DRIVEN COMMUNITY

Finally, connect with a purpose-driven community of some kind. Many in our modern society long for a real community and a feeling of belonging because, to an extent never seen throughout human history, community is no longer a given. The disconnection from real community so pervasive in modern life leaves many of us feeling lost, anxious, and depressed, and this is one of the primary forces behind the meaninglessness crisis.

This is why the cultivation of community, and the feeling of belongingness it provides, is Turquoise's third answer to the meaninglessness crisis. For Turquoise, connecting with community is essential. A basic reason is that the project of creating a more beautiful world is not ultimately something that you can do in isolation. For Turquoise, everything in life consists of relationships, and so you only come to know your own wholeness through your relationships with the beings around you. So, while it is possible to amass great intellectual, artistic, or spiritual attainments on your own, in the end, such attainments have more impact and meaning when they are the result of your connection with your human and more-than-human community.

For Turquoise, community is also essential to both personal and societal change. At the personal level, community is essential in that the very best support for your own personal growth and healing comes from being around people who model and value the same kind of growth and healing as you do. Societal change is best supported through the development of an increasingly interconnected meta-community, one that consists of a mosaic of local projects that are energized by a shared vision. For Turquoise, community reaches its true purpose when it allows us, in the words of spiritual teacher Ram Dass, to "walk each other home."

How do you go about effectively creating a community ? The key is to have a shared purpose of some kind. Think back to all the times when you may have felt a real sense of belonging—perhaps during a school play, in a team sport, while in the military, or at church or school. What is common to these examples is that the togetherness they provide comes through doing something worthwhile together. So, when seeking out or creating a community, first start by reflecting on what purpose you most deeply want to carry out in your own life. Then, just follow your purpose with an attitude of humility and openness. Doing so will allow you to find your community without undue effort; following your own purpose, by itself, acts like a prayer to the universe that sets in motion certain forces that will organically draw to you the right people at the right time, just as a flower, through its display of color and scent, attracts its pollinator friends without grasping or clinging.

THE NEXT NATURAL STEP

> *"The basis of our collective judgment as a culture may need to be transmuted from logic to that which guides the hand of an artist. And this does not need to be so difficult: deep inside, we all have an innate, intuitive notion of what is harmonious, beautiful, and fulfilling; if only we can give this innate impulse unfiltered and unbiased expression."*
>
> — BERNARDO KASTRUP, *MEANING IN ABSURDITY*

As a matter of a widespread phenomenon, second-tier artistry is only now being born. We do not yet know its full ramifications for the lives of artists, the kinds of art we make, or the role of the arts in society. An exciting possibility of living in this time is that you get to be a trailblazer, one whose discoveries and resultant system updates will shape the nature of artistry for generations to come. In this way, growing into second-tier artistry is not ultimately something you do solely for yourself as an individual. Instead, your thoughts, actions, and creations set a foundation for future artists to build upon. When you're a second-tier artist, you create for the benefit of all living beings.

Being a trailblazer is not always easy. You will very likely encounter resistance within the parts of yourself, and the people and institutions around you, that are more comfortable with first-tier ways of thinking. There may be times when you feel alone or when you doubt yourself, your abilities, or your second-tier vision. This is all to be expected. Encountering resistance on your way toward the things you care most about is the very definition of being a trailblazer, and is therefore no impediment to a satisfying, meaningful life.

As you can see from the examples given in this chapter, there are countless ways to step into second-tier artistry—perhaps to the point of being overwhelming. How do you choose among all these options in a way that works for your daily life as it is? There are two basic steps.

Firstly, get in touch with your artistic purpose. Thoroughly inquire into your deepest and highest values, your vision of the kind of world you want to create, and the energy most authentic to who and what you are. Spend some time every day just touching into and making space for your authentic values, vision, and energy. This is who you are, where you're headed, and what matters to you.

Secondly, whether as a standalone practice or in moments of making important choices, simply ask yourself, *What's the next natural step I can take today toward my artistic purpose?* Then, just wait for a response to spontaneously arise from your psyche. Don't edit what comes up for you. Instead, be curious about the messages you receive from inside and see if there's a simple action step that you can take today to actualize those messages.

It doesn't matter how incremental or seemingly inconsequential such steps might be. The creation of a more beautiful, life-giving world needn't happen solely through monumental shifts. Certainly, monumental shifts are great when they happen, but to expect or solely rely on such shifts to create change is just a holdover from the Story of Separation. Could you really prove, for instance, that "small" actions are truly inconsequential, or is that idea just an artifact of your inherited ways of thinking about the world? The Story of Interbeing suggests another way. It says, in the words of Charles Eisenstein, that "there is no way to the more beautiful world; the more beautiful world is the way." So, let go of your "shoulds" and the story that you are not enough. Instead, listen for the kind of world you were born to create and follow the next natural step.

In the final chapters of this book, we will explore a variety of tangible and more outward-facing examples of second-tier artistry. These include how to effectively address physical and emotional challenges common to musicians and artists, specific methods of practicing, creating, and teaching, as well as how to build a satisfying, sustainable, and purpose-driven career as an artist in the twenty-first century.

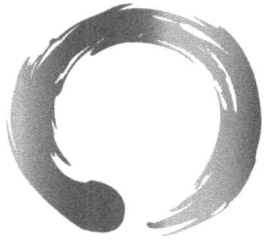

MIND-BODY INTERLUDE #6

THE FOUR PERMISSIONS

"'Existence' and 'nonexistence' are both extremes. 'Pure' and 'impure' are the same. Therefore, abandon all extremes. The wise do not even abide in the middle."

— KHENPO TSULTRIM GYAMTSO, *THE SUN OF WISDOM: TEACHINGS ON THE NOBLE NAGARJUNA'S FUNDAMENTAL WISDOM OF THE MIDDLE WAY*

As a spiritual practice, Buddhism is sometimes called "the middle way." This refers to the central insight of Buddhism, also found at the core of many other mystical traditions, that you find liberation from suffering when you no longer cling to or repel any sensory experience. For Buddhists, *suffering* has a very specific meaning that is distinct from *pain*. Suffering is a resistance to sensory experience that amplifies pain through futile attempts to escape. Suffering diminishes pleasure through gnawing addiction.

Rather than be caught in an endless cycle between these unsatisfactory extremes, Buddhists put forth that liberation from suffering can be found amid daily pains and pleasures by resisting neither. Free from the necessity of escaping your sensory experience, you subsequently feel an immense relief, like putting down a burden you've carried your whole life. This relief is called *nirvana*, which means the extinguishing of the gnawing resistance and dissatisfaction that didn't need to be there in the first place.

The middle way is not a state of disempowerment, laziness, or disengagement with life. It is not to be found in becoming a helpless doormat or even in trying to create some equal mixture of pleasure and pain. Any of these options are themselves extreme positions that negate the possibility of nirvana. To paraphrase Khenpo Tsultrim Gyamtso's quote, the ultimate truth is neither this, nor that, nor both, nor neither. In other words, liberation from suffering happens when you give yourself full permission to feel, do, know, or be anything, and at the same time feel no compulsion that you must feel, do, know, or be anything in particular.

This is the pathless path to nirvana, and the basis of what I call the Four Permissions.

Why is it a "pathless" path? Because nirvana is your original state of being. You don't need to meditate in a cave for thirty years to experience nirvana. In fact, being your original state, you probably experience it many times in each day without recognizing it. One of the easiest ways to cultivate nirvana is through the Four Permissions. The Four Permissions are four easy-to-remember phrases that immediately grant access to nirvana by freeing you from any extreme in how you currently feel, what you're doing, what you're thinking about, and who you believe yourself to be.

When you practice the Four Permissions, you notice a freedom and creative renewal that seems to come out of nowhere. You first find yourself letting go of burdens you didn't even realize you were carrying. Then, your anxiety, stress, and tension melt away to allow space for your true self to arise. Reconnected to your true self, you experience a creative renewal that provides new insights and energy to your art. What's vital to remember is that deliberately seeking the fruits of this creative renewal will inevitably backfire because to do so is the same clinging to an outcome that caused your constriction and suffering in the first place. Remember, creativity is something you are and that you allow, rather than something you make happen.

THE FOUR PERMISSIONS

Sit or lie comfortably as you take in each of these phrases. Say each to yourself slowly and let them sink in fully. Simply notice what happens to your quality of being as you hold both portions of each phrase at once. Any release you experience is a little taste of nirvana.

- **Feeling.** I'm welcome to feel anything I want right now, and I also don't have to feel anything in particular.
- **Doing.** I'm welcome to do anything I want right now, and I also don't have to do anything in particular.
- **Knowing.** I'm welcome to know anything I want right now, and I also don't have to know anything in particular.
- **Being.** I'm welcome to be anything I want right now, and I also don't have to be anything in particular.

Feel free to make these your own, substituting the operative word as fits your own habits and activities. For instance, if "knowing" doesn't do much for you, try "figuring out." You can also make a permission for a specific activity: "You're welcome to paint in any way that you'd like right now, and you also don't have to paint in any way in particular."

As always, adapt rather than adopt. Experiment and notice what comes up for you. Practice the Four Permissions both amid daily activities and as a quiet meditation; the more you release the clinging to extremes that now governs certain areas of your life, the more Soulforce can flow through you.

"Transfusions from living primordial traditions empower the artist ... take the artist to the heights and depths needed to find the medicine of the moment."

— ALEX GREY, *THE MISSION OF ART*

CHAPTER 11

ANCIENT ROOTS, NEW LIFE

"For years, the hamster wheel of the liturgy and the confines of church traditions have felt like a bear claw clamped around my musical expression," John, a church music director, told me. "But Playing from the Heart and spacious awareness have changed everything. During last week's service, it occurred to me to let the room breathe, to let myself breathe, and then I allowed the music to move in the direction that the breathing was moving. I had the bravery to step outside my usual confines and create a musical, spiritual—even theatrical—experience. I was fully engulfed, fully present, and the music just got deeper and more emotional as we went on. When I stopped playing, I could hear the audience gasp to take in a breath. I looked over at my husband and saw that he was crying. People stayed around in receiving lines at the end for me and my husband for almost thirty minutes. This experience confirmed what I have always known: that music changes molecules to bring healing to our bodies and planet. It was very powerful."

John's experience moved me on multiple levels. Of course, I was pleased that Playing from the Heart and spacious awareness had worked so well for him, but I was also struck by how closely his experience matched descriptions I had read of the enactment of shamanic ritual powers. Did John's new approach to music allow him to temporarily become a modern-day shaman?

Sabrina, a writer, had chronic back pain and carpal tunnel syndrome that flared when she sat and wrote for long periods. The presence of her symptoms made perfect sense when I saw her write with pen and paper: she hunched over the desk and held her pen in a white-knuckled snarl of fingers. When I used my Alexander Technique hands on work to gently guide her torso into a state of poise and her writing hand into a conduit for bodily flow, Sabrina spoke to me in a state of semi-shock. "Wow. This feels totally different! I can actually feel how my legs and back are affecting my handwriting. The body really is an interconnected web! More than that, I somehow now feel that my words are writing themselves, like they have a life of their own, and I'm just the conduit." After she spoke, Sabrina sat for a moment in awed contemplation of her pen as if seeing it for the first time.

Just as with John, I had multiple reactions to Sabrina's experience. I was happy that she now had a path to physical ease as she wrote. Plus, I was also struck by how closely her description of interconnectedness and aliveness resonated with the animistic, ecological worldview so prevalent throughout human history, but discarded in our own age. Did we just stumble on an ancient truth, hidden under layers of tension and effort?

Eva, an actor, spoke to me of the sadness and creative malaise she had long felt. "I want to get back to acting. It's been too long. Yes, I have a job and I'm a mom, but the real reason I've kept away is that acting sometimes seems so frivolous and not worthwhile financially. I long to be creative, but what stops me is the question, 'What am I even doing here? Is this even useful?'"

This began a long conversation about the wound our society's commodification of the arts inflicted on her, giving rise to her sadness and malaise. As we explored, Eva discovered that at the bottom of her sadness was a beautiful inner child filled with many creative gifts: enthusiasm, light, love, and a mischievous joy. Eva immediately recognized these as some of her greatest creative assets. I then put her recovered creative gifts in a larger context, speaking about the true purpose of the arts, Spiral Dynamics, and the ways artists are uniquely well-suited to help people in our society evolve their consciousness.

I saw tears well up in Eva's eyes as she took all this in. "Oh! My pain has a purpose!" she said. "I now see that my purpose in life is to help others heal the wounds in their hearts through my creativity, whether I'm onstage or off. I want to be a part of the solution in our society, breaking the chain of trauma and helping people into a greater awareness of our fragile planet."

Once more, at the same time I was pleased that Eva was feeling relief from her sadness and creative malaise, I also was amazed at the connection I saw between the process she just underwent and the ancient ideas of alchemy, sacred purpose, and transformation. Did we just practice a modern form of alchemy, turning Eva's existential lead into gold?

The spontaneous appearance of ancient wisdom and practices amid contemporary artistic contexts can raise perplexing questions for many in today's world. To the rigorously scientific-minded, shamanism, mysticism, animism, and alchemy seem like backward superstition and dogma with no place in serious intellectual discourse other than as curious historical footnotes that we've now, thankfully, grown past.

Is such a dismissal truly warranted? Or are experiences like those of my students signs that many ancient traditions still have something to offer us? What if, in our society's understandable haste to be free from stifling religious dogmatism, we've thrown the baby out with the bathwater? What if some of these ancient traditions, far from being outdated relics, are, in fact, the keys to our artistic Soulforce and even our collective survival and thriving?

Let's address these questions at a societal and planetary level first.

The global, industrialized society that currently dominates the earth is at a crossroads. We are increasingly becoming aware that the story of technological progress that currently animates our way of life is not bringing the life of ease and prosperity it promised. Many are increasingly horrified at the destruction wrought by our way of life. At the same time our technology has brought unparalleled prosperity and longer lifespans for many, its unbridled use now threatens to destroy the very basis of life on earth. As we come to terms with this destruction, our horror grows as we realize that our familiar answers are not just failing to stop the destruction, but often make it worse. As a result, many feel disillusioned, helpless, hopeless, and full of despair. What can we possibly do when the ways we know how to help only result in hurt?

I call this state the **Great Humbling**. It is the process of fully taking account of the fact that our current answers are insufficient to meet our challenges and that we need to look elsewhere for guidance. As overwhelming and final as it might seem at times, the Great Humbling is not the end of the story, but a necessary prelude that clears the way for new answers to arise.

Thankfully, the answers to all our collective challenges already exist; the catch is that they will necessarily come from uncommon and unfamiliar sources. Opening ourselves to these new sources requires that we humble ourselves and reintegrate some of the very things we once held in contempt and fear. These sources take many forms: nature, the soul, the feminine, the body, the psychological shadow, altered states of consciousness, near-death experiences, indigenous and esoteric wisdom traditions—even UFO encounters, ancient monuments, and conspiracy theories. Each has their wisdom to offer in our search for new answers to our collective challenges; as Charles DuBois wrote in *Approximations*, "The important thing is to be able at any moment to sacrifice what we are for what we could become."

While many of the sources of the answers we seek have ancient roots, this doesn't mean that to access them we need to entirely give up our modern way of life and live as our ancestors did. The earth couldn't support seven billion hunter-gatherers, after all. Instead, the invitation

Chapter 11 | ANCIENT ROOTS, NEW LIFE

is to bring these ancient sources into the internet age, giving them new life as we navigate our current challenges. This is the essential mission of Spiral Dynamics stages Yellow and Turquoise.

There is a Great Humbling in the art world, as well. More and more artists are discovering that our usual ways of creating, performing, practicing, teaching, and making a living are not working. Instead, these usual ways are often the very source of our creative, physical, emotional, and spiritual challenges. As each artist (and arts institution) fully takes account of this fact and moves through the ordeal of facing their own pain, disillusionment, and despair, they can, with the proper support, be initiated into a new kind of artistry; one that is dynamic, flexible, soul-led, spiral-informed, and whole. One that can take what has worked well in the past and give it new life in addressing current challenges. In short, they become Soulforce Artists.

You become a Soulforce Artist when you go through your personal Great Humbling and come out the other side capable of creating transformative, evolutionary art. The purpose of the Soulforce Arts Approach is to provide the intellectual, spiritual, and practical support necessary for you to do so. As you progress through the Soulforce Arts Approach on your way to full-fledged Soulforce Artistry, you may discover that your creative process blends the old and the new, giving new life and contemporary forms to the ancient and timeless source of creativity and wisdom within. Your art then goes beyond the merely pretty, popular, provocative, or virtuosic to take on a unique power shared with the greatest works of art throughout history. It empowers others to navigate their own great humblings and come out the other side feeling more whole, connected, alive, and free from the pain of separation. Delivering this experience is your highest calling as an artist.

> You become a Soulforce Artist when you go through your personal Great Humbling and come out the other side capable of creating transformative, evolutionary art.

This chapter explores several ancient archetypes of transformation and creativity, and provides the practical tools necessary to give them new life in your artistic practices.

We begin with the magical source of art's power.

ART AS ENCHANTMENT

> *"To produce their finest works, artists lose themselves in the energetic flow of creation, become possessed by an art spirit ... Like the seers and oracles of old, Art sings and shouts from the axis of truth to wake us up to who we are and where we are going."*
>
> — ALEX GREY, THE MISSION OF ART

As we've explored throughout this book, art has a unique power to transform, heal, inspire, and connect. The source of this power is nothing less than the living universe itself and finds unique form within everyone. A Soulforce Artist is one who directly participates with this source, has the skills to give it exquisite form, and shares it with others to enchanting effect.

Who else in human societies has similar powers and intentions? Magicians. More than silly people in top hats or bestarred robes with tricks up their sleeves, magicians carry unique insights into the inner workings of the universe and the ability to enact those insights to transformative effect.

The magician's power and that of the artist's are one and the same, a truth reflected in the enchanting art left to us by many ancient societies. Why do millions flock to Stonehenge, Angkor Wat, or the Sphinx every year? It's because the people who built them understood timeless truths about the human condition and possessed the skills to invoke those truths through their creations. As we explored in Chapter 4, the creative act is a celebration, and to regard it as such grants access to the same insight held by the builders of some of the most transformative works of art ever created: that there is no difference between magic and art.

The characteristic effect of the magician/artist's power is the experience of enchantment. According to author Patrick Curry in *Art and Enchantment*, enchantment is a state of wonder that can range in intensity from "charm, through delight, to full-blown joy."[1] It occurs with the release of control and the will to power that provokes a state of mutual apprehension, appreciation, and love with the enchanting other. Curry again: "With art, [enchantment] happens when you find yourself in the picture you're looking at, to the music you're hearing, or the story you're reading. Going deeply into it carries you away to somewhere else, which turns out to be at the heart of where you already were."[2]

Intentionally cultivating enchantment is the key to the magician's power and requires understanding the inner workings of enchantment. Enchantment is wild, meaning that it can't be controlled or made to happen. It is a form of "concrete magic," meaning that it exists in the liminal space where matter and spirit are one.[3] It is highly personal and dependent on the uniqueness of that moment's circumstances, while at the same time conveying a sense of timelessness, universality, and connection with mysterious forces beyond the individual ego. It is also relational, providing an experience of meeting a lovable other across a gap or veil. Its etymology suggests a participatory nature; *enchantment* literally means "to be in a song." In addition, enchantment often feels fateful and takes on mythic significance; you feel as though your whole life has led you specifically to this encounter, and that you have somehow entered a realm previously thought to be inhabited solely by gods, saints, and heroes.

> The builders of the most transformative works of art ever created understood a timeless truth: that there is no difference between magic and art.

Enchantment's relationship with art is complex. Not all forms of enchantment have the same emotional valence; there are dark and light forms of enchantment. For example, Debussy's *Pavane for a Dead Princess* and the landscape paintings of the Chinese Song dynasty invoke a light enchantment: these pieces are like stepping into a heavenly realm full of delicious wonder. True light enchantment is not a vapid scene of rainbows and daisies, however. For light enchantment to work, there must also be an element of transiency, poignancy, and mystery that goes beyond the merely cheerful. In contrast, Alfred Hitchcock's *The Birds*, Edgar Allen Poe's *The House of Usher*, and Hieronymus Bosch's *Last Judgement* invoke a dark enchantment: they are deeply moving works whose enthralling power draws the audience in despite the feelings of dread and even horror they elicit. Both light and dark enchantment are artistically valid and draw on the same source of power: the apprehension of an animate universe, the lived experience of the Story of Interbeing.

There is also false enchantment, which is marked by obsession, glamor, and the desire to possess or be possessed.[4] Advertising, public relations, the newest technological gadgets, political and ideological trends, popularity and fads, AI art, the merely pretty or virtuosic, and the profit motive all result in falsely enchanting art. Examples include Andy Warhol's *Campbell's Soup Cans*, most pop music, and romance novels. These are often eye- or ear-catching but ultimately unsatisfying.

Not all of art's power comes from enchantment. Sometimes a piece's most powerful effect is disenchantment. The value of Penderecki's *Threnody for the Victims of Hiroshima* and Picasso's *Guernica* is their disenchantment of war. There is a danger in creating disenchanting art, however. Disenchantment is the evaporation of wonder that leaves behind the apprehension of a lifeless, inert world filled with meaningless stuff; it is the world seen from the Story of Separation. Disenchantment is the materialist's voice saying, "That cloud isn't *really* alive; it's just a bunch of water vapor randomly blown about by the wind!" Or "Art doesn't *do* anything; it's just a bunch of blobs on a canvas!"

Chapter 11 | ANCIENT ROOTS, NEW LIFE

Much modernist and postmodernist conceptual art, as well as any created in service of the lesser gods, is deeply disenchanting and thus fails to move us into the mysterious depths our souls long for. Art created in this way can have a certain power, but it is limited to the power to disenchant; as the journalist Cyril Connolly wrote, "One cannot serve both [the will to power] and beauty."[5] Thus, disenchantment is antithetical to art's only true—and magical—source of power: the power to enchant and bring alive.

There is no formula to create enchanting art. Enchantment is more like a gift, arising unbidden only after you've released any kind of formula, agenda, or program. However, you can invite it into your artistic life by setting the right conditions. The first is to understand its characteristics. The second is to recall experiences of enchantment so that you become more attuned it its presence in your life. The third is to remember that to enchant your audiences, you must be attuned to enchantment as you create; a shift that turns a performance, for example, into a scene of mutual enchantment. And the fourth is to develop effortlessness skills, such as those in the Mind-Body Interludes. Lovingkindness practices, such as Buddhist metta meditations, are also useful. These involve wishing the best for yourself or others to tap into the enchanting effect of love. With these in place, you make yourself more available to the magician's power and the transformative potential characteristic of all truly great art.

SOULFORCE INQUIRY 11.1
CULTIVATING THE MAGICIAN'S POWER

Recall experiences of enchantment, artistic and otherwise, from your life. These may include experiences in nature, art, spiritual practices, loving relationships, food and drink, or psychedelics. What was unique about these experiences and how have they informed your life and art?

What is your relationship with the creative process? Overall, is it more characterized by enchantment or disenchantment, and why?

Spend some time over the next few weeks deliberately practicing the lessons in the Mind-Body Interludes. What happens to your experience of enchantment when the creative act is truly effortless? In addition, listen to guided metta or loving-kindness meditations. These are widely available on the internet and can reliably release the hidden emotional attachments that block enchantment's presence in your life and art.

THE SHAMANIC INITIATION

"We are called to become hollow bones for our people and anyone else we can help, and we are not supposed to seek power for our personal use and honor."

— FRANK FOOLS CROW, LAKOTA MEDICINE MAN, IN *FOOLS CROW* BY THOMAS MAILS

Connecting with the ancient archetype of the magician provides valuable insight into art's magical power. However, learning to step into this archetype carries certain dangers. Remember the story of *The Sorcerer's Apprentice*, in which the young adept loses control over his magical water-carrying brooms and almost loses his life and his master's house to the ensuing deluge? If you don't think this can happen to you as an artist, simply look at the all-too-short and painful lives of many 1960s rock stars; these were people with great artistic power who didn't know how to get the brooms to stop.

The presence of this danger has been known since time immemorial. As a result, all indigenous wisdom traditions, the great mystery schools, and even some modern institutions require their prospective students to go through a process of initiation. Initiation is an ordeal that tempers the prospect's overeager enthusiasm, reveals the society's innermost understandings and practices, and teaches the humility required for the wise handling of the powers on offer. It is the absolute prerequisite to full acceptance within the tradition or community, to adulthood, and to magicianhood.

An initiation, whether formal or informal, is also necessary to become a full-fledged Soulforce Artist. An artist who has not gone through the ordeal of initiation is in danger of remaining a child forever; creative, perhaps, but irresponsible, lacking a meaningful direction, and unable to be of service to their world. In contrast, an artist who has completed their initiation becomes an awakened adult—one who is connected to their artistic purpose, balances discipline and freedom, and whose art meets the world's hunger.

What does the process of initiation look like and how might it affect your artistic life? Let's examine the initiatory process of another ancient archetype closely related to that of the magician: the shaman.

The process of becoming a shaman involves two initiations, both centered around a healing journey. In shamanic cultures, such as those of the Eskimos and the Siberian tribes, the first sign that someone was destined to become a shaman was a prolonged childhood illness.[6] Far from being solely a calamity, such an illness was regarded as an initiatory process that, if successfully navigated (often with the help of experienced elders), armed the young person with first-hand knowledge of certain healing powers. In *The Death and Resurrection Show: From Shaman to Superstar*, author Rogan Taylor writes, "It is the shaman's own susceptibility to sickness that paradoxically leads toward the experience which not only cures himself, but also provides the power to cure others."[7]

The second initiation came when it was time to claim the official role of shaman in their tribe. This consisted of gaining the trust and admiration of their community through a display of their powers. According to Taylor, this display is what eventually became our contemporary show-business and artistic performance practices. In other words, the historical root of modern "showmanism" (including that of theater, comedy, stage magic, escape artistry, rock concerts, film, medicine shows, and others) is shamanism. He writes, "It could be that the whole phenomenon of entertainment has its roots in the variety of methods and devices that ancient shamans employed to both exhibit and validate their extraordinary experiences ... Showbusiness originates in demonstrations of spirit-power which give a teaching about the supernatural, an instruction in the art of transformation from sickness into health." [8]

While Taylor's focus in *The Death and Resurrection Show* is on the historical origins of performance and entertainment, the shaman's initiatory display may also be the origin of all other forms of art. Do contemporary painters owe their lineage to those who painted deep in the caves of Lascaux? Or contemporary poets to their ancestral forebears who illuminated deep truths through campfire enactments of myth and story? It's likely.

Once accepted in their official role, ancient shamans would then work to bring healing to the members of their tribe. This they would do by re-enacting their own healing journey in the presence of the patient and with the active participation of the entire tribe. For the shaman, all illnesses have the same root cause: soul loss, which is a form of anxiety that comes from being separated from one's divinity, community, or purpose. "Far from being a naïve superstition, soul loss, and its sickness-inducing effect, now has scientific support. Studies now show how one contemporary manifestation of soul loss, adverse childhood events, clearly have negative long-term health outcomes, such as chronic diseases."[9] Thus, the shaman's cure was one for the human condition in general, and its efficacy rested on the shaman's ability to produce an ecstatic condition in themselves, their patient, and everyone else present. According to Taylor, the shaman's main healing force came from the power their performance had to:

Chapter 11 | ANCIENT ROOTS, NEW LIFE

> *"... Abolish temporarily the psychic boundaries between the mundane and the supernatural worlds. The shaman leads those present into direct experiential contact with the 'spirit powers,' primarily those that dwell in the 'Underworld.' He knows how therapeutically effective such experiences can be because the cure of his own sickness was accomplished through precisely such a magical journey. [His] show dramatically imitates initiation ... [seducing] both patient and audience into a mini descent-into-hell and simultaneously invites them to accomplish their own act of self-renewal.* (10)

Using chanting, drumming, singing, dancing, storytelling, and divination, the shaman gradually brought everyone present into an ecstatic trance. This trance dissolved psychological barriers between individuals, leaving any distinction between performer and audience nonexistent. In this altered state, encounters with spirit powers became possible and, guided by the shaman's experience and learning, messages from archetypal realms could surface about how best to treat the patient. By the end of the experience, everyone gathered would feel refreshed and rejuvenated, better able to meet life's challenges through a renewed sense of connection with something larger than themselves.

> Shamanism teaches us that the creative act is not merely an act of entertainment nor the creation of a luxurious commodity. Rather, it is the magical invocation of superhuman realities via the performer's extraordinary artistic abilities in service of the healing and wholeness of both the artist and audience.

What is the creative act other than just such a journey to archetypal realms? The shaman's healing act reveals that the creative act is not merely an act of entertainment nor the creation of a luxurious commodity. Rather, it is the magical invocation of superhuman realities via the performer's extraordinary artistic abilities in service of the healing and wholeness of both the artist and audience.

Your journey into full-fledged Soulforce Artistry is greatly supported by learning about the shaman's initiations and powers. Even if you are not currently an active member in an indigenous wisdom tradition or mystery school, you can seek out initiatory experiences offered by other communities, as well as enact your initiation using practices like the one below. The wisdom, healing, and sense of connection with the cosmos you potentially gain from these experiences are a vital source of the creative inspiration and energy necessary to the magical, spine-tingling, and transformative art both you and your audiences desire.

One more note. To complete your initiations and to learn the shaman's skills is not reliant on any one tradition or modality. It is rather an inner alchemical transformation that can be undertaken in multiple ways, and which ultimately leads to a shared human experience. The historical context offered above implies that all contemporary artists already draw upon the shaman's powers when up on stage or in the studio, only without being aware that they are doing so.[11] Therefore, the process of developing shamanic powers is, in a sense, inescapable and takes nothing away from others so long as it helps you connect with our common humanity. We live in a time when many in our contemporary society have little to no connection with their own cultural heritage, and for some, this disconnection is a source of crushing depression and existential anxiety. We long for a deeper cultural heritage than what is currently on offer. We crave acceptance into something like the mystery schools of yore; we want to be humbled before a great and mysterious power, to know the secrets of the universe, to participate in their inner workings, and to thereby inhabit our proper place in the cosmos. Without initiation, society devolves into narcissism, nihilism, and chaos. Completing your own initiations and otherwise embracing the shaman's take on the creative act allows your art to be a vehicle for

Chapter 11 | ANCIENT ROOTS, NEW LIFE

connection to deeper sources of cultural and mystical connection, and thereby bringing healing to our fractured world.

**SOULFORCE INQUIRY 11.2
DISCOVERING YOUR OWN SHAMANIC
JOURNEY IN A SOUL CAVE MEDITATION**

Sit comfortably and close your eyes. Imagine yourself at the edge of an ancient forest; feel the warm breeze, smell the fresh scent of greenery, and feel your feet on the grass. You notice a path leading into the forest and follow it into the cool darkness.

After a while following this path, you find yourself at the edge of a clearing in the forest. Enjoying the birdsong and shafts of light coming through the trees, you notice something curious: a little door in the forest floor. It looks inviting and you decide to find out where it goes. You open the door and walk down a beautiful spiral staircase into the earth.

You find yourself standing in a long, cool, dark hallway. At the far end you see a light, and as you slowly walk toward it you find yourself in a large, magical cave with a glowing pool at its center. You realize that this pool is your deepest, wisest self, your very soul. It holds all the important experiences, symbols, memories, feelings, desires, and truths that you now carry as an artist. It speaks to you, inviting you to ask any questions you may have.

You ask this pool of light about your first artistic initiation, the pivotal challenging events from your childhood that have since fed your creative inspiration and drive. How have these challenging events shaped your outlook on life and your creative activities? What were their hidden gifts? Were there moments of initiation that had a more positive feeling, as well, such as being inspired to learn to write or by certain concerts? Stay open to whatever the pool of light wishes to reveal to you and remember you can always come back another time.

When you receive answers about your first artistic initiation, ask about your second initiation. This is the one where you began to prove your artistic powers in front of others. Was there a moment when you gained the trust of your audiences in your skills as an artist, and when you said to yourself, *Yes, I really can do this*? What are your special powers as a performer? What are the challenges you overcame on the way to proving to yourself and others that you "have what it takes"?

Finally, ask about the most magical moments in your artistic training, as well as those you've had as a more mature artist. What was transformed inside you or your audiences because of those moments? How have those moments informed your artistic purpose?

When you're finished, you thank the glowing pool for sharing its wisdom with you. You walk back down the long, dark hallway to the beautiful spiral staircase. As you climb back up, you see the sunlight above and step out into the forest clearing. Taking a deep breath, you follow the path out of the forest and back to the open field where you began.

Make some notes in your journal about what you discovered about your own artistic initiations. Then find a simple action you can take in the coming few days that helps you makes space in your current artistic life for what you discovered in the soul cave.

Even if the idea of the creative act as a shamanic rite is currently unfamiliar to you, realize now that any power you've conveyed in any creation nonetheless stems from the very same skills and supernatural sources as did those of countless shamans throughout history and across the globe. This power is your Soulforce.

How might you cultivate greater connection with your Soulforce through a shamanic lens? Firstly, you need to have successfully navigated the two initiations of your own healing journey and that of proving your skills as an artist. Secondly, like the shaman, you need a reason to create that goes beyond serving your individual self. Thirdly, you need to be in front of an audience who trusts you and who is willing to get swept up in your creations. Fourthly, you need to be in touch with something larger than yourself during the creative act so that the transformative and healing power of the archetypal realms have a chance to work their magic. With these conditions in place, your art will go beyond the mundane, and will instead reveal, in the words of the poet Hafiz, "the astonishing light of your own being."

A HOLISTIC HEALING JOURNEY

"Where there is ruin, there is hope for a treasure."
— JALALLUDIN RUMI, *DIVAN-E SHAMS-E TABRIZI*

One of the primary functions of the arts is to heal. This is evidenced by the widespread use of the arts in healing practices around the world, from the ancient didgeridoo medicine of the Australian aborigines to the development of art therapy. While to the modern scientific materialist the healing power of the arts is considered suspect at best, there are nonetheless countless people who can testify to the catharsis on offer when surrounded, for example, by the rhythmic thumping of a blues tune whose ache perfectly matches the one in their own hearts. Where does the healing power of the arts come from, and how can you, as an artist, cultivate it to its greatest effect?

The answer lies in the archetype of the wounded healer. The **wounded healer** is one who has suffered an injury or ailment that is not easily treated by conventional means, and who then embarks upon a journey of self-healing. You will recognize this as the same journey every shaman completes. Such a journey is often difficult, but if completed successfully, it yields two invaluable treasures: the return of your full life force and the knowledge of how to heal others.

The archetype of the wounded healer stands in contrast to the usual attitude toward ailments in our society, which is to regard them as aberrations that need to be quickly eradicated and then, hopefully, forgotten about forever. The wounded healer understands sickness differently, saying that the cracks are where the light comes through. The lessons learned from their journey from sickness to health turns their ailments into a source of power. This source of power then becomes their greatest gift, the precious treasure that they then share with others.

The archetype of the wounded healer lends new meaning to the physical, emotional, or spiritual challenges you currently face as an artist. For instance, it gives a deeper, more nuanced perspective on the common debate between the story of the struggling artist and that of the happy artist. The story of the struggling artist looks at the tortured lives of many of the great artists throughout history and draws the conclusion that difficult life circumstances must be necessary to produce great art, and, moreover, that becoming happy and whole may threaten your creative inspiration. This may be what writer Anaïs Nin meant when she wrote in her *Diaries of Anaïs Nin* that, "Life is truly known only to those who suffer, lose, endure adversity and stumble from defeat to defeat."[12]

In contrast, the story of the happy artist says that the creative inspiration to be found in joy and love is every bit as great—if not greater—than that to be found in pain, and furthermore that not all great artists throughout history have been tortured souls. It also says that letting yourself fully feel and express joy and love can be just as difficult, transformative, and generative a process as plumbing the depths of your pain. Painter Bob Ross's aphorisms from his show *The Joy of Painting* were the epitome of the happy artist: "Let us build a happy little cloud which floats around the sky!" (13)

At first glance, these two stories seem to be irreconcilable. To the story of the struggling artist, the story of the happy artist seems hopelessly naïve and risks falling prey to the fake happiness so common in our society and which is antithetical to art that has any power to move us. To the story of the happy artist, on the other hand, the story of the struggling artist misses the ways in which pleasure and joy can lead to illumination. In its mature form, the story of the happy artist says, "Yes, suffering is powerful, but have you ever had a mystical experience where every atom of your being was annihilated by God's Love for ten thousand eternities? Yeah, I didn't think so."

The wounded healer archetype offers a third, more balanced perspective. It says that yes, pain is necessary to the creative process, but the goal is not to wallow in it forever. Rather, your pain can be composted to bring forth greater wholeness and healing than you previously thought possible. As an artist, when you embrace the archetype of the wounded healer, the life force energy and healing skills you acquire along the way will find form in your art, giving you the best of both worlds: the fertile richness of the darkness and the life-affirming vision that comes from making it to the other side more resilient and alive than before. Alex Grey knew this potential well when he wrote in *The Mission of Art*, "Artists offer the world the pain and beauty of their soul as a gift to open the eyes of and heal the collective."

As a practical matter, your healing journey will be best supported by a holistic approach. This means that, instead of focusing on just one part of your body, mind, or life, attend to your well-being on all levels simultaneously. You can do this by engaging in practices that support all your physical, emotional, mental, spiritual, and interpersonal needs.

Here are some examples of self-care practices that support each level of your being:

- **Physical:** Exercise, yoga, a diet free from processed foods, fasting, sauna, cold exposure, breathwork, Alexander Technique, getting plenty of deep sleep
- **Emotional:** Trauma work, shadow work, somatic psychotherapy, group therapy, soul retrieval, time in nature
- **Mental:** Being a life-long learner, studying philosophy and spirituality, meditation
- **Energetic:** Reiki, yoga, visualization, listening to healing music, forest bathing, acupuncture, intuitive healing, chanting
- **Spiritual:** Meditation, the thoughtful use of psychedelics under skilled supervision, time in nature, other spiritual practices
- **Interpersonal:** Immersive concerts, religious gatherings, book clubs, knitting circles, Circling, Authentic Relating,[14] meditation or yoga retreats, "noble friends and noble conversations"[15]

SOULFORCE INQUIRY 11.3
SELF-CARE CALENDAR

There's no need to take part in every practice listed here. Instead, choose one from each level and practice it at regular intervals. Schedule some on a daily basis (such as meditation or exercise), some on a weekly basis (such as psychotherapy or book club), some on a monthly basis (such as a hike in nature or a special class), some on a quarterly basis (such as a weekend getaway or psychedelics), and some on a yearly basis (such as a vacation or meditation retreat that leaves you feeling fully refreshed). Write down which practices speak to you and when you'll do them, and then enter them into your personal calendar so you don't forget.

The ultimate lesson of the wounded healer is illustrated by the linguistic root of the word *healing*. *Healing* comes from *holos*, which is a Greek root found in other words like "holistic," "wholeness," and "holy." It's no wonder these words are connected. When you take a holistic approach to healing yourself, you step into a greater wholeness that can initiate moments of truth and healing that put your audiences in touch with something larger than themselves—an experience, if poignant enough, may be accurately described as holy. This is the artistic treasure that lies waiting within your wounds.

ACCESSING THE MYSTICAL

"Our whole business in this life is to restore to health the eye of the heart whereby God may be seen."
— SAINT AUGUSTINE, SERMON 88.5.5

One of the greatest potentials of the arts is their ability to provoke mystical experiences. A mystical experience is one in which the feeling of your normal, everyday self dissolves to reveal your preexisting connection with all that is. Mystical experiences form the core, esoteric knowledge of every great wisdom tradition, and it may be fair to say that all religion and spirituality is an attempt to preserve knowledge about these states and to provide practices to reliably reach them. Mystical experiences can be life-changing and are often rated among the most important experiences of a person's life, ranked alongside marriage, childbirth, and the death of loved ones.[16] The practices used to induce mystical experiences are incredibly varied, and include meditation, prayer, breathwork, shamanic drumming, psychedelics, fasting, and, of course, the arts.

Mystical experiences come in a variety of forms and characteristics. They are ineffable, meaning that they can't be fully put into words and have a noetic quality, meaning that they reveal previously hidden knowledge and feelings. They come in and out of awareness and can't be held onto. You often feel that the experience is somewhat passive, coming to you instead of being created through your willpower. They reveal the unity of opposites, meaning that you experience a profound sense of the oneness behind all dualities. Mystical experiences can involve visions of archetypal or heavenly realms and carry profound messages that blend personal and cosmic significance. They are timeless, placing your attention in the deep now and dissolving the sense of time passing. Also, they often have a peaceful and joyful quality in which your usual struggles seem to resolve themselves into the larger, sacred dance of life. Finally, mystical experiences reveal the true self, that which is an expression of the divine and beyond any sense of separation, ego, birth, or death.[17],[18]

In *Nurtured by Love: The Classical Approach to Talent Education*, renowned violin teacher Shinichi Suzuki wrote about a mystical state he experienced during a performance of Mozart's Clarinet Quintet. You will find within it several of the above characteristics of mystical experiences:

> *That evening I seemed to be gradually drawn into Mozart's spirit, and, finally I was not conscious of anything else, not even of my own being, I became so immersed. Of course, I did not realize this until afterward. After the performance I tried to applaud. But there was no feeling from the shoulders down, and I could not move either hand. I don't know when the clapping stopped. During the applause I just sat there in a trance. Finally, I got my*

hands back, but even when the feeling came back, I still just stared into space. An indescribable, sublime, ecstatic joy had taken hold of my soul. I had been given a glimpse into Mozart's high spiritual world. Through sound, for the first time in my life, I had been able to feel the highest pulsating beauty of the human spirit, and my blood burned within me. It was a moment of sublime eternity when I, a human being, had gone beyond the limits of my physical body. That night I couldn't sleep at all. Mozart, the man, had shown me immortal light.[19]

Not all art is mystical, nor does it need to be to have value. However, the incredible power of mystical experiences, like Suzuki's, reveal why they are so often sought after in both spiritual and artistic contexts.

There are many ways in which mystical experiences are induced or depicted in art. Some art is notable for its complete lack of spiritual presence, as in advertising. Some use spiritual imagery to transmit an ambiguous or anti-spiritual message, such as Felicien Rops's pornographic crucifixions. Some use traditional spiritual symbols, but transmit little mystical power, such as the commercialized reproductions of religious saints and deities. Some use traditional spiritual symbols to transmit substantive mystical power, such as Islamic calligraphy, Hindu temples, and Buddha sculptures. Some use no spiritual symbols but nonetheless transmit the personally realized mystical knowledge of the artist, such as Zen paintings, the paintings of Van Gogh, and instrumental music like the Mozart Clarinet Quintet described above. Some use spiritual symbols in nontraditional ways to convey mystical power, such as the work of Michelangelo, William Blake, and Claude Debussy. Yet others bring together sacred archetypes of many spiritual traditions, such as Edward Moor's *The Hindu Parthenon*, *Interfaith Song Book: One World, Many Voices*, and the paintings of Alex Grey.

Learning about mysticism and the varieties of mystical art is the first step to being able to create mystical art yourself. However, more important than such intellectual learning are firsthand experiences of mystical connection with all that is. Without direct experience, any art with mystical pretentions will fall flat and fail to resonate with the potential for mystical experiences that now lies dormant in your audiences. With direct experience, however, your art will naturally be infused with your new experiences and understandings and will act to induce similar experiences in your audiences.

SOULFORCE INQUIRY 11.4
CULTIVATING MYSTICAL EXPERIENCES

There are countless ways to cultivate mystical experiences. These include yoga, breathwork, meditation (especially on long retreats), psychedelics, time in nature, fasting, certain forms of psychotherapy, shamanic drumming, trance dancing, and art, among many others.

To begin your path into mysticism, first explore stories of mystical experiences and learn about the many mystical traditions that now exist. Notice which ones call to you and dive deep into those. Don't worry about choosing the right path; in many ways, all roads lead to Rome. In addition, all paths have their pros and cons, so always use your best judgment.

The path to mysticism can be dangerous. It requires you to leave behind the usual ways you've known yourself and the world. You may even feel at times that you're losing your mind. While uncomfortable, these "dark nights of the soul" are normal and even desirable. Seek guidance from experienced elders to navigate difficult experiences.

Finally, keep in mind that mystical experiences, like enchanting ones, are wild and cannot be willed into existence. Indeed, they often only show up when you've fully discovered that, as a path to mystical experiences, your willpower is a dead end. When the paradox of willing yourself to surrender comes to fruition, mystical experiences cannot help but arrive in your life.

PRACTICING AS MAGICAL PLAY

"Learn the alchemy true human beings know. The moment you accept what troubles you've been given the door will open."

— JALALLUDIN RUMI, "THE GUEST HOUSE"

The alchemist is another ancient archetype with direct relevance to the creative act. Alchemy is an ancient form of natural philosophy and the ancestor to modern chemistry. Its main objective is to harness esoteric powers to transmute base materials into gold. While many of the literal beliefs of ancient alchemy have little place in a modern scientific context, their metaphorical and transformational principles still hold true and contain valuable lessons for contemporary artists.[20]

The source of the alchemist's power lies in transmuting lead (what is dark, heavy, painful, stressful, and so on) into gold (what is empowering, full of life, flowing, easeful, and pleasurable). In contemporary artistic contexts, this is accomplished by two basic means. The first we have already explored in the previous sections on shamanism and the wounded healer: when transmuted by certain healing practices, your emotional, physical, and spiritual wounds reveal creative gold.

The second form of transmutation available to contemporary artists happens with a holistic approach to practicing your artistic skills. Common issues in practicing like tension, boredom, burnout, and creative blocks cannot be addressed by the conventional, narrow focus on technique, tradition, and achievement. It is precisely this narrow focus that causes these issues in the first place. Instead, a holistic approach is needed. Taking account of the mind-body connection while practicing, for example, leads to seemingly magical results such as an increased speed of learning, the development of unforeseen skills, surprising effortlessness, and the fullest expression of your knowledge of the soul. The modern mind often dismisses the possibility of such magical results because they do not occur via scientific materialist notions of causality, force, and control. However, the alchemical approach does not require that we lie to ourselves about what's possible; it's rather an invitation into more comprehensive vantage point from which the real possibilities that were previously hidden suddenly become obvious, available, and workable.

What does a holistic approach to practicing look like? It turns out to have a similar relationship to the culminating creative act as does foreplay to sex. For example, to Paul Joannides, author of the popular manual on sex *The Guide to Getting It On*, foreplay is more than merely some fun techniques prior to the "main event" of intercourse. Instead, Joannides takes a more holistic outlook, saying that foreplay is everything that happens in a relationship since the last orgasm.[21]

The same is true of your art. A truly holistic outlook on practicing includes not just the time spent in your studio, but your health, relationships, spiritual outlook, career, and community. In short, practicing includes everything that happened in your life since your last gig.

From this holistic perspective, practicing is more than just trying to learn a particular piece or technique. It's about improving the quality of your system update so that your Soulforce can more easily shine through. Since your Soulforce is an energy inherent to the totality of who and what you are, your approach to practicing should likewise reflect all the ways your art connects to your whole self.

The following are two practical approaches to developing your artistic skills that reveal the alchemical potential of holistic practicing.

Chapter 11 | ANCIENT ROOTS, NEW LIFE

QUANTUM PRACTICING

Quantum practicing is a method of rehearsing a particular passage or technique that draws on the idea of quantum superposition from quantum field theory. A quantum superposition is the ability of a quantum system to be in multiple states at the same time until it is measured.

If, for example, you are a sculptor preparing to execute a delicate and challenging piece, through a process of improvising with various chisels, angles of approach, degrees of striking force, mediums, and other elements, you can create a sort of quantum superposition in yourself comprising all the elements. This yields a feeling of a field of possibilities where you can draw upon any element at will rather than being limited to just trying to recreate a linear, predetermined creative pathway. When you play around with the elements necessary to execute your piece in different combinations as you would with a toy, you no longer feel the pressure of trying to get them all perfect, and instead enjoy the assurance of knowing that any of them are available to you at any moment.

Quantum practicing's nonlinear approach can, at first, seem unfamiliar or paradoxical. However, creating this quantum-like state is the ideal preparation for giving form to any passage or technique because of the openness, resilience, effortlessness, and playfulness it affords.

There are three main ways quantum practicing is superior to the more common method of inculcating the correct procedures. Firstly, inculcating a passage or technique from beginning to end is highly linear. The trouble with this is that there's nothing linear about your mind, body, or creativity, and so trying to impose linearity on yourself is counterproductive. In contrast, quantum practicing honors the nonlinear, interconnected, and fractal-like nature of your mind, body, and creativity, and thereby avoids the pitfalls of imposed linearity.

Secondly, linear ways of practicing encourage mindless repetition, which often produces a state of boredom, fatigue, and tension. For some, this state poses a barrier to practicing that must then be overcome by the excessive use of willpower. Quantum practicing, on the other hand, allows for real creativity and a sense of play while practicing, which naturally encourages internal and intrinsic motivation. Thirdly, repetitious and linear ways of practicing don't reflect the spontaneity, heart, and joy that makes a performance or other creative act truly great. Quantum practicing encourages these qualities and is thus more aligned with the truth that how you practice becomes how you perform.

Here's a real-life example of quantum practicing in music. My violin student Andy, who's ten years old, can play Gossec's Gavotte quite well and with verve, but he often rushes through the sixteenth notes such that he drops the last few notes of each passage. This tendency has shown up only recently in his process of bringing the whole piece up to performance tempo. In previous lessons, I suggested that he practice the passages very slowly, but this clearly hasn't worked; even though he has done this for a few weeks, every time he tries to play the passage quickly again, he still drops those last few notes.

So, in one lesson I said, "Okay, Andy, let's do our improv practicing," which is what I call quantum practicing with my younger students. "Why don't you pick the hardest measure and name the notes from lowest to highest?"

He did this: "C, D, E, F#, G, and high E."

"Alright," I said. "Now play those notes like they were a funny little scale from lowest to highest, and then highest to lowest." He did this without difficulty. "Now let's use those notes to make up little songs. We'll take turns."

He and I then took about half a dozen turns each, making up fun little songs using only the notes in that one measure. At a certain point I asked him to add in some four-note slurs (a violin technique that uses one bow stroke to play four different notes) because that's a technique featured in each of these tricky sixteenth-note passages. After I saw that he could easily improvise using those notes with occasional four-note

Chapter 11 | ANCIENT ROOTS, NEW LIFE

slurs, I asked him to play the passage again as written. And wouldn't you know it—he played it perfectly! Three times in a row!

Then I asked him, "Now tell me—what did you notice about your body when you played the measure as written this time? Did you get tighter or freer?"

"Freer," he replied.

"And what happened to the fun factor? Was it more fun or more boring to practice in this way?"

"More fun!" he said.

"Great!" I replied. "And did you have to work really hard to get the notes right?"

"No," he replied.

"That's right. This is why we call it 'playing music,' not 'working music.' Just notice how practicing this way helped you feel more free, have more fun, and be better able to get the notes right."

What I often tell students like Andy is that quantum practicing is like finding your way through a new neighborhood. If you only ever take one route from your house to the market, you might feel a bit anxious and tense because if you ever took a wrong turn, you'd be totally lost! If you instead took a different route every time you went to the market, you'd probably feel totally confident and at ease, even if you had to navigate blindfolded.

There is a sense of effortlessness, confidence, and delicious presence that comes from practicing in this way. When you do quantum practicing right, practicing feels less like unicycling across a mile-high tightrope, and more like lying on a divan, plucking ripe fruit from a tree.

SOULFORCE INQUIRY 11.5
A STEP-BY-STEP GUIDE TO
QUANTUM PRACTICING

- **Find the critical moment.** Locate the trickiest section of whatever piece or technique you're working on. You can also think of finding the spot where you get most tense or stressed out. Choose to work on the few notes/words/gestures just before and after the critical moment.
- **Organize the elements.** For music, organize the notes from lowest to highest. For dance, organize the movements from simplest to most complex, or from slowest to quickest. For poetry, organize your words in alphabetical order or from shortest to longest.
- **Practice in order.** Let yourself get comfortable with the elements by going through them simply and slowly in the order you've selected.
- **Improvise.** Play around with the notes/words/gestures in various ways that feel fun. Use varying styles, tempos, rhythms, and articulations. If desired, include other elements that are particular to the passage you've selected.
- **Go back to the original critical moment.** Once you've reached a certain level of fluidity, ease, and fluency with the improvisations, play the passage as you would in the final product. Notice if anything feels, sounds, or looks different. Did you get tighter or freer? Did you have more fun or less? Was it more expressive or more mechanical?

Chapter 11 | ANCIENT ROOTS, NEW LIFE

STEWARDING THE KNOWLEDGE OF THE SOUL

The second example of a holistic form of practicing is **stewarding the knowledge of the soul**. As mentioned in Chapter 4, the knowledge of the soul is the non-conceptual embodiment of what is uniquely yours to express in your lifetime. It is kind of like a living library inside you. Depending on your life's experiences, your training, and where and when you live, your library will have different resources inside it that will inform the quality of, and approach to, your creative life. Every time you experience something new—whether in your art or elsewhere in your life—your library gets updated. Then, when you create, perform, practice, or teach, this new information becomes a part of what you bring to the creative act.

The stewardship of the knowledge of the soul is a truly holistic process, one that is only partly dependent on the time you intentionally spend on your art. Many other aspects of your life inform your knowledge of the soul:

- What you pay attention to, and with what quality of attention
- Your personality traits, which can include your degree of extroversion, agreeableness, openness, conscientiousness, and neuroticism[22]
- Your beliefs and habits
- The amount of trauma you carry and how much healing work you've done
- How much and what kind of artistic training you've had
- The knowledge of the soul of your teachers, mentors, and childhood caretakers
- Your cultural heritage

- Your friendships and relationships
- The kinds of music and art you've been exposed to
- Your awareness of what's happening in the world at large
- The attitudes of the people around you toward you as an artist
- Your inborn degree of sensitivity
- Your health and well-being overall
- The possible influence of past lives
- Your genetic disposition
- Your age

To be a good steward, you must realize that your knowledge of the soul has a life of its own, and that imposing your will upon it won't do nearly as much good as trying to bring life to what's already there. Stewardship starts with a clear-eyed assessment of what's already within your knowledge of the soul. Then, you adopt an attitude of reverence toward your charge and make choices based on what would be most life-giving. Finally, you take the long view, both in the past and into the future, and have a clear vision or mission to work toward.

SOULFORCE INQUIRY 11.4
STEWARDING YOUR KNOWLEDGE OF THE SOUL

As an artist, you can steward your knowledge of the soul in a variety of ways. For example:

- Listening to music or taking in art that speaks to you deeply and letting it work on you

- Spending time with people whom you admire
- Meditation and contemplation
- Healing your trauma
- Playing from the Heart
- Making your built and natural environments more beautiful
- Discovering and living your life purpose
- Deepening your capacity for love through conscious relationships
- Spending more time in places of natural beauty

Write down twenty ideas for stewarding your knowledge of the soul. Then, choose the two or three that feel the most lively, fun, and satisfying, and decide to engage in those in the coming weeks.

Essentially, stewarding the knowledge of the soul is the same as what's required to live fully and deeply. Every time you wholeheartedly give yourself over to the ten thousand joys and ten thousand sorrows of life, your knowledge of the soul deepens. Any time you wake up, grow up, clean up, or show up,[23] your knowledge of the soul becomes richer through your growing capacity for love, joy, pleasure, fun, truth, goodness, connection, beauty, and insight into the nature of life. Through stewarding the knowledge of the soul and quantum practicing, your artistic sessions will take on a new richness, depth, and pleasure. They will empower you to meet the challenges of your life, artistic and otherwise, from a place of greater wholeness and vitality, and this is what will allow you to create with Soulforce.

TEACHING THE PATH

"[Kids] don't remember what you try to teach them. They remember what you are."

— JIM HENSON, *IT'S NOT EASY BEING GREEN: AND OTHER THINGS TO CONSIDER*

Note: This section is meant to put forth an example of the Soulforce Arts Approach applied to teaching. If you're not a teacher, feel free to skip it. Even so, you may still wish to read it because its core lesson can help you connect more with peers, colleagues, and audiences, in addition to students.

Every great mystery school puts forth three basic layers of truth. The first layer contains the outward-facing truths that are easy to understand by the lay population. The second layer contains the truths that require serious practice and discipline to attain. The third layer contains the deepest, most secret, and most esoteric knowledge that cannot be understood without having fully digested the first two layers. All three layers have their own valid take on the ultimate truth, and each one builds on its predecessor to provide learners with the appropriate perspectives and skills necessary for their stage of development. The ultimate purpose of this multi-layered model is to provide spiritual adepts with a viable, step-by-step path to humanity's deepest wisdom.

This is a model not just for spiritual teachers, but for arts teachers as well. The first layer of teaching an art form concerns outward-facing skills, such as technique, body mechanics, theory, history, and the rituals that comprise the creative act. The second layer goes deeper and builds on the first by addressing the physical tension, mindset, and emotional blocks that cannot be resolved by applying yet more of the first layer. The third layer concerns the innermost lessons of any art form, such

Chapter 11 | ANCIENT ROOTS, NEW LIFE

as the ultimate purpose of the arts, and how art can serve to remind people of who we are and what we're here to do. All three have their valid take on how to create great art, and each builds on the previous to provide students with developmentally appropriate perspectives and skills. Ultimately, and as we saw with the three stories that began this chapter, a multi-layered approach to teaching provides arts students with a viable, step-by-step path to humanity's deepest wisdom.

While many arts teachers acknowledge the value of the two deeper layers, few have the skills or understanding to implement anything beyond the first layer in their day-to-day lessons. The reason for this is not hard to understand: the first layer is the easiest to see and deal with; if you see your student holding their brush at the wrong angle, you can easily correct it to the right one. However, as important as the first layer is, to ignore the other two leaves you without the skills and understanding necessary to effectively address the two greatest creative hindrances most students face: excess effort and tension that come from trying hard and the focus on "just getting it right," as we've discussed throughout the book. Lacking fluency in these deeper layers, you may feel helpless to lead your students through these hindrances and into their greatest artistic potential. As a result, you may end up either leaving these potentials to chance or giving up on the possibility of conveying these deeper layers at all, saying, "Either you have it or you don't."

Thankfully, there is a simple and effective method of helping your students release their over-efforting and to go beyond just getting it right. I call it **transmitting your quality of being**. It's a method of conveying your own effortlessness and knowledge of the soul to your students, directly and nonverbally. It's based on the reality that you and your students are interconnected, and that you can rely on that interconnectedness to effectively transmit your inner state to your students.

Developing the ability to transmit your quality of being comprises three basic components. The first component is a process of personal growth; you need to develop your own knowledge of the soul and effortlessness to a sufficient degree, so you have something of real value to transmit to your students. This we have already explored extensively. The second component involves sensory appreciation; you need to develop your ability to reliably sense your students' degree of soulfulness and effortlessness in real time. The third component is a well-defined process by which the transmission of your own knowledge of the soul and effortlessness can take place. We will now explore these latter two components.

Transmitting your quality of being to your students requires reliably sensing their degree of soulfulness and effortlessness in real time. For this, you need to practice **see-sensing**. See-sensing is a term coined by one of my primary Alexander Technique teachers, and Director of the Philadelphia School for the Alexander Technique, Martha Hansen Fertman, Ed.D. It is a skill that focuses your attention in two ways. The first is an embodied focus, meaning that when you see or hear your student, you attend not just to your visual or auditory experience of them, but to your bodily response to them as well. The second is an open focus, just like we explored in Mind-Body Interlude 1 on spacious awareness. An open focus lets you pick up on the subtleties of what's happening in your student better than if you tried to pick out specific details with a narrower focus.

To practice see-sensing while teaching, simply sense your whole body, including your Inner Audience Member, while you watch your student demonstrate their art. When you notice that your body becomes tighter, it could be that your student just got tighter. Likewise, when your body becomes freer, it could be that your student just got freer, too. The more sensitive you become to your own body while your student plays, the better your ability to pick up on what's happening in your student's body-mind while they play.

When you've covered the first two components of transmitting your quality of being, you are then ready for the third component: a specific process by which you can directly guide your students into greater effortlessness and a deeper knowledge of the soul.

Chapter 11 | ANCIENT ROOTS, NEW LIFE

**SOULFORCE INQUIRY 11.5
TRANSMITTING YOUR QUALITY OF BEING**

- Have your student demonstrate their current skills or pieces while you practice see-sensing. Compare notes on what each of you noticed: Did each of you get tighter or freer? Was their creative act more expressive or mechanical? Was it more fun for them or more boring? What happened in your respective inner audience members?

- Ask your student what they were paying attention to while playing. If it was some version of "just trying to get it right," continue to the next step.

- Perform your student's skill or piece in two ways and ask them to notice their Inner Audience Member as you do so. First, perform it while just trying to get it right, and then ask your student what their Inner Audience Member said or felt while you performed. Next, perform it while Playing from the Heart or while employing a method of effortlessness. Have a conversation about what your student noticed in their Inner Audience Member this time.

- Say the following to your student: "Now it's your turn. Perform the skill or piece in such a way where you feel the same way you felt when I Played from the Heart/used a spacious awareness." It often helps to use their language. If they described feeling "happy and relaxed," then you can modify the sentence above and say, "Perform the piece in such a way where you feel happy and relaxed, just like you did when I was playing." You can also use a more general prompt such as, "Play in a way where your Inner Audience Member feels good."

- Afterward, have a brief conversation about what your student noticed. Asking your students what they notice is a powerful way to reinforce their new experiences. If they had a clear experience of being in touch with their knowledge of the soul, ask them how they accomplished it. Often, young students will fish about for answers, so keep directing them back to the simple fact that they were paying attention to the feelings of their Inner Audience Member while playing.

- Finally, share what you felt in your own body and Inner Audience Member while you heard your student play. For example, you might describe how you noticed they were listening to themselves in a new way, how that affected the quality of their artistic output, and how all of that affected you at an emotional and physical level. Such feedback is immensely valuable to your students' artistic development because it helps them bring awareness and language to the vital, and hard-to-describe, emotional, physical, and spiritual sensations that comprise their knowledge of the soul and effortlessness.

By adopting this method, you can effectively transfer your knowledge of the soul and degree of effortlessness you have inside yourself to your students. When you practice it regularly, you and your students will notice greater enjoyment, creativity, and connection in your lessons together. With time, you will both get to enjoy the full flowering of what can be a surprising depth of feeling in their creations. In essence, this method allows for the transmission of your own Soulforce to your students—and this may be one of the greatest gifts you can give to them as a teacher.

Chapter 11 | ANCIENT ROOTS, NEW LIFE

THE MAGIC OF RESONANCE

*"In the Story of Interbeing, all we can give
to each other is our attention."*

— STELLA OSOROJOS EISENSTEIN, DEVELOPER
OF RESONANT ATTENTION

There is a paradox at the heart of reaching outside our society's current paradigm to ancient and unorthodox sources of wisdom: it's that humanity's deepest wisdom already resides within you. It's just that you don't fully realize it yet.

Your job as an artist, then, is to discover the wisdom within, illuminate it through your art, and, by so doing, guide others into their own inner sources of wisdom.

Art guided by your inner wisdom is a force for healing, harmony, and sanity. It breaks down the barriers between what you thought was separate and allows you, and those around you, to share in the wisdom thus discovered. This kind of art has a transformative potential that few in our society fully realize, one capable of ringing in a new and more beautiful world. By what means can your art bring the gifts of your inner wisdom to wider conscious awareness?

Here we turn to the magic of resonance, though to illustrate how this works, let's look at an example of literal resonance. Imagine that you are playing a Tibetan singing bowl by stroking its rim gently with a leather-bound mallet. Around and around you go, and, gradually, the bowl's vibration increases until it rings with a clear, loud tone. Now imagine that you have not just one bowl in front of you, but many. You notice that some of the other bowls are beginning to sing as well, their own vibrations being stimulated by those from the one bowl you're playing. Pretty soon, nearly all the bowls are ringing, and you realize that the collective sound is louder and more sustained than could have been accomplished if you had instead expended the greater effort of trying to ring them all separately. The magic of resonance works the same way, revealing how the smallest, simplest acts can have an outsized effect if they resonate with the potential latent in those around you.

To tap into the magic of resonance you must realize that art is not a one-way street, an emanation from the artist as a separate individual to the audience members as separate individuals. This is something many musicians, for example, already know firsthand: if you play for an audience who ignores you, you feel deflated because you know instinctually that your gifts must be both given well and received well for the essential function of art to take place. On the other hand, if you play for an audience who listens to you deeply, then their deep listening draws out of you the very magic that they wanted to hear from you—and that you wanted to give in the first place. Thus, as Henri Matisse said, "In art, what is most important is the relationship between things."[24]

Becoming a more powerful creator rests largely on your ability to magnify the magic of resonance between you and your audiences. To do this, you need to have two conditions in place. The first, as just mentioned, is to find audiences who will resonate with the frequencies that come through in your system updates. We will explore how to find such audiences in the following chapter. The other condition is listening deeply to yourself during the creative act.

Deep listening is a state of absorption that uses the simple act of paying attention to tap into the magic of resonance. Attention is like the mallet for your singing bowl, and deep listening is what allows you to use that mallet to the greatest effect. When you listen deeply to yourself in a performance, for example, your movements, stage presence, and sound will take on the quality of deep listening. Deep listening is a very attractive quality, one that exerts a strong gravitational pull on your audiences' attention. From the point of view of deep listening, a performance doesn't consist so much of the specific acts taken on stage, but of the relationship of the qualities of listening between you and your audience—a state of mutual enchantment. The performance, then, starts not with the first notes, but rather in the first moment you and your audience become coupled through listening to one another. Likewise, a performance ends not with the last notes, or even with a series of catastrophic mistakes, but when either you or your audience stop listening. Ultimately, the more deeply you listen, the greater your creative power. You know you have become a great performer when your listening is so deep that all you have to do is walk out on stage and your audience is immediately entranced.

The magic of resonance, and the deep listening that magnifies it, have direct relevance to creating a more beautiful, harmonious world. As we explored previously, a more beautiful world cannot be brought about by force and control. Instead, it can only be brought forth from the Story of Interbeing, whose mode of action relies on attention and resonance. From this story, for your art to carry the greatest transformative effect, it needs to come from listening deeply to a longing or knowing shared by you and your audiences. What is the longing or knowing latent in our society that has the greatest potential of bringing about a more beautiful world?

It is the longing for wholeness that comes from the painful illusion of separation and the related, sometimes subconscious, knowledge of our inherent wisdom. It is our unrequited longing for our wholeness that energizes the destruction all around us, and it is our latent inner wisdom which inspires us to acts of beauty and healing. Drawing on the singing bowl analogy, this longing and this knowledge are like a tone fundamental to all singing bowls. When you create something that resonates with this tone, it may have a far greater transformative power than you realize.

Do not underestimate the power of resonance to initiate radical change. It is the same power that leads the builders of mighty bridges to fear the synchronized steps of seemingly innocent marching bands and parades. You, as an artist, can tap into this power by creating from the knowledge of, and your longing for, your inherent wholeness and wisdom. This you can do by connecting with sources of ancient wisdom and giving them new form in your artistic life as it is. When you do so, you turn the simple act of creation into one suffused with sufficient Soulforce to move mountains.

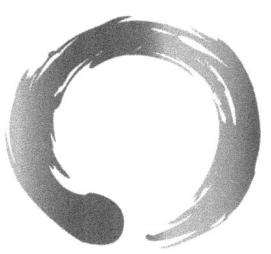

MIND-BODY INTERLUDE #7

THE MAGIC PAUSE

"Sometimes all it takes is a little bit of nothing."

— MARJORIE BARSTOW,
ALEXANDER TECHNIQUE TEACHER

The premise of the Soulforce Arts Approach is that your creative magic, your Soulforce, already lies in wait within you, just waiting to burst forth. The Alexander Technique offers a crucial insight into how to allow it to do so. It reveals that your body is the channel through which your Soulforce pours. If you unlock your body, you unlock your Soulforce.

The Magic Pause is my take on the very core of the Alexander Technique. It is the single most powerful, useful, and adaptable method of releasing the muscular tension that constricts your Soulforce and leads to musculoskeletal discomfort and overuse injuries. It's the first thing I teach to all my new Alexander Technique students because it's so easy to implement and has such outsized and far-reaching benefits. With it, you'll be able to quickly and easily release the muscular tension that interferes with your technique, creative expression, and well-being.

What is the source of the Magic Pause's power? It allows you to exercise more choice over the body movement habits that are the root cause of tension. Here's how it works.

Every day, you use your body in ways that are familiar. You employ habitual movements to walk, sit, stand, create, and brush your teeth. You formed these habits long ago through repetition; at first you had to consciously learn these behaviors, but over time they became automatic and somewhat unconscious. Sometimes, habits are great—they allow you to tie your shoes without having to relearn every time you put them on. However, what makes habits useful is also what makes them hard to change. When they become automatic and unconscious, habits like holding excess tension can cause physical damage and creative blocks.

The key to changing these habits is to understand their hidden leverage point. Every habit functions according to stimulus and response. The stimulus is whatever initiates the habit, whether it's something you're reacting to (like the conductor raising her baton) or something you want to do (like practicing your lines). The response is whatever comes next in terms of bodily movement. To create a response of ease of movement in place of one of tension, you must pause just after the stimulus and before the response.

This pause is your leverage point. It allows you to interrupt and prevent your old habits from starting so that you can exercise renewed choice over your bodily movements. I call it the Magic Pause because when you interrupt your old habits of tension, your body automatically and organically moves more freely. You don't have to make anything happen. You don't even have to try to relax. It happens all by itself. *Voila!*

THE MAGIC PAUSE

Let's apply the Magic Pause to three simple arm movements to experience how it works. The first time you do these movements, don't pause or try to relax. Instead, set a baseline by noticing your body movement habits as they are. Do the movements as you normally would and at the same time notice your whole body—do you get tighter or freer at any point during the sequence?

- *Movement 1.* Sit with your hands in your lap. Think "one" to yourself and raise your hands to about chest height with your elbows bent comfortably and your hands facing down.

- *Movement 2.* Think "two" and then lift your hands above your head so that your palms face forward as if you're about to give someone a two-handed high five.

- *Movement 3.* Think "three" and then bring your hands back down to your lap.

In this sequence, saying the number is the stimulus and your arm movements are the response. To allow for greater ease of movement, simply pause for a few seconds after each stimulus and before you move. Think to yourself, "One, pause ... [then move]. Two, pause ... [then move]. Three, pause ... [then move]." What do you notice now?

During the pause, you may notice your old habits wanting to creep in so that you get tense even before you start moving your arms. I call this anticipatory tension. If your anticipatory tension starts and you move anyway, you'll be carrying that tension throughout your following movements. But if you wait for that anticipatory tension to subside (which may take three to five seconds, and less with practice), your body will relax all by itself and your subsequent movements will be free and fluid. The unearned gift of this freedom is the magic of the Magic Pause.

To apply the Magic Pause to other activities, you must identify the critical moment. The critical moment is when your body gets tighter than you'd like, usually just before you do the hard thing. So, choose an activity that makes your body tight and identify the critical moment. Then, proceed with the activity until the critical moment and then take a nice, long pause. After the anticipatory tension has subsided, then continue the activity. What do you notice now?

The deeper lesson of the Magic Pause is that it addresses the real issue behind excess tension: treating your body like a machine, a thing to be manipulated. To address this issue, you need a moment of aliveness. There's nothing more alive than awareness, which is why pausing and bringing awareness to your body during the critical moment has such powerful benefits. Because of its focus on aliveness, the Magic Pause accomplishes what no amount of bodily interventions like exercise, stretching, or tissue manipulation can do by themselves. It allows your inner aliveness to spontaneously burst forth.

This is the power of a "little bit of nothing!"

"How is an artist to nourish himself in an age whose values are market values?"

— **LEWIS HYDE,** *THE GIFT*

CHAPTER 12

SOULFORCE LIVELIHOOD

"The best part of being a kid is that you just get to play!" my six-year-old niece recently told me, and she is right. When I was a child, one of my greatest pleasures was the freedom to get lost in my creativity and play. I loved to spend endless hours drawing, building, exploring, and creating. In my innocence, I thought that when I grew up, I would still be able to create and play all day, just in grown-up ways. However, I gradually became aware that this wasn't necessarily so.

I noticed how few of the grown-ups around me enjoyed a life of creativity and play. Worse, many of them were hostage to money. They mortgaged their present to fulfill an imagined future of plenty that never came. I was horrified by the toll their lives of drudgery took on their well-being, the stress they felt and then inflicted on those around them, and how the money they earned never made them happy. The lesson my younger self learned from this was that money is antithetical to love, creativity, and play.

When it came time to choose my own career, I resolved to avoid the trap these unfortunate grown-ups had fallen into. Since I was gifted with violin, I decided to become a professional musician. At the time,

I enjoyed visions of becoming a famous, and presumably wealthy, concert violinist. However, conflicting with this vision was the deeply ingrained belief that money meant drudgery. I thought, *Surely, being an artist will mean that I won't have to deal with money. I'll just get to play and create all day! Then, maybe the money will come, somehow ...*

It wasn't until I graduated from music school that I realized how naïve this assumption was.

In those first weeks and months on my own, I faced a stark reality. I was penniless and without the means to support myself effectively with my music. It dawned on me that my education had given me absolutely no skills to find work as a musician beyond the ability to play my instrument. The orchestral and concert soloist careers my schooling had trained me for were few, dwindling in number, and exceedingly hard to get. The ongoing injuries in my arms precluded auditioning for such jobs, in any case, and moreover, I realized that being an orchestral musician would probably stifle my creative soul—so why bother? I felt incredibly discouraged.

This began a long journey of trying to find a satisfying way of supporting myself with music. I did all the usual things young artists do: working odd jobs, finding occasional gigs, and teaching on the side. Years later, I was supporting myself with a steady stream of performances and students—but only just. I felt shame and fear about not earning much money, but I was also unwilling to seek more because I was so afraid that doing so would inevitably entail a life of drudgery and thereby betray my core, life-giving values of play, love, and creativity.

My dilemma was brought into greater focus when I became an Alexander Technique teacher. I was inspired to help other musicians more easily relieve their injuries, and so I felt determined to move past my money blocks and empower myself with basic business and marketing skills so I could reach a wider audience. However, the hard-selling tactics and superficial values on offer in the business books and courses I found made me nauseous. I intuited that using their tactics would result in yet more betrayals: that of the depth of connection possible with my prospective clients, as well as the integrity of my art and other offerings. Even the more spiritually oriented marketing methods, such as those offered by Law of Attraction coaches, were dissatisfying because they often promoted the same superficial values, just under a different banner. Without exception, the business offerings I encountered just felt too *icky*, so I continued my search.

A turning point came when I learned about the underlying economic forces that drive many of the issues I cared about most. I stumbled across alternative economics books that led me to the surprising insight that there was a single factor behind ecological destruction, pollution, poverty, political corruption, the disintegration of communities, corporate overreach, the rise of chronic diseases, and even the cheapening of the arts, among countless other issues. This was the infinite growth imperative inherent to our extractive economic system. Because of fundamental structures few are aware of, for our economic system to work at all, we need constantly to seek new sources of wealth. Where are these new sources to be found? By taking more and more from our planet, by initiating wars, and by monetizing the network of favors that had formerly tied community members together. The hidden truth is that our economic system is a giant Ponzi scheme, a world-devouring machine whose purpose is to turn everything that is good and green into lifeless money.

Learning about these underlying economic forces put the shame, fear, and ick I had felt, as well as my long years of penury, into a new light. It wasn't that there was something wrong with me, that I hadn't tried hard enough, that money simply wasn't for me, that I should just get over my distaste of selling and drudgery, or even that I hadn't said my Law of Attraction affirmations with enough fervor. I instead understood that my hesitation to engage more with business, money, and selling came from a correct perception of the harm caused by our economic system. If making more money meant contributing to a destructive system, I wanted nothing to do with it. My values of ecological and societal healing and the integrity of my art came first.

Learning about these economic forces was, on the one hand, deeply empowering; I finally understood the hidden-in-plain-sight forces that drive our society to so much destruction. On the other hand, I still felt at a loss for what to do about it because, despite my extensive research, I had found so few business and marketing resources that take account of these forces. I was left with many questions: How do I support myself in ways that are aligned with my deepest values while surrounded by an extractive system? How do I relate to money and livelihood in ways that feel good and enhance community ties? What does wealth mean outside of the hoarding and greed that are so caustic a force in society? Is it even possible to increase my wealth in ways that promote, rather than erode, the integrity of my art and teaching?

I know I am not alone in my search for answers to these questions. Countless artists and others feel the ick of money, business, and selling. We correctly intuit that, in our system as it is, there is an inherent conflict between the drive for more money and that which we value most like artistic integrity and societal and planetary healing. The lack of satisfying solutions to this conflict leaves many of us in a disempowered state. Some simply try to avoid the issue altogether and accept the life of a starving artist. Others pursue as much money as they can, ignoring the ick and accepting the loss of a degree of artistic integrity as a necessary, if regrettable, cost of business. Yet others work hard in artistic jobs they only half enjoy and, in the never-ending struggle to pay their bills and ensuing burnout, are sometimes left wondering why it is they became artists in the first place. Clearly, artists, and their art, are suffering from a lack of satisfying answers to this dilemma.

So, even though I have often experienced money, business, and selling to be distasteful, I have also realized that, as a community of artists, we must face these issues squarely and from a place of wholeness, aliveness, and connection—in other words, with Soulforce. If we don't,

Chapter 12 | SOULFORCE LIVELIHOOD

we risk running our artistic livelihoods according to societal defaults of extraction, commodification, and greed. We risk the creative death that comes from our artistic gifts being ignored, squashed, or twisted in service of the profit motive. We risk the world not benefiting from our creative Soulforce, a resource we can rest assured it needs.

> The "ick" of money stems from the correct intuition that, in our current systems, there is an inherent conflict between the drive for more money and that which we value most like artistic integrity, and societal and planetary healing.

If, on the other hand, we do discover a new relationship between art and money, we may be able to achieve what many of us long for the most: a means of supporting ourselves that affords the freedom to create and play and aligns with our Soulforce. This kind of livelihood, instead of playing into the extractive incentives that surround us, supports our well-being, our art, and the world that receives us. The great challenge is that the path to this new relationship is not readily found because the most visible resources on livelihood are often the ones that most affirm the values of our extractive system. So, we must look to uncommon sources to regard our livelihood as a worthy realm for our creativity. Discovering this new relationship may be the greatest artistic challenge of our time, and we are as capable and worthy as anyone to bring it forth. To make this discovery is more than an act of individual benefit; our art, communities, and planet depend on us doing so.

My intention for this chapter is to explore these issues and spark curiosity about what a new relationship between art and money could look like. I will give no hard and fast answers, nor any five-step method to guarantee success. In fact, I only consider this chapter to be a success if it leaves you with more curiosity and questions than which you started. While I will be sharing valuable insights I've gleaned from conventional and unconventional sources, I do not claim to be an expert on money and business. Rather, my intention with this chapter is to make an offering to the knowledge my heart, and maybe yours, carries that a more life-giving way of supporting ourselves as artists is possible. I will offer a variety of approaches, some inner and some outer, with the intention that doing so will call a more life-giving artistic livelihood out of the mists of the merely aspirational and into something viable, joyful, and full of Soulforce.

Some final notes. I understand that not everybody's story around money is the same as mine, and so not everybody feels the same ick around money that I have felt. If this is the case for you, then you may not resonate with everything in this chapter, but I hope you still find some valuable insights along the way. Also, you do not need to be a professional artist to benefit from this chapter. Rather, what you will find herein is useful to all artists (and perhaps all people), whether or not you actually earn money from your art. Instead of offering advice specific to certain artistic careers, or to professional artistry in general, this chapter explores a method of aligning your livelihood with your deepest and most authentic truths and desires, and this is something that will enrich and enliven your artistic life, regardless of if you're a tenured university theater professor, a professional studio musician, or a hobbyist painter.

We begin with the terrible choice between love and survival.

TO STARVE OR TO SELL OUT? THAT IS THE QUESTION

"If you would know what the Lord God thinks of money, you have only to look at those to whom He gives it."

— MAURICE BARING, QUOTED IN "AN INTERVIEW WITH DOROTHY PARKER," *THE PARIS REVIEW*, ISSUE 13

For many artists, money and art are unhappy bedfellows. On the one hand, we love being able to make a living from our art because it affords

Chapter 12 | SOULFORCE LIVELIHOOD

us the time and energy to go deep into our creativity and to share it with others. On the other, what it takes to make enough money to survive and thrive in our society is so rarely in alignment with our love, authenticity, and creativity. Given this conflict, the choice for many artists can at first seem stark: Do you become a "starving artist" and accept penury as the price for artistic purity? Or do you instead choose a life of greater financial stability and risk becoming a sell-out?

At its root, the seeming conflict between art and money is one between the true purpose of the arts and the demands of our economic system. As we've already seen throughout this book, the true purpose of the arts is to provide avenues to beauty, aliveness, growth, healing, connection, and wholeness. The trouble is that our economic system can't put a price on any of these qualities. As a result, it demands we turn our art into a commodity, a stomach-turning conversion that effectively saps our art of its full aliveness and transformative potential. This leaves artists in a terrible bind. To survive, it seems we must, to a certain extent, accede to the values of the system and commodify our art. For this, we are rewarded with money, but the greater survival capacity it confers comes at the expense of the very thing that makes our art truly valuable. In an economic system that pits our love and creativity against our survival, is it any wonder that so many artists try to avoid matters of money, business, and marketing as much as possible?

While this avoidance is understandable, it ignores three important truths. The first truth is that your livelihood is an inextricable part of your system update. For your art to have its fullest impact, it must be shared. The medium through which you share your art shapes what you create and how it's received. In our society, sharing your art often means selling it, and the way you sell inevitably finds reflection in your art's ultimate impact. Therefore, you cannot separate your art from your livelihood. Not only is this separation impractical (because those without basic business skills will struggle), but it's also disempowering and dishonors the gift that your art is. To strive for artistic purity and regard money, business, and marketing as inherently distasteful results not in a life-giving and abundant livelihood, but merely in the smug security that, despite your failure to reach your full potential as an artist, at least you retained your purity. Is this the kind of system update you wish to propagate?

The second truth is that, in the Story of Interbeing, to reject money is to reject yourself. Despite the reality that many of us experience it in other ways, money is a symbol of love, value, worth, safety, security, life, and the divine. When you reject money—or just as problematic, cling to it—you reject that which is lovable, valuable, safe, and divine in yourself. Surely, this isn't the road to Soulforce. Moreover, to reject money is to tacitly agree that our current form of money, and the extractive system that supports it, is the only one possible. If that were so, perhaps it would make sense to reject money altogether, but as we will see in the coming sections, this is not the case.

These first two truths reveal that the real question is not whether to become a starving artist or a rich sell-out. This is a false duality that masks a higher order understanding and the third, yet deeper truth: that your livelihood can be just as much a channel for your Soulforce as your time with paintbrush in hand. Just as you might with any other artistic challenge, you can create a **Soulforce Livelihood** when you face your survival challenges from a place of wholeness, aliveness, and connection.

At one level, a Soulforce Livelihood empowers you to better survive and thrive in our current economic system through an approach to basic money and business decisions that keeps your artistic purpose in mind. In connection with your artistic purpose, your financial decisions will feel more meaningful and in alignment with your artistic integrity because their guiding light will be your deepest truths and desires. While making decisions in this way may at times feel unfamiliar or even scary, doing so is a practical place to start cultivating a Soulforce Livelihood in your life, exactly as it is.

Chapter 12 | SOULFORCE LIVELIHOOD

On a deeper level, a Soulforce Livelihood is an act of joyful rebellion against an extractive economic system that incentivizes us to buy things we don't need while destroying the things we do. It is a step into the Story of Interbeing that realigns what's good for yourself, your art, and your world.

> A **Soulforce Livelihood** is one in which you face your survival challenges as an artist from a place of wholeness, aliveness, and connection.

I can make no promise that a Soulforce Livelihood will lead to greater financial success. Of course, it very well might because a life full of Soulforce leads to great art and is thus very attractive to your audiences. However, it often entails a step outside the values and incentives that normally lead to financial success in our society. The good news is that taking this step won't leave you destitute because it will allow you to meet more and more of your needs through genuine human connection, rather than money. Sometimes the result may very well be less money, but keep in mind that money in itself, while useful, meets no human needs and is therefore not true wealth. A Soulforce Livelihood is one in which the lesser god of money is replaced by a truer form of wealth: all the love, creativity, play, and connection you can handle.

The greatest barriers to enjoying this latter form of wealth are the belief that our current economic system is the only viable option, the mental and emotional conditioning our system inflicts, and the lack of practical steps to bring forth an alternative. To overcome these barriers, you need to learn the inner workings of our current system, what viable alternatives exist, how to heal the wounds that act to keep our system in place, and the ways reconnecting with the true purpose of the arts can help you create new forms of artistic livelihood that allow you to play your highest role as an artist in today's world.

STEPPING OUT OF THE RAT RACE

> *"When everything is subject to money, then the scarcity of money makes everything scarce, including the basis of human life and happiness. Such is the life of the slave—one whose actions are compelled by the threat to survival. Perhaps the deepest indication of our slavery is the monetization of time."*
>
> — CHARLES EISENSTEIN, *SACRED ECONOMICS*

Have you noticed how everything seems to be moving faster and faster these days? The frantic news media cycle, the constant release of novel technologies, the daily tsunami of new social media content, the race to beat the traffic, the replacement of children's free play with endless after-school activities ... It's like we're trapped in the Red Queen's world in *Alice in Wonderland*—we're all running faster and faster to stay in the same place.

The frantic pace of modern life can be stressful, exhausting, and even maddening. Where are we all racing to, anyway? The weekend? The next vacation? The grave? Why is it that, even when we arrive at the beach, margarita in hand, our mind still races and we can't relax enough to truly enjoy the sand and waves? It seems that all our best efforts and time-saving technology haven't made a difference. The rat race continues apace and, as a result, we find ourselves doing more and more of what we don't like to secure less and less of what we do. So much for "progress."

If it all seems a bit insane, that's because it is. As mentioned, our economic system requires constant growth to maintain our current way of life. Centuries ago, when our modern economic system first developed, this growth imperative did, indeed, bring greater ease and plenty; at that time, our economic growth led to a global population boom. However, what started with promise has now become like an addiction, such that we now must work harder and grow faster just to remain in the same place. As the return on our efforts continues to diminish, our way of life will eventually require infinite economic growth—an obvious insanity on a finite planet.

What is driving the rat race? Many say capitalism, corruption, and greed, but these are non-answers that hide the deeper forces at work. A cursory glance at hunter-gatherer ways of life reveals that the greed that now threatens our world is not inherent to humanity.[1] For countless millennia, our ancestors lived (more or less) in harmony with the planet. What accounts for the difference? It comes down to the sense of self.

Our ancestors saw themselves as part of a larger whole, participants in the flow of the earth's gifts, and their economic model (if it can be called that) reflected this worldview. For them, what made for a good economy was one in which the flow of gifts among community members and neighboring groups was kept running smoothly and in accord with nature's cycles. In *The Gift*, Lewis Hyde said this about the traditional Maori hunting ritual: "The circle of gifts enters the cycles of nature and, in so doing, manages not to interrupt them and not to put man on the outside. The forest's abundance is in fact a consequence of man's treating its wealth as a gift."[2]

In contrast, we moderns regard ourselves as separate from the earth, isolated individuals rationally seeking to maximize our self-interest. For us, what makes for a good economy is one in which individual actors spend needlessly while simultaneously hoarding as much wealth as possible to safeguard against the vagaries of nature's cycles, even if that wealth comes at the expense of others and the planet. Each worldview results in a different economy with manifestly different results.

A defining feature of our rat race is an all-pervasive sense of scarcity. Have you noticed how it seems like there's never enough money to go around, regardless of the amount in your bank account? Money is not the only thing in scarce supply these days. Despite the globalized West's mind-boggling financial wealth, we nonetheless suffer from a poverty of everything that makes life worth living: time, attention, beauty, connection, belonging, love, ease, play, fresh foods, silence, night skies dark enough to see the stars, experiences of wild nature, and, of course, genuine creativity. Scarcity is paradoxical. Why is it, despite the trillions of dollars that exist in bank accounts worldwide, that so few of us feel wealthy? The surprising truth is that even billionaires worry about money and suffer from these other forms of poverty. How could that be? It's because scarcity is the natural result of a money system founded on the separate sense of self.

Scarcity goes hand in hand with the sense of separation. Separation is a scary place to be, after all. How do you secure your long-term survival when the world around you seems like an untrustworthy other? You hoard as much as you can for you and yours. This is a scarcity mindset that finds reflection in our very definition of economics, which we regard to be the study of how people behave under conditions of scarcity. As Marshall Sahlins wrote in *Stone Age Economics*, "Modern capitalist societies, however richly endowed, dedicate themselves to the proposition of scarcity."[3] However, the scarcity mindset is not something that you can undo solely with positive thinking, as many Law of Attraction teachers would have you believe. Instead, it is a correct perception of the very real scarcity inherent to the way money is created in our system. To relieve scarcity and its mindset, we must understand that system.

There is a slant to our economic playing field. In our system, money is not created freely. Instead, it is made artificially scarce by the rules of the system. Money is created by central banks as interest-bearing debt. In essence, the central bank says, "Here's some money, but when it comes due I want a little extra in return." Interest-bearing debt is the tilt in the playing field that explains why the wealthy keep getting wealthier while the poor keep getting poorer. Our form of money accrues to those who already have it because of the little bit extra that interest demands. Where does that little bit extra come from? By extracting value from our natural, social, intellectual, and spiritual capital. Because of the way money is created in our system, there's always more debt than money, and so there's never truly enough to go around. To survive, we must extract more and more at any cost. Sound familiar? This is the rat race.

A good analogy is the game of musical chairs.[4] In this game, there are always fewer chairs than players. To succeed, each player vies against the others for access to the chairs, which are made artificially scarce by the rules of the game. While there is little consequence when this is played as a children's game, in our real-world version, when you don't get a chair, you lose your house, your kids go hungry, and you end up mired in debt. Who wouldn't resort to greed, corruption, and even violence to prevent this from happening? Far from being attributes of bad actors who use their economic might to oppress helpless others, greed, corruption, and violence are intelligent, if narrowly focused, responses to the maladaptive incentives baked into the very foundations of our way of life.

One of the great moral imperatives of our time is to establish a new, more life-giving relationship with money. We must step out of the rat race to heal our planet, society, and even our art. While the source of the rat race is collective, and so ultimately requires collective solutions, discovering these solutions begins with each of us as individuals. In involves a process of both learning and unlearning. Our first step has been to learn about the inner workings of the rat race. Our next step is to connect with money's secret, sacred purpose.

There's nothing inherently wrong with money. It is not the root of all evil, as the saying goes. In fact, many of our ancient ancestors used money, albeit in forms we may not recognize. Their economy was a **gift economy**, and so for them, money was a sacred gift that facilitated the flow of shared resources and brought people closer together.[5] What was true for them is still true for us—it just no longer seems that way because our own form of money has been instrumentalized, brutalized, and cheapened by the Story of Separation and its will to power. In its current form, money can't help but erode what is life-giving. But as a sacred gift, money can fulfill its true purpose: to bring forth more life.

> A **gift economy** is one in which money is a sacred gift that facilitates the flow of shared resources and brings people closer together.

Here we find a perfect analogy to what has been done to art in our society. As we've seen, art is best regarded not as a commodity, but as a gift. However, the rat race demands that we turn our art, our gifts, into commodities, a conversion that makes money at the expense of art's life-giving power. This is why we feel torn between art and money; what's good for the rat race is all too often bad for art. Not all is lost, however. The purpose of this book has been to reveal art's indelible resilience to the corrosive effects of the lesser gods. All that's required is to face those effects from a place of connection with art's true identity as a sacred gift and its true purpose to bring forth more life. To do so transforms the corrosive effects of our system from a burden to be escaped into the very source of creative fulfillment, our Soulforce.

The same is true of money. By reconnecting with money's hidden identity as a sacred gift and its true purpose of bringing forth more life, you can reverse the harmful effects of our current form of money and instead use it to promote what is life-giving. This process of reconnection, and its results, are the same as those regarding art's true purpose: a livelihood in which what's good for your finances is also what's good for your art and for the world around you. This is the ultimate aspiration of a Soulforce Livelihood.

SOULFORCE INQUIRY 12.1
WHAT IF MONEY WERE A SACRED GIFT?

In our current system, money is regarded as a thing to be manipulated. In this worldview, anything money touches becomes lifeless and expendable. In contrast, throughout most of our history, money was regarded

> as a being to be honored. In this worldview, anything money touches becomes more vibrant and precious. It's all in how you hold it.
>
> The good news is that you needn't be limited by the way our society holds money. You can reclaim money's sacred purpose by shifting your relationship with it during any transaction. Begin by contemplating the possibility that money is a sacred gift, a being to be honored. How would that change how you feel and what you believe about money? How would that change how you use it? The next time you spend or receive money, take a moment to regard it for the sacred gift that it is.

If discovering the place where your well-being (financial and otherwise), art, and the world's hunger meet now seems to you like a naïve fairy tale, I wouldn't blame you. It does to me, too, as often as not. The corrosive effects of the rat race are all-pervasive and make any attempt to escape it exceedingly difficult. There's a reason why so many nonprofits, eco-villages, and time banks (all examples of economic alternatives) fail to survive in the long run; our system is inhospitable to anything not created to extract endless profits.

However, you don't need to tear down the system and craft an entirely new one to take meaningful steps toward a Soulforce Livelihood. Nor do you need to know exactly what the destination looks like or how to get there. Nobody does. We are all in this together, searching for something only our hearts know the shape of, bringing into being a world that may be entirely unrecognizable. How do we discover something that doesn't yet exist?

It begins with a step into the Story of Interbeing. Any action taken from within a certain story results in the furthering of that story. To end the rat race, to end the ick that results from commodifying your art, to enjoy all the freedom to create your heart longs for—in other words, to create a Soulforce Livelihood—you must approach money and livelihood from the Story of Interbeing. This is something you can do in your life, exactly as it is. Any step toward this makes yet further steps more tangible and possible, so even the smallest step into the Story of Interbeing matters.

While, again, I make no claim on the finality or completeness of what I'm putting forth in this chapter, I do feel confident in laying out at least some of what can help you step into a new relationship between your art and your money. Despite its pervasive influence, you don't need to accede to the values of the rat race to survive. You don't need to sell yourself, commodify your art, or strive endlessly to gain a million social media followers. Any of these activities may only act to further propagate the rat race and in the long run may leave you burnt out and unable to share your artistic Soulforce. Instead, you need to make space for new answers to arise, and this begins with reviewing your relationship with money and the self-beliefs you've picked up as a result.

SOULFORCE INQUIRY 12.2
YOUR MONEY STORY

Get out your journal and set aside plenty of time for the following prompts. Go into as much detail as you can. To regain freedom from the values of the rat race, you must make your unconscious money beliefs conscious. Otherwise, you risk those unconscious beliefs continuing to drive the bus.

- What emotions do I have around money, business, and selling?
- What negative beliefs do I have about money?
- What are some of the harms I've seen because of the way money is used in society?
- What are the beliefs about myself I've taken in as a result?

- What beliefs get in the way of me achieving financial prosperity?
- What does wealth mean to me, and what kind of person would I be if I were wealthy?

SOULFORCE INQUIRY 12.3
PRACTICING SELF-LOVE IN AN EXTRACTIVE SYSTEM

Seeing the harm of our extractive system, you may have taken in the belief that you are somehow bad or wrong for participating in it. The truth, however, is that none of us (at least in a conventional sense) chose to be born into this system. Its harm does not define who you are, but, being surrounded by it your whole life, you may subconsciously believe that it does. Holding onto this belief is part of what keeps our system in place. Pry loose the underpinnings of this belief through this self-love meditation.

Sit comfortably and repeat the following phrases to yourself. Feel free to adapt them to better fit your own beliefs and conditioning.

- Even though our economic system causes harm, I choose to love and accept myself anyway.
- Even though I'm sick of the rat race, I choose to love and honor myself.
- Even though the system forces me to commoditize my art, I choose to love, honor, and accept myself, as well as anyone else who might be involved in this system.
- Even though the thought of money, selling, and business scare me and make me nauseous, I choose to regard myself, my art, our economic system, and our planet as beings to be honored, loved, and accepted.

Finally, spend a moment feeling compassion for the ways you and all the other beings in our world have been harmed by our system. Repeat this to yourself several times: "We're all in this together."

THE YOGA OF MONEY

"Realize that money is completely the side effect and byproduct of finding the real thing you are looking for. What you're looking for is you."
— KYLE CEASE, *THE ILLUSION OF MONEY*

I've always had a love-hate relationship with money. For a long time, there was a part of me that thought that money was evil, or at least that our extractive economic system was. After all, look at its effects! The profit motive has led to endless destruction of the rainforests, the presence of toxic PCBs in every living cell on earth, and the cheapening of everything good and green. At the very same time, there was another part of me that loved being paid well for my work and recognized that, unless I was to go live on a farm, I'd have to meet my needs through money. For years, I struggled to reconcile my need and desire for money with its seemingly inevitable deleterious effects.

Then I had an insight that radically changed my relationship with money. I realized that the challenge of meeting my survival needs in an extractive economic system was the same as reaching for Soulforce Artistry in arts institutions still dominated by the Story of Separation. After all, my path to Soulforce Artistry had taught me that I could remain connected with my Soulforce even when the system around me, however unintentionally, incentivized me to disconnect. What if the same was possible with my financial challenges?

As mentioned previously, while my university musical training had many positive aspects, the Soulforce I channeled at that time happened despite my education, not because of it. Its focus was primarily on technical perfection and fitting myself into the cramped artistic boxes offered by an outdated system. The message I received was that artistic success required controlling the outcome, maximizing personal gains, and expending effort at the cost of my well-being. The stress and pain this approach resulted in left such a bad taste in my mouth that, for a long time afterward, I was unwilling to advance my technique—or, sometimes, even to practice at all.

What I later discovered while recovering from the Soulforce-stifling effects of my education is that I didn't need to adopt a stressful, painful approach to reach the artistic mastery I desired. Instead, what helped most was to expand my definition of mastery to include my well-being because only that allowed me to create art I loved, and which was ultimately good for the world. Seeing my musical Soulforce flower as a result, I realized there was nothing inherently wrong with technique, effort, or even arts institutions that are a bit stuck in the past. As long as I remembered that technique and effort could be used as avenues to deeper self-connection, I could create with Soulforce in any situation. You will recognize this as the essence of the Yoga of Art.

The turning point in my financial life came when I realized that this same shift was possible in my relationship with money. The core problem is the same: the maximization of a narrow goal at the expense of the whole. In the creative process, disconnection from Soulforce comes from maximizing the values of the lesser gods at the expense of your well-being and creative aliveness. It's the same with money. All the harm due to our use of money comes not from some inherent evil, but from its use to maximize the short-term security and prosperity of the few at the expense of the long-term well-being of the whole. Any time you use money in this narrow, controlling way, you add to the harm our system does. That harm can be avoided, however, not by avoiding money, but by using it to connect more deeply with your self. This is the **Yoga of Money**, which is the practice of using every financial decision, whether large or small, to connect with your inner aliveness—your deepest truths, desires, and values.

The Yoga of Money is the foundation of an ethical approach to money in an unethical system. Its ethics are based on two facets of interbeing. The first is non-duality. Non-duality means that there is no separation between your individual actions and the well-being of the whole. What you do to others, you do to yourself. Your every purchase and earning, no matter how small or invisible, impacts the whole world because you and your money are whirlpools indivisible from the larger river of life. Non-duality invites you to take account of your impact on the whole world; what kind of world are you saying "yes" to with each purchase or earning?

> The **Yoga of Money** is the practice of using every financial decision, whether large or small, to connect with your inner aliveness—your deepest truths, desires, and values. It is the foundation of an ethical approach to money in an unethical system.

Secondly, interbeing offers a definite direction to ethics. What is good? It's whatever enhances the amount, complexity, richness, and vibrancy of life. If your actions bring more aliveness into the world, then they are ethical. How do you know which purchase or earning is going to bring more life into the world? Whichever ones bring you truly alive. You are not separate from life, after all, which means that your deepest truths and desires are inherently life-giving. Some hear this and fear that guiding financial decisions based on your aliveness may lead to a bank-breaking spending spree—but is that true? Or are unhinged spending sprees more an attempt to remedy the deadness you feel inside? Just as with the Yoga of Art, the Yoga of Money leads not to addictive behaviors, but to wisdom and sanity.

Interbeing reveals that an ethical approach to money is possible, even when surrounded by an extractive and unethical system. You can

Chapter 12 | SOULFORCE LIVELIHOOD

reclaim an ethical relationship with money when you take account of the whole and connect with what brings you alive. How do you do this in practice?

The Yoga of Money is made possible by four shifts. The first is to see through the lie that controlling money will make you safer. Just as tightening your body does nothing to ensure the success of your next dance move, and in fact makes its completion harder, tightening your grip on your finances does nothing to ensure your future survival, and in fact makes it harder. What is the point of scrimping and self-denial? To ensure your comfort and survival in an imagined future. This is a wise enough move in a society without the true social safety net of an intact community in living relationship with nature. But at what point does a scrimping mindset interfere with your quality of life and your sense of freedom and possibility? At what point does it prevent you from a livelihood suffused with Soulforce?

As much as we might like to wish otherwise, regardless of your finances, nobody makes it out of this life alive, and as the saying goes, you can't take it with you. So, why are you holding on so tightly? Is it because of genuine financial constraints or are you living from inherited fears? In what way do your anxieties serve you when you already have a roof over your head, food to eat, water to drink, air to breathe, and friends to connect with? This isn't to say that you shouldn't build a nest egg; it's rather an invitation to recognize that doing so in no way guarantees a joyful life or your survival.

The second shift is to regard your true value as stemming from your inner wisdom, not your possessions and accomplishments. At every turn, our system invites us to disconnect from our true value as sacred beings and to instead believe that we will only be worthy, lovable, and complete if we have a certain bank balance or buy the next new thing. Lacking sufficient cultural messages to the contrary, we end up with a giant hole in our souls that we then try to fill by buying more stuff we don't need—a habit of over-spending just as harmful as scrimping.

Money, possessions, and accomplishments are manifestly useful but, obviously, no amount of these can fill the hole inside. The only thing that can is the rock-solid, embodied knowledge of your worthiness, lovability, goodness, and completeness. Only this knowledge can plug the hole inside, end the gnawing hunger that drives both scrimping and over-spending, and allow you to make financial decisions from a place of true self-sufficiency and abundance.

The third shift is to fully process your grief at the harm caused by our system. For instance, one of the biggest blocks to my own healthier relationship with money was my grief at the ecological destruction its mindless pursuit has collectively wrought. My belief was that having more money would make me culpable for yet more destruction, but processing my grief allowed for a new understanding to arise: by rejecting money I was rejecting part of my larger self. At first, this understanding was difficult to digest. It conflicted with my subconscious identity as someone who cares about the planet by rejecting our economic system. I found resolution to this difficulty in an unexpected source: single-use plastics.

Single-use plastics have become essential to the way of life for globalized, industrialized peoples, to the great detriment of our oceans and other ecosystems. I often cringed and felt sad each time I threw one away, which, unfortunately, was nearly a daily occurrence. The shift to a more empowered relationship with plastic came when I realized that plastic, like money, is a gift, a precious resource that should be used with reverence. When I started treating it as such, saying a little "thank you" every time I threw some away, I felt relieved because at least I was able to honor our planet in a small way. I realized that the planet doesn't need my shame, but my wholeness, aliveness, and connection. I felt lighter as a result, no longer weighed down by the belief that I was wrong for using plastic.

Far from merely being a "get out of jail free card" that released me from responsibility and allowed the unbridled continuation of our system, this shift has made me more sensitive to my use of plastic; more responsible, not less. It has further opened my heart to the tragedy of it all, but without the weight of needless guilt. Instead, I find myself empowered with a more life-giving stance to a pragmatic reality. This mirrors what is possible with money. When you fully grieve the harms of our current economic system, you create the space within yourself to treat money, and by extension our planet, as the precious gift that it is. This is a shift that lets you provide what the world truly needs from you; not your fear, shame, and guilt, but your joy, reverence, and Soulforce.

The fourth shift into the Yoga of Money is faith. It is the faith that you'll be held if you relinquish control and certainty over the outcome of your financial decisions. This is not easy to do in our current system, as failing to secure the next gig may result in not being able to pay your bills. This stark reality often produces an understandable result: the belief that your financial safety is solely ensured by a tighter grip on your finances. This is partly true; a tight grip can provide safety, but only in a limited, short-term way. The other part of the truth is that, again, no amount of gripping is ever sufficient to provide the safety and prosperity you desire. Instead, it often paradoxically leads to spending binges and is, collectively, the very source of the scarcity that now drives the rat race. So, while financial control is an understandable response to the very real scarcity that afflicts many artists and others, the safety and prosperity it promises is ultimately illusory and leads to unethical choices.

The answer is a leap of faith made possible by certain inner and outer resources that help you feel safe stepping off the rat race. The foundation of your inner resources is connection with your inner sacred self, a direct experience of your inherent wholeness, goodness, and sufficiency. It is only with this felt experience that you can fully trust that you're going to be okay, regardless of financial circumstances. Other inner resources include listening to the financial wisdom of your Inner Audience Member, harnessing the power of synchronicities to fulfill your desires, and clearing out your inherited financial conditioning. Outer resources can include non-monetized ways of meeting your needs (such as buy-nothing groups and collective daycares), holistic business practices, and marketing that succeeds by honoring the true value of your art.

The rest of this chapter explores each of these resources. Combined, they can help you relinquish stringent financial control and the need for certainty, a shift that is critical because, as Financial Alchemy coach Morgana Rae says, "Change happens at the speed of safety." With experimentation and attunement to what truly feels safe, these resources can transform what at first seems like a frightening leap into the unknown into the source of a livelihood full of self-trust, self-love, and magic.

SOULFORCE INQUIRY 12.4
LEARNING TO TRUST THAT YOU'LL BE HELD

Necessary to a Soulforce Livelihood is the process of learning to let go of rigid control and certainty over your money, possessions, and career accomplishments. This prospect can bring up intense survival fears, so the next step is to compassionately investigate these questions:

- What do I need to trust that I'll be held if I let go of my current form of financial control?
- What do I need to trust to allow my inner wisdom, my Inner Audience Member, to guide my financial decisions?
- What would I need to trust that I'll be sustained financially if I guide my livelihood through what brings me alive?
- What do I need to trust that financial decisions, guided by my IAM, will bring the world more alive as well?

Asking these questions is not an invitation to abandon your current means of surviving as an artist. They are rather a means to soften the ways you may now be unduly acceding to the values of the rat race.

SOULFORCE INQUIRY 12.5
THE YOGA OF MONEY

The practice of the Yoga of Money is just like that for the Yoga of Art. When you're about to make a purchase, check in with your Inner Audience Member. Will this purchase bring you more alive? If so, it's probably a good idea. If not, save it for another time. Be aware that there are many levels to aliveness and that sometimes your inherited conditioning will masquerade as something more genuine.

Use this inquiry with payments that feel like a burden, like utilities or taxes. What happens when you connect with what's life-giving about having electricity and roads that get paved? Use it with purchases that are fun by letting yourself revel in the joy of your purchase. It's also revealing for purchases that come from a place of disconnection; what happens to your craving to buy your fiftieth pair of shoes when you include your heart's guidance in the conversation?

You can also use this practice when you receive money. How does your Inner Audience Member feel about receiving a paycheck from these people, in this amount, or for that piece of art? What situations genuinely bring you more alive and which are motivated by the lesser gods? Don't judge yourself for the latter; they are an inescapable part of contemporary life. Instead, see what happens when you hold the parts of you motivated by the lesser gods with love and compassion.

Again, there are no right or wrong answers here. The Yoga of Money is simply a path to financial sanity that allows you to access a source of inner wisdom that might otherwise be ignored in your rush to secure your survival. Simply let yourself relax and be open to what comes up. You get to decide whether to act on it.

YOU ARE THE ONE YOU'VE BEEN LOOKING FOR

"You have the right to work, but never to the fruit of work. You should never engage in action for the sake of reward, nor should you long for inaction. Perform work in this world, Arjuna, as a man established within himself without selfish attachments, and alike in success and defeat."

— *THE BHAGAVAD GITA*, TRANSLATED BY EKNATH EASWARAN

The Bhagavad Gita is a cornerstone text of Hinduism and one of humanity's most revered sources of wisdom. Its resonance throughout history and for millions worldwide is a testament to its profound insight into the human condition. The story it tells is directly relevant to Soulforce Livelihood. It reveals the way connection with the divine drama of life can lead to an empowered acceptance of challenging circumstances and the joyful fulfillment of your purpose.

The Bhagavad Gita tells the story of Arjuna, an Indian prince who is trying to bring order to his kingdom after its long period of decay. The story begins with Arjuna standing on the edge of a battlefield, about to engage forces with his enemy—whose ranks include members of his own family. Despairing of the task in front of him, which would involve killing family members he cares about, he turns to his chariot driver for advice. Thankfully, his chariot driver is none other than the god Krishna who offers an ultimate perspective on Arjuna's dilemma.

Krishna encourages Arjuna to engage in battle as a means of embracing his purpose. Balking, Arjuna asks how the bloody task ahead of him could possibly lead to anything good. Krishna then provides Arjuna with a larger context to help him make sense of his otherwise confusing life circumstances. Krishna paints a picture of life as a vast, divine drama. Arjuna is an actor on the stage of this drama, and his most life-giving path forward is not to stop the action on stage, but to participate in it fully, knowing that, ultimately, every aspect of the drama is the divine in action. Arjuna himself is the divine in human form, as are his enemies. There is nothing else he must strive to attain. The divine essence whose search has been the unconscious motivation behind his political aspirations is already within. Given this reality, and despite his inability to intellectually grasp the forces that have led him to this place, Arjuna finally realizes that there is nothing to do but embrace his part in the divine drama and joyfully join the fray.

What's true for Arjuna is also true for us as artists. Our extractive economic system is like Arjuna's battlefield, but instead of a literal army, we face our financial challenges, the cheapening effect money often has on the arts, and the grief many of us feel at not being fully supported as we share our artistic gifts. Similarly, Arjuna's desire for a thriving kingdom is like our own desire for a more prosperous, fulfilling artistic livelihood. Arjuna's dilemma is mirrored in the ick that many artists feel around money and selling, and like Arjuna, many artists balk at joining the fray. Our way through this dilemma is not to either run from it or judge ourselves or our circumstances as bad. Instead, we can follow Krishna's advice and locate ourselves within the divine play of life.

Regarding ourselves as divine actors upon the stage of life allows for a more empowered and purposeful stance toward our financial challenges. It begins with acceptance of our situation. Yes, our economic system is often harmful, and yes, what is good for money is often bad for art. However, this is the situation in front of us. It is inescapable. To judge our economic machine as bad and expend our energy trying to escape it is often fruitless and, moreover, dishonors the divine energy that moves in all things. Who are we to judge what is good or bad, given our infinitesimal and brief part in our universe's vast and mysterious drama? Moreover, without challenges like this, how could we possibly fulfill our greatest artistic purpose? Why else would we have been born in this time other than to face these very challenges with courage, honor, and love? What if our circumstances within the divine play are perfect, just as they are?

Far from being a disempowered stance, acceptance rests on the truth that action is inescapable. Trying to escape action for fear of the consequences is itself an action with consequences. The only question is what you are in service to as you act. Do your actions bring more life into the world, or less? By all means, fight the good fight. Simply remember the paradox that the divine play of life is perfect as it is, even as you exert every effort to better your circumstances. You may even discover that connection with the divine is the best place from which to create change. It is only when we recognize our true divine nature and locate ourselves within the larger divine play that our true purpose and capability as Soulforce Artists becomes fully apparent.

Many in our secular society may find a discussion of the divine, especially as relates to money, a difficult pill to swallow. After all, money is just money, right? Cold, hard cash has nothing to do with the divine. Wouldn't it make more sense to focus this chapter on building a business plan, budgeting, marketing, advertising, and other conventional business practices? Why bring the divine into the conversation at all? Besides, isn't connection with the divine a luxury only available to the privileged few?

I hope by now you can recognize the fingerprints of the Story of Separation in these objections. Why do we need the divine? Because the story of a de-sacralized universe is what got us into this mess in the

Chapter 12 | SOULFORCE LIVELIHOOD

first place. The rat race is what survival looks like in a universe devoid of spirit. You cannot step outside the rat race or make it stop by using its own values, methods, and worldview. Nor can you do so from some halfway divinity of an ascendent realm of pure spirit, which is merely the reverse side of the coin from materialism. Instead, you must tap into a new game, a new story, a new experience of self, one based on something larger than the rat race and whose very existence radiates transcendent significance and value. And, no, connection with the divine isn't a luxury for the privileged few. As the inspiring content and effect of African American spirituals attest, among countless other examples, connection with the divine is available to all and may be the one thing that can get you through hard times.

> It is only when we recognize our true divine nature and place ourselves within the larger divine play that our true purpose and capability as Soulforce Artists becomes fully apparent.

It is for these reasons that a direct experience of the divine is an absolute prerequisite for a Soulforce Livelihood. Without it, you will never be able to see the rat race for what it is: a dream, or perhaps a nightmare. Experiencing your divine self is like waking from that dream. It's like being an actor who suddenly realizes that the drama you were caught up in is just a play. It puts the rat race in context; no longer taken for granted as the only game in town, it becomes the set on a stage. Because you sense how all things come in and out of existence within the divine self without ever threatening to destroy it, much of your survival fear lessens. The rat race doesn't magically disappear, and you still play your part in the drama, only now it's a lot more fun because you're not taking it so seriously.

When you experience your divine self, you realize that this is what you've been looking for all along. You thought you were looking for more money, new relationships, or better opportunities, but what you were truly looking for was you, your divine self.

What's more, you realize the whole rat race is based on a false belief: that if you get more money, then you'll finally know yourself as the divine. When you realize that this is who you've been all along, all you can do is laugh! You can finally relax. You've made it. You've discovered the great secret of existence and now you just get to play. Of course, unlike a production at your local theater, the drama of making a living in our system has real consequences. There is real pain and suffering possible in this production and what happens on this stage is for keeps. What's different is that now you can come at it from a totally different angle, buoyed by a purpose and significance that were previously simply unimaginable.

So, what does this all mean for your livelihood? While there are many implications, including some we covered in the previous section, here's a simple example. One of the main reasons artists have a hard time getting paid well (even with top-quality art) is that we have taken in the values of our system and now fear that we and our art don't matter. When we take in our system's values, we forget our true worth, and so we sell ourselves for less. The experience of the divine changes all this. It reveals our true worth in no uncertain terms: it shows us that we are children of the Universe. Connected with that truth, we are enabled to create art that serves to remind others of that same fact. This is an experience that is truly priceless and, if shared in the right contexts, it can lead your audiences to shower you with gifts in return.

The value of your art, in other words, is in direct proportion to your connection with the divine. The paradox is that, as soon as you try to monetize it, your connection with the divine will vanish. The divine exists for its own sake, its integrity being its true source of value. The ideal is to hold both truths simultaneously: that your inner sacred self is the source of your artistic and financial value, and at the same time, that to regard it solely in those terms destroys that value.

Chapter 12 | SOULFORCE LIVELIHOOD

SOULFORCE INQUIRY 12.6
TOUCHING THE DIVINE WITHIN

Do the following meditation someplace comfortable and quiet, preferably in wild nature.

Firstly, imagine that everything you own has been taken away from you; your money, home, clothes, art, food, and everything else. Imagine that your friends and family have left you, that you are utterly alone. Imagine that your personal history has been taken away, your memories, and even your name. What's left? Who are you with nothing at all?

Now imagine that you've been given everything you could ever hope for. You have all the money you'll ever need, a beautiful home, the best clothes and food, the most masterful artistic skills, the ideal soulmate, and thousands of adoring fans. You are surrounded by loving friends and family in a vibrant community. Your history, memories, and name feel rich and full of meaning. Who are you now? What do you notice about who and what you are, now that you have everything you could desire?

The paradox this meditation reveals is that the experiential truth of who and what you are—the inner sacred self—remains the same, regardless of your outer circumstances. Underlying the fear of loss is the fear that we'll lose connection with the inner sacred self, and underlying the joy of every gain is the promise of connecting with it more fully. The ultimate truth is that no loss can take away your inner sacred self, nor can any gain bring you closer to it. Do an experiment and check in with your inner sacred self the next time you lose or gain something—have your outer circumstances truly changed your inner divinity?

STEERING THE DIVINE HAND

"Standing in the middle between the idea of an event and the actual event is a strange kind of physical reality just in the middle between possibility and reality."

— WERNER HEISENBERG, QUANTUM PHYSICIST

Famed twentieth-century psychologist Carl Jung once relayed a story of a surprising and meaningful coincidence that occurred during a session with a patient. Progress with his patient's issues had recently stalled because her "highly polished Cartesian rationalism" had prevented the softer, more human understanding necessary for relief from her neuroses.[6] During one session, she spoke of a recent dream in which one of her dream characters had given her a priceless piece of jewelry: a golden scarab. Just as she was describing the dream, Jung heard a tapping at the window. Investigating its source, he opened the window to discover a live scarab beetle, which promptly flew into the room. He brought it to her and declared, "Here is your scarab."

Combined with its rarity given Vienna's distance from the usual habitat for scarab beetles, its appearance at the exact moment of her dream's retelling made a lasting impression on both Jung and his patient. The result? The stunning, meaningful, and undeniable presence of the beetle pierced his patient's mental armoring and provided a means for the psychological progress she desired and which Jung's previous efforts had failed to bring about.

Jung became fascinated with this phenomenon and called them **synchronicities**, meaningful coincidences that links distinct people, places, things, or events that otherwise have no discernable causal connection. Synchronicities are like a mirror; they occur when something you've been thinking about or paying attention to finds reflection in unusual, and often funny, references elsewhere in your life. While many dismiss synchronicities as mere coincidences, or perhaps enjoy them as spontaneous oddities, correctly harnessed, synchronicities have the potential to help you cultivate a desirable life.

The intentional cultivation of synchronicities is a valuable part of your Soulforce Livelihood. As a practice, it can help you bring about career and financial goals that might otherwise seem impossible to reach through the values and means of the rat race. The cultivation of synchronicities is a mode of action within the Story of Interbeing, which regards their occurrence as a sign of your interconnectedness with a living, responsive, intelligent universe. Synchronicities can help you achieve challenging goals without force and control, they invite a process of healing your wounds of unworthiness, and they fill your life with enchantment. Most importantly, with practice, the cultivation of synchronicities allows you to trust that you'll be held when you relinquish the anxious search for certainty over your finances and career, and instead act in service to life.

> A Soulforce Livelihood intentionally cultivates synchronicities to bring about career and financial goals that might otherwise seem impossible to reach through the values and means of the rat race.

Are synchronicities "real"? From the Story of Separation's point of view, no—they are but meaningless coincidences in whose significance only fools believe. However, this dismissal is unwarranted because it ignores three important pieces of information. The first is that there is no scientific evidence that mind is separate from matter or that the universe we inhabit is unresponsive to our thoughts, emotions, and desires. Just try to imagine a double-blind, placebo-controlled trial that could prove these assertions. It can't be done, which only proves that Cartesian rationalism is a belief, not a fact.

The second piece of information skeptics ignore is that the evidence they use to support their claims is itself the result of synchronicities.

Skeptics pay attention to, and are emotionally involved with, a story that says that synchronicities are meaningless, and so the universe generously provides them with synchronicities that prove this story to be true! This is what confounds so many experiments on psi phenomena—the field of study that investigates extrasensory perception, precognition, and psychokinesis. When skeptics pay attention to an experiment, their thoughts and beliefs spark synchronistic changes in the results. This is not a fringe claim. The ability of an observer's attention to change experimental results is well known in quantum physics. It is what physicist Max Planck was referring to when he wrote in *Where Is Science Going?* that "Science cannot solve the ultimate mystery of nature. And that is because, in the last analysis, we ourselves are a part of the mystery that we are trying to solve."[7]

The third piece of information the Cartesian dismissal of synchronicities ignores is the vast mountain of rigorous scientific evidence that supports their reality. Countless high-quality studies have been completed on psi phenomena, often with needlessly rigorous standards, such as triple-blind protections against bias. Far from comprising delusional claims by quack researchers, the field of psi phenomena has demonstrated proven—and often jaw-dropping—results.

For instance, one study by researcher Stephan Schwartz investigated whether human intention could affect the results of computerized random number generators.[8] In this study, participants thought about the computers and visualized them generating certain numbers and not others. The Cartesian mind would expect that the participants' visualizations shouldn't have had an effect—but they did. The random number generators subject to the visualizations gave non-random results. While the overall affect size was small (on the order of three to five percentage points), the results were nonetheless astonishingly significant.[9] According to Schwartz, the odds that the change in numerical output was due to chance was billions to one. Countless other rigorous studies on psi phenomena have shown a similar statistical significance, leading to the undeniable conclusion that human thought and attention affects material reality.[10]

Studies like this reveal an exciting possibility: that through focusing your thoughts and attention, you can change the world around you. Using the power of attention to create change is how you harness synchronicities. By placing your attention on, and getting emotionally involved in, what you want, synchronicities related to your desire will begin showing up in your life. With practice, you can steer the divine hand that moves in all things, tilting the scale a few percentage points in your desired direction. Over time, those few percentage points can lead to massive change.

So, how do you use the power of synchronicities to create a Soulforce Livelihood? The first thing to realize is that you already use the power of synchronicities every day, only without knowing it. Your life is the way it is largely because you pay attention to certain things each day. Your attention calls forth the people, events, and money that come your way. To the extent you didn't force anything to happen, these occurrences are synchronicities. If they don't feel special or unusual, it's probably because you're too familiar with them to notice their presence. When you focus your attention on new desires and possibilities, and learn to spot synchronicities when they happen, the synchronicities that show up will bring you closer to the livelihood you want.

The process of cultivating synchronicities will be familiar to those who study manifestation techniques like the Law of Attraction. However, while the Law of Attraction does have certain truths, its proponents often miss yet other important truths. The first is that not all your attention is conscious. Some, and maybe most, of your attention is subconscious. This means that when your stated desires aren't showing up through synchronicities, it might be that subconscious parts of you have conflicting desires. We will explore how to resolve these conflicts in the following section.

Another truth popular proponents of the Law of Attraction often miss is that just because you use a "spiritual" technique to achieve financial goals doesn't necessarily mean you've escaped the values of the system or that your relationship with money is automatically ethical. Too many proponents of the Law of Attraction purvey the values of the rat race by framing synchronicities as a get rich quick scheme. This can be just as damaging to people and the planet as more conventional business practices. Furthermore, the rat race conflicts with the life inside us, and so purveying its values can lead to inner resistance and confusion as to why our goals aren't manifesting. In such cases, our inner resistance isn't an obstacle to be bulldozed, but our larger self speaking to us with hidden wisdom.

They also miss that, ultimately, you don't get to choose your desires. Every desire is a discovery. If you ask people what they want most in life, many probably won't be able to tell you. Sure, they could come up with some answers, but often those answers are just guesses based on their cultural programming, which can sometimes be toxic. It takes a long process of peeling back the layers of programming to get to the authentic, soul-level desires core to your being. Often, difficulties in the cultivation of synchronicities come from reaching for desires that aren't truly your own, a situation that only creates more inner conflict and disappointment. In a sense, the authentic, soul-level desires that are necessary to your Soulforce Livelihood are like the slogan for the old Ford Model T: you could have it in any color you want, just so long as you want black. The promise of synchronicities is that you can have anything you want, and the paradox is that you don't get to choose what you want.

SOULFORCE INQUIRY 12.7
CULTIVATING SYNCHRONICITIES

There are many methods for cultivating synchronicities. These are sometimes known as manifestation techniques. You can find them online as well as in the Recommended

Reading section at the end of this book. Here's the essence of the process.

First, ask yourself what you want most for your livelihood. Write out all the answers that come up for you. Humbly inquire which are authentic desires and which are inherited from your culture (the things you think you should want). For ideas, refer to your artistic purpose.

Next, imagine yourself in the future, having everything you want. Make this a vivid, multi-sensory experience. Then imagine this future coming toward you into your present moment. The feeling should be that you already have what you desire, not that you're in a state of still wanting it. Continue holding the image of your desires presently fulfilled until a positive emotion arises. Then, enjoy that emotion for as long as it lasts. Emotional involvement is essential to stimulating synchronicities. Practice this for about twenty minutes a day for at least two weeks.

Finally, pay special attention to any synchronicities that show up, even tiny ones. Make note of them in your journal, describing the event, its context, what you were thinking and feeling, who else was involved, and any other details. The more you feed these experiences with your attention, the stronger and more frequent they will become.

Some final thoughts on cultivating synchronicities. Relying on synchronicities to manifest your desires is not an invitation to laziness. Synchronicities are the universe providing you the opportunities necessary for your growth, healing, and prosperity. If you don't gratefully accept the opportunities that come your way and honor them with your hard work, then you send a message to the universe that you don't truly want what you say you want. The same goes for your artistic purpose and creative gifts. These appear in your life because they are necessary to the growth, healing, and prosperity of those around you. If you don't develop them fully, they will atrophy and pass on to someone else.

Finally, the deeper truth about synchronicities is not so much that you steer the divine hand, but that you are the divine hand. All the universe is your doing. It just doesn't feel that way for the same reason you don't take credit for your heart's pumping. To cultivate synchronicities is to awaken to the reality that there is but one divinity, one universal field, that moves through you and all other beings.

YOUR INNER MONEY GURU

"Money and love are inextricably linked. You can't separate the two. So, love yourself and make what you want safe, and then it becomes easy."

— MORGANA RAE, *FINANCIAL ALCHEMY*

What's the solution for when you're doing everything right, but you're still not getting the results you want in your livelihood? While there are countless factors involved, the one you have most agency over is your inner landscape. As mentioned, subconscious parts of you may hold certain beliefs and painful feelings that conflict with your consciously stated goals. Until you understand and clear out those beliefs and feelings, the conflict will remain, and so you may fail to reach your goals. Once you do understand and clear out those beliefs and feelings, an alchemical process can take place that transforms your pain and conflict into a sense of personal fulfillment that magnetizes the wealth you seek.

Money is an outer reflection of an inner reality. In a sense, money is neutral, so any beliefs and feelings you have related to money are projections from within your psyche. If you believe money is great, it's because money has become a mirror of your own greatness. If you believe money is evil, it's because money has become a mirror of your own evil. What you believe and feel about money, you believe and feel about yourself.

Money is also a potent symbol. As mentioned at the beginning of this chapter, it signifies value, love, safety, security, worth, life, and the

Chapter 12 | SOULFORCE LIVELIHOOD

divine. Your personal experiences with these signifiers shape how you regard money. If you felt loved and valued in your life, you may have warmer, less conflicted feelings toward money. If you felt unlovable and undervalued, you may have a more difficult relationship with money. Change your relationship with these signifiers and you change your relationship with money.

Money's symbolic and psychological nature suggests that if you want more money in your life, you must improve your inner relationship with money. This begins with a process of emotional and spiritual healing. Many believe that gaining money is best supported by learning financial literacy and business skills, but this is only partly true. Without a corresponding inner transformation that can support financial skills, these may in the end be of little use.

One of the most potent means I have found for improving your inner relationship with money comes from Morgana Rae's *Financial Alchemy*. Rae's method involves personifying money and developing a healthy relationship with that personification. She calls this personification your "money honey" and recommends visualizing it as an ideal lover. My own journey has led me to emphasize the divine qualities of money, so I call this personification your **inner money guru**. Your inner money guru is an imaginal being that resides in your psyche. It is an experiential anchor for the symbol of money and provides a source of wisdom with whom you can have a living, ongoing relationship. Developing a positive relationship with your inner money guru requires an attitude of humility and receptivity. Instead of following your inherited programming and muscling through your financial fears, you listen to your inner money guru's guidance, feelings, desires, and messages.

> Your **inner money guru** is an imaginal being that resides your psyche. It is an experiential anchor for the symbol money and provides a source of wisdom with whom y have a living, ongoing relationship.

Improving your relationship with your inner money guru offers many benefits. The first is the healing of your wounds around love, value, security, and money's other signifiers. The second is the discovery of your authentic truths and desires regarding livelihood and a more values-aligned definition of wealth. The third is a source of guidance on how to support your authentic truths, desires, and values through real-world action. The fourth is the initiation of synchronicities that make your Soulforce Livelihood a reality. The following Soulforce Inquiry offers a way to discover your inner money guru and develop a more life-giving relationship with it.

**SOULFORCE INQUIRY 12.8
YOUR INNER MONEY GURU**

The following inquiry is inspired by one of Rae's processes. Begin by considering your relationship with money's symbolic signifiers: value, love, safety, security, worth, life, and the divine. Ask yourself these questions:

- What important events in my life have shaped my relationship with these signifiers?
- What do I believe about myself or the world as a result?
- What emotions come up for me?
- How have these impacted my relationship with money?
- Does my current relationship with money make sense, given my personal history with its signifiers?

Next, personify your relationship with money and its signifiers. If money were a person, animal, or deity, what would they look like? How would they feel, smell, and sound? For many, this personification can at first seem ugly, frightening, or even revolting. That's okay. By getting to know it better, it may transform into something more positive.

Get to know your personification of money by first warmly welcoming it to your inner landscape and then asking it the following questions.

- What do you want me to know about you?
- How did you come to be this way?
- What are your biggest needs, fears, and desires?
- What secret wish do you hold that prevents me from meeting my financial and career goals?
- What positive wish underlies your current painful form?
- Do you enjoy your current job of protecting me in this way? If not, what would you like to do instead?
- What do you need from me to feel safe enough to relax and step into a new role in my psyche?

If you get to know it well enough and it begins to relax and trust you more, your personification may transform into something new. It may appear as a wise inner child, a spirit animal, a lover, or a representation of divinity or nature. This new form is your inner money guru. Ask your inner money guru:

- What do you want me to know about yourself in this form?
- What do you need from me to feel safe staying with me?
- What do you want me to do today to improve our relationship?

Let yourself be surprised by the answers you receive. Maintain an attitude of reverence toward your inner money guru. Listen to its messages and act upon its wishes, even if its wishes at first seem unrelated to money. Improving this relationship may result in monetary gain, but it's about more than that. Your inner money guru will show you the true meaning of wealth, the one in alignment with Soulforce Livelihood: connection to the flow of life within and around you.

AN ECOLOGICAL MODEL OF BUSINESS

"All flourishing is mutual."

— DELLA DUNCAN, RENEGADE ECONOMIST

In a culminating scene in the movie *The Matrix*, the antagonist Agent Smith delivers a damning diagnosis of the human condition. He states how other kinds of mammals live in balance with nature while humans use up and destroy everything. He ends his speech saying, "Human beings are a disease, a cancer of this planet."

The truth this metaphor contains is that the infinite growth our economic system demands is, indeed, overwhelming our planet's capacity to adapt. However, this metaphor assumes that our current way of life is the only one possible. If that were so, then Agent Smith would be right; humanity truly would be a cancer. However, other ways of living, and importantly of doing business, are possible. If implemented more widely, these alternatives can potentially resolve the overconsumption that is now placing our planet in peril. They may even be able to restore and enhance ecological and social well-being. What might these alternatives look like and how can you implement them in your Soulforce Livelihood?

For answers, let's examine the difference between conventional, industrial agriculture and its alternative, permaculture, also known as regenerative agriculture. In conventional agriculture, farmers cultivate crops through imposing their will onto the land via tilling, pesticides, and herbicides. While these methods can secure temporary gains in yield, they have considerable downsides, including pollution, soil degradation, beneficial insect die-offs, and the disruption of ecosystems.

In contrast, permaculture farmers cultivate crops by working with the natural forces already at work in the land. Instead of bulldozing a hill to make room for a uniform crop, they plant a variety of crops that can thrive in different locations. Instead of using poisons to control pests, they use biodiversity to balance insect populations. Instead of disrupting beneficial soil mycorrhizae and releasing tons of carbon dioxide into the atmosphere through tilling, they create food forests that build soil health and capture carbon.

While permaculture is time-intensive and difficult to scale, it makes up for these shortcomings by producing higher quality food in a way that is good for the land. Done with skill and a good business sense, a permaculture can be vastly more productive per acre than its conventional counterparts. What's more, its higher-quality products garner higher prices on the market, thus providing a more sustainable and fulfilling livelihood for farmers.

What's true for permaculture farmers is also true for artists. By adopting permaculture principles, you can create an artistic business that is profitable and fulfilling while building better relationships with your community. Plus, it enhances your artistic Soulforce.

Here are four basic permaculture principles and the ways in which they might apply to artistic livelihood.

RELATIONSHIP

Permaculture is based on relationship. In the same way, artists do not best create or make a living in a vacuum. Rather, your most valuable insights, creative inspiration, and financial well-being will come from the relationships you foster. You can begin by observing and interacting with your audiences. What do they say they need from artistic experiences? Are you meeting those needs through your art? Build life-giving relationships with the people and institutions you resonate with and their enthusiasm for your art will be all the advertising you need.

CIRCULATION

Permaculture circulates resources, rather than draining them. As an artist, you can imitate this in two main ways: eliminating waste and building a community-based emergency fund. One way of eliminating waste is to question your habits of overconsumption and seek ways to flourish with less. Another way is to learn to say no to opportunities that don't truly serve you or your art and which may interfere with opportunities that do. A third way is to compost your money-related wounds into creative projects that inspire others to a more ecological way of life. The conventional idea of an emergency fund is to build a personal stockpile of money. As useful as this is at times, this kind of emergency fund doesn't build what you truly need in an emergency: the flow of resources, energy, and love that comprise community. In fact, a stockpile is only ever needed because of the very absence of real community. A more ecological approach would be to develop stronger ties with friends and neighbors, as well as to elicit the good will of your audiences through generously sharing your artistic gifts when you have bonus energy. The best emergency fund is, as Slow Money founder Woody Tasch says, the "mutually assured affection" of strong community.

FERTILITY

The purpose of permaculture isn't to make a profit, although it can excel at that. Rather, it's to cultivate crops in such a way as to promote the fertility of the entire ecosystem. The same is true of your livelihood. When you focus on the flourishing of yourself, your art, and your community, your financial flourishing will tend to take care of itself. For example, if you host an art showing that brings artists and audiences together, they benefit through making new connections and you benefit by becoming known as an authority and community hub. Because all flourishing is mutual, when you help others, you help yourself. Ultimately, the purpose of a Soulforce Livelihood is the flourishing of all life. What kinds of opportunities can you pursue that align with this purpose?

RENEWABLE RESOURCES AND BIODIVERSITY

A permaculture farmer creatively uses the renewable resources at hand to accomplish the job. In addition, they encourage biodiversity to enhance the resilience of their farm. As an artist, you can create a renewable, resilient livelihood in several ways. A familiar means is by cultivating multiple income streams, such as with performances, selling artistic products, teaching, patronage, grants, and others. A step into a more ecological approach would be to build a network of friends and colleagues who exchange skills, abilities, and resources through reciprocity and favors. Community, trust, love, connection, and reciprocity are renewable resources in that, so long as you tend them, you reap a surplus of support in return. A Soulforce Livelihood is not a solo endeavor; it is an act of mutual flourishing that depends on the interchange of gifts by people motivated by a common cause.

Ultimately, the cultivation of an ecological business model is a step into a gift economy and thus a return to a society based on connection and community. Whereas our conventional transactional model often results in the ick of separation, a gift resolves this ick by enhancing interpersonal connection. The caveat is that a livelihood based on the flow of gifts requires an intact community to function properly. The witnessing of gifts by a close-knit group of others is the bank account of a gift economy; when you give generously, your account goes up in the eyes of others, and so they naturally feel inclined to support you in return. Your stinginess results in your account going down in the eyes of others. In a gift economy, those who give the most are the wealthiest.[11]

Since so few of us live in an intact community, fully basing your livelihood on a gift economy can be impractical. Until we collectively shift to a gift economy, you may always need to sell your offerings via transactions to survive. However, it is still possible in our system as it is to take small, yet significant, steps into a gift economy and thereby enjoy greater closeness with your community and audiences. How is this done?

Again, we can look at the difference between art and commodities. Art is anything more beautiful than it needs to be for the money. That extra bit of beauty is the gift that distinguishes it from a commodity. Any time you create something more beautiful than it needs to be for its price, you are offering a precious gift to your audiences. They will naturally feel grateful for this gift and be inclined to support you in return. While their return support may very well be financial, it will also extend beyond that to the human connection that ties communities together. In this way, when you create genuine art, its surplus beauty becomes an antidote to fragmentation and a catalyst for the true wealth that is connection and community.

SACRED MARKETING

*"Money is not a gift. It's the replacement for a gift.
The only true gift is a portion of thyself."*

— RALPH WALDO EMERSON

"I recently had the opportunity to play at a men's retreat," my friend, singer-songwriter Wyatt Rogers recently told me. "It just fell in my lap; three different friends recommended me for it out of the blue and so I reached out to the retreat leader. I use narrative, storytelling, and comedy to create songs that reflect the lessons I've learned in my journey of personal growth, and at first, I felt unsure that the participants would get my material. As soon as I started playing, however, I knew

I was in the right place. The men were very receptive, very quiet, and this is exactly the sort of environment I need as a performer. Soon, they were asking questions, hooting and hollering, and laughing and crying along with me.

"After the show, I was flooded with interest. So many men told me how moved they were by my performance, about all the emotions and memories that came up for them, how my expressivity and vulnerability gave them the courage to step into their own, and how the heartache in my songs touched theirs. I became a source of connection for them, for a part of themselves that hadn't been expressed, which, I believe, was the entire point of their men's retreat! I got so much from this experience. It reminded me of my own value and gave me renewed confidence in my music. I also got paid very well! I made more money from this show than any other I've ever played, and the great thing was that it all felt so effortless and fun. One guy even offered to help market me to other wellness events! I feel inspired to market myself now so I can find similar performances and share this same gift."

I love this story because it's a perfect example of what I call sacred marketing. **Sacred marketing** is the process of aligning the kinds of artistic "products and services" you provide, as well as the way you communicate about them, with the true purpose of the arts and your unique artistic purpose. Sacred marketing entails fully honoring the guidance from your soul and allows you to spread the word about your offerings in a way that supports your Soulforce.

Sacred marketing reveals that you don't have to fit yourself into the conventional artistic livelihood boxes to survive. Instead, you can rely on the fact that what your audiences want most from you, and what they are most willing to reward you for, is your Soulforce. For these reasons, sacred marketing doesn't feel like conventional marketing. Instead of pulling you away from your core values and disconnecting you from your community through sleazy sales tactics, it lets you get closer to your values and community. This is how you can enjoy the true wealth possible in an artistic livelihood: creative fulfillment, material abundance, and genuine human connection.

> **Sacred marketing** is the process of aligning the kinds of artistic "products and services" you provide, as well as the way you communicate about them, with the true purpose of the arts and your unique artistic purpose.

Let's examine Wyatt's story to discover real-world examples of sacred marketing. One example is the synchronistic emergence of an opportunity that came to him through a close network of friends and colleagues, rather than one that he *made* happen through his solo efforts or paid advertising. Another is the creation of a new context for his art in alignment with his artistic purpose. Instead of merely providing background music to an anonymous audience, the personal growth context and intimate setting of the retreat brought out the best in his unique artistic gifts. Another is the feeling of being carried by events so that the artistic act and its monetary return felt more like an exchange of gifts rather than a cold transaction. Yet another example is that the return gift for his artistic generosity went beyond the money to include intimacy and connection, artistic fulfillment, and the opening of a promising new direction for his artistic career. All these examples functioned to preserve and enhance what was life-giving and sacred about Wyatt's art, while at the same time facilitating greater financial, social, and spiritual wealth. This is the goal of sacred marketing.

To achieve this goal involves five main transformations. The first is faith in the true value and purpose of your art. Without such faith, you enter a vicious cycle in which you unconsciously perpetuate the very stories of scarcity and unworthiness you're trying to escape. For instance, if you're stuck in survival fear, when it comes time to sell your art you may be tempted to seek financial security by focusing on your art's ability to meet certain utilitarian needs, such as those of money, entertainment, social status, or political power. The trouble with this is that, while art can sometimes meet such needs, its real value is more transcendent, lying in its ability to awaken, enliven, heal, and connect. So, when you regard your art in merely utilitarian terms, you diminish the value of your art in the eyes of your audiences and clients. As a result, they will feel less inspired by your work and less willing to pay what your art is truly worth. The truth is that even the greatest work of art will garner little earnings or recognition if it is presented this way. Want a new sculpture to liven up your dining room? Why not try Michelangelo's "David"? Want a new relaxing tune to play in your hotel lobby? Why not try Fauré's "Pavane"? Act now and get two for the price of one!

Sacred marketing says the answer to your financial struggles as an artist is not to accede to the utilitarian values of our economic system. It is rather to create art that so abundantly meets the needs of your audience members for transcendence that—after they recover from being stunned into awed silence—they are so grateful that they fall over themselves to give back to you in return. A new, more life-giving avenue to success opens when you trust your art to have this effect and when you skillfully convey this value through your marketing. The function of your marketing efforts, then, is to let your ideal audiences know you exist so they can choose to have this kind of experience with you.

The second transformation is discovering or creating new kinds of artistic opportunities that align with your art's true purpose. Doing so addresses the fact that many of the conventional venues, careers, and contexts for sharing your art exist solely to serve financial concerns. These conventional contexts can sometimes feel degrading and lead you to think, *I was meant for more than this*. Sacred marketing reminds you that the true purpose of the arts is to bring us more alive. It invites you to build your business and career to serve that purpose, rather than compromising to fit into more familiar, limited, and outdated artistic opportunities. Sometimes you can serve this purpose in conventional artistic contexts, and other times you can serve it in what seem like unrelated fields. A third and exciting possibility is to imagine new artistic contexts custom-built to enhance and transmit your Soulforce.

The third transformation is in how you communicate the true value of your art. A classic marketing mistake is to tell people about what you offer, rather than what need of theirs your offering fulfills. Notice the difference in emotional impact between these two descriptions: "I make clay pots using slip casting techniques and decorative glazes," versus, "My clay pots bring the earthy, funky tone that will make your living room finally feel like home." Or "See Maestro X lead orchestra Y playing Z," versus, "Treat your loved one to a classy, romantic evening of music that will bring the two of you closer together." Which descriptions are more inviting and enlivening? Which clay pot or concert ticket would you buy? When you communicate based on how your art meets the genuine needs of your audiences, selling no longer feels sleazy. Instead of an effortful attempt to convince people of your value, your marketing will feel like a flower opening and saying, "Here I am! Aren't I a beautiful way to meet your needs?"

The fourth transformation is to regard marketing as the development of genuine relationships. The truth about marketing techniques and advertising is that you only need them when people don't know you. When people know you, all the marketing you need is to connect with people while you do what you do best. When people don't know you, you need to expend more effort spreading the word and convincing others of your value. To regard marketing as the development of genuine relationships feels better than conventional marketing because it builds human connection, rather than eroding it through high-pressure tactics. It's also more effective and efficient because a network of people who both know your ideal audience members and are enthusiastic about your art will do most of the work of spreading the word for you.

The final transformation is to regard marketing not as an attempt to get others to add to your personal stockpile of wealth, but as a means of playing your part in the circulation of resources. This requires a step

Chapter 12 | SOULFORCE LIVELIHOOD

out of the linear, infinite growth machine of the rat race and into a circular or gift economy. In a gift economy, you release certainty and control over the outcome of your actions. For your sacrifice, you receive relationships that are more intimate and the source of spontaneous return gifts. Stepping into the gift in an extractive system poses many challenges. One is that you can't truly do it alone; you need a network of trustworthy others to make it work. A further challenge are the misconceptions you will face from those unfamiliar with gift economy, such as equating "gift" with "free." While freely given, a gift only works with the promise of eventual return. While taking this step can be frightening for the separate self, it truly is a step into interbeing, one that enhances your artistic Soulforce, brings you material and social wealth, and is ultimately an act of service to life.

SOULFORCE INQUIRY 12.9
EXPLORING SACRED MARKETING

Using your journal, explore sacred marketing through the following prompts:

- In what ways does my current artistic livelihood align or misalign with the true purpose of the arts and my unique artistic purpose?
- What beliefs and feelings stand in the way of my faith about the deeper purpose and value of my art?
- When did sharing my Soulforce lead to material, social, or spiritual gain?
- Is my marketing focused more on individual effort for individual gain, or on building relationships with enthusiastic supporters who know your ideal audience members?

- When I communicate about my art, do I focus on what my art is or on what needs my art meets?
- In what ways do I already engage in the circle of the gift?

SOULFORCE INQUIRY 12.10
ALIGNING YOUR LIVELIHOOD WITH YOUR ARTISTIC PURPOSE

The following inquiry will help you more fully align your livelihood with your artistic purpose.

Make a list of every activity you do in your artistic livelihood, including budgeting, marketing, creating, networking, paying bills, and so on. Then take some time to review the artistic purpose statements you created in Chapter 5. Let the feeling of your artistic purpose sink into your body.

Reflect on your current approach to each activity in your list. Rate your approach to each activity on a scale of one to ten, giving a one to those activities in which your approach is completely out of alignment with your artistic purpose, and giving a ten to those in which your approach is completely in alignment.

For those activities with the lowest scores, return to *Soulforce Inquiry 8.5: Making an Offering to the Mystery* and ask the Mystery for guidance on how to either change your approach to better align with your artistic purpose or how to find ways of delegating those activities.

For those activities with the highest scores, strengthen the alignment that already exists by celebrating in some way. For ideas on how to celebrate, ask the Mystery.

Chapter 12 | SOULFORCE LIVELIHOOD

ART AND TRUE WEALTH

> *"Early European accounts of [North America's] opulence border on the unbelievable. Time and again we read of 'goodly woods, full of Deere, Conies, Hares, and Fowle ... in incredible abundance,' of islands 'completely covered with birds' ... and of rivers so full of salmon that 'at night one is unable to sleep, so greate the noise they make.'"*
>
> — DERRICK JENSEN, *A LANGUAGE OLDER THAN WORDS*

Within our economic system, you will always face two equally unsavory options: to starve or sell out. So long as you accede to the values and goals of the system, you will never escape these two options. Money and art will always seem to conflict, and no option will feel fully aligned with the life inside you. The promise of a Soulforce Livelihood is that you can transcend this dichotomy. It comprises a new set of values and goals that will align what makes money with the life inside you. Even a Soulforce Livelihood carries a price, however. You must surrender some of the ways you've known yourself and kept yourself safe.

Included in what you must surrender is what money and wealth mean to you. What is wealth? Is it just the accumulation of money, as is commonly thought? Surely not, because money is just an abstraction, a means of exchange that satisfies no human needs. Moreover, to define wealth solely as money invites the myopic pursuit of yet more money. It creates a world of isolated individuals, each on their separate islands of money. The result is the world we see around us, in which so much that is good and green has been destroyed to create lifeless cash.

It's time to expand wealth's definition. For this, we can look to the linguistic root of the word *wealth*, which comes from the Middle English *wele*. Wealth shares this root with other modern English words like *health*, *wholeness*, and *well-being*.⁽¹²⁾ There is a place inside all of us that already knows this. Our hearts know that true wealth is to be surrounded by beauty, to have plenty of time to play and wander aimlessly, to enjoy ripe tomatoes still warm from the sun, to laugh and sing songs around a campfire with loved ones, and to sleep soundly at the day's end knowing that you've given your gifts well and that they were well-received. True wealth, in other words, is a life well-lived. In this definition, to build wealth is to make the world more alive.

You will recognize this as the true purpose of art as well. Art's purpose is to create this expanded kind of wealth—the true, juicy, poignant, flowing wealth that our hearts long for. The whole ick of money and selling regarding art is that we are wired for true wealth, but to create its simulacrum—money—we must betray wealth's fullest definition. We long to give our gifts freely and be supported in return; to enjoy the freedom, to create, to enjoy life's bounty and—as my niece put it—to just get to play.

True wealth is the vibrant circulation of gifts. The ick of our system's form of money is that the circle of the gift has been broken, so we must hold our artistic gifts hostage by only giving them when we're certain we'll receive money in return. No amount of this diminished form of money can resolve its ick, only the reclamation of wealth's fullest definition.

The ultimate purpose of a Soulforce Livelihood is to expand your ability to serve life through your artistic gifts. Perhaps you can do this without relying on your art as a source of income, but this isn't necessarily an advantage. If you want your artistic Soulforce to propagate more widely, you may need to spend more of your time creating, and unless you're independently wealthy, this will probably entail turning pro. While taking this step may involve certain survival challenges, you needn't accept penury as the price for artistic purity nor add to the rat race by commoditizing your art.

Chapter 12 | SOULFORCE LIVELIHOOD

A Soulforce Livelihood offers a third, more empowered choice. By facing your survival challenges from connection with your divine nature and your art's true purpose, you create something that is truly priceless: the more vibrant, loving, enchanting, and abundant world we know is possible for all of us.

"Our deepest fear is not that we are inadequate. Our deepest fear is that we are powerful beyond measure. It is our light, not our darkness that most frightens us …We were born to make manifest the glory of God that is within us … As we let our own light shine, we unconsciously give other people permission to do the same."

— MARIANNE WILLIAMSON, *A RETURN TO LOVE*

CONCLUSION

THE MIRACULOUS POWER OF SENSELESS ACTS OF BEAUTY

Sherrie, a retired elementary school art teacher, told me a story about a drawing assignment she once gave to her students. After handing out paper, pens, and markers, she asked her class to imagine the future and then draw what they thought it would be like. The results were not what she expected. Instead of the youthful, light-hearted, and optimistic visions she thought she might see, most of the drawings comprised scenes of destruction and catastrophe.

It's not hard to imagine why these young students shared such a dark vision of the future. Collectively, we are awakening to a multitude of complex and intractable crises. Our media and entertainment reflect our fears and overflow with end-of-the-world narratives. For many, the future is a place of uncertainty, anxiety, and even despair.

While such feelings are understandable, failing to address them carries a risk. Our imaginations are a powerful force, and what we imagine can eventually come into being. If we don't start imagining a new future—a future where humans and nature can flourish together—then it may not happen.

This is where artists come in. Artists have long given form to the imagination of society, both by expressing the current mood as well as by calling others into newly emerging possibilities. This means that the future you personally envision matters because the art you create from that vision has the potential to influence and inspire those around you. You are a node in the imagination of society. As such, one of your highest callings is to help society dream into existence a new vision of the world. One that works for all life on earth. One that unflinchingly considers all our current horrors while never taking its eyes off a more life-giving vision of what is possible.

We began this book inquiring whether art truly matters because while many artists wish to make a positive impact, they secretly fear themselves or their art incapable of doing so. What we've discovered along the way is that, in an interconnected world, there is no escape from impact. You don't need to agonize over how to make a difference because you make one every day. The only question is what kind of impact you want to have, a question best answered with an understanding of interbeing. You are neither a separate agent acting upon the world, nor a helpless victim of larger forces. Instead, you are the world evolving and finding expression through your unique being. From this larger perspective, your art matters when you contribute positively to the world's evolutionary process, enabling life and consciousness to become more complex, whole, and alive.

The Soulforce Arts Approach was created to help you accomplish just this. It is an evolutionary artistic pedagogy with a truly inclusive outlook. It reveals that none of the usual areas of focus of artistry today—tradition, achievement, self-expression, money, or status—are sufficient by themselves to contribute meaningfully to our world's healing and evolution. Far from implying that we throw these areas of focus away, the Soulforce Arts Approach says that each has their place in our artistic lives. Their true value is revealed with an evolutionary perspective. When each of these contributes to your artistic evolution, they

Conclusion | THE MIRACULOUS POWER OF SENSELESS ACTS OF BEAUTY

function to bring the world more alive through your art.

As powerful as it is, the Soulforce Arts Approach is not a panacea for the world's problems. Indeed, to rely too heavily on this, or any other set of solutions, may only serve to disconnect you from the only thing that can reliably guide you through times of uncertainty: your heart's wisdom. Trusting your heart's guidance requires a leap of faith, but what other options are available in a world gone mad, where all our usual institutions and ways of making sense are crumbling before our eyes?

The way through our uncertain times is not to look to outward authorities, but to notice what makes your spine tingle, what enchants you, and what resonates with and confirms what your heart secretly knows. These are the breadcrumbs that will lead you, and then those around you, out of the dark forest. You are as worthy a vehicle for the world's evolution as anyone else, so you can trust that your heart knows the way. No matter how bad things get, never settle for less than what your heart knows to be possible. This is your sacred task as an artist today.

In this book, I have argued that art has a function and purpose. However, this is only half the truth—a necessary medicine to address the distorted purposes and nihilism of the lesser gods. The other half is that art has no function or purpose whatever. In this, it is like life. What is the purpose of a tree, a baby, the sky, a mushroom, or the stars? These have no definable function; they exist for their own sake only. The same is true of a fugue, dance, poem, or drawing. To create these furthers no utilitarian function, and so—from the point of view of the lesser gods, at least—they are utterly senseless.

However, it is art's very senselessness that provides its transformative power. The wounds so many of us carry are the result of imposing the values and imperatives of the lesser gods upon ourselves and the world. So, when we encounter a truly great work of art, its sheer, wanton, profligate, and senseless beauty carries a miraculous power to heal those wounds. Such art says to us, "Your time of imprisonment and drudgery is over. It's okay—let go of your agenda, your plan, and control. Unshackle yourself and come play with me in the divine dance of life."

Embracing art's senselessness paradoxically reveals a deeper purpose: to re-enchant the world. Great art brings forth the direct realization that, yes, the kingdom of heaven truly has been here on earth all the while. To paraphrase Michelangelo: "My soul can find no staircase to Heaven unless it be through Earth's loveliness."[1] He lived in an enchanted world, and the lasting appeal of his many works attests to this fact. His works, and those of countless other great artists, put the lie to the conceit of the lesser gods that enchantment is useless frippery. Author J.R.R. Tolkien also knew the value of enchantment. He said that it "is as necessary for the health and complete functioning of the Human as is sunlight for physical life."[2] Given that our society's disenchanted worldview is what's responsible for the destruction all around us, re-enchanting the world through our creations is, in fact, the most sensible thing we can do right now and our most urgent task.

That art's power comes from both its sensibleness and senselessness is not a contradiction. It accords with Niels Bohr's maxim that, "There are trivial truths and there are great truths. The opposite of a trivial truth is plainly false. The opposite of a great truth is also true."[3] So it is with the function and purpose of the arts. Their senselessness and purposelessness are precisely what gives them their enchanting, transformative power. They are a glorious sort of nonsense that function to free us of trivial truths and allow us to experience the great truths revealed by the coincidence of yet other great truths. How do you create such art? By embracing all the seemingly contradictory truths within yourself as you meet your creative challenges.

You, as an artist, truly have a vital and potent role to play in re-enchanting the world. This book has provided a solid foundation for embracing this role with an intellectual and spiritual framework supported by many ideas for practical steps. If you find the number and variety of steps provided overwhelming, don't fret. There's no need to do them all at once or even get to all of them. They're all connected with

Conclusion | THE MIRACULOUS POWER OF SENSELESS ACTS OF BEAUTY

one another anyway, so just pick the ones that are the most fun and which feel like a balm to your soul. These steps are like the front end of your golden thread; follow them deeply enough and you're bound to discover your Soulforce.

This leaves us with our final inquiry. Underlying the dark vision for the future so many of us carry is the question, "Will we make it?" The answer is yet another paradox. On the one hand, yes, we will make it. It is utterly certain. In the field of potential that the future represents, the more beautiful, harmonious, and evolved world our hearts know is possible is already on its way. It is fully formed, ready and waiting. It knows that we're coming and can't wait to meet us.

At the very same time, a more evolved world will only come about with our most dedicated and passionate efforts. To bring it about will require nothing less than everything we have, everything we are. In this effort, everyone has a part to play, and no act is too small to matter. The great mistake many make is to believe that a more evolved world lies sometime in the future. The truth is that it's already here, available every time you pick up your pen, practice your pliés, or strum a chord. It's up to you to remember its presence and give it form in your creations.

When you do so, your creations will shine forth with Soulforce. You and your art will be a force that evolves the world's consciousness into more holistic values, and which brings us all more alive through the enchantment of soulfulness. Suffused with your Soulforce, your art will have a value far beyond its technical virtuosity, conceptual novelty, prettiness, ability to entertain, or price tag. It's true value will instead be as a beacon of compassion and wisdom that allows us, in the words of Ram Dass, to "walk each other home."[4]

This is the value of Soulforce.

Have no doubt that the world needs yours.

Joseph Arnold
Philadelphia, Pennsylvania, June 2024

RESOURCES

Now that you've finished this book, you may be wondering, "What's next? How do I further develop myself as a Soulforce Artist?" Here are some possible steps.

You can begin with my webpage containing additional materials relevant to this book. These include a guided meditation into your creative Soulforce, recordings of the Mind-Body Interludes that go into greater detail than space allowed in this book, plus other bonus content that will be updated on occasion and which won't be available elsewhere. You can find all of this at **SoulforceArts.com/bookextras**.

Another option that is free of charge includes following me on social media (@soulforcearts) so you can learn from my blog posts and videos. In addition, when you sign up for my monthly email newsletter, you can download the Soulforce Arts Starter Kit, a free mini-course designed to help you discover your artistic purpose. Learn more at **SoulforceArts.com**.

In this book, I've made the point that we can't reach Soulforce Artistry alone; we need others to share support and inspiration as we walk this path together. This is why I created the Soulforce Arts Community, an online community and learning platform that brings together conscious, purpose-driven artists of all kinds, abilities, and backgrounds to help you embrace your artistic purpose, create free from blockages, and make art that matters to a world in need—together. Learn more at **SoulforceArts.com/community**.

I also offer private lessons and group programs, both online and in person, as well as online courses that feature distillations of the most effective methods for enhancing your artistic well-being and for channeling your Soulforce. Learn more at **SoulforceArts.com/learn**.

I am also available for speaking engagements online and in person. Often, these feature both a violin performance as well as an inspiring talk on Soulforce in the arts. To invite me to your school, podcast, arts venue, or home, contact me at **joseph@soulforcearts.com**.

RECOMMENDED READING

ALEXANDER TECHNIQUE AND OTHER SOMATIC MODALITIES

- Alexander, Frederick Matthias. *The Use of the Self*, 1932. Details his pioneering method of improving the 'use' of his body musculature in all positions and movements, which he developed after almost completely losing his voice.
- Fehmi, Les. *Open Focus*, 2007. Presents a method to reduce stress and enhance well-being by altering attentional skills.
- Jones, Frank Pierce. *Body Awareness in Action*, 1979. An introduction to the life and ideas of Frederick Matthias Alexander, describing and assessing the essential features of his technique of body/mind coordination.
- Myers, Thomas. *Anatomy Trains*, 2001. A guide to understanding body movement and functions through the study of interconnected myofascial lines within the musculoskeletal system.
- Sweigard, Lulu. *Human Movement Potential*, 1974. An innovative teaching method for better postural alignment and body coordination which emphasizes the neural aspects of movement.

SPIRITUALITY AND THE COSMOS

- Eisenstein, Charles. *The More Beautiful World Our Hearts Know is Possible*, 2013. A deeply moving book that explores the concept of interbeing, and how small acts of courage, kindness, and self-trust can change our culture's narrative of separation, ultimately leading us toward a more beautiful world.
- Foster, Jeff. *You Were Never Broken*, 2020. A collection of poetry and teachings on personal transformation and self-acceptance.

- Gober, Mark. *An End to Upside Down Thinking*, 2018. Challenges traditional materialistic thinking by presenting compelling scientific evidence from various disciplines, suggesting that consciousness creates all material reality.
- Murchie, Guy. *The Seven Mysteries of Life*, 1978. A fascinating, heartfelt, and rich exploration into the interconnectedness of all life and various fields such as biology, geology, sociology, mathematics, and physics.
- Plotkin, Bill. *Soulcraft*, 2003. A guide to purpose discovery, blending psychology, ecology, mythology, and indigenous traditions.
- Alan Watts. *The Book*, 1966. A philosophical exploration of human consciousness and its relationship to the universe, challenging readers to question their assumptions and seek a more profound understanding of existence.
- Wilber, Ken. *Integral Spirituality*, 2006. A visionary work that presents a comprehensive understanding of human experience from multiple perspectives by integrating various spiritual traditions, disciplines, and practices.

SPIRAL DYNAMICS & DEVELOPMENTAL PSYCHOLOGY

- Beck, Don. *Spiral Dynamics: Mastering Values, Leadership and Change*, 1996. Delves into a transformative framework for understanding complex human behaviors and societal changes, focusing on innovative leadership and management in a diverse, globalized era.
- Cook-Greuter, Susanne. *Ego Development: A Full-Spectrum Theory Of Vertical Growth And Meaning Making*, 2021. Outlines a theory of ego development detailing nine progressive stages of increasing complexity in meaning-making and self-understanding.
- Kegan, Robert. *In Over Our Heads*, 1994. Examines the mismatch between modern life's demands and our mental capabilities, suggesting that adult development is a necessary response to these challenges
- Wilber, Ken. *Integral Spirituality*, 2006. A visionary work that presents a comprehensive understanding of human experience from multiple perspectives by integrating various spiritual traditions, disciplines, and practices.

WELLNESS AND SHADOW WORK

- Berry, Dr. Ken. *Lies My Doctor Told Me: Medical Myths That Can Harm Your Health,* 2017. Dispels medical myths and misinformation perpetuated by the medical and food industries, emphasizing that nutritional therapy is often overlooked in medical school and the information provided to physicians is often outdated.

- Capacchione, Lucia. *Recovery of Your Inner Child*, 1991. A guide to reconnecting with our 'Inner Child' through art therapy and journaling, leading to improved well-being and unlocking creativity.
- Hof, Wim. *The Wim Hof Method*, 2020. A guide to unlocking physical and spiritual potential through conscious breathing, cold exposure, and the power of the mind.
- Morter, Dr. Sue. *The Energy Codes,* 2019. A guide to awaken your spirit, heal your body, and live your best life through energy healing practices.
- Schwartz, Richard. *No Bad Parts,* 2021. Presents the Internal Family Systems (IFS) therapy, emphasizing that all our internal parts are sacred and that even the most painful parts have life-giving intentions.
- Wade, Paul. *Convict Conditioning*, 2010. A comprehensive guide to bodyweight exercise that promises to help readers build muscle, strength, and endurance through a series of six progressive calisthenics sequences.

ARTISTRY

- Curry, Patrick. *Art and Enchantment*, 2023. Explores the experience of enchantment in art, its dynamics, and how it shapes our understanding of art and life.
- Grey, Alex. *The Mission of Art*, 1998. An inspirational exploration of art's spiritual power, combining art history and personal experiences to challenge conventional consciousness.
- Hyde, Lewis. *The Gift*, 1983. Explores the role of gifts in the arts, ancient human history, mythology, and spirituality.
- Leland, Kurt. *Music and the Soul*, 2004. Introduces the concept of Transcendent Musical Experiences, exploring how music can guide us toward greater self-awareness.
- Nachmanovitch, Stephen. *Free Play*, 1990. Explores the importance of improvisation and spontaneous creativity in life and the arts, emphasizing its role in personal development and fulfillment.
- Taylor, Rogan P. *The Death and Resurrection Show: From Shaman to Superstar,* 1985. Explores the origins of modern show business in the rituals of shamanism.
- Werner, Kenny. *Effortless Mastery*, 1996. A guide that challenges conventional skill perception, advocating for effortless creativity and a shift in mindset for artistic expression.

COMMUNITY, SOCIETY, AND PLANET

- Abrams, David. *The Spell of the Sensuous*, 1997. Explores the subtle dependence of human cognition on the natural environment, drawing from diverse sources like philosophy and shamanism.
- Eisenstein, Charles. *Climate: A New Story*, 2018. Reimagines climate change, advocating for a broader focus beyond carbon emissions to healing from ecological destruction.
- Martin, Eric. *Your Leadership Moment*, 2020. Provides practical tools and techniques to discover your leadership potential, emphasizing authentic, adaptive, and non-authoritarian forms of leadership.
- McGilchrist, Iain. *The Matter With Things*, 2021. Explores the differing worldviews of the brain's hemispheres, critiquing the left hemisphere's dominant, reductionist approach and its impact on our world.
- West, John Anthony. *Serpent in the Sky*, 1993. A revolutionary reinterpretation of Ancient Egypt, revealing hermetic messages, sophisticated sciences, and evidence of a highly advanced civilization.
- Wheal, Jamie. *Recapture the Rapture*, 2021. Proposes Hedonic Engineering, a practice combining neuroscience and psychology, to mend trauma, inspire, and connect, addressing the crisis of meaning.

MONEY AND MANIFESTATION

- Cease, Kyle. *The Illusion of Money*, 2019. Challenges our relationship with money, promoting a fulfilling, authentic life beyond monetary definitions of wealth.
- Eisenstein, Charles. *Sacred Economics*, 2011. Reimagines money and exchange, advocating for a gift economy—a system based on abundance and interconnectedness.
- Rae, Morgana. *Financial Alchemy*, 2012. Offers a transformative process to change your relationship with money, fostering enrichment and life transformation.
- Silver, Tosha. *It's Not Your Money*, 2019. Guides readers through an eight-week transformative process to release financial fears and embrace abundance by offering everything back to Love.
- Surprise, Dr. Kirby. *Synchronicity*, 2012. Explores how our minds influence the occurrence of meaningful coincidences and create our reality.
- Twist, Lynn. *The Soul of Money*, 2006. Explores the connection between money and soul, challenging beliefs about scarcity and sufficiency.

ENDNOTES

CHAPTER 1

1. https://www.ipcc.ch/report/ar6/wg1/. Accessed June 2024.
2. Future Thinkers Podcast, episode 122. https://futurethinkers.org/live-qa-jamie-wheal/. Accessed June 2024.
3. Welcome address to freshman parents at Boston Conservatory. 2004. https://www.bc.edu/content/dam/files/centers/boisi/pdf/s091/Welcome_address_to_freshman_at_Boston_Conservatory.pdf. Accessed June 2024.
4. Dawkins, Richard. *River Out of Eden*, 1995. p.133
5. West, John Anthony. *Serpent in the Sky*, 1993. p.73
6. Brown, Joseph Epes. *Teaching Spirits*, 2001. p.42
7. See the account of a Siberian shaman's séance for a vivid account of the use of a variety of artistic forms to induce this effect in Taylor, Rogan P. *The Death and Resurrection Show*, 1985. 211.

CHAPTER 2

1. Brown, Brené. *Daring Greatly*, 2012. p.8.
2. Campbell, Joseph. *The Power of Myth*, 1991. p.162.
3. Hyde, Lewis. *The Gift*, 1979. p.XIII.
4. https://www.washingtonpost.com/posteverything/wp/2014/06/27/wanna-write-a-pop-song-heres-a-fool-proof-equation/. Accessed June 2024.
5. https://www.londonsinginginstitute.co.uk/history-of-autotune/. Accessed June 2024.

6. https://www.metmuseum.org/toah/hd/shak/hd_shak.htm. Accessed June 2024.

CHAPTER 3

1. Hanh, Thich Nhat. *The Heart of Understanding: Commentaries on the Prajnaparamita,* 1987. p.3.
2. *The Bible* (New International Version), Genesis, 1:31.
3. Tse, Lao. *Tao Te Ching.* Translated by Ralph Alan Dale, 2002. Verse 1.
4. From the work of Amanda Krichbaum, creator of The Heart of Now.

CHAPTER 4

1. The Joe Rogan Experience, episode 852. https://www.youtube.com/watch?v=Iqro15wGByM. Accessed June 2024.
2. Sacred Design Lab www.sacred.design. Accessed June 2024.
3. Wheal, Jamie. *Recapture the Rapture,* 2021. p.80
4. Kotler, Steven. *The Rise of Superman: Decoding the Science of Ultimate Human Performance.* 2021.
5. Shakespeare, William. *Hamlet.* Act 3, Scene 1.
6. https://www.cigna.com/static/www-cigna-com/docs/about-us/newsroom/studies-and-reports/combatting-loneliness/cigna-2020-loneliness-factsheet.pdf. Accessed June 2024.
7. Wheal, Jamie. *Recapture the Rapture,* 2021. p.82.
8. Buechner, Frederick. *Wishful Thinking: A Seeker's ABC,* 1973.

CHAPTER 5

1. Buechner, Frederick. *Wishful Thinking: A Seeker's ABC,* 1973.
2. Campbell, Joseph. *The Hero with a Thousand Faces,* 1949. p.245.
3. Beery, Itzhak *The Gift of Shamanism: Visionary Power, Ayahuasca Dreams, and Journeys to Other Realms,* 2015.
4. Muraresku, Brian C. *The Immortality Key: Uncovering the Secret History of the Religion with No Name,* 2020.
5. Taylor, Rogan P. *The Death and Resurrection Show: From Shaman to Superstar,* 1985.
6. https://www.electricsheepcomix.com/chrysalis/. Accessed June 2024.

ENDNOTES

CHAPTER 6

1. https://www.britannica.com/topic/Muse-Greek-mythology. Accessed June 2024.
2. Schwartz, Richard. *No Bad Parts,* 2021.
3. West, John Anthony. *Serpent in the Sky,* 1993. p. 89.
4. West, John Anthony. *Serpent in the Sky,* 1993. p. 78

MIND-BODY INTERLUDE #2

1. https://youtu.be/PRkeahelZHM. Accessed June 2024.

CHAPTER 7

1. From the collection of Alan Watts' lectures, available at https://alanwatts.com/products/the-works. Accessed June 2024.

CHAPTER 8

1. This characterization of the gift comes from Charles Eisenstein's online course "Living in the Gift." www.CharlesEisenstein.org
2. Hyde, Lewis. *The Gift: How the Creative Spirit Transforms the World*, 2019.
3. Graphic adapted from McGilchrist, Iain. *The Matter With Things*, 2021. p.241.

CHAPTER 9

1. "Trends in the diagnosis of diseases of despair in the United States, 2009–2018: a retrospective cohort study" doi:10.1136/bmjopen-2020-037679. Accessed June 2024.
2. Jenkins, Sarah. "Postmodern Art Definition Overview and Analysis." 2023. https://www.theartstory.org/definition/postmodernism/. Accessed June 2024.
3. Mann, Jon. "How Duchamp's Urinal Changed Art Forever." 2017. https://www.artsy.net/article/artsy-editorial-duchamps-urinal-changed-art-forever\. Accessed June 2024.
4. Vanhoenacker, Mark. "Requiem: Classical Music in America is Dead." 2014 https://slate.com/culture/2014/01/classical-music-sales-decline-is-classical-on-deaths-door.html. Accessed June 2024.

5. Wilber, Ken. *A Brief History of Everything*, 2001.
6. https://www.researchgate.net/publication/356357233EgoDevelopment_A_Full-Spectrum_Theory_Of_Vertical_Growth_And_Meaning_Making. Accessed June 2024.
7. https://www.spiral-dynamics.com/faq_colors.htm. Accessed June 2024.
8. Wilber, Ken. *A Brief History of Everything*, 2001.
9. Graves, Clare W. *The Futurist*, 1974. p.72.
10. Sources for this analysis: www.SpiralDynamicsIntegral.nl; https://www.thenextevolution.com/spiral-dynamics/; https://youtube.com/playlist?list=PLFfM65xLnO-G2ytmWV1A6WBNrvLte92kN; https://www.researchgate.net/publication/356357233_Ego_Development_A_Full-Spectrum_Theory_Of_Vertical_Growth_And_Meaning_Making. All accessed June 2024.

CHAPTER 10

1. Rozmaryn LM. "Upper extremity disorders in performing artists." Md Med J. 1993 Mar;42(3):255-60. PMID: 8350684. Accessed June 2024.
2. Ackermann B, Driscoll T, Kenny DT. "Musculoskeletal pain and injury in professional orchestral musicians in Australia." Med Probl Perform Art. 2012 Dec;27(4):181-7. PMID: 23247873. Accessed June 2024.
3. Sarver, Jon Jr. "ECU study reveals the mental health needs of music students." https://www.witn.com/2021/07/07/ecu-study-reveals-mental-health-needs-music-students/. Accessed June 2024.
4. https://pirate.com/en/blog/news/sixty-six-percent-of-artists-have-experienced-burnout/. Accessed June 2024.
5. Beck, Don Edward and Cowan, Christopher. *Spiral Dynamics: Mastering Values, Leadership, and Change*, 2006. p.3.
6. Beck, Don Edward and Cowan, Christopher. *Spiral Dynamics: Mastering Values, Leadership, and Change*, 2006. p.3.
7. Laszlo, Dr. Ervin. *Reconnecting to the Source: The New Science of Spiritual Experience, How It Can Change You, and How It Can Transform the World*, 2020. p.3.
8. https://spiraldynamicsintegral.nl/en/turquoise/. Accessed June 2024.
9. Grey, Alex. *The Mission of Art*. Shambhala Publications, 2017.
10. The term "holon" was first coined by Arthur Koestler in his book *Ghost in the Machine* (1967) and was later expanded upon by Ken Wilber in *A Brief History of Everything* (2001).
11. Lady Wallace. *Beethoven's Letters (1790–1826)* Vol. II.

12. Beck, Don Edward and Cowan, Christopher. *Spiral Dynamics: Mastering Values, Leadership, and Change,* 2006. p.290.
13. Beck, Don Edward and Cowan, Christopher. *Spiral Dynamics: Mastering Values, Leadership, and Change,* 2006. p.291.
14. "The New Jazz." Newsweek. December 12, 1966. p.108.

CHAPTER 11

1. Curry, Patrick. *Art and Enchantment*, 2023. p.8.
2. Curry, Patrick. *Art and Enchantment*, 2023. p.8.
3. Curry, Patrick. *Art and Enchantment*, 2023. p.15.
4. Auden, W.H. *A Certain World,* 1971. p.159.
5. Connoley, Cyril, *The Unquiet Grave*, 1981. p.55.
6. Taylor, Rogan. *The Death and Resurrection Show: From Shaman to Superstar*, 1985. p.21.
7. Taylor, Rogan. *The Death and Resurrection Show: From Shaman to Superstar*, 1985. p.37.
8. Taylor, Rogan. *The Death and Resurrection Show: From Shaman to Superstar*, 1985. p.33.
9. https://developingchild.harvard.edu/resources/aces-and-toxic-stress-frequently-asked-questions/. Accessed June 2024.
10. Taylor, Rogan. *The Death and Resurrection Show: From Shaman to Superstar*, 1985. p.43.
11. Taylor, Rogan. *The Death and Resurrection Show: From Shaman to Superstar*, 1985. p.12.
12. Anais Nin. *The Diary of Anaïs Nin, Vol. 4.*
13. https://youtu.be/YLO7tCdBVrA?si=yVMuAVmKJof9AzSy. Accessed June 2024.
14. Circling and Authentic Relating are forms of interpersonal meditation that encourage authenticity, connection, and vulnerability as a means for personal growth and collective emotional healing.
15. The phrase "noble friends and noble conversations" comes from the Buddha's discourse in *Samyutta Nikaya* 45.2
16. Griffiths RR, Johnson MW, Richards WA, Richards BD, McCann U, Jesse R. "Psilocybin occasioned mystical-type experiences: immediate and persisting dose-related effects." *Psychopharmacology* (Berl). 2011 Dec;218(4):649-65. doi: 10.1007/s00213-011-2358-5. PMID: 21674151; PMCID: PMC3308357. Accessed June 2024.

17. Shrader, Douglas W. "Seven Characteristics of Mystical Experiences," 2007.
18. Griffiths RR, Johnson MW, Richards WA, Richards BD, McCann U, Jesse R. "Psilocybin occasioned mystical-type experiences: immediate and persisting dose-related effects." Psychopharmacology (Berl). 2011 Dec;218(4):649-65. doi: 10.1007/s00213-011-2358-5. PMID: 21674151; PMCID: PMC3308357. Accessed June 2024.
19. Suzuki, Shinichi. *Nurtured by Love: The Classic Approach to Talent Education*, 1993.
20. https://www.britannica.com/topic/alchemy/The-chemistry-of-alchemy. Accessed June 2024.
21. Joannides, Paul. *The Guide to Getting It On*, 2009. p.9.
22. Costa, Paul and McCrae, Robert. "Personality in Adulthood: A Five-Factor Theory Perspective." *Management Information Systems Quarterly*, 2002.
23. Future Thinker's Podcast. Episode 113. "Clean Up, Wake Up, Grow Up, Show Up—Ken Wilber." Accessed June 2024.
24. Flam, Jack. *Matisse on Art*, 1995. pp.89, 211.

CHAPTER 12

1. Sahlins, Marshall. *Stone Age Economics*, 1974. p.4.
2. Hyde, Lewis. *The Gift*, 1983. p.19.
3. Sahlins, Marshall. *Stone Age Economics*, 1974. pp.3–4.
4. Eisenstein, Jimi. "Our Economy: A Game of Musical Chairs" https://www.youtube.com/watch?v=7BZ-WGnZMXM&pp=ygUeamltaSBlaXNlbnN0ZWluIG11c2ljYWwgY2hhaXJz. Accessed June 2024.
5. Hyde, Lewis. *The Gift*, 1983. p.28.
6. Jung, Carl. *Synchronicity: An Acausal Connecting Principle*, 1960. p.22.
7. Planck, Max. *Where Is Science Going?* 1932. p.217.
8. Schwartz, S. (July/August 2015). "Six protocols, neuroscience, and near death: An emerging paradigm incorporating nonlocal consciousness." *Explore*, 11(4), pp. 252–260.
9. Surprise, Dr. Kirby. *Synchronicity: The Art of Coincidence, Choice, and Unlocking Your Mind*, 2012.
10. For instance, one study showed that pianists who practiced via visualizations alone made just as much progress as did those who put their hands on an actual piano. [Pascual-Leone, A., Dang, N., Cohen, L.G., Brasil-Neto, J.P., Cammarota, A. and Hallett, M., 1995. "Modulation of muscle responses evoked by transcranial magnetic stimulation during the acquisition of new fine motor skills." *Journal of Neurophysiology*, 74(3), pp.1037–1045.] Another

study showed that visualization of exercise alone can build muscle strength by up to 13.5%. [Cohen, P., 2001. "Mental gymnastics increase bicep strength." *New Scientist,* 2001. https://www.newscientist.com/article/dn1591-mental-gymnastics-increase-bicep-strength/. Accessed June 2024].] Yet another study showed that the intentions of newly hatched chicks dramatically influenced the movements of a robot guided by a random event generator. [Cohen, P. "Mind over matter," *Wired,* April 1995. https://www.wired.com/1995/04/pear/. Accessed June 2024] One study showed that the coordinated efforts of people meditating en mass can reduce crime rates in major cities by up to 18%. [Follow-up study suggests group meditation reduced murder rates in large US cities'" *Institute of Science, Technology and Public Policy*, March 2017. http://istpp.org/news/2017_03-new-research-group-meditation-reduced-murder-rates.html Accessed June 2024.] Many studies have shown the profound effect of stress on gene expression, and others have shown how parents' trauma can be passed down to children epigenetically. [Neuropsychopharmacology REVIEWS (2016) 41, 1–2], [Yehuda R, Lehrner A. "Intergenerational transmission of trauma effects: putative role of epigenetic mechanisms." *World Psychiatry.* October 2018;17(3):243-257. doi: 10.1002/wps.20568. PMID: 30192087; PMCID: PMC6127768. Accessed June 2024.]

11. "The Kuma "big men" or "men of strength" ... who command much wealth, are entrepreneurs in the sense they control the flow of valuables between clans by making fresh presentations on their own account and choosing whether or not to contribute to others. Their profit in these transactions is incremental reputation ... The aim is not simply to be wealthy, nor even to act as only the wealthy can act: it is to be known to be wealthy." (Reay, Marie. *The Kuma*, 1959. p.96.)

12. https://www.etymonline.com/word/wealth. Accessed June 2024.

CONCLUSION

1. Rebay, Luciano. *Invitation to Italian Poetry*, 1969. p.77
2. Tolkein, J.R.R. *Smith of Wooten Major*, 2005. p.101.
3. Quoted by Hans Bohr in Stefan Rozental (ed.) *Niels Bohr: His Life and Work*, 1967. p.328.
4. Dass, Ram, and Bush, Mirabai. *Walking Each Other Home: Conversations on Loving and Dying*, 2018.

ACKNOWLEDGMENTS

They say it takes a village to raise a child, and so it is with a book. My own village made this book so much richer, deeper, and more vibrant than could have been possible had I written it alone.

I would first like to thank my teachers and mentors who guided me through some of my most challenging moments with love, wisdom, and compassion. Thank you to Diane Egli, Arnold Liver, and my other violin teachers for imparting your love for music and the means to express my own love through the violin.

I am eternally grateful to all my Alexander Technique teachers. To Maria Caruso, my first teacher, who showed me that I had a body and that freedom from my overuse injuries was possible. To Martha Hansen Fertman, whose compassionate teaching fostered so much healing and growth. To Zoana Gepner-Muller who showed me the utter importance of magic, fun, and play.

I'd like to thank Patsy Eisenstein for immediately seeing my gifts and supporting me in the self-knowledge necessary to share those gifts effectively and joyfully. To Charles Eisenstein for holding the vision of a more beautiful world so steadfastly and with such integrity. To the New and Ancient Story community for holding that vision alongside me.

To Judy Nielsen for being an unending source of love and light in my life, and for the countless hours listening to me read the drafts of this book aloud. May you know that you are loved in every moment.

I'd also like to thank my friends who supported me by reading early drafts and providing feedback. To Larry Massett for reading so many of my first drafts and helping me grow as a writer. To Jason Howard, Emma Back, Raji Malik, Kyle Sensenig, Alyssa Lahoda, and Eric Martin for your gracious readership. To Aaron Bigeleisen for initial help in developing the ideas and practices that became this book and the Soulforce Arts Institute. To Johannes Fischerkeller who challenged my ideas about livelihood and provided a glimpse into a contemporary and practical take on gift economy.

Thank you, as well, to Julian Lauzanna, Sumanya Narra, Laura Seidman, and the others whose generous donations and friendship helped support me financially during my long writing process.

To Lucy Rist, Em Onorato, Raquel Boucher, and Carl Hemenway for initial editorial support that brought my message and writing style into greater clarity.

A very special thanks to Bryna Haynes, my publisher and primary editor, for believing in me so strongly and providing the guidance that has helped this book become better than I could possibly have imagined. Having benefited from your help, I now stand ready to become a World Changer, too.

Finally, I want to thank all my students, both in violin and Alexander Technique. You provided the training grounds that honed my teaching skills, and which led to the development of the Soulforce Arts Approach. Thank you for your willingness to trust me to guide you into your own Soulforce.

ABOUT THE AUTHOR

Joseph Arnold is a Creative Soulforce Mentor and the Director of the Soulforce Arts Institute. Through this platform, he provides artists of all kinds and backgrounds with tools to reconnect with their Soulforce, helping them navigate physical discomfort, manage emotional challenges, enhance their creative spirit, and contribute positively to their communities.

Beyond his directorial role, Joseph is a versatile violinist with a rich repertoire that includes jazz, fiddle, rock, and classical styles. He has played for varied audiences across the U.S. As an Alexander Technique teacher, Joseph assists fellow artists in relieving physical tension and discomfort while promoting ease and fluidity of movement.

Currently residing in Philadelphia, Joseph spends his time playing gypsy jazz with the Hot Club of Philadelphia, Irish fiddle with the Birmingham Six, volunteering at his local food forest, and exploring the outer reaches of inner space.

Learn more about Joseph and his work at **SoulforceArts.com**.

ABOUT THE PUBLISHER

Founded in 2021 by Bryna Haynes, WorldChangers Media is a boutique publishing company focused on "Ideas for Impact." We know that great books change lives, topple outdated paradigms, and build movements. Our commitment is to deliver superior-quality transformational nonfiction by, and for, the next generation of thought leaders.

Ready to write and publish your thought leadership book? Learn more at **www.WorldChangers.Media**.

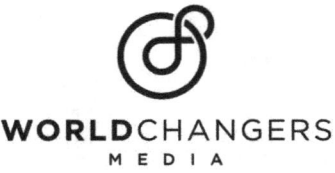